Nelson English

Literature & Media 10

D1616249

Nelson English

Literature & Media 10

Authors
Neil Andersen, ON
James Barry, ON
Robert Bilan, MB
John DiLeonardo, ON
Martha DiLeonardo, ON
Ian Mills, ON
Donna Nentwig, MB
David Normandale, MB
Janeen Werner-King, AB

Literature Consultant
Anthony Luengo

Reviewers
Bill Anderson, Toronto, ON
Sandie Bender, Ottawa, ON
Anne Carrier, Toronto, ON
Owen Davis, London, ON
Rocco Di Ianni, Burlington, ON
Lori Rog, Regina, SK
Jim Satterthwaite, Vancouver, BC
Terry Swift, Erickson, MB
Peter Weeks, Stettler, AB

Aboriginal/Equity Consultants
Linda Laliberté, Edmonton, AB
Rocky Landon, Napanee, ON

NELSON

NELSON

Literature & Media 10

Director of Publishing:
David Steele

Publisher:
Carol Stokes

Executive Editor:
Jessica Pegis

Managing Editor:
Norma Kennedy

Senior Project Editor:
Irene Cox

Production Supervisor:
Isobel Stevenson

Production Editors:
Jerry Cowan
Susan McNish
Stephen Sanborn
Susan Selby

Editorial Consultant:
Rebecca Vogan

Text Researchers:
Monika Croydon
Glen Herbert
Todd Mercer
Dayne Ogilvie
Catherine Rondina
Jennifer Sweeney
Rebecca Vogan

Project Coordinator:
Alex Moore

Activities Editor:
Susan Skivington

Production Manager:
Renate McCloy

Production Coordinator:
Julie Preston

**Permissions Editor and
Photo Researcher:**
Vicki Gould

Art Director:
Angela Cluer

Interior Design:
Anne Goodes
Suzanne Peden

Cover Design:
Anne Goodes

Composition Manager:
Marnie Benedict

Formatters:
Art Plus
Susan Calverley

Canadian Cataloguing in Publication Data

Literature & media 10

(Nelson English)
Western Canada ed.
ISBN 0-17-619174-7 (bound)
ISBN 0-17-618794-4 (pbk.)

1. Readers (Secondary).
I. Barry, James, 1939– .
II. Title: Literature and media
III. Series.

PE1121.L57 2000   428.6
C00-930019-8

TABLE OF CONTENTS

Unit 2: Nonfiction 120

Unit 3: Poetry 200

Plays

Monologues

Unit 5: Media

Print Media

Audio Media

Visual Media

Cyberspace

THEMATIC INDEX

Environmental Change

Technological Change

Design

Recreation

Adventure

Tragedy

Comedy

The tenth-century Japanese writer Murasaki Shikibu once said that people write because they have been "moved to an emotion so passionate" they "can no longer shut it up in their heart." The same could be said for contributors to *Literature & Media 10*, an international anthology of writing and visual texts. Whether communicating through fiction, nonfiction, poetry, drama, or media, every author and artist represented here needed to say something. Now you have the opportunity to read, listen, and respond to their words and images.

This anthology is organized by genre and by theme. Unit openers introduce the main sections, describe each genre, and include arresting quotations and key terms. Other important terms, and their definitions, appear in a glossary. Short biographies of the authors or artists provide a context for the selections.

Four activities are provided for every selection, beginning on page 369. These activities focus on understanding the meaning of the text; analyzing its style, structure, and technique; and using new information to create an original work or to extend the meaning of the selection.

Some of the texts are accompanied by photographs and paintings, and there are two full-colour sections of visuals: The Arts, a section of fine art and photography, and Media Images, a section of advertisements, posters, and other examples of media works. Texts in the Media unit are reproduced as they would appear in their original form—often with accompanying photos, pull-quotes, and graphics.

The Media unit is supported by a video that includes a variety of clips, such as a public service announcement, author profile, and interview. The texts in this anthology are complemented by additional models with an integrated language skills focus in *Language & Writing 10*, the companion volume to *Literature & Media 10*.

We hope your journey through *Literature & Media 10* will let you connect with all the voices represented here, and that you in turn will be moved to connect with others about what you have read and seen.

Fiction

"When you're creating a character, you make
him or her as interesting as you can, and
once you start doing that you move
from the obvious to something individual."

–Michael Ondaatje

"When I write a story I'm always trying to
figure out what the story is all about. This
to me is the pleasure of writing."

–Alice Munro

Short stories and novels are works of fiction, which means that they deal with imagined worlds based on human experience.

Writers of fiction work with a number of key elements to craft their stories. The broadest element is the **theme**, the main idea that emerges from the story as a whole. To develop the theme, writers have to work with other elements. These include locating the story in a specific setting in time and place, and assembling a group of characters.

The writer also creates a plot, which usually involves conflict in the form of tensions or problems. The story develops as the characters react to this conflict. When you read short stories or novels written from the **first-person point of view**, you watch the plot develop through the eyes of one of the characters. In most other works of fiction, you observe the action through the eyes of a **narrator**.

Like all writers, every fiction writer has a distinct **style**—a way of using language that marks the work as her or his own.

theme: the key point, meaning, or purpose of a story

first-person point of view: a literary term which indicates that events in a text are being observed through the eyes of one character, who is telling the story

narrator: a fictional voice that describes the sequence of events in a literary work

style: a writer's choice and arrangement of words, which create a distinctive literary expression

A Catch Tale

retold by Charlie Slane

YOU DON'T SEE BEARS AROUND as often as you used to. But I remember seeing one once when I was out picking raspberries. It was the end of August and it was hot. It was a real scorcher! And there I was, down on my knees making my way around the raspberry canes. Suddenly, I came nose to nose with this great black bear.

He was doing the same thing, of course. He was eating the raspberries, stripping them off with his big paw and stuffing them in his mouth. He was surprised and annoyed that I was picking his berries, because he growled and got up on his hind legs. Well, I didn't hang around.

I took off down the old woods road, and when I looked back he was coming along after me on all fours. Bears can run pretty fast. I can run pretty fast too. I was running the mile in about two minutes, at least. But so was the bear and he was right behind me.

I ran and ran and ran. It was awful hot. The sweat was just pouring off me. I'd look back every once in a while, and the bear seemed to be getting a little closer. So I put on a little more effort and I ran for an awful long time. I was getting tired too. But the bear was still coming on. He wasn't getting any farther away. In fact, he was just as close as he could be.

So I ran and ran and ran. I ran for an awful long time. And just when I thought I couldn't run another step, I came to this lake. It was frozen over a little bit. There was just an inch of ice over it, and I knew that it would hold me if I ran over it real fast, and I knew if the bear followed me, it wouldn't hold him.

So I ran out onto the ice, and I stopped in the middle. And there came the bear, charging after me. He paused for a minute when he saw me out there, then he ran right out on the ice. He got just about halfways when the ice cracked and gave way and down he went and drowned. That was the end of him.

"Hey! That can't be true. You said it was summertime and awful hot. There couldn't be any ice on the lake then!"

Yup, it's true all right. It was summertime when I started running. But like I said, I ran for an awful long time.

A Catch Tale

A Man Told Me the Story of His Life

Grace Paley

VICENTE SAID: I wanted to be a doctor. I wanted to be a doctor with my whole heart.

I learned every bone, every organ in the body. What is it for? Why does it work?

The school said to me: Vicente, be an engineer. That would be good. You understand mathematics.

I said to the school: I want to be a doctor. I already know how the organs connect. When something goes wrong, I'll understand how to make repairs.

The school said: Vicente, you will really be an excellent engineer. You show on all the tests what a good engineer you will be. It doesn't show whether you'll be a good doctor.

I said: Oh, I long to be a doctor. I nearly cried. I was seventeen. I said: But perhaps you're right. You're the teacher. You're the principal. I know I'm young.

The school said: And besides, you're going into the army.

And then I was made a cook. I prepared food for two thousand men.

Now you see me. I have a good job. I have three children. This is my wife, Consuela. Did you know I saved her life?

Look, she suffered pain. The doctor said: What is this? Are you tired? Have you had too much company? How many children? Rest overnight, then tomorrow we'll make tests.

The next morning I called the doctor. I said: She must be operated immediately. I have looked in the book. I see where her pain is. I understand what the pressure is, where it comes from. I see clearly the organ that is making her trouble.

The doctor made a test. He said: She must be operated at once. He said to me: Vicente, how did you know?

Grace Paley (*Born 1922, Bronx, New York*), poet and short-story writer, is an activist in the anti-war and feminist movements. A teacher of creative writing and literature, Paley was declared the official New York State Author from 1986 to 1988.

The Dinner Party

Mona Gardner

THE COUNTRY IS INDIA. A colonial official and his wife are giving a large dinner party. They are seated with their guests—army officers and government attachés and their wives, and a visiting American naturalist—in their spacious dining room, which has a bare marble floor, open rafters, and wide glass doors opening onto a veranda.

A spirited discussion springs up between a young girl who insists that women have outgrown the jumping-on-a-chair-at-the-sight-of-a-mouse era and a colonel who says that they haven't.

"A woman's unfailing reaction in any crisis," the colonel says, "is to scream. And while a man may feel like it, he has that ounce more of nerve control than a woman has. And that last ounce is what counts."

The American does not join in the argument but watches the other guests. As he looks, he sees a strange expression come over the face of the hostess. She is staring straight ahead, her muscles contracting slightly. With a slight gesture she summons the native boy standing behind her chair and whispers to him. The boy's eyes widen, and he quickly leaves the room.

Of the guests, none except the American notices this or sees the boy place a bowl of milk on the veranda just outside the open doors.

The American comes to with a start. In India, milk in a bowl means only one thing—bait for a snake. He realizes there must be a cobra in the room. He looks up at the rafters—the likeliest place—but they are bare. Three corners of the room are empty, and in the fourth the servants are waiting to serve the next course. There is only one place left—under the table.

His first impulse is to jump back and warn the others, but he knows the commotion could frighten the cobra into striking. He speaks quickly, the tone of his voice so arresting that it sobers everyone.

"I want to know just what control everyone at this table has. I will count three hundred—that's five minutes—and not one of you is to move a muscle. Those who move will forfeit fifty rupees. Ready!"

The twenty people sit like stone images while he counts. He is saying "... two hundred and eighty ..." when, out of the corner of his eye, he sees the cobra emerge and make for the bowl of milk. Screams ring out as he jumps to slam the veranda doors safely shut.

"You were right, Colonel!" the host exclaims. "A man has just shown us an example of perfect control."

"Just a minute," the American says, turning to his hostess. "Mrs. Wynnes, how did you know that cobra was in the room?"

A faint smile lights up the woman's face as she replies: "Because it was crawling across my foot."

Mona Gardner (*Born 1900; died 1981*), novelist and short-story writer, wrote many works of fiction, and lived in Hong Kong, South Africa, and the United States.

Gratitude

Andrew E. Hunt

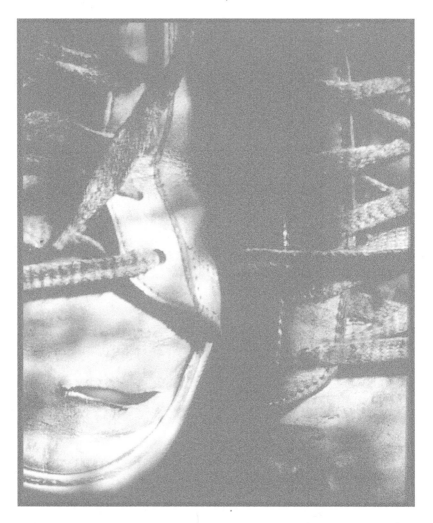

THE STREETLIGHTS were a warm welcome from the oncoming chill of darkness.

The park bench's curvature felt familiar under his tired old spine.

The wool blanket from the Salvation Army was comfortable around his shoulders and the pair of shoes he'd found in the dumpster today fit perfectly.

God, he thought, isn't life grand.

The Wall

Gilles Vigneault

A FORMER MASON, sentenced to twenty years' hard labour, was repairing with surprising care the exterior wall of his prison. He was of course closely guarded, and although the work was compulsory and under scrupulous surveillance, the taste for perfection he exhibited at it was a source of amazement to passers-by and even to his two guards. Someone expressed his surprise and the former mason, without lifting his eyes from his work, replied as if he had expected the question all along: "What pleasure would there be in escaping from a prison that was poorly built?"

Then, before the anxious prison guards who had become more watchful than ever, he went on as though talking to himself: "When you've put your own hand to the making of a wall, it tells you more about human freedom than all the philosophers put together."

This saying spread far and wide until it reached the ears of a monk. The monk came to visit the mason. They talked together at length. And the mason, without disturbing a soul, left the prison by the main gate wearing a habit and a rope belt.

The prison director, a subtle man though he didn't show it, recently asked a professional burglar to repair a window sash. The work was so well done that one feels something is bound to happen, despite the formal order issued that day forbidding anyone to speak to a prisoner at work.

Gilles Vigneault (*Born 1928, Natashquan, Quebec*), singer-songwriter, poet, and publisher, wrote the rousing song *Mon Pays* that has become an important part of Quebec's heritage. Associated with the Quiet Revolution of Quebec in the 1960s, Vigneault was instrumental in promoting Quebec culture abroad and was awarded the Legion d'honneur by France. In 1993, he received the Governor General's Performing Arts Award for lifetime achievement.

Just Lather, That's All

Hernando Téllez

HE SAID NOTHING WHEN HE ENTERED. I was passing the best of my razors back and forth on a strop. When I recognized him I started to tremble. But he didn't notice. Hoping to conceal my emotion, I continued sharpening the razor. I tested it on the meat of my thumb, and then held it up to the light. At that moment he took off the bullet-studded belt that his gun holster dangled from. He hung it up on a wall hook and placed his military cap over it. Then he turned to me, loosening the knot of his tie, and said, "It's hot as hell. Give me a shave." He sat in the chair.

I estimated he had a four-day beard. The four days taken up by the latest expedition in search of our troops. His face seemed reddened, burned by the sun. Carefully, I began to prepare the soap. I cut off a few slices, dropped them into the cup, mixed in a bit of warm water, and began to stir with the brush. Immediately the foam began to rise. "The other boys in the group should have this much beard, too." I continued stirring the lather.

"But we did all right, you know. We got the main ones. We brought back some dead, and we've got some others still alive. But pretty soon they'll all be dead."

"How many did you catch?" I asked.

"Fourteen. We had to go pretty deep into the woods to find them. But we'll get even. Not one of them comes out of this alive, not one."

He leaned back on the chair when he saw me with the lather-covered brush in my hand. I still had to put the sheet on him. No doubt about it, I was upset. I took a sheet out of a drawer and knotted it around my customer's neck. He wouldn't stop talking. He probably thought I was in sympathy with his party.

"The town must have learned a lesson from what we did the other day," he said.

"Yes," I replied, securing the knot at the base of his dark, sweaty neck.

"That was a fine show, eh?"

"Very good," I answered, turning back for the brush. The man closed his eyes with a gesture of fatigue and sat waiting for the cool caress of the soap. I had never had him so close to me. The day he ordered the whole town to file into the patio of the school to see the four rebels hanging there, I came face to face with him for an instant. But the sight of the mutilated bodies kept me from noticing the face of the man who had directed it all, the face I was now about to take into my hands. It was not an unpleasant face, certainly. And the beard, which made him seem a bit older than he was, didn't suit him badly at all. His name was Torres. Captain Torres. A man of imagination, because who else would have thought of hanging the naked rebels and then holding target practice on certain parts of their bodies? I began to apply the first layer of soap.

With his eyes closed, he continued. "Without any effort I could go straight to sleep," he said, "but there's plenty to do this afternoon."

I stopped the lathering and asked with a feigned lack of interest: "A firing squad?"

"Something like that, but a little slower."

I got on the job of lathering his beard. My hands started trembling again. The man could not possibly realize it, and this was in my favour. But I would have preferred that he hadn't come. It was likely that many of our faction had seen him enter. And an enemy under one's roof imposes certain conditions. I would be obliged to shave that beard like any other one, carefully, gently, like that of any customer, taking pains to see that no single pore emitted a drop of blood. Being careful to see that the little tufts of hair did not lead the blade astray. Seeing that his skin ended up clean, soft, and healthy, so that passing the back of my hand over it I couldn't feel a hair. Yes, I was secretly a rebel, but I was also a conscientious barber, and proud of the preciseness of my profession. And this four-days' growth of beard was a fitting challenge.

I took the razor, opened up the two protective arms, exposed the blade and began the job, from one of the sideburns downward. The razor responded beautifully. His beard was inflexible and hard, not too long, but thick. Bit by bit the skin emerged. The razor rasped along, making its customary sound as fluffs of lather mixed with bits of hair gathered along the blade. I paused a moment to clean it, then took up the strop again to sharpen the razor, because I'm a barber who does things properly. The man, who had kept his eyes closed, opened them now, removed one of his hands from under the sheet, felt the spot on his face where the soap had been cleared off, and said, "Come to the school today at six o'clock."

"The same thing as the other day?" I asked horrified.

"It could be better," he replied.

"What do you plan to do?"

"I don't know yet. But we'll amuse ourselves." Once more he leaned back and closed his eyes.

I approached him with the razor poised. "Do you plan to punish them all?" I ventured timidly. *rut rè*

"All."

The soap was drying on his face. I had to hurry. In the mirror I looked toward the street. It was the same as ever: the grocery store with two or three customers in it. Then I glanced at the clock: two-twenty in the afternoon. The razor continued on its downward stroke. Now from the other sideburn down. A thick, blue beard. He should have let it grow like some poets or priests do. It would suit him well. A lot of people wouldn't recognize him. Much to his benefit, I thought, as I attempted to cover the neck area smoothly. There, for sure, the razor had to be handled masterfully, since the hair, although softer, grew into little swirls. A curly beard. One of the tiny pores could be opened up and issue forth its pearl of blood. A good barber such as I prides himself on never allowing this to happen to a client. And this was a first-class client. How many of us had he ordered shot? How many of us had he ordered mutilated? It was better not to think about it. Torres did not know that I was his enemy. He did not know it, nor did the rest. It was a secret shared by very few, precisely so that I could inform the revolutionaries of what Torres was doing in the town and of what he was planning each time he undertook a rebel-hunting excursion. So it was going to be very difficult to explain that I had him right in my hands and let him go peacefully—alive and shaved.

The beard was now almost completely gone. He seemed younger, less burdened by years than when he had arrived. I suppose this always happens with men who visit barber shops. Under the stroke of my razor Torres was being rejuvenated—rejuvenated because I am

14   Short Stories

a good barber, the best in the town, if I may say so. A little more lather here, under his chin, on his Adam's apple, on this big vein. How hot it is getting! Torres must be sweating as much as I. But he is not afraid. He is a calm man, who is not even thinking about what he is going to do with the prisoners this afternoon. On the other hand I, with this razor in my hands, stroking and re-stroking this skin, trying to keep blood from oozing from these pores, can't even think clearly.

Damn him for coming, because I'm a revolutionary and not a murderer. And how easy it would be to kill him. And he deserves it. Does he? No! What the devil! No one deserves to have someone else make the sacrifice of becoming a murderer. What do you gain by it? Nothing. Others come along and still others, and the first ones kill the second ones and they the next ones and it goes on like this until everything is a sea of blood. I could cut this throat just so, zip! zip! I wouldn't give him time to complain and since he has his eyes closed he wouldn't see the glistening knife blade or my glistening eyes. But I'm trembling like a real murderer. Out of his neck a gush of blood would spout onto the sheet, on the chair, on my hands, on the floor. I would have to close the door. And the blood would keep inching along the floor, warm, ineradicable, uncontainable, until it reached the street, like a little scarlet stream. I'm sure that one solid stroke, one deep incision, would prevent any pain. He wouldn't suffer. But what would I do with the body? Where would I hide it? I would have to flee, leaving all I have behind, and take refuge far away, far, far away. But they would follow until they found me. "Captain Torres' murderer. He slit his throat while he was shaving him—a coward." And then on the other side. "The avenger of us all. A name to remember. (And here they would mention my name.) He was the town barber. No one knew he was defending our cause."

And what of all this? Murderer or hero? My destiny depends on the edge of this blade. I can turn my hand a bit more, press a little harder on the razor, and sink it in. The skin would give way like silk, like rubber, like the strop. There is nothing more tender than human skin and the blood is always there, ready to pour forth. A blade like this doesn't fail. It is my best. But I don't want to be a murderer, no sir. You came to me for a shave. And I perform my work honourably ... I don't want blood on my hands. Just lather, that's all. You are an

*đao phủ*⁹

plan

executioner and I am only a barber. Each person has his own place in the scheme of things. That's right. His own place.

Now his chin had been stroked clean and smooth. The man sat up and looked into the mirror. He rubbed his hands over his skin and felt it fresh, like new.

"Thanks," he said. He went to the hanger for his belt, pistol and cap. I must have been very pale; my shirt felt soaked. Torres finished adjusting the buckle, straightened his pistol in the holster and after automatically smoothing down his hair, he put on the cap. From his pants pocket he took out several coins to pay me for my services. And he began to head toward the door. In the doorway he paused for a moment, and turning to me he said:

"They told me that you'd kill me. I came to find out. But killing isn't easy. You can take my word for it." And he headed on down the street.

Hernando Téllez (*Born 1908, Bogotá, Colombia; died 1966*), essayist, short-story writer, and journalist, was a senator in the Colombian government before joining the diplomatic corps to serve as Consul General in France, and as the Colombian Ambassador to UNESCO. Téllez's stories have been described as "living history."

Dancer

Vickie Sears

Eagles, *Robert Davidson, 1991*

TELL YOU JUST HOW IT WAS WITH HER. Took her to a dance not long after she come to live with us. Smartest thing I ever done. Seems like some old Eaglespirit woman saw her living down here and came back just to be with Clarissa.

Five years old she was when she come to us. Some foster kids come with lots of stuff, but she came with everything she had in a paper bag. Some dresses that was too short. A pair of pants barely holding a crotch. A pile of ratty underwear and one new nightgown. Mine was her third foster home in as many months. The agency folks said she was *so-cio-path-ic*. I don't know nothing from that. She just seemed like she was all full up with anger and scaredness like lots of the kids who come to me. Only she was a real loner. Not trusting nobody. But she ran just like any other kid, was quiet when needed. Smiled at all the right times. If you could get her to smile, that is. Didn't talk much, though.

Had these ferocious dreams too. Real screamer dreams they were. Shake the soul right out of you. She'd be screaming and crying with her little body wriggling on the bed, her hair all matted up on her woody-coloured face. One time I got her to tell me what she was seeing, and she told me how she was being chased by a man with a long knife what he was going to kill her with and nobody could hear her calling out for help. She didn't talk too much about them, but they was all bad like that one. Seemed the most fierce dreams I ever remember anybody ever having outside of a vision seek. They said her tribe was Assiniboin, but they weren't for certain. What was for sure was that she was a fine dark-eyed girl just meant for someone to scoop up for loving.

Took her to her first dance in September, like I said, not long after she came. It wasn't like I thought it would be a good thing to do. It was just that we was all going. Me, my own kids, some nieces and nephews, and the other children who was living with us. The powwow was just part of what we done all the time. Every month. More often in the summer. But this was the regular first Friday night of the school year. We'd all gather up and go to the school. I was thinking on leaving her home with a sitter cause she'd tried to kill one of the cats a couple of days before. We'd had us a big talk and she was grounded, but, well, it seemed like she ought to be with us.

Harold, that's my oldest boy, he and the other kids was mad with her, but he decided to show her around anyhow. At the school he went through the gym telling people, "This here's my sister, Clarissa." Wasn't no fuss or anything. She was just another one of the kids. When they was done meeting folks, he put her on one of the bleachers near the drum and went to join the men. He was in that place where his voice cracks but was real proud to be drumming. Held his hand up to his ear even, some of the time. Anyhow, Clarissa was sitting there, not all that interested in the dance or drum, when Molly Graybull come out in her button dress. Her arms was all stretched out, and she was slipping around, preening on them spindles of legs that get skinnier with every year. She was well into her seventies, and I might as well admit, Molly had won herself a fair share of dance contests. So it wasn't no surprise how a little girl could get so fixated on Molly. Clarissa watched her move around-around-around. Then all the rest of the dancers after Molly. She sure took in a good eyeful. Fancy dance. Owl dance. Circle dance. Even a hoop

dancer power b/c connect herself — her back nostalgity

dancer was visiting that night. Everything weaving all slow, then fast. Around-around until that child couldn't see nothing else. Seemed like she was struck silent in the night, too. Never had no dreams at all. Well, not the hollering kind anyways.

Next day she was more quiet than usual only I could see she was looking at her picture book and tapping the old one-two, one-two. Tapping her toes on the rug with the inside of her head going around and around. As quiet as she could be, she was.

A few days went on before she asks me, "When's there gonna be another dance?"

I tell her in three weeks. She just smiles and goes on outside, waiting on the older kids to come home from school.

The very next day she asks if she can listen to some singing. I give her the tape recorder and some of Joe Washington from up to the Lummi reservation and the Kicking Woman Singers. Clarissa, she takes them tapes and runs out back behind the chicken shed, staying out all afternoon. I wasn't worried none, though, cause I could hear the music the whole time. Matter of fact, it like to make me sick of them same songs come the end of three weeks. But that kid, she didn't get into no kind of mischief. Almost abnormal how good she was. Worried me some to see her so caught up but it seemed good too. The angry part of her slowed down so's she wasn't hitting the animals or chopping on herself with sticks like she was doing when she first come. She wasn't laughing much either, but she started playing with the other kids when they come home. Seemed like everybody was working hard to be better with each other.

Come March, Clarissa asks, "Can I dance?"

For sure, the best time for teaching is when a kid wants to listen, so we stood side to side with me doing some steps. She followed along fine. I put on a tape and started moving faster, and Clarissa just kept up all natural. I could tell she'd been practising lots. She was doing real good.

Comes the next powwow, which was outside on the track field, I braided Clarissa's hair. Did her up with some ermine and bead ties, then give her a purse to carry. It was all beaded with a rose and leaves. Used to be my aunt's. She held it right next to her side with her chin real high. She joined in a Circle dance. I could see she was watching her feet a little and looking how others do their steps, but mostly she was doing wonderful. When Molly Graybull showed up beside her, Clarissa took to a seat and stared. She didn't dance again that night, but I could see there was dreaming coming into her eyes. I saw that fire that said to practise. And she did. I heard her every day in her room. Finally bought her her very own tape recorder so's the rest of us could listen to music too.

Some months passed on. All the kids was getting bigger. Clarissa, she went into the first grade. Harvey went off to community college up in Seattle, and that left me with Ronnie being the oldest at home. Clarissa was keeping herself busy all the time going over to Molly Graybull's. She was coming home with Spider Woman stories and trickster tales. One night she speaks up at supper and says, right clear and loud, "I'm an Assiniboin." Clear as it can be, she says it again. Don't nobody have to say nothing to something that proud said.

Next day I started working on a wing dress for Clarissa. She was going to be needing one for sure real soon.

Comes the first school year powwow and everyone was putting on their best. I called for Clarissa to come to my room. I told her, "I think it's time you have something special for yourself." Then I held up the green satin and saw her eyes full up with glitter. She didn't say nothing. Only kisses me and runs off to her room.

Just as we're all getting out of the car, Clarissa whispered to me, "I'm gonna dance with Molly Graybull." I put my hand on her shoulder to say, "You just listen to your spirit. That's where your music is."

We all danced an Owl dance, a Friendship dance, and a couple of Circle dances. Things was feeling real warm and good, and then it was time for the women's traditional. Clarissa joined the circle. She opened her arms to something nobody but her seemed to hear. That's when I saw that old Eagle woman come down and slide right inside of Clarissa, scooping up that child. There Clarissa was, full up with music. All full with that old, old spirit, letting herself dance through Clarissa's feet. Then Molly Graybull come dancing alongside Clarissa, and they was both the same age.

Vickie Sears (*Born 1941*) is a poet, writer, therapist, and teacher. Of Cherokee, Spanish, and English descent, she grew up in the Pacific Northwest. Her poetry and short stories have appeared in several journals and collections, including *Spider Woman's Granddaughters: Traditional Tales and Contemporary Writing by Native American Women*.

Lifeguard

Barbara Scott

I'M NOT ALL THAT CRAZY ABOUT SMALL KIDS. That might seem strange coming from a guy who's a lifeguard at the Bridgeland Community Swimming Pool, but the job gives me free pool time, and I'm training for the city tryouts. Keeping snot-nosed kids from drowning themselves and one another is the only price I have to pay. I made it pretty clear to the kids the first couple days that I wasn't hired as their babysitter or their buddy, and most of them gave me a wide berth after that. Fine by me. I had my own problems that summer.

For one thing, my mom got this great job offer that she couldn't turn down, never mind that this was the year I finally had a chance to make the city team. After four years of being told, You're too small, too thin, not strong enough. Four years of push-ups and sit-ups in the dark in my bedroom after Mom said lights out, of countless lengths in the mornings before school. So I flat out refused to move, and wound up living on my own in Calgary while she and my kid brother lived in Vancouver and kept in touch through weekly phone calls that all went pretty much the same way. Mom would ask how I was doing, and then she'd start to cry and remind me that none of this was her fault, that the Vancouver job paid almost twice as much as her old job and if Dad hadn't run off like he did everything would be just great. Which, when I thought about the time before he took off, made me wonder whether her mind hadn't been cracked by the move. I suppose the good thing about it was that there wasn't much room for me to get too upset, what with her getting upset enough for the both of us. I'd tell her about practice and how my time was really improving and she'd ask if I was remembering to eat right. A few words with the kid bro and that was it for another week.

All of which I was OK with, for the most part. But then, right out of the blue, my dad shows up. After running out on us six years before. I had to look twice to be sure it was him behind the glass in the viewing area, watching me. Watching me watching him. And he doesn't wave or move or even crack a smile. Typical.

I'd been diving before they opened up the pool for the free swim. I get a kick out of doing my dives then, surfacing to catch the kids staring at me with open mouths. I hadn't told anybody, not even my mom, but I wasn't only trying out for the swim team. My real goal was to be on the diving team. High diving. I like everything about it, the swing of my back as I climb the ladder, the metal steps and rungs cold under my feet and hands. I even like the way my stomach falls away when I get to the top and feel the pebbly grain of the platform under my feet. And no matter how many times I dive, my gut always does fall away. Butterflies, my mom calls it. "Butterflies," she used to sing out into the back seat whenever we hit a big bump driving down into the States on holidays. And my kid brother, who was practically a baby still, would laugh like crazy, with his snorty little laugh that sounds like a sneeze, and try to say, "Butterflies," with her while she reached over from the front seat to tickle his tummy. That was when we were all still a family. I don't remember much about my dad, even though I was old enough to remember. I guess he was just there, hands on the wheel, eyes on the road. I don't really know. I try to picture him doing anything else and that's the best I can do.

I stand at the edge of the platform for a minute, smelling the chlorine and staring into the blue-green square, gathering everything I've got into the centre of my body. A couple of bends at the knee, then up and out, with all the tension in my legs pouring through my chest and straight *simile*

out the top of my head. Try to hang there forever, stretched out and motionless, then make the body arrow-straight and knife-steady and slice open that pool like it was a melon. There isn't anything like it. When the dive is right it's just you and the air racing away from everything, even from your body.

So anyway, I sploosh out of the pool after a dive and there's a whole bunch of kids jostling in the viewing room. And Dad. We barely lock eyeballs when the doors burst open and all the little creeps cannonball into the pool, yelling fit to break glass. And I'm blowing my whistle and yelling too, so I don't have a lot of time to think about why he's here and what exactly I'm supposed to do about it.

I just get things slightly under control when a finger pokes my arm. I look down and there's Mike. Ever since he first saw me dive, that kid stuck to me like a leech no matter how hard I tried to shake him loose. He was always after me, "How's my crawl doin', Chris?" and "Watch me do the butterfly." So every once in a while, to get some peace, I'd watch him thrash his way around the shallow end of the pool. He was lousy, but no amount of telling him so would get him off my back.

Mike was so scrawny he barely had enough butt to hang swim trunks on, and without his glasses, his eyes were always slightly out of focus, like he was looking at something just beyond you. For all the times I saw him at the pool, and that was almost every day for the whole summer, I don't think I ever saw him with anybody—he was always off by himself, puffing and blowing like a baby whale. His mom would drop him off at the gate. She looked a bit like my mom. First time I saw her, I thought for a minute Mom had changed her mind about taking the job in Vancouver. After his mom left, Mike spent all his time paddling in the shallow end. And bugging me. Like I didn't have better things to do with my time.

comparison

So I'm scanning the viewing room to see if my dad's still there, only my eyes keep getting snagged on one of the babes that hang out at the pool in a bathing suit that's a clear signal they don't come for the swimming, and she looks away and laughs with her friends and I'm hoping she was watching when I made that dive. I hadn't taken my eyes off the pool for more than a few minutes but all of a sudden I see Mike splashing around in the deep end. So I'm in the pool like a flash, hauling him to the surface and throwing him onto the edge like a dead mackerel. "You idiot! What do you think you're doing down this end of the pool? You could've drowned!"

He stands there streaming with water and this weird, shining kind of look.

"Wow! That is so cool!"

I glance over to the viewing area. No sign of my dad, and the girls have moved on too.

I poke Mike in the chest, hard. "Button it, kid. What were you doing down in the deep end?"

"You gotta try it, Chris."

"Try what?" The little snot has gone off the deep end in more ways than one.

"Look, I'll show you." And he starts off back to where I've just finished hauling him out. Some people you have to hit over the head with a sledgehammer. I yank him back by the arm.

"Haven't you heard a word I've been saying? You're not allowed down there unless you can swim a length."

"Why should I have to swim a length?" the kid asks. "Anybody knows that even if you fall in the middle of the pool, the most you'd have to swim is half a width."

"Yeah, well, for you that'd still be pushing it."

"If I swim the width will you let me show you?"

"Show me what?"

He answered with the slow patience you'd treat someone with who wasn't wrapped too tight. "If I have to show you, I can't tell you, can I?" And then before I can say anything, in he dives—into the deep end again, couldn't prove his point in the shallow end, not Mike. Well, he's moving like an eggbeater, churning up the water and looking like he'll go down any minute. But I have to admit that he's made it when he comes back up to me.

"Now watch," he says, like he's going to open me up to some kind of miracle.

What I see convinces me that the little squirt is definitely a little bent. He crouches down at the edge of the pool and rolls himself up into a ball, then slowly tips himself off the edge backward, gradually unfolding as he sinks deeper and deeper into the water. I keep waiting for some sort of trick, but all he does is a limp deadman's float underneath the surface of the water, not moving, only wafting like a fleshy seaweed. The longer he stays there the more nervous I get, and I'm just thinking I'm going to have to go in after him a second time when he slowly rises to the surface, bursting through near the ladder. He comes running up to me with the same goofy expression, like a pup that figures it's been really clever. "Did you see, Chris? Did you see?"

"See *what*?"

He stares at me like *I'm* the moron.

"It's like ... like falling into a ... a cloud, and it ..." I tap my forehead with one finger and draw circles in the air. Mike's voice fizzles. "I guess you have to do it yourself to figure it out." He tugs at my finger. "Why don't you try it, Chris? It feels really neat."

"I have to get back to work, kid. I can't stand around all day listening to weirdos." I start to walk away. But he's a persistent guy and you've got to admit he doesn't take an insult. He tags along, saying, "Yeah, but you will try it, won't you, Chris?"

"Yeah, yeah, sure, kid." I keep walking.

That Sunday the usual phone call took an unusual turn.

"Dad came by the pool last week."

"How on earth did he find you? After six years!" Mom clamps down on this outburst and there's a long, murky pause; then she says, too carefully, "What did you two talk about?"

"We didn't. He just stood there. He watched me practise and then he left."

"If that isn't exactly like him, to wait for you to make the ..." She reins in her voice hard, and takes a minute before going on. "What do you think you'll do about it?"

"I don't know. He left."

"He'll be back." Her voice is too neutral, gives nothing away, and I feel like I'm straining to see her face, to find out what she thinks I should do, but all I can see is the blank wall of the kitchen.

"Dammit, Mom, I don't know."

"Don't swear, Chris," but she says it automatically, not like she's mad. "Honey, I don't know either. You have to do what's best for you."

Thanks a lot, I think. All the times she couldn't keep her nose out of my business, telling me what to do, and for the first time in ages, when I'd actually like at least a hint, now I'm grown up enough to decide for myself.

"Yeah, well. I guess I'll let you know."

"OK, dear." Another pause and then, almost like a question, "I love you."

"I know, Mom. I know."

"Do you want to talk to your brother?"

"Naw, I'll catch him next time. I gotta go."

She was right of course. He came back. Every few days I'd look up from the water and see him behind the glass. He never came beyond it and never waved or motioned in any way. And I knew he was leaving it up to me to decide. The jerk, I thought. Serve him right if one of these days I walk up to that viewing room, shove open the door and pop him one right in the mouth. Tell him exactly what I've been thinking of him in the years he's been gone. I had a lot of fantasies like that, and they got my blood boiling pretty good, but the ones that made me even madder were the ones that snuck in when I was off my guard, the ones where he looked at me and half smiled, a little nervous, and said he was sorry for everything.

"So how does he look?" Mom asked on one of my calls.

Old, I think. Seeing not only the greying hair that dipped across his forehead, but the lines around the eyes and mouth, deep enough to see even through glass. "He looks OK, I guess." For a minute I think, why not tell the truth, dummy? You don't have to protect him. And then I realize it's not him I'm protecting. I remember what it was like when he was around. Mom talking all the time, especially toward the end. Dad barely talking at all. Me shunted between the two of them, Mom pushing Dad to take me to the park, then pulling me aside and asking me what he said, whether he left me alone there. It was almost a relief when he took off. Almost but not quite. The first couple of years I used to see him everywhere, only it was never him. It was so typical that he'd finally show up once I got used to the fact that he was gone. And that thought would get me boiling all over again.

Mike was at the pool almost every day, not swimming, just playing his strange little game. Every so often he'd bug me to watch him, but my temper was not the best and usually I told him to buzz off. I was spending every spare minute at the pool, even helping to clean up after the last Belly-Burner Aquacise class ended at eleven. I'd come back early in the morning and spend hours swimming lengths, paring precious seconds off my time. At the end of one of these sessions I could barely stand. I pushed myself with diving too, leaping harder, trying to go higher, come down faster, cleaner, deeper. One day, Keith, one of the older lifeguards who also did some diving, yelled at me to get out of the pool and then dragged me into the office, wet and shivering. Didn't even give me time to get my towel. He glared at me and plugged in a video of the Olympic Games a few years back. A Russian diver miscalculated his dive and hit the platform on his way down. The moment of impact didn't look like anything much; he barely glanced off the edge, nothing dramatic at all. But you could tell he was in trouble the minute he hit. His body. It just dropped, like there was no one inside it any more. And then the water bloomed red from the bottom of the pool. I felt sick. Keith switched off the VCR. "I don't know what you're thinking about out there, kid," he said, "but it isn't diving. And if you're not thinking about diving, stay the hell off the platform."

I barely opened my mouth to say something when he stared me down and said, "I don't want to hear about it. Stop fooling around out there or I'll have you banned from this pool."

It's hard to try for righteous indignation when you're practically naked and shaking with cold and anger, so I slammed out of the office, and straight into Mike.

"Hi, Chris. You OK? Did he chew you out?"

I swear, I tried to keep walking and not talk to him, but he grabbed my hand and something snapped. I turned around with my fist raised, like I was going to smack him, and yelled straight into his nerdy face, "Leave me alone, you little geek. Just clear off and leave me alone!" I stomped off to the changing rooms without even a glance at the viewing area. Just my luck my dad'd be there in time to see me practically cream some kid a quarter my size. Well, I didn't want to know about it, thank you very much.

So naturally, when Mike stopped coming to the pool, I figured it had to be because I'd yelled at him. I felt pretty bad but, honestly, he was such a pain in the neck, and I figured he'd get over it. Then one day I overheard a couple of parents talking while their kids were getting showered. Talking about Mike's family, in that hush-hush, greedy voice people use when they go over gory details. Mike and his parents had been driving up to Saskatchewan to see some relatives. Just out of Drumheller they'd been hit head-on by a kid out joyriding, playing chicken with another guy. The idiot pulled out to pass on a curve and hit Mike's family doing about a hundred klicks. His buddy didn't even stop, but a Greyhound bus driver saw the whole thing and radioed the police. When they got there Mike's mom was squashed like an accordion under the dashboard, and his dad was walking in big crazy circles all over the road, muttering to himself in gibberish and flapping his arms like a chicken. Mike had crawled into the corner farthest from his mom, in the back seat, and was staring from behind his shattered glasses, from one parent to the other, folded in on himself like a tight, hard ball.

Well, you can imagine what a jerk I felt then. The pool is right near the hospital they had Mike at, so I went over to see him after work. I talked to a nurse there, and she filled me in on the rest of the story. Mike's mom was killed on impact; his dad took a few days more to go. They did a whole bunch of tests on Mike, and apart from some cuts and a big bruise on his forehead he was OK. Physically.

Since they'd brought him in he hadn't said a word or looked like he could hear anyone. They couldn't even tell if he knew his parents were dead. He didn't move, didn't speak, barely blinked. There wasn't a friend or a relative who could take him—he had to be dressed and changed like a baby—so they were sending him to a Home a few blocks away.

I went up to his room and it was spooky the way he just sat there, staring at nothing. He didn't even look at me. I felt funny trying to talk to him, so I only stayed a few minutes that day. But the Home was even closer to the pool than the hospital, so I got into the habit of dropping in on him every couple of days. He got on pretty well there. In a few weeks he was walking again, and going to the toilet himself. But nobody could get a peep out of him. I almost gave up going, but I couldn't get him out of my head, he looked so scrawny and small behind his glasses. And apart from feeling sorry for the guy, I found out it's actually pretty cool talking to somebody who can't talk back. Easier to open up when the person doesn't say anything stupid to shut you back down again. Or when they don't have a stake in what's on your mind. It got so I'd talk to Mike a lot, and I even looked forward to it.

Things went on this way for most of the summer. The last week in August were my tryouts. The swimming one went great. All those lengths stood me in good stead and I was solidly in the middle range for the team. But my diving tryout was a total bomb. I got to the edge of the platform and nothing went the way it usually does. No butterflies, no rush from the smell of chlorine. The pool looked too close, too real, my legs and arms felt too big, gangly, in the way. And what clinched it was my dad. There again, behind the viewing glass. No smile, no wave. I'll show you, I thought, and I flung myself into my dive like a knife-thrower. It was a disaster. No hang-time, in fact I felt so rushed I barely had time to straighten out and avoid the total humiliation, not to mention pain, of a belly-flop. I knew as soon as I got out of the water that I'd blown it. I wanted to ask for a second chance, but I was afraid I'd start blubbering all over the place if I opened my mouth, so I had to just stand there tight-lipped, my chest clenched like a fist, while the coach told me really nicely that I was trying too hard, I had to learn to let go and let the dive take me with it. I couldn't even thank her when she suggested I come to some training sessions she was giving at the Y. By the time I headed for the showers my dad was gone.

I didn't go see Mike for five days after that. I showed up for work and went home and that was about it. My dad didn't show up either. I was watching for him. Then the nurse called me. She'd gotten my name from the sign-in sheet and looked up my number in the phone book. Just wanted to know how I was doing, she said, but I knew she wanted to know why I'd suddenly stopped visiting. Typical, I thought, even when he can't speak the kid finds a way to hassle me. But I told her I'd be by the next day.

I stopped at the door of his room, and watched him for a minute, breathing that pale washed-out smell you get in hospitals. Lying in that big white square of a bed he looked like he had been swallowed whole. The fist in my chest squeezed tighter and I thought, it's too much, I can't do it. But I pasted a big smile on my face, walked to the side of the bed and sat down.

"Hey, Mikey," I said.

He looked at me. Turned his head and looked at me. And when I figured out he really was in there somewhere, I couldn't help it, I started to cry. And I told him about the tryouts and my dad and how awful it was, what with my mom being no help at all and me not knowing whether I wanted to talk to him or kill him. And the whole time I was thinking, good going, Chris, the kid just lost both his parents and may never get a chance at a normal life, and you're busy telling him all your stupid little problems, but I just couldn't help it.

Finally I scrubbed my face and said, "Sorry, kid. Guess you've got problems of your own, eh?" But he was gone again, not a flicker in his eyes, staring beyond me. "Well, at least I still have my day job. They've asked me to teach swimming a couple nights a week. Most of the kids are worse swimmers than you, and boy, is that saying something." Still nothing. And suddenly it became the most important thing in the world to get him to look at me again. "Listen, Mikey, they're putting in a whirlpool for sports injury therapy. Looks pretty neat. Why don't you come to the pool sometime? Would you like that?"

He touched my face with one finger.

Well, I was like a crazy man, running up to the nurse all excited, shouting my head off. And she was just as bad. So that was how he started coming to the pool again, only this time a volunteer attendant brought him. The guy would sit Mike in the shallow end and kind of play with him, splashing him lightly with water, letting him walk around. Mike seemed to be quite happy just to sit or paddle. He was tired and old looking, too feeble to resist when the attendant steered him away from the deep end. I began to think that this might be the best he'd ever do.

Then one day, while the attendant is talking to one of the girls in the new Jacuzzi, I see Mike head for the deep end, walking close to the edge, jerkily, like he's on automatic pilot. The deep end is near the Jacuzzi and I figure it's only a matter of moments before the volunteer sees what the kid's up to and hauls him away, so I casually wander over to the whirlpool and block his view. All the time I'm watching Mike out of the corner of my eye and trying to convince myself that if he starts to get into trouble I can get him out of it, but I'm still pretty nervous. How do I really know why he's off to that end of the pool, anyway? But another part of me, lower down, is drumming out this message over and over, telling him to go for it, go for it, and I don't even know what I mean. Well, Mike gets to the deep end and, sure enough, the attendant looks over my shoulder and freaks. He leaps out of the whirlpool as Mike crouches down, but I hold him back by one arm. "Leave him alone, man."

"Are you crazy?" he says. "You're gonna get me fired."

"Back off," I say, eyes glued to the kid.

Mike tips himself backward into the pool.

"Get him out!" yells the volunteer and hurls himself toward the pool, only to come smack up against me. I'm ready to punch him out if he takes one more step toward that kid. Mike is floating like a dead man, loose and motionless beneath the water. My heart is thrashing the inside of my chest when I think of what could be happening if I'm wrong. The attendant is staring at me like I'm a murderer, and I'm grunting with the strain of holding him back when suddenly I realize I haven't been keeping track of my breathing. I don't know how long he's been in there.

Maybe this is what he intended all along. Maybe he figured he could trust me to let him go.

Maybe he's two steps above vegetable and whatever's left of him is somewhere in there screaming for help.

"MIKEY!" I yell at the pool. But I don't move one step closer.

The attendant is practically crying, and a ragged group is forming behind us, trying to figure out what's happening, what we're staring at.

Mike's arms and legs start to move. He looks like he's feeling his way through some invisible tunnel, then he bursts through into the open air, climbs out of the pool and walks back to the same spot, more confidently, almost eagerly. He tips himself backward again, eyes closed.

My hands are still digging into the attendant's arms—he'll have a huge bruise, and I think I've strained a muscle in my wrist. We breathe in our first wild gulps, and stand there panting for a few seconds after I let him go. "See," I say while he rubs the red spots, "it's just his game. He's OK. I'll watch him." We dance around a little, 'cause I've wounded the guy's pride, but basically he's cool.

I turn away to check the rest of the pool, and there's my dad in the viewing room. He's seen the whole thing. I can tell because his face is twisted like he's in pain, and he looks like he's ready to step through the glass like it's nothing but air. Our eyes lock, and his hands rise to the glass and press against it, fingers spread wide open. And it's like what he's feeling is so strong it pulls my hand toward it all by itself. But that's where it ends. Every muscle in my body aches. I need to sit down, rub my wrists. I need. And all he does is stand there.

I still spend a lot of time at the pool. My dad comes by, but not so often, and I find myself looking for him less and less. When he does show, I don't make a move to go talk to him. I figure there are some things you have to work out on your own. Maybe he will, maybe he won't. Maybe he'll just disappear again. But that's up to him. In the meantime, I have things to get on with. My diving lessons at the Y. And Mike. Like I promised, I watch him, every day, while he tips himself into the depths of that big fluffy cloud or living pool or whatever his bent little brain thinks is there. Most days he doesn't give any sign that he knows I'm here. But I know I am, and I guess that's what matters. And I'll tell you something else. Every time he breaks water it's like some kind of underwater flower bursting into the sunlight, and I swear I can feel the touch of something warm on my face.

Barbara Scott (*Born 1957, Saskatoon, Saskatchewan*), writer. Her work has been published in literary magazines and in several anthologies. A collection of her short stories, *The Quick*, was published in 1999. In her writing she draws on her varied experiences as a matron in a girls' boarding school in England, a jug-hustler on a seismic crew, an itinerant singer, and an instructor at the Alberta College of Art and Design.

   Selection Activities, p. 371

The Concert Stages of Europe

Jack Hodgins

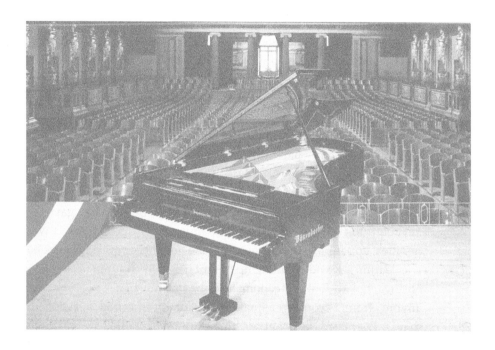

Now I KNOW CORNELIA Horncastle would say I'm blaming the wrong person. I know that. I know too that she would say thirty years is a long time to hold a grudge, and that if I needed someone to blame for the fact that I made a fool of myself in front of the whole district and ruined my life in the process, then I ought to look around for the person who gave me my high-flown ideas in the first place. But she would be wrong; because there is no doubt I'd have led a different sort of life if it weren't for her, if it weren't for that piano keyboard her parents presented her with on her eleventh birthday. And everything— everything would have been different if that piano keyboard hadn't been the kind made out of stiff paper that you unfolded and laid out across the kitchen table in order to do your practising.

I don't suppose there would have been all that much harm in her having the silly thing, if only my mother hadn't got wind of it. "What a fantastic idea," she said. "You could learn to play without even making a sound! You could practise your scales without having to hear that awful racket when you hit a wrong note! A genius must have thought of it," she said. Certainly someone who'd read his Keats: *Heard melodies are sweet, but those unheard are sweeter.* "And don't laugh," she said, "because Cornelia Horncastle is learning to play the piano and her mother doesn't even have to miss an episode of *Ma Perkins* while she does it."

That girl, people had told her, would be giving concerts in Europe some day, command performances before royalty, and her parents hadn't even had to fork out the price of a piano. It was obvious proof, if you needed it, that a person didn't have to be rich to get somewhere in this world.

In fact, Cornelia's parents hadn't needed to put out even the small amount that paper keyboard would have cost. A piano teacher named Mrs. Humphries had moved onto the old Dendoff place and, discovering that almost no one in the district owned a piano, gave the keyboard to the Horncastles along with a year's free lessons. It was her idea, apparently, that when everyone heard how quickly Cornelia was learning they'd be lining up to sent her their children for lessons. She wanted to make the point that having no piano needn't stop anyone from becoming a pianist. No doubt she had a vision of paper keyboards in every house in Waterville, of children everywhere thumping their scales out on the kitchen table without offending anyone's ears, of a whole generation turning silently into Paderewskis without ever having played a note.

They would, I suppose, have to play a real piano when they went to her house for lessons once a week, but I was never able to find out for myself, because all that talk of Cornelia's marvellous career on the concert stages of Europe did not prompt my parents to buy one of those fake keyboards or sign me up for lessons with Mrs. Humphries. My mother was born a Barclay, which meant she had a few ideas of her own, and Cornelia's glorious future prompted her to go one better. We would buy a real piano, she announced. And I would be sent to a teacher we could trust, not to that newcomer. If those concert stages of Europe were ever going to hear the talent of someone from the stump ranches of Waterville, it wouldn't be Cornelia Horncastle, it would be Barclay Desmond. Me.

My father nearly choked on his coffee. "But Clay's a boy!"

"So what?" my mother said. *All* those famous players used to be boys. What did he think Chopin was? Or Tchaikovsky?

My father was so embarrassed that his throat began to turn a dark pink. Some things were too unnatural even to think about.

But eventually she won him over. "Think how terrible you'd feel," she said, "if he ended up in the bush, like you. If Mozart's father had worked for the Comox Logging Company and thought piano-playing was for sissies, where would the world be today?"

My father had no answer to that. He'd known since before his marriage that though my mother would put up with being married to a logger, expecting every day to be made a widow, she wouldn't tolerate for one minute the notion that a child of hers would follow him up into those hills. The children of Lenora Barclay would enter the professions.

She was right, he had to agree; working in the woods was the last thing in the world he wanted for his sons. He'd rather they take up ditch-digging or begging than have to work for that miserable logging company, or take their orders from someone like Tiny Beechman, or get their skulls cracked open like Stanley Kirck. It was a rotten way to make a living, and if he'd only had a decent education he could have made something of himself.

Of course, I knew he was saying all this for my mother's benefit. He didn't really believe it for a minute. My father loved his work. I could tell by the way he was always talking about Ab Jennings and Shorty Cresswell, the men he worked with. I could tell by the excitement that mounted in him every year as the time grew near for the annual festival of loggers' sports where he usually won the bucking contest. It was obvious, I thought, that the man really wanted nothing more in this world than that one of his sons should follow in his footsteps. And much as I disliked the idea, I was sure that I was the one he'd set his hopes on. Kenny was good in school. Laurel was a girl. I was the obvious choice. I even decided that what he'd pegged me for was a high-rigger. I was going to be one of those men who risked their necks climbing hundreds of feet up the bare lonely spar tree to hang the rigging from the top. Of course I would fall and kill myself the first time I tried it, I knew that, but there was no way I could convey my hesitation to my father since he would never openly admit that this was really his goal for me.

And playing the piano on the concert stages of Europe was every bit as unattractive. "Why not Kenny?" I said, when the piano had arrived, by barge, from Vancouver.

"He's too busy already with his school work," my mother said. Kenny was hoping for a scholarship, which meant he got out of just about everything unpleasant.

"What about Laurel?"

"With her short fat fingers?"

In the meantime, she said, though she was no piano player herself (a great sigh here for what might have been), she had no trouble at all identifying which of those ivory keys was the all-important Middle C and would show it to me, to memorize, so that I wouldn't look like a total know-nothing when I showed up tomorrow for my first lesson. She'd had one piano lesson herself as a girl, she told me, and had learned all about Mister Middle C, but she's never had a second lesson because her time was needed by her father, outside, helping with the chores. Seven daughters altogether, no sons, and she was the one who was the most often expected to fill the role of a boy. The rest of them had found the time to learn chords and chromatic scales and all those magic things she'd heard them practising while she was scrubbing out the dairy and cutting the runners off strawberry plants. They'd all become regular show-offs in one way or another, learning other instruments as well, putting on their own concerts and playing in dance bands and earning a reputation all over the district as entertaining livewires—The Barclay Sisters. And no one ever guessed that all the while she was dreaming about herself at that keyboard, tinkling away, playing beautiful music before huge audiences in elegant theatres.

"Then it isn't me that should be taking lessons," I said. "It's you."

"Don't be silly." But she walked to the new piano and pressed down one key, a black one, and looked as if I'd tempted her there for a minute. "It's too late now," she said. And then she sealed my fate: "But I just know that you're going to be a great pianist."

When my mother "just knew" something, that was as good as guaranteeing it already completed. It was her way of controlling the future and, incidentally, the rest of us. By "just knowing" things, she went through life commanding the future to fit into certain patterns she desired while we scurried around making sure that it worked out that way so she'd never have to be disappointed. She'd had one great disappointment as a girl—we were never quite sure what it was, since it was only alluded to in whispers with far-off looks—and it was important that it never happen again. I was trapped.

People were always asking what you were going to be when you grew up. As if your wishes counted. In the first six years of my life the country had convinced me it wanted me to grow up and get killed fighting Germans and Japanese. I'd seen the coils of barbed wire along the beach and knew they were there just to slow down the enemy while I went looking for my gun. The teachers at school obviously wanted me to grow up and become a teacher just like them, because as far as I could see nothing they ever taught me could be of any use or interest to a single adult in the world except someone getting paid to teach it to someone else. My mother was counting on my becoming a pianist with a swallow-tail coat and standing ovations. And my father, despite all his noises to the contrary, badly wanted me to climb into the crummy every morning with him and ride out those gravelly roads into mountains and risk my life destroying forests.

I did not want to be a logger. I did not want to be a teacher. I did not want to be a soldier. And I certainly did not want to be a pianist. If anyone had ever asked me what I did want to be when I grew up, in a way that meant they expected the truth, I'd have said quite simply that what I wanted was to be a Finn.

Our new neighbours, the Korhonens, were Finns. And being a Finn, I'd been told, meant something very specific. A Finn would give you the shirt off his back, a Finn was as honest as the day is long, a Finn could drink anybody under the table and beat up half a dozen Germans and Irishmen without trying, a Finn was not afraid of work, a Finn kept a house so clean you could eat off the floors. I knew all these things before ever meeting our neighbours, but as soon as I had met them I was able to add a couple more generalizations of my own to the catalogue. Finnish girls were blonde and beautiful and flirtatious, and Finnish boys were strong, brave, and incredibly intelligent. These conclusions were reached immediately after meeting Lilja Korhonen, whose turned-up nose and blue eyes fascinated me from the beginning, and Larry Korhonen, who was already a teenager and told me for starters that he was actually Superman, having learned to fly after long hours of practice off their barn roof. Mr. and Mrs. Korhonen, of course, fitted exactly all the things my parents had told me about Finns in general. And so I decided my ambition in life was to be just like them.

I walked over to their house every Saturday afternoon and pretended to read their coloured funnies. I got in on the weekly steam bath with Larry and his father in the sauna down by the barn. Mr. Korhonen, a patient man whose eyes sparkled at my eager attempts, taught me to count to ten—*yksi, kaksi, kolme, neljä, viisi, kuusi, seitsemän, kahdeksan, yhdeksän, kymmenen.* I helped Mrs. Korhonen scrub her linoleum floors and put down newspapers so no one could walk on them, and I gorged myself on cinnamon cookies and *kala loota* and coffee sucked through a sugar cube. If there was something to be caught from just being around them, I wanted to catch it. And since being a Finn seemed to be a full-time occupation, I didn't have much patience with my parents, who behaved as if there were other things you had to prepare yourself for.

The first piano teacher they sent me to was Aunt Jessie, who lived in a narrow, cramped house up a gravel road that led to the mountains. She'd learned to play as a girl in Toronto, but she had no pretensions about being a real teacher, she was only doing this as a favour to my parents so they wouldn't have to send me to that Mrs. Humphries, an outsider. But one of the problems was that Aunt Jessie—who was no aunt of mine at all, simply one of those family friends who somehow get saddled with an honorary family title— was exceptionally beautiful. She was so attractive, in fact, that even at the age of ten I had difficulty keeping my eyes or my mind on the lessons. She exuded a dreamy sort of delicate femininity; her soft, intimate voice made the hair on the back of my neck stand on end. Besides that, her own playing was so much more pleasant to listen to than my own stumbling clangs and clunks that she would often begin to show me how to do something and become so carried away with the sound of her own music that she just kept right on playing through the rest of my half-hour. It was a simple matter to persuade her to dismiss me early every week so that I'd have a little time to play in the creek that ran past the back of her house, poling a homemade raft up and down the length of her property while her daughters paid me nickels and candies for a ride. At the end of a year my parents suspected I wasn't progressing as fast as I should. They found out why on the day I fell in the creek and nearly drowned, had to be revived by a distraught Aunt Jessie, and was driven home soaked and shivering in the back seat of her old Hudson.

Mr. Korhonen and my father were huddled over the taken-apart cream separator on the veranda when Aunt Jessie brought me up to the door. My father, when he saw me, had that peculiar look on his face that was halfway between amusement and concern, but Mr. Korhonen laughed openly. "That boy lookit like a drowny rat."

I felt like a drowned rat too, but I joined his laughter. I was sure this would be the end of my piano career, and could hardly wait to see my mother roll her eyes to the ceiling, throw out her arms, and say, "I give up."

She did nothing of the sort. She tightened her lips and told Aunt Jessie how disappointed she was. "No wonder the boy still stumbles around on that keyboard like a blindfolded rabbit; he's not going to learn the piano while he's out risking his life on the *river*!"

When I came downstairs in dry clothes Aunt Jessie had gone, no doubt wishing she'd left me to drown in the creek, and my parents and the Korhonens were all in the kitchen drinking coffee. The Korhonens sat at either side of the table, smoking hand-rolled cigarettes and squinting at me through the smoke. Mrs. Korhonen could blow beautiful white streams down her nostrils. They'd left their gumboots on the piece of newspaper just inside the door, of course, and wore the same kind of grey work-socks on their feet that my father always wore on his. My father was leaning against the wall with both arms folded across his chest inside his wide elastic braces, as he sometimes did, swishing his mug gently as if he were trying to bring something up from the bottom. My mother, however, was unable to alight anywhere. She slammed wood down into the firebox of the stove, she rattled dishes in the sink water, she slammed cupboard doors, she went around the room with the coffee pot, refilling mugs, and all the while she sang the song of her betrayal, cursing her own stupidity for sending me to a friend instead of a professional teacher, and suddenly in a flash of inspiration dumping all the blame on my father. "If you hadn't made me feel it was somehow pointless I wouldn't have felt guilty about spending more money!"

From behind the drifting shreds of smoke Mr. Korhonen grinned at me. Sucked laughter between his teeth. "Yust *teenk*, boy, looks like-it you're saved!"

Mrs. Korhonen stabbed out her cigarette in an ashtray, picked a piece of tobacco off her tongue, and composed her face into the most serious and ladylike expression she could muster. "Yeh! Better he learn to drive the tractor." And swung me a conspirator's grin.

"Not on your life," my mother said. Driving a machine may have been good enough ambition for some people, she believed, but the Barclays had been in this country for four generations and she knew there were a few things higher. "What we'll do is send him to a real teacher. Mrs. Greensborough."

Mrs. Greensborough was well known for putting on a public recital in town once a year, climaxing the program with her own rendition of Grieg's Piano Concerto—so beautiful that all went home, it was said, with tears in their eyes. The problem with Mrs. Greensborough had nothing to do with her teaching. She was, as far as I could see, an excellent piano teacher. And besides, there was something rather exciting about playing on her piano, which was surrounded and nearly buried by a thousand tropical plants and dozens of cages full of squawking birds. Every week's lesson was rather like putting on a concert in the midst of the Amazon jungle. There was even a monkey that swung through the branches and sat on the top of the piano with the metronome between its paws. And Mrs. Greensborough was at the same time warm and demanding, complimentary and hard to please—though given a little, like Aunt Jessie, to taking off on long passages of her own playing, as if she'd forgotten I was there.

It took a good hour's hard bicycling on uphill gravel roads before I could present myself for the lesson—past a dairy farm, a pig farm, a turkey farm, a dump, and a good long stretch of bush—then more washboard road through heavy timber where driveways disappeared into the trees and one dog after another lay in wait for its weekly battle with my right foot. Two spaniels, one Irish setter, and a bulldog. But it wasn't a spaniel or a setter or even a bulldog that met me on the driveway of the Greensboroughs' chicken farm, it was a huge German shepherd that came barking down the slope the second I had got the gate shut, and stuck its nose into my crotch. And kept it there, growling menacingly, the whole time it took me to back him up to the door of the house. There was no doubt in my mind that I would come home from piano lesson one Saturday minus a few parts. Once I had got to the house, I tried to get inside quickly and shut the door in his face, leaving him out there in the din of cackling hens; but he always got his nose between the door and the jamb, growled horribly and pushed himself inside so that he could lie on the floor at my feet and watch me hungrily the whole time I sat at the kitchen table waiting for Ginny Stamp to finish off her lesson and get out of there. By the time my turn came around my nerves were too frayed for me to get much benefit out of the lesson.

Still, somehow I learned. That Mrs. Greensborough was a marvellous teacher, my mother said. The woman really knew her stuff. And I was such a fast-learning student that it took less than two years for my mother to begin thinking it was time the world heard from me.

"Richy Ryder," she said, "is coming to town."

"What?"

"Richy Ryder, CJMT. *The Talent Show.*"

I'd heard the program. Every Saturday night Richy Ryder was in a different town somewhere in the province, hosting his one-hour talent contest from the stage of a local theatre and giving away free trips to Hawaii.

Something rolled over in my stomach.

"And here's the application form right here," she said, whipping two sheets of paper out of her purse to slap down on the table.

"No thank you," I said. If she thought I was going in it, she was crazy.

"Don't be silly. What harm is there in trying?" My mother always answered objections with great cheerfulness, as if they were hardly worth considering.

"I'll make a fool of myself."

"You play beautifully," she said. "It's amazing how far you've come in only two years. And besides, even if you don't win, the experience would be good for you."

"You have to go door-to-door ahead of time, begging for pledges, for money."

"Not begging," she said. She plunged her hands into the sink, peeling carrots so fast I couldn't see the blade of the vegetable peeler. "Just giving people a chance to vote for you. A dollar a vote." The carrot dropped, skinned naked, another one was picked up. She looked out of the window now toward the barn and, still smiling, delivered the argument that never failed. "I just know you'd win it if you went in, I can feel it in my bones."

"Not this time!" I shouted, nearly turning myself inside out with the terror. "Not this time. I just can't do it."

Yet somehow I found myself riding my bicycle up and down all the roads around Waterville, knocking at people's doors, explaining the contest, and asking for their money and their votes. I don't know why I did it. Perhaps I was doing it for the same reason I was tripping over everything, knocking things off tables, slamming my shoulder into doorjambs; I just couldn't help it, everything had gone out of control. I'd wakened one morning that year and found myself six feet two inches tall and as narrow as a fence stake. My feet were so far away they seemed to have nothing to do with me. My hands flopped around on the ends of those lanky arms like fish, something alive. My legs had grown so fast the bones in my knees parted and I had to wear elastic bandages to keep from falling apart. When I turned a corner on my bicycle, one knee would bump the handlebar, throwing me into the ditch. I was the same person as before, apparently, saddled with this new body I didn't know what to do with. Everything had gone out of control. I seemed to have nothing to do with the direction of my own life. It was perfectly logical that I should end up playing the piano on the radio, selling myself to the countryside for a chance to fly off to Hawaii and lie on the sand under the whispering palms.

There were actually two prizes offered. The all-expense, ten-day trip to Hawaii would go to the person who brought in the most votes for himself, a dollar a vote. But lest someone accuse the radio station of getting its values confused, there was also a prize for the person judged by the panel of experts to have the most talent. This prize, which was donated by Nelson's Hardware, was a leatherette footstool.

"It's not the prize that's important," people told me. "It's the chance to be heard by all those people."

I preferred not to think of all those people. It seemed to me that if I were cut out to be a concert pianist it would be my teacher and not my parents encouraging me in this thing. Mrs. Greensborough, once she'd forked over her two dollars for two votes, said nothing at all. No doubt she was hoping I'd keep her name out of it.

But it had taken no imagination on my part to figure out that if I were to win the only prize worth trying for, the important thing was not to spend long hours at the keyboard, practising, but to get out on the road hammering at doors, on the telephone calling relatives, down at the General Store approaching strangers who stopped for gas. Daily piano practice shrank to one or two quick run-throughs of "The Robin's Return," school homework shrank to nothing at all, and home chores just got ignored. My brother and sister filled in for me, once in a while, so the chickens wouldn't starve to death and the woodbox would never be entirely empty, but they did it gracelessly. It was amazing, they said, how much time a great pianist had to spend out on the road, meeting his public. Becoming famous, they said, was more work than it was worth.

And becoming famous, I discovered, was what people assumed I was after. "You'll go places," they told me. "You'll put this place on the old map." I was a perfect combination of my father's down-to-earth get-up-and-go and my mother's finer sensitivity, they said. How wonderful to see a young person with such high ambition!

"I always knew this old place wouldn't be good enough to hold you," my grandmother said as she fished out a five-dollar bill from her purse. But my mother's sisters, who appeared from all parts of the old farmhouse in order to contribute a single collective vote, had some reservations to express. Eleanor, the youngest, said she doubted I'd be able to carry it off, I'd probably freeze when I was faced with a microphone, I'd forget what a piano was for. Christina announced she was betting I'd faint, or have to run out to the bathroom right in the middle of my piece. And Mabel, red-headed Mabel who'd played accordion once in an amateur show, said she remembered a boy who had made an utter fool of himself in one of these things. "Don't be so morbid," my grandmother said. "The boy probably had no talent. Clay here is destined for higher things."

From behind her, my grandfather winked. He seldom had a chance to contribute more than that to a conversation. He waited until we were alone to stuff a five-dollar bill in my pocket and squeeze my arm.

I preferred my grandmother's opinion of me to the aunts'. I began to feed people lies so they'd think that about me—that I was destined for dizzy heights. I wanted to be a great pianist, I said, and if I won that trip to Hawaii I'd trade it in for the money so that I could go and study at the Toronto Conservatory. I'd heard of the Toronto Conservatory only because it was printed in big black letters on the front cover of all those yellow books of finger exercises I was expected to practise.

I don't know why people gave me their money. Pity, perhaps. Maybe it was impossible to say no to a six-foot-two-inch thirteen-year-old who trips over his own bike in front of your house, falls up your bottom step, blushes red with embarrassment when you open the door, and tells you he wants your money for a talent contest so he can become a Great Artist. At any rate, by the day of the contest I'd collected enough money to put me in the third spot. I would have to rely on pledges from the studio audience and phone-in pledges from the radio audience to rocket me up to first place. The person in second place when I walked into that theatre to take my seat down front with the rest of the contestants was Cornelia Horncastle.

I don't know how she managed it so secretly. I don't know where she found the people to give her money, living in the same community as I did, unless all those people who gave me their dollar bills when I knocked on their doors had just given her two the day before. Maybe she'd gone into town, canvassing street after street, something my parents wouldn't let me do on the grounds that town people already had enough strangers banging on their doors every day. Once I'd got outside the vague boundaries of Waterville I was to approach only friends or relatives or people who worked in the woods with my dad, or stores that had—as my mother put it—done a good business out of us over the years. Cornelia Horncastle, in order to get herself secretly into that second place, must have gone wild in town. Either that or discovered a rich relative.

She sat at the other end of the front row of contestants, frowning over the sheets of music in her hands. A short nod and a quick smile were all she gave me. Like the other contestants, I was kept busy licking my dry lips, rubbing my sweaty palms together, wondering if

I should whip out to the bathroom one last time, and rubbernecking to get a look at people as they filled up the theatre behind us. Mrs. Greensborough, wearing dark glasses and a big floppy hat, was jammed into the far corner at the rear, studying her program. Mr. and Mrs. Korhonen and Lilja came partway down the aisle and found seats near the middle. Mr. Korhonen winked at me. Larry, who was not quite the hero he had once been, despite the fact that he'd recently beat up one of the teachers and set fire to the bus shelter, came in with my brother Kenny—both of them looking uncomfortable—and slid into a back seat. My parents came all the way down front, so they could look back up the slope and pick out the seats they wanted. My mother smiled as she always did in public, as if she expected the most delightful surprise at any moment. They took seats near the front. Laurel was with them, reading a book.

My mother's sisters—with husbands, boyfriends, a few of my cousins—filled up the entire middle section of the back row. Eleanor, who was just a few years older than myself, crossed her eyes and stuck out her tongue when she saw that I'd turned to look. Mabel pulled in her chin and held up her hands, which she caused to tremble and shake. Time to be nervous, she was suggesting, in case I forgot. Bella, Christina, Gladdy, Frieda—all sat puffed up like members of a royal family, or the owners of this theatre, looking down over the crowd as if they believed every one of these people had come here expressly to watch their nephew and for no other reason. "Look, it's the Barclay girls," I heard someone behind me say. And someone else: "Oh, *them*." The owner of the first voice giggled. "It's a wonder they aren't all entered in this thing, you know how they like to perform." A snort. "They *are* performing, just watch them." I could tell by the muffled "Shhh" and the rustling of clothing that one of them was nudging the other and pointing at me, at the back of my neck. "One of them's son." When I turned again, Eleanor stood up in the aisle by her seat, did a few steps of a tap dance, and quickly sat down. In case I was tempted to take myself seriously.

When my mother caught my eye, she mouthed a silent message: stop gawking at the audience, I was letting people see how unusual all this was to me, instead of taking it in my stride like a born performer. She indicated with her head that I should notice the stage.

As if I hadn't already absorbed every detail. It was exactly as she must have hoped. A great black concert grand with the lid lifted sat out near the front of the stage, against a painted backdrop of palm trees along a sandy beach, and—in great scrawled letters—the words "Richy Ryder's CJMT Talent Festival." A long blackboard leaned against one end of the proscenium arch, with all the contestants' names on it and the rank order of each. Someone named Brenda Roper was in first place. On the opposite side of the stage, a microphone seemed to have grown up out of a heap of pineapples. I felt sick.

Eventually Richy Ryder came out of whatever backstage room he'd been hiding in and passed down the row of contestants, identifying us and telling us to get up on to the stage when our turns came without breaking our necks on those steps. "You won't be nervous, when you get up there," he said. "I'll make you feel at ease." He was looking off somewhere else as he said it, and I could see his jaw muscles straining to hold back a yawn. And he wasn't fooling me with his "you won't be nervous" either, because I knew without a doubt that the minute I got up on that stage I would throw up all over the piano.

Under the spotlight, Richy Ryder acted like a different person. He did not look the least bit like yawning while he told the audience the best way to hold their hands to get the most out of applause, cautioned them against whistling or yelling obscenities, painted a glorious picture of the life ahead for the talented winner of this contest, complimented the audience on the number of happy, shiny faces he could see out there in the seats, and told them how lucky they were to have this opportunity of showing off the fine young talent of the valley to all the rest of the province. I slid down in my seat, sure that I would rather die than go through with this thing.

The first contestant was a fourteen-year-old girl dressed up like a gypsy, singing something in a foreign language. According to the blackboard she was way down in ninth place, so I didn't pay much attention until her voice cracked open in the middle of a high note and she clutched at her throat with both hands, a look of incredulous surprise on her face. She stopped right there, face a brilliant red, and after giving the audience a quick curtsy hurried off the stage. A great beginning, I thought. If people were going to fall to pieces like that through the whole show no one would even notice my upchucking on the Heintzman. I had a vision of myself dry-heaving the whole way through "The Robin's Return."

Number two stepped up to the microphone and answered all of Richy Ryder's questions as if they were some kind of test he had to pass in order to be allowed to perform. Yes sir, his name was Roger Casey, he said with a face drawn long and narrow with seriousness, and in case that wasn't enough he added that his father was born in Digby, Nova Scotia, and his mother was born Esther Romaine in a little house just a couple blocks up the street from the theatre, close to the Native Sons' Hall, and had gone to school with the mayor though she'd dropped out of Grade Eight to get a job at the Safeway cutting meat. And yes sir, he was going to play the saxophone because he'd taken lessons for four years from Mr. D. P. Rowbottom on Seventh Street though he'd actually started out on the trumpet until he decided he didn't like it all that much. He came right out to the edge of the stage, toes sticking over, leaned back like a rooster about to crow, and blasted out "Softly As in a Morning Sunrise" so loud and hard that I thought his bulging eyes would pop right out his head and his straining lungs would blast holes through that red-and-white shirt. Everyone moved forward, tense and straining, waiting for something terrible to happen—for him to fall of the stage or explode or go sailing off into the air from the force of his own fantastic intensity—but he stopped suddenly and everyone fell back exhausted and sweaty to clap for him.

The third contestant was less reassuring. A kid with talent. A smart-aleck ten-year-old with red hair, who told the audience he was going into show business when he grew up, started out playing "Swanee River" on his banjo, switched in the middle of a bar to a mouth organ, tap-danced across the stage to play a few bars on the piano, and finished off on a trombone he'd had stashed away behind the palm tree. He bowed, grinned, flung himself around the stage as if he'd spent his whole life on it, and looked as if he'd do his whole act again quite happily if the audience wanted him to. By the time the tremendous applause had died down my jaw was aching from the way I'd been grinding my teeth the whole time he was up there. The audience would not have gone quite so wild over him, I thought, if he hadn't been wearing a hearing aid and a leg brace.

Then it was my turn. A strange calm fell over me when my name was called, the kind of calm that I imagine comes over a person about to be executed when his mind finally buckles under the horror it has been faced with, something too terrible to believe in. I wondered for a moment if I had died. But no, my body at least hadn't died, for it transported me unbidden across the front of the audience, up the staircase (with only a slight stumble on the second step, hardly noticeable), and across the great wide stage of the theatre to stand facing Richy Ryder's enormous expanse of white smiling teeth, beside the microphone.

"And you are Barclay Philip Desmond," he said.

"Yes," I said.

And again "yes," because I realized that not only had my voice come out as thin and high as the squeal of a dry buzz saw, but the microphone was at least a foot too low. I had to bend my knees to speak into it.

"You don't live in town, do you?" he said. He had no intention of adjusting that microphone. "You come from a place called ... Waterville. A logging and farming settlement?"

"Yes," I said.

And again "yes" because while he was speaking my legs had straightened up, I'd returned to my full height and had to duck again for the microphone.

He was speaking to me but his eyes, I could see, were busy keeping all that audience gathered together, while his voice and mind were obviously concentrated on the thousands of invisible people who were crouched inside that microphone, listening, the thousands of people who—I imagined now—were pulled up close to their sets all over the province, wondering if I was actually a pair of twins or if my voice had some peculiar way of echoing itself, a few tones lower.

"Does living in the country like that mean you have to milk the cows every morning before you go to school?"

"Yes."

And again "yes."

I could see Mrs. Greensborough cowering in the back corner. I promise not to mention you, I thought. And the Korhonens, grinning. I had clearly passed over into another world they couldn't believe in.

"If you've got a lot of farm chores to do, when do you find the time to practise the piano?"

He had me this time. A "yes" wouldn't be good enough. "Right after school," I said, and ducked to repeat. "Right after school. As soon as I get home. For an hour."

"And I just bet," he said, throwing the audience an enormous wink, "that like every other red-blooded country kid you hate every minute of it. You'd rather be outside playing baseball."

The audience laughed. I could see my mother straining forward; she still had the all-purpose waiting-for-the-surprise smile on her lips but her eyes were frowning at the master of ceremonies. She did not approve of the comment. And behind that face she was no doubt thinking to herself "I just know he's going to win" over and over so hard that she was getting pains in the back of her neck. Beside her, my father had a tight grin on his face. He was chuckling to himself, and sliding a look around the room to see how the others were taking this.

Up at the back, most of my aunts—and their husbands, their boyfriends—had tilted their chins down to their chests, offering me only the tops of their heads. Eleanor, however, had both hands behind her neck. She was laughing harder than anyone else.

Apparently I was not expected to respond to the last comment, for he had another question as soon as the laughter had died. "How old are you, son?"

"Thirteen."

For once I remembered to duck the first time.

"Thirteen. Does your wife like the idea of your going on the radio like this?"

Again the audience laughed. My face burned. I felt tears in my eyes. I had no control over my face. I tried to laugh like everyone else but realized I probably looked like an idiot. Instead, I frowned and looked embarrassed and kicked at one shoe with the toe of the other.

"Just a joke," he said, "just a joke." The jerk knew he'd gone too far. "And now seriously, one last question before I turn you loose on those ivories over there."

My heart had started to thump so noisily I could hardly hear him. My hands, I realized, had gone numb. There was no feeling at all in my fingers. How was I ever going to play the piano?

"What are you going to be when you grow up?"

The thumping stopped. My heart stopped. A strange cold silence settled over the world. I was going to die right in front of all those people. What I was going to be was a corpse, dead of humiliation, killed in a trap I hadn't seen being set. What must have been only a few seconds crawled by while something crashed around in my head, trying to get out. I sensed the audience, hoping for some help from them. My mother had settled back in her seat and for the first time that surprise-me smile had gone. Rather, she looked confident, sure of what I was about to say.

And suddenly, I was aware of familiar faces all over that theatre. Neighbours. Friends of the family. My aunts. People who had heard me answer that question at their doors, people who thought they knew what I wanted.

There was nothing left of Mrs. Greensborough but the top of her big hat. My father, too, was looking down at the floor between his feet. I saw myself falling from that spar tree, high in the mountains.

"Going to be?" I said, turning so fast that I bumped the microphone with my hand, which turned out after all not to be numb.

I ducked.

"Nothing," I said. "I don't know. Maybe ... maybe nothing at all."

I don't know who it was that snorted when I screwed up the stool, sat down, and stood up to screw it down again. I don't know how well I played, I wasn't listening. I don't know how loud the audience clapped, I was in a hurry to get back to my seat. I don't know what the other contestants did, I wasn't paying any attention, except when Cornelia Horncastle got up on the stage, told the whole world she was going to be a professional pianist, and sat down to rattle off Rachmaninoff's *Rhapsody on a Theme of Paganini* as if she'd been playing for fifty years. As far as I know it may have been the first time she'd ever heard herself play it. She had a faint look of surprise on her face the whole time, as if she couldn't quite get over the way the keys went down when you touched them.

As soon as Cornelia came down off the stage, smiling modestly, and got back into her seat, Richy Ryder announced a fifteen-minute intermission while the talent judges made their decision and the studio audience went out into the lobby to pledge their money and their votes. Now that the talent had been displayed, people could spend their money according to what they'd heard rather than according to who happened to come knocking on their door. Most of the contestants got up to stretch their legs but I figured I'd stood up once too often that night and stayed in my seat. The lower exit was not far away; I contemplated using it; I could hitchhike home and be in bed before any of the others got out of there.

I was stopped, though, by my father, who sat down in the seat next to mine and put a greasy carton of popcorn in my lap.

"Well," he said, "that's that."

His neck was flushed. This must have been a terrible evening for him. He had a carton of popcorn himself and tipped it up to gather a huge mouthful. I had never before in my life, I realized, seen my father eat popcorn. It must have been worse for him than I thought.

Not one of my aunts was anywhere in sight. I could see my mother standing in the far aisle, talking to Mrs. Korhonen. Still smiling. She would never let herself fall apart in public, no matter what happened. My insides ached with the knowledge of what it must have been like right then to be her. I felt as if I had just betrayed her in front of the whole world. Betrayed everyone.

"Let's go home," I said.

"Not yet. Wait a while. Might as well see this thing to the end."

True, I thought. Wring every last drop of torture out of it.

He looked hard at me a moment, as if he were trying to guess what was going on in my head. And he did, he did, he always knew. "My old man wanted me to be a doctor," he said. "My mother wanted me to be a florist. She liked flowers. She thought if I was a florist I'd be able to send her a bouquet every week. But what does any of that matter now?"

Being a part of a family was too complicated. And right then I decided I'd be a loner. No family for me. Nobody whose hearts could be broken every time I opened my mouth. Nobody *expecting* anything of me. Nobody to get me all tangled up in knots trying to guess who means what and what is it that's really going on inside anyone else. No temptations to presume I knew what someone else was thinking or feeling or hoping for.

When the light had flickered and dimmed, and people had gone back to their seats, a young man with a beard came out on to the stage and changed the numbers behind the contestants' names. I'd dropped to fifth place, and Cornelia Horncastle had moved up to first. She had also, Richy Ryder announced, been awarded the judges' footstool for talent. The winner of the holiday in sunny Hawaii would not be announced until the next week, he said, when the radio audience had enough time to mail in their votes.

"And that," my mother said when she came down the aisle with her coat on, "is the end of a long and tiring day." I could find no disappointment showing in her eyes, or in the set of her mouth. Just relief. The same kind of relief that I felt myself. "You did a good job," she said, "and thank goodness it's over."

As soon as we got in the house I shut myself in the bedroom and announced I was never coming out. Lying on my bed, I tried to read my comic books but my mind passed from face to face all through the community, imagining everyone having a good laugh at the way my puffed-up ambition had got its reward. My face burned. Relatives, the aunts, would be ashamed of me. Eleanor would never let me forget. Nor would Mabel. I lay awake the whole night, torturing myself with these thoughts. But when morning came and the hunger pains tempted me out of the bedroom as far as the breakfast table, I decided the whole wretched experience had brought one benefit with it: freedom from ambition. I wouldn't worry any more about becoming a pianist for my mother. Nor would I worry any more about becoming a high-rigger for my father. I was free at last to concentrate on pursuing the only goal that ever really mattered to me: becoming a Finn.

Of course I failed at that too. But then neither did Cornelia Horncastle become a great pianist on the concert stages of Europe. In fact, I understand that once she got back from her holiday on the beaches of Hawaii she announced to her parents that she was never going to touch a piano again as long as she lived, ivory or cardboard, or any other kind. She had already, she said, accomplished all she'd ever wanted from it. And as far as I know, she's kept her word to this day.

Jack Hodgins (*Born 1938, Comox, British Columbia*), writer of novels, short stories, and nonfiction, is influenced in much of his writing by his Vancouver Island neighbours and surroundings. He has received several awards including the Governor General's Award for Fiction in 1980 for *The Resurrection of Joseph Bourne.*

Selection Activities, p. 372

Tunnel

Sarah Ellis

WHEN I WAS A KID and I imagined myself older, with a summer job, I thought about being outdoors. Tree planting, maybe. Camping out, getting away from the parents, coming home after two months with biceps of iron and bags of money. I used to imagine myself rappelling down some mountain with a geological hammer tucked into my belt. At the very worst I saw myself sitting on one of those tall lifeguard chairs with zinc ointment on my lips.

I didn't know that by the time I was sixteen it would be the global economy and there would be no summer jobs, even though you did your life-skills analysis as recommended by the guidance counsellor at school. Motivated! Energetic! Computer-literate! Shows initiative! Workplace-appropriate hair! What I never imagined was that by the time I got to be sixteen, the only job you could get would be babysitting.

I sometimes take care of my cousin, Laurence. Laurence likes impersonating trucks and being held upside down. I am good at assisting during these activities. This evidently counts as work-related experience.

Girls are different.

Elizabeth, who calls herself Ib, is six-and-one-quarter years old. I go over to her place at 7:30 in the morning and I finish at one o'clock. Then her dad or her mum or her gran (who is not really her gran but the mother of her dad's ex-wife) takes over. Ib has a complicated family. She doesn't seem to mind.

Ib has a yellow plastic suitcase. In the suitcase are Barbies. Ib would like to play with Barbies for five-and-one-half hours every day. In my babysitting course at the community centre they taught us about first aid, diapering, nutritious snacks, and how to jump your jollies out. They did not teach Barbies.

"You be Wanda," says Ib, handing me a nude Barbie who looks as though she is having a bad hair life.

I'm quite prepared to be Wanda if that's what the job requires. But once I am Wanda, I don't know what the heck to do.

Ib is busy dressing Francine, Laurice, Betty, and Talking Doll, who is not a Barbie at all, but a baby doll twice the size of the Barbies.

"What should I do?" I ask.

Ib gives me The Look—an unblinking stare that combines impatience, scorn, and pity.

"*Play*," she says.

When you have sixteen-year-old guy hands, there is no way to hold a nude Barbie without violating her personal space. But all her clothes seem to be made of extremely form-fitting stretchy neon stuff, and I can't get her rigid arms with their poky fingers into the sleeves.

Playing with Barbies makes all other activities look good. The study of irregular French verbs, for example, starts to seem attractive. The board game Candyland, a favourite of Laurence and previously condemned by me as a sure method for turning the human brain to tofu, starts to seem like a laff-riot.

I look at my watch. It is 8:15. The morning stretches ahead of me. Six weeks stretch ahead of me. My life stretches ahead of me. My brain is edging dangerously close to the idea of eternity.

I hold Wanda by her hard, clawlike plastic hand and think of things that Laurence likes to do. We could notch the edge of yogurt lids to make deadly star-shaped tonki for a Ninja attack, but somehow I don't think that's going to cut it with Ib. She's probably not going to go for a burping contest, either.

A warm breeze blows in the window—a small wind that probably originated at sea and blew across the beach, across all those glistening, slowly browning bodies, before it ended up here, trapped in Barbie World. I'm hallucinating the smell of suntan oil. I need to get outside.

I do not suggest a walk. I know, from Laurence, that "walk" is a four-letter word to six-year-olds. Six-year-olds can run around for seventy-two hours straight, but half a block of walking and they suffer from life-threatening exhaustion. I therefore avoid the W-word.

"Ib, would you like to go on an exploration mission?"

Ib thinks for a moment. "Yes."

We pack up the Barbies.

"It's quite a long walk," I say. "We can't take the suitcase."

"I need to take Wanda."

We take Wanda.

We walk along the overgrown railway tracks out to the edge of town. Ib steps on every tie. The sun is behind us and we stop every so often to make our shadows into letters of the alphabet.

("And what sort of work experience can you bring to this job, young man?"

"Well, sir, I spent one summer playing with Barbie dolls and practising making my body into a K."

"Excellent! We've got exciting openings in that area!")

We follow the tracks as the sun rises high in the sky. Ib walks along the rail, holding my hand. My feet crunch on the sharp gravel and Ib sings something about ducks. I inhale the dusty smell of sun-baked weeds, and I'm pulled back to the summer when we used to come out here, Jeff and Danielle and I. That was the summer that Jeff was a double agent planning to blow up the enemy supply train.

The sharp sound of a pneumatic drill rips through the air, and Ib's hand tightens in mine.

"What's that?"

I remember. "It's just a woodpecker."

There was a woodpecker back then, too.

"Machine-gun attack!" yelled Jeff. And I forgot it was a game and threw myself down the bank into the bushes. Jeff laughed at me.

"No lit-tle ducks came swimming back." Ib's high thin voice is burrowing itself into my brain, and there is a pulse above my left eye. I begin to wish I had brought something to drink. Maybe it's time to go back.

And then we come to the stream. I hear it before I see it. And then I remember what happened there.

Ib jumps off the tracks and dances off toward the water.

I don't want to go there. "Not that way, Ib."

"Come *on*, Ken. I'm exploring. This is an exploration mission. You said."

I follow her. It's different. The trees—dusty, scruffy-looking cottonwoods—have grown up, and the road appears too soon. But there it is. The stream takes a bend and disappears into a small culvert under the road. Vines grow across the entrance to the drainage pipe. I push them aside and look in. A black hole with a perfect circle of light at the end.

It's so small. Had we really walked through it? Jeff and Danielle and finally me, terrified, shamed into it by a girl and a double-dare.

I take a deep breath and I'm there again. That smell. Wet and green and dangerous.

There I was, feet braced against the pipe, halfway through the tunnel at the darkest part. I kept my mind up, up out of the water where Jeff said blackwater bloodsuckers lived. I kept my mind up until it went right into the weight of the earth above me. Tons of dirt and cars and trucks and being buried alive.

Dirt pressing heavy against my chest, against my eyelids, against my legs which wouldn't move. Above the roaring in my ears, I heard a high snatch of song. Two notes with no words. Calling. I pushed against the concrete and screamed without a sound.

And then Jeff yelled into the tunnel, "What's the matter, Kenny? Is it the bloodsuckers? Kenton, Kenton, where are you? Ve vant to suck your blood." Jeff had a way of saying "Kenton" that made it sound like an even finkier name than it is.

By this time I had peed my pants, and I had to pretend to slip and fall into the water to cover up. The shock of the cold. The end of the tunnel. Jeff pushed me into the stream because I was wet anyway. Danielle stared at me and she knew.

"Where does it go?" Ib pulls on my shirt.

I'm big again. Huge. Like Talking Doll.

"It goes under the road. I walked through it once."

"Did you go to that other place?"

"What other place?"

Ib gives me The Look. "Where those other girls play. I think this goes there."

Yeah, right. The Barbies visit the culvert.

Ib steps right into the tunnel. "Come on, Kenton."

I grab her. "Hey! Hold it. You can't go in there. You'll ... you'll get your sandals wet. And I can't come. I don't fit."

Ib sits down on the gravel and takes off her sandals. "I fit."

Blackwater bloodsuckers. But why would I want to scare her? And, hey, it's just a tunnel. So I happen to suffer from claustrophobia. That's my problem.

"Okay, but look, I'll wait on this side until you're halfway through and then I'll cross over the road and meet you on the other side. Are you sure you're not scared?"

Ib steps into the pipe and stretches to become and X. "Look! Look how I fit!"

I watch the little X splash its way into the darkness.

"Okay, Ib, see you on the other side. Last one there's a rotten egg." I let the curtain of vines fall across the opening.

I pick up the sandals and climb the hill. It's different, too. It used to be just feathery horsetail and now skinny trees grow there. I grab onto them to pull myself up. I cross the road, hovering on the centre line as an RV rumbles by, and then I slide down the other side, following a small avalanche of pebbles. I kneel on the top of the pipe and stick my head in, upside down.

"Hey, rotten egg, I beat you."

Small, echoing, dripping sounds are the only answer.

I peer into the darkness. She's teasing me.

"Ib!"

Ib, Ib, Ib—the tunnel throws my voice back at me. A semi-trailer roars by on the road. I jump down and stand at the pipe's entrance. My eyes adjust and I can see the dim green O at the other end. No outline of a little girl.

A tight heaviness grips me around the chest.

"Ibbie. Answer me right now. I mean it." I drop the sandals.

She must have turned and hidden on the other side, just to fool me.

I don't remember getting up the hill and across the road, except that the noise of a car horn rips across the top of my brain.

She isn't there. Empty tunnel.

"Elizabeth!"

She slipped. She knocked her head. Child drowns in four inches of bath water.

I have to go in. I try walking doubled over. But my feet just slip down the slimy curved concrete and I can only shuffle. I drop to my hands and knees.

Crawl, crawl, crawl, crawl.

The sound of splashing fills my head.

Come back, Elizabeth.

Do not push out against the concrete. Just go forward, *splash, splash.*

Do not think up or down.

Something floats against my hand. I gasp and jerk upward, cracking my head. It's Wanda. I push her into my shirt. My knee bashes into a rock, and there is some sobbing in the echoing tunnel. It is my own voice.

And then I grab the rough ends of the pipe and pull myself into the light and the bigness.

Ib is crouched at the edge of the stream pushing a floating leaf with a stick. A green light makes its way through the trees above.

She looks up at me at sees Wanda poking out of my shirt. "Oh, good, you found her. Bad Wanda, running away."

My relief explodes into anger.

"Ib, where were you?"

"Playing with the girls."

"No, quit pretending. I'm not playing. Where were you when I called you from this end of the tunnel? Were you hiding? Didn't you hear me call?"

"Sure I heard you, silly. That's how they knew my name. And I was going to come back but it was my turn. They never let me play before, but this time they knew my name and I got to go into the circle. They were dancing. Like ballerinas. Except they had long hair. I get to have long hair when I'm in grade two."

My head is buzzing. I must have hit it harder than I realized. I hand Wanda to Ib and grab at some sense.

"Why didn't you come when I called you?"

"They said I wasn't allowed to go, not while I was in the circle, and they were going to give me some cake. I saw it. It had sprinkles on it. And then you called me again but you said 'Elizabeth.' And then they made me go away."

Ib blows her leaf boat across the stream. And then she starts to sing.

"Idey, Idey, what's your name,
What's your name to get in the game."

The final puzzle piece of memory slides into place.

That song, the two-note song. The sweet high voice calling to me in the tunnel. The sound just before Jeff yelled at me. The sound just before Jeff called me back by my real name.

They wanted me. They wanted Ib. I begin to shiver.

I find myself sitting on the gravel. The stream splashes its way over the lip of the pipe into the tunnel. I stare at Ib, who looks so small and so solid. My wet jeans with their slime-green knees begin to steam in the sun. A crow tells us a thing or two.

"Ken?"

"Yes?"

"I don't really like those girls."

"No, they don't sound that nice. Do you want to go home?"

"Okay."

I rinse off my hands and glance once more into the darkness.

"Put on your sandals, then."

Ib holds onto the back belt loops of my jeans, and I pull her up the hill, into the sunshine.

Sarah Ellis (*Born 1952, Vancouver, British Columbia*), short-story writer and novelist, was an avid reader as a child, and later studied librarianship and children's literature. She won the 1992 Governor General's Award for Children's Literature (text) for *Pick-up Sticks*. In addition to writing, Ellis teaches and works as a part-time reference librarian.

The First Day

Edward P. Jones

ON AN OTHERWISE UNREMARKABLE SEPTEMBER MORNING, long before I learned to be ashamed of my mother, she takes my hand and we set off down New Jersey Avenue to begin my very first day of school. I am wearing a checkered-like blue-and-green cotton dress, and scattered about these colours are bits of yellow and white and brown. My mother has uncharacteristically spent nearly an hour on my hair that morning, plaiting and replaiting so that now my scalp tingles. Whenever I turn my head quickly, my nose fills with the faint smell of Dixie Peach hair grease. The smell is somehow a soothing one now and I will reach for it time and time again before the morning ends. All the plaits, each with a blue barrette near the tip and each twisted into an uncommon sturdiness, will last until I go to bed that night, something that has never happened before. My stomach is full of milk and oatmeal sweetened with brown sugar. Like everything else I have on, my pale green slip and underwear are new, the underwear having come three to a plastic package with a little girl on the front who appears to be dancing. Behind my ears, my mother, to stop my whining, has dabbed the stingiest bit of her gardenia perfume, the last present my father gave her before he disappeared into memory. Because I cannot smell it, I have only her word that the perfume is there. I am also wearing yellow socks trimmed with thin lines of black and white around the tops. My shoes are my greatest joy, black-patent-leather miracles, and when one is nicked at the toe later that morning in class, my heart will break.

I am carrying a pencil, a pencil sharpener, and a small ten-cent tablet with a black-and-white speckled cover. My mother does not believe that a girl in kindergarten needs such things, so I am taking them only because of my insistent whining and because they are presented from our neighbours, Mary Keith and Blondelle Harris. Miss Mary and Miss Blondelle are watching my two younger sisters until my mother returns. The women are as precious to me as my mother and sisters. Out playing one day, I have overheard an older child, speaking to another child, call Miss Mary and Miss Blondelle a word that is brand new to me. This is my mother: When I say the word in fun to one of my sisters, my mother slaps me across the mouth and the word is lost for years and years.

All the way down New Jersey Avenue, the sidewalks are teeming with children. In my neighbourhood, I have many friends, but I see none of them as my mother and I walk. We cross New York Avenue, we cross Pierce Street, and we cross L and K, and still I see no one who knows my name. At I Street, between New Jersey Avenue and Third Street, we enter Seaton Elementary School, a timeworn, sad-faced building across the street from my mother's church, Mt. Carmel Baptist.

Just inside the front door, women out of the advertisements in *Ebony* are greeting other parents and children. The woman who greets us has pearls thick as jumbo marbles that come down almost to her navel, and she acts as if she had known me all my life, touching my shoulder, cupping her hand under my chin. She is enveloped in perfume that I only know is not gardenia. When, in answer to her question, my mother tells her that we live at 1227 New Jersey Avenue, the woman first seems to be picturing in her head where we live. Then she shakes her head and says that we are at the wrong school, that we should be at Walker-Jones.

My mother shakes her head vigorously. "I want her to go here," my mother says. "If I'da wanted her someplace else, I'da took her there." The woman continues to act as if she has known me all my life, but she tells my mother that we live beyond the area that Seaton serves. My mother is not convinced and for several more minutes she questions the woman about why I cannot attend Seaton. For as many Sundays as I can remember, perhaps even Sundays when I was in her womb, my mother has pointed across I Street to Seaton as we come and go to Mt. Carmel. "You gonna go there and learn about the whole world." But one of the guardians of that place is saying no, and no again. I am learning this about my mother: The higher up on the scale of respectability a person is—and teachers are rather high up in her eyes— the less she is liable to let them push her around. But finally, I see in her eyes the closing gate, and she takes my hand and we leave the building. On the steps, she stops as people move past us on either side.

"Mama, I can't go to school?"

She says nothing at first, then takes my hand again and we are down the steps quickly and nearing New Jersey Avenue before I can blink. This is my mother: She says, "One monkey don't stop no show."

Walker-Jones is a larger, new school and I immediately like it because of that. But it is not across the street from my mother's church, her rock, one of her connections to God, and I sense her doubts as she absently rubs her thumb over the back of her hand. We find our way to the crowded auditorium where grey metal chairs are set up in the middle of the room. Along the wall to the left are tables and other chairs. Every chair seems occupied by a child or adult. Somewhere in the room a child is crying, a cry that rises above the buzz-talk of so many people. Strewn about the floor are dozens and dozens of pieces of white paper, and people are walking over them without any thought of picking them up. And seeing this lack of concern, I am all of a sudden afraid.

"Is this where they register for school?" my mother asks a woman at one of the tables.

The woman looks up slowly as if she has heard this question once too often. She nods. She is tiny, almost as small as the girl standing beside her. The woman's hair is set in a mass of curlers and all of those curlers are made of paper money, here a dollar bill, there a five-dollar bill. The girl's hair is arrayed in curls, but some of them are beginning to droop and this makes me happy. On the table beside the woman's pocketbook is a large notebook, worthy of someone in high school, and looking at me looking at the notebook, the girl places her hand possessively on it. In her other hand she holds several pencils with thick crowns of additional erasers.

"These the forms you gotta use?" my mother asks the woman, picking up a few pieces of the paper from the table. "Is this what you have to fill out?"

The woman tells her yes, but that she need fill out only one.

"I see," my mother says, looking about the room. Then: "Would you help me with this form? That is, if you don't mind."

The woman asks my mother what she means.

"This form. Would you mind helpin' me fill it out?"

The woman still seems not to understand.

"I can't read it. I don't know how to read or write, and I'm askin' you to help me." My mother looks at me, then looks away. I know almost all of her looks, but this one is brand new to me. "Would you help me, then?"

The woman says "Why sure," and suddenly she appears happier, so much more satisfied with everything. She finishes the form for her daughter, and my mother and I step aside to wait for her. We find two chairs nearby and sit. My mother is now diseased, according to the girl's eyes, and until the moment her mother takes her and the form to the front of the auditorium, the girl never stops looking at my mother. I stare back at her. "Don't stare," my mother says to me. "You know better than that."

Another woman out of the *Ebony* ads takes the woman's child away. "Now," the woman says upon returning, "Let's see what we can do for you two."

My mother answers the questions the woman reads off the form. They start with my last name, and then on to the first and middle names. This is school, I think. This is going to school. My mother slowly enunciates each word of my name. This is my mother: As the questions go on, she takes from her pocketbook document after document, as if they will support my right to attend school, as if she has been saving them up for just this moment. Indeed, she takes out more papers than I have ever seen her do in other places: my birth certificate, my baptismal record, a doctor's letter concerning my bout with chicken pox, rent receipts, records of immunization, a letter about our public assistance payments, even her marriage licence— every single paper that has anything even remotely to do with my five-year-old life. Few of the papers are needed here, but it does not matter and my mother continues to pull out the documents with the purposefulness of a magician pulling out a long string of scarves. She has learned that money is the beginning and end of everything in this world, and when the woman finishes, my mother offers her fifty cents, and the woman accepts it without hesitation. My mother and I are just about the last parent and child in the room.

My mother presents the form to a woman sitting in front of the stage, and the woman looks at it and writes something on a white card, which she gives to my mother. Before long, the woman who has taken the girl with the drooping curls appears from behind us, speaks to the sitting woman, and introduces herself to my mother and me. She's to be my teacher, she tells my mother. My mother stares.

We go into the hall, where my mother kneels down to me. Her lips are quivering. "I'll be back to pick you up at twelve o'clock. I don't want you to go nowhere. You just wait right here. And listen to every word she say." I touch her lips and press them together. It is an old, old game between us. She puts my hand down at my side, which is not part of the game. She stands and looks a second at the teacher, then she turns and walks away. I see where she has darned one of her socks the night before. Her shoes make loud sounds in the hall. She passes through the doors and I can still hear the loud sounds of her shoes. And even when the teacher turns me toward the classrooms and I hear what must be the singing and talking of all the children in the world, I can still hear my mother's footsteps above it all.

Edward P. Jones (*Born 1950*), short-story writer, won the PEN/Hemingway Award for Best First Fiction for his collection *Lost in the City*. His stories have been published in numerous magazines. Jones has had teaching appointments at several universities, including Princeton and the University of Maryland.

   Selection Activities, p. 373

What Language Do Bears Speak?

Roch Carrier

FOLLOWING OUR OWN MORNING RITUAL, to which we submitted with more conviction than to the one of saying our prayers when we jumped out of bed, we ran to the windows and lingered there, silent and contemplative, for long moments. Meanwhile, in the kitchen, our mother was becoming impatient, for we were late. She was always afraid we'd be late ... Life was there all around us and above us, vibrant and luminous, filled with trees; it offered us fields of daisies and it led to hills that concealed great mysteries.

The story of that morning begins with some posters. During the night, posters had been put up on the wooden poles that supported the hydro wires.

"Posters! They've put up posters!"

Did they announce that hairy wrestlers were coming? Far West singers? Strong men who would carry horses on their shoulders? Comic artists who had made all America collapse with laughter? An international tap-dance champion? A sword swallower? Posters! Perhaps we'd be allowed to go and see a play on the stage of the parish hall—if the curé declared from the pulpit that the play wasn't immoral and if we were resourceful enough to earn the money for a ticket. Posters! The artists in the photographs would gradually come down from the posters until they inhabited our dreams, haunted our games, and accompanied us, invisible, on our expeditions.

"There's posters up!"

We weren't allowed to run to the posters and, trembling, read their marvellous messages; it was contrary to maternal law to set foot outside before we had washed and combed our hair. After submitting to this painful obligation we were able to learn that we would see, in flesh and blood, the unsurpassable Dr. Schultz, former hunter in Africa, former director of zoos in the countries of Europe, former lion-tamer, former elephant-hunter and former freestyle wrestling champion in Germany, Austria, and the United Kingdom, in an unbelievable, unsurpassable show—"almost unimaginable." Dr. Schultz would present dogs that could balance on balls, rabbit-clowns, educated monkeys, hens that could add and subtract; in addition, Dr. Schultz would brave a savage bear in an uneven wrestling match "between the fierce forces of nature and the cunning of human intelligence, of which the outcome might be fatal for one of the protagonists."

We had seen bears before, but dead ones, with mouths bleeding, teeth gleaming. Hunters liked to tell how their victims had appeared to them: "... standing up, practically walking like a man, but a big man, hairy like a bear; and then it came at me roaring like thunder when it's far away behind the sky, with claws like knives at the end of his paws, and then when I fired it didn't move any more than if a mosquito'd got into its fur. Wasn't till the tenth bullet that I saw him fall down ..." Loggers, too, had spotted bears and some, so they said, had been so frightened their hair had turned white.

Dr. Schultz was going to risk his life before our eyes by pitting himself against this merciless beast. We would see with our own eyes, alive before us, not only a bear but a man fighting a bear. We'd see all of that!

A voice that reached the entire village, a voice that was magnified by loudspeakers, announced that the great day had arrived: "At last you can see, in person, the unsurpassable Dr. Schultz, the man with the most scars in the world, and his bear—a bear that gets fiercer and fiercer as the season for love comes closer!"

We saw an old yellow bus drive up, covered with stars painted in red, pulling a trailer on whose sides we could read: DR. SCHULTZ AND ASSOCIATES UNIVERSAL WONDER CIRCUS LTD. The whole thing was covered with iron bars that were tangled and crossed and knotted and padlocked. A net of clinking chains added to the security. Between messages, crackling music made curtains open at the windows and drew the children outdoors. Then the magical procession entered the lot where we played ball in the summer. The motor growled, the bus moved forward, back, hesitated. At last it found its place and the motor was silent. A man got out of the bus. He stood on the running board; twenty or thirty children had followed the circus. He considered us with a smile.

"Hi, kids," he said.

He added something else, words in the same language, which we'd never heard before.

"Either he's talking bear," said my friend Lapin, "or he's talking English."

"If we can't understand him," I concluded, "it must be English."

The man on the runningboard was still talking; in his strange language he seemed to be asking questions. Not understanding, we listened, stupefied to see Dr. Schultz in person, alive, come down from the posters.

"We talk French here," one of us shouted.

Smiling again, Dr. Schultz said something else we didn't understand.

"We should go get Monsieur Rancourt," I suggested.

Monsieur Rancourt had gone to Europe to fight in the First World War and he'd had to learn English so he could follow the soldiers in his army. I ran to get Monsieur Rancourt. Panting behind his big belly, he hurried as fast as he could. He was looking forward to speaking this language. He hadn't spoken it for so many years he wasn't sure, he told me, that he could remember it. As soon as he saw the man from the circus he told me: "I'm gonna try to tell him hello in English."

"Good day sir! How you like it here today?" ("I remember!" Monsieur Rancourt rejoiced, shouting with delight. "I didn't forget!")

Dr. Schultz moved toward Monsieur Rancourt, holding out his hand. A hand wearing a leather glove, in the middle of summer.

"It's because of the bear bites," my friend Lapin explained to me.

"Apparently the *Anglais* can't take the cold," said one of our friends whose mother's sister had a cousin who worked in an *Anglais* house in Ontario.

The man from the circus and Monsieur Rancourt were talking like two old friends meeting after a number of years. They even laughed. In English, Monsieur Rancourt laughed in a special way, "a real English laugh," we judged, whispering. In French, Monsieur Rancourt never laughed; he was surly. We listened to them, mouths agape. This English language which we'd heard on the radio, in the spaces between the French stations when we turned the tuning knob, we were hearing now for real, in life, in our village, spoken by two men standing in the sun. I made an observation: instead of speaking normally, as in French, instead of spitting the words outside their lips, the two men were swallowing them. My friend Lapin had noticed the same thing, for he said:

"Sounds like they're choking."

Suddenly something was overturned in the trailer; we could hear chains clinking, a bump swelled out the canvas covering, and we saw a black ball burst out—the head of a bear.

Dr. Schultz and Monsieur Rancourt had rolled up their shirt-sleeves and they were comparing tattoos.

"The bear's loose!"

The animal ran out on the canvas, came down from the roof of the bus, and jumped to the ground. How could we tell that to Dr. Schultz who didn't understand our language, whose back was turned to the trailer, and who was completely absorbed in his conversation?

"Monsieur Rancourt" I shouted. "The bear's running away!"

There was no need to translate. The man from the circus had understood. Waving a revolver, he sped toward the bear, which was fleeing into a neighbouring field. He shouted, pleaded, threatened.

"What's he saying?" we asked Monsieur Rancourt.

"Words that English children don't learn till they're men."

"He must be saying the same words my father says when a cow jumps over the fence. They aren't nice."

Dr. Schultz, whom we had seen disappear into the oats, came back after a long moment and spoke to Monsieur Rancourt, who ran to the village. The men who were gathered at the general store rushed off to find other men; they took out traps, rifles, ropes. While the mothers gathered up their children who were scattered over the village, the men set out, directed by fat Monsieur Rancourt. Because of his experience in the war, he took charge of the roundup. Dr. Schultz had confided to him, we learned later:

"That bear's more important than my own wife."

They mustn't kill it, then, but bring it back alive.

The show was to begin in the early afternoon. Dr. Schultz, who had gone with the men into the forest, came back muttering; we guessed that he was unhappy. At his trailer he opened the padlock, unfastened the crossed iron bars, pulled out the pegs, and undid the chains. We saw him transform his trailer into a stage with the help of a system of pulleys, ropes, and tripods. Suddenly we were working with the circus man: we carried boxes, held out ropes, unrolled canvas, stuck pickets in the ground, lined up chairs. Dr. Schultz directed our labours. Small, over-excited men that we were, we had forgotten he was speaking a language we didn't understand.

A piece of unrolled canvas suspended from a rope, which was held in place by stakes, formed a circular enclosure. It resembled a tent without a roof; we had built it. We were proud; would we, as long as we lived, ever have another day as beautiful as this one? From now on we were part of the circus.

At last it was time for the show. The music cried out as far as the horizon. In the stands there were mostly women: the men were still pursuing the lost bear.

In gleaming leather boots, in a costume sparkling with gilt braid, Dr. Schultz walked out on the stage. He said a few words and the crowd applauded fervently; the spectators no doubt considered it a mark of prowess to speak with such ease a language of which they couldn't utter a single word.

He opened a cage and a dozen rabbits came out. On the back of each he hung a number. At the other end of the platform was a board with holes cut out of it. Above each hole, a number. The man from the circus gave an order and the rabbits ran to the holes that bore their numbers. Unbelievable, wasn't it? We all raised rabbits, but our animals had never learned anything more intelligent than how to chew clover. Our hands were burning, so much had we applauded our friend Dr. Schultz. Next came the trained dogs' act: one danced a waltz; another rode around a track on a bicycle while his twin played a drum. We applauded our great friend hard enough to break our metacarpals.

The acrobatic chimpanzee's act had scarcely begun when a great uproar drowned the music from the loudspeakers. The canvas wall shook. It opened, and we saw the captured bear come in. The men from the village were returning it to its master, roaring, furious, screaming, clawing, kicking, gasping, famished. The men from the village, accustomed to recalcitrant bulls and horses, were leading it with strong authority; they had passed ropes around its neck and paws so the furious animal had to obey. Monsieur Rancourt was speaking French and English all at once.

When he saw his bear, Dr. Schultz let out a cry that Monsieur Rancourt didn't translate. The men's hands dropped the ropes: the bear was free. He didn't notice immediately. We heard his harsh breathing, and his master's too. The hour had come: we were going to see the greatest circus attraction in the Americas; we were going to see with our own eyes the famous Dr. Schultz, our friend, wrestle a giant black bear.

No longer feeling the ropes burning its neck, no longer submitting to the strength of the men who were tearing it apart, the bear stood up, spread its arms, and shot forward with a roar. The bear struck Dr. Schultz like a mountain that might have rolled onto him. The bear and our friend tumbled off the stage. There was a ripple of applause; all the men together would never have succeeded in mustering half the daring of Dr. Schultz. The bear got up again, trampled on the great tamer of wild beasts and dived into the canvas enclosure, tearing it with one swipe of its claws before disappearing.

Dr. Schultz had lost his jacket and trousers. His body was streaked with red scratches. He was weeping.

"If I understand right," said Monsieur Rancourt, "he's telling us that the bear wasn't his bear ..."

"It isn't his bear ..."

The men shook and spluttered with laughter as they did at the general store when one of them told a funny story.

The men laughed so hard that Monsieur Rancourt could no longer hear Dr. Schultz's moans as he lay bleeding on the platform. The undertaker apologized for the misunderstanding.

"That bear was a bear that talked English, though, because I didn't understand a single word he said."

Roch Carrier (*Born 1937, Sainte-Justine-de-Dorchester, Quebec*), novelist and children's author, is one of Canada's most read Quebec writers. Carrier is known for his use of dark humour and autobiographical references. His collection of short stories, *Prayer of a Very Wise Child*, won the 1991 Stephen Leacock Medal for Humour. Carrier is currently head of the National Library of Canada.

  Selection Activities, p. 373

Excerpted from How to Write a Serious Novel About Love

Diane Schoemperlen

BEGIN WITH A MAN AND A WOMAN. Many famous novels begin with this familiar combination. Although it may at first strike you as rather trite, in fact, once you get going, you will find that it presents a vast array of possibilities.

First of all, your man and woman will need names. Consider their selection very carefully. Vinny and Ethel cannot possibly live out the same story as Alphonse and Olivia. The reader may well have trouble taking seriously the fates of Mitzi and Skip. Sometimes neutral names are best. After much deliberation, decide to name your characters John and Mary.

Describe John.

John has brown hair and brown eyes. John has blond hair and blue eyes. John has black hair and green eyes. John has no hair and no eyes. Pick one. Make John short or tall, fat or thin, pale or rosy-cheeked. Does John have a hairy chest? How big are John's ears, feet, nose, biceps? Give some thought to dimples, facial hair, birthmarks, scars, and tattoos.

Move from character description to development. John wears grey sweatpants. John wears black, always black, with a black beret. What does John see when he looks in the mirror? How does John feel about the shape of his chin, the colour of his teeth, the size of his biceps?

Do not make John perfect. The reader, who is not perfect, will lose interest. And you, the writer, also not perfect, will lose credibility. Remember, this is supposed to be a serious novel. Above all else, make John human.

Describe Mary.

Again, hair, eyes, height, weight. Be sure the choices you make for Mary coordinate well with the ones you've made for John. How big are Mary's lips, hands, eyes? Give some thought to cheekbones, crow's-feet, beauty marks, facial hair, and tattoos. How long is Mary's neck? How graceful are her arms when she throws them around John or pushes him away?

Move from description to development. Mary goes barefaced into the world, her cheeks scrubbed smooth and shining. Mary spends an hour constructing a new face each morning with a sophisticated battery of potions, lotions, pencils, and brushes. Does Mary believe in cosmetic surgery, aromatherapy, aerobics, vitamins, God? Does Mary have low self-esteem? Does Mary love herself more than anybody else in the whole wide world? Does Mary love herself more than she loves John?

You must describe John and Mary in such detail because readers want to have pictures of them in their heads. Speaking of heads ...

Decide from whose point of view you will tell the story, into whose head the reader will be allowed access. Decide whose brain you are most interested in picking, whose thoughts will underscore, interpret, and otherwise illuminate the action. This narrator may tell the truth or lies. You decide.

Avoid using the phrase *she thought to herself*. The reader will wonder who else she might have thought to. Remember that no matter how witty, intelligent, or perceptive John and Mary may be, they cannot read each other's minds. If you decide to tell the story through Mary's eyes, remember that she cannot see through walls. She cannot know for sure what John is doing when he is out of her sight. She can only speculate. Remember that every point of view harbours its own limitations.

If you wish to dispense with this handicap entirely, choose the omniscient point of view. This narrator, like God, sees all, knows all, and feels free to tell all too. This eye in the sky can see what's happening in Outer Mongolia, Brooklyn, and Brazil, while also being privy to the thoughts of John and Mary and anyone else who happens along. The omniscient narrator also knows the future and the past so be careful.

No matter who is telling their story and/or their future, John and Mary still have to live somewhere. Do not make this decision lightly. Your choice will make all the difference in the world to John and Mary.

If, for instance, you set your novel in the country, its pages will fill up with the smell of freshly turned earth, the growl of tractors and combines, the bleating of baby goats, the twinkling of stars in the vast black sky. John and Mary never lock their doors. Mary bakes apple pies in the sunny farmhouse kitchen. John chops the heads off chickens. They sit together for hours on the front porch in straight-backed wooden chairs, peering at the pastoral evening sky, praying for rain.

If, on the other hand, you decide to set your novel in a big city, its chapters will be laced with the exhaust fumes of rush-hour traffic jams, the hum of a million air conditioners, the urgent heart-stopping wail of sirens, the click of high heels on concrete, the grunts and sighs of impatient consumers lined up at ringing cash registers, the slick purr of men and women in power suits conducting high finance in hermetically sealed buildings. At night the office towers glow like radioactive monoliths.

John and Mary live in the fast lane. They work hard to pay for the condo, the alarm system, the cleaning lady, the sailboat, the Christmas vacation in Switzerland. John is a corporate lawyer. Mary is a bond trader. They own a silver BMW. While John drives and curses the traffic all around them, Mary pops open her laptop and sends faxes all over the world.

On weekends in the city, John and Mary are always busy. They have many friends but they never have time to see them. They go to films, plays, operas, ballets, art exhibits, and antique auctions. They eat complicated international cuisine in expensive elegant restaurants.

Of course John and Mary know full well that not everyone in the city is as privileged as they are. They know all about the poverty, the crime, the drugs, the homeless, the powerless, the helpless, children abducted and abused, women raped and battered, innocent people murdered for no reason. They see it on the evening news. They read all about it in the morning paper. They are appropriately shocked. Sometimes they see the evidence around them: a man sleeping in a doorway, a bullet hole in a plate-glass window, a bloodstain on a white wall, once the chalk outline of a victim like a hopscotch game on the sidewalk. But they know these things in a haphazard way, the way they know about hurricanes, famine, and war. They see them through a wall of shatterproof glass.

Realizing that you know a lot about city life and virtually nothing about the country, decide to set your novel in the city. After all, you have always been told to write about what you know.

Admit that you don't know much about lawyers, bond traders, BMWs, or life in the fast lane. Admit that you have never had a cleaning lady, a sailboat, or a vacation in Switzerland. On weekends you do chores and get groceries at the mall. Then you have a nap.

Make John and Mary ordinary people. Make Mary a teacher. Make John an employee of the railroad. Remember that all ordinary people are extraordinary in their own way. Remember that *ordinary* does not mean *simple*.

Always bear in mind that in a serious novel, only trouble is interesting. This means tension, obstacles, conflicts, danger, and desire. This means plot. If John and Mary are happy at the beginning of the book, they must become unhappy later on. By the end, they may be happy again, still unhappy, or else one or both of them may die. A perfectly happy life is, no doubt, a wonderful thing to live, but in fiction it is boring.

Don't forget the villain. Every novel needs a villain. Male or female, make the villain despicable but interesting, vicious but exciting, evil but fond of children and small animals. In a serious novel, the bad guys do not wear black hats. Be careful not to make the villain more interesting than John and Mary.

Inner torment is an essential ingredient in a serious novel. The reader will relate well to a character who has emotional problems, who sometimes does not know what she wants, who senses that something is missing from her life but cannot put her finger on exactly what.

Mary has everything a woman could want. She is married to the only man she has ever loved. He loves her as much as she loves him. He is a good provider. He is not physically, verbally, or emotionally abusive. He never forgets to bring her flowers on their anniversary. He never forgets to take out the garbage, hang up the wet towels, or put his dirty socks in the hamper. He vacuums without being asked. They live in a bright, spacious suburban home on a quiet, safe cul-de-sac. They are not wealthy but they are comfortable. They both enjoy their jobs. Their children are healthy, smart, and well-behaved. Mary is a good cook and pursues many hobbies including knitting, stamp collecting, and bowling. John loves golf, swimming, and woodworking. Mary has never had a broken heart or any broken bones. Her children do not have allergies or learning disabilities. John does not have high cholesterol or a family history of heart disease. Mary does not suffer from migraine headaches or excessive weight. Her friends envy her. They say she is leading a charmed life.

Mary knows her friends are right. But still ... but still ...

Mary knows she is not as happy as she should be. Sometimes she feels frustrated, dissatisfied, unfulfilled, empty, and bored. Sometimes she gets tired of giving, caring, looking after; tired of wiping counters, tables, noses, and bums; tired of washing clothes, floors, dishes, and her children's hair. Sometimes she even gets tired of washing her own hair. Sometimes she resents always having to be reasonable, reliable, and responsible.

Mary feels the kettle of discontent bubbling inside her. Sometimes she wishes she had become an acrobat instead of the perfect wife and mother. She imagines a skimpy gold outfit with sequins, a thrilling drumroll, the whole crowd holding its breath while she performs death-defying acts before them. Or else maybe Mary wishes she had become an artist. She could have lived in a garret, worn outlandish clothing, and gone to scintillating bohemian parties.

Now Mary, in her real life, feels trapped. Mary knows that *cul-de-sac* is just a fancy way of saying *dead end*.

In fiction, as in real life, most people want their lives to amount to something even if they're not sure what.

Any minute now the whistle on that kettle of discontent is going to blow. Mary is going to either break out of her own life or get up and make herself a pot of tea.

John and Mary, of course, will both have many memories which occasionally surface within the context of their current lives. In fiction these are called *flashbacks*. Generally speaking, their function is to give your story history and depth. They help the reader understand how John and Mary came to be who they are today.

In fiction, as in real life, a flashback may be triggered by any little thing:

The look of a fried egg on a blue plate, a black umbrella dripping in the vestibule, an old woman in a babushka weeding her garden. The sound of a shovel on pavement after a snowstorm, a song on the radio at the hairdresser's, tires squealing in the night. The smell of shampoo on a strange woman in a crowded elevator, a cigarette lit outside in the winter at night, a woollen jacket in the rain. The feel of a child's hand on your arm, a fat cat in your lap, a silk scarf against your cheek. The taste of an orange, a pomegranate, bitter chocolate, sweet potatoes, the pink eraser on the end of a pencil.

Any one of these things may lead your character back through the doorway of time. The reader will go along gladly into the labyrinth of the past.

In fiction, time is of the essence. In a serious novel, the strings connecting the past, the present, and the future are explicit and articulate. It is only in real life that you may well hang yourself on those same sticky strands. Your readers will likely feel much more comfortable in John's and Mary's past lives than they do in their own.

In fiction, time is finite. Consider how much time your novel will cover: a day, a week, a month, a year, two years, ten, one hundred? All stories must start and end somewhere. The same can be said of individual lives, although not necessarily of time itself. In fiction, as opposed to real life, you control time. It does not control you.

Remember to use concrete language. Be specific. Give all objects the dignity of their names. You owe them that much at least.

Avoid vague, limp words like *good, bad, pretty,* and *nice*. Especially be careful around the word *nice*. There is little or no place in a serious novel for a nice man and a nice woman having a nice picnic on a nice day. Even if you say the woman is pretty, the man is good, and the bugs are bad, it is still not enough. You can do better than that.

Especially avoid the use of clichés. If you are going to use metaphors and similes in your novel (of course you are—everybody does), you must search for more original comparisons.

The best way to accomplish this is to lie down in a quiet darkened room and free your mind from the prison of everyday thinking. Forget about the dishes that need doing, the dog that needs walking, the lawn that needs mowing, and your family that needs feeding again and again. Concentrate. Push away the obvious choices, the easy answers. Dispense with women who are pretty as pictures, with lips like cherries, eyes like diamonds, and skin as white as snow. Dispense with men who are sly as foxes, strong as bulls, quick as whips, thick as bricks, or as slow as molasses in January. Dispense entirely with all of these ideas, which are as old as the hills. Instead, train your mind to float away to a higher plane where all thoughts are made new again.

In order to get to the heart of the matter, you must forget all about hearts that look like valentines and pound like hammers.

Go to the place where John's heart is like a piece of celery: crispy, juicy, a pale green stick run through with strings upon which Mary will choke if she's not careful. Go to the place where Mary's heart is like a purse, a soft leather bag in which she carries a jumble of small but vital necessities. When she doesn't need it, she hangs it from the bedroom doorknob.

Go to the place where *love* has nothing to do with hearts, flowers, violins, chocolates, or weddings. Go to the place where *love* is like charcoal, apricots, a helicopter, peppermints, the sound of fingernails on a chalkboard, a bucket of blood under the bed. This is the place where good writing comes from.

Learn to love language. It, after all, is both the tool and the raw material with which you must work. It, fortunately, turns out to be a renewable resource. Make a list of all the words you love and then use them. Words like: *simulacrum, erstwhile, luscious, lunatic, ambush, salubrious, sanctuary.* Do not neglect the power of verbs: *ignite, coddle, holler, galvanize, capitulate, sink, saddle, expire.*

Remember that ordinariness is only in the eye of the beholder. Remember that ordinary does not mean simple or dull. You, as writer, have the power to reveal the extraordinary which lies within (behind, beneath, or beyond) the ordinary. Pay attention to details. Hone your vision. Rekindle the marvel, the innocence, and/or the menace of the mundane. All things have presence. Study the particulars of tables, sidewalks, ceilings, bricks, curtains, crockery, knives. Look out the kitchen window for an hour. See everything. Stare all night at the sky.

If you look long enough at an ordinary cup of tea, it too will become a figment of your imagination. Remember that kettle of discontent about to boil.

Describe the clear hot liquid filling the cup, the white steam rising in the kitchen on a bright March Thursday afternoon. Describe the cup: the white bone china so thin it is nearly translucent, the perfect curves of the handle, the delicate pattern of red and gold around the saucer. Describe Mary stirring a spoonful of honey into her tea and then licking the hot spoon. Describe the shape of her lips as she takes the first sweet sip and breathes in the aromatic steam with her eyes closed. Describe the sound of the cup being placed carefully back on the saucer. Then describe the silence.

Think of everything you know about tea, about cups, about tea in cups. Think about tea leaves and the future.

Ask yourself why Mary is not at work. She should be standing in front of her Grade Four class right now, teaching them about the solar system, the names of the nine planets in order, the position of the earth in the greater scheme of things. Why is Mary at home? Is she sick? Has she lost her job in the latest round of budget cuts? Has she been fired for insubordination?

Mary, sipping her tea, has a wistful look on her face. Remember that it is possible to feel wistful about almost anything. It is even possible to feel wistful about pain, especially an old pain caused by great love, great loss.

After Mary has finished her tea, she rinses the cup and leaves it on the drainboard to dry. Describe the drainboard and the sound of the warm water running into the stainless steel sink. Think about the fact that warm water makes a different sound than cold water.

Where is John while Mary is having her tea? Mary assumes, correctly, that John is at work. She imagines the train station: the echoing noise of the crowd, all those people crying goodbye and hello, the trains grinding and blowing off steam, the announcements of departures and arrivals, the amplified voice so distorted that no one can understand what is being said but everybody looks up anyway at the high domed ceiling from which the voice seems to emanate.

Mary imagines John looking up at the giant clock on the station wall: it will soon be time to go home. Does John look forward to coming home? Does John come home because he wants to or because he has to? Mary doesn't know and has never thought to ask.

Remember that this all started with an ordinary cup of tea. Look at how far your story has travelled from there. Ask yourself where it will go from here. Remember that, as your novel unfolds, you must always strive to create tension and suspense. That is what keeps the reader turning the pages, always wanting to know what happens next. Suspense in a serious novel does not mean car chases, killer tomatoes, or a serial killer on the loose. It is also probably better to avoid aliens, UFOs, talking animals, ghosts, and vampires as these elements are seldom appropriate or believable in a serious novel. A murder is okay as long as it is not handled in a spuriously sensational manner.

The building emotion of your story is what will lead the reader forward. Along the way, feel free to run the reader through the gamut of delight, surprise, disgust, anger, disbelief, sympathy, sorrow, lust, and so on.

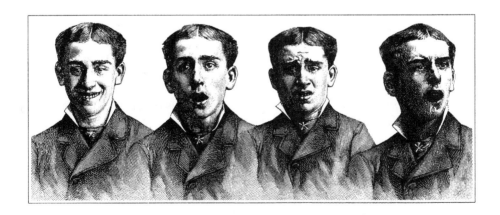

What the action in your novel must build inexorably toward is called *the crisis*. At this point the various strands of tension and emotion running through your story will come to a head. Although a cataclysmic crisis is more dramatic, it is not absolutely necessary. John and Mary need not end up tearing their own or each other's hair out. Think about the difference between *calamity* and *cataclysm*.

In fiction, as opposed to real life, what follows the crisis is called the *resolution* by which the loose ends of the story are tied up. In a serious novel, do not tie up all these ends too neatly. The reader will find this hard to believe because in real life, after the crisis, things just tend to go on and on.

The day will eventually come when your novel is finished. Years have passed. You have tinkered with the commas, deleted the word *nice* seventeen times, worked in all the words you love, and then some, words like: *permafrost, paradigm, abacus, sanguine, frugal, stark*. You have rewritten, reworked, and revised as much as you can. You have read the whole book out loud to your cat. You know this novel is as good as it's going to get. You know it's time to stop. On the last page of the last draft, type the words *THE END*. By now these have become the words you love best.

Sit back and admire your manuscript. Tap its many pages into a perfect pile and pat it lovingly. Rest your head upon it and grin. Put your manuscript in a sturdy box and send it to a prestigious publisher.

For a month or so, believe that you are brilliant. Sit back and admire yourself. Decide what you will wear to accept the Nobel Prize. Watch for the mailman every morning. Resist the urge to kill him when he brings back your novel in its now battered box. Send it out to another (perhaps slightly less prestigious) publisher in a new sturdier box.

Remind yourself that you love writing more than anything else in the world. Read *People* magazine, *National Geographic*, and *The Guinness Book of World Records*. Do not read any other serious novels about love.

Realize that you have a lot more to say. Think about seismology and the power of love. Feel your veins filling up with words again. Think of all the words you love that you haven't used yet. Words like: *fugitive, iconoclast, wedlock, pendulum, labyrinth, pestilence, shark*. Realize that you will have to write another novel. What else can you do?

Begin with a man and a woman. Many famous novels begin with this familiar combination. Although it may at first strike you as rather trite, in fact, once you get going, you will find that it presents a vast array of possibilities.

Diane Schoemperlen (*Born 1954, Thunder Bay, Ontario*) is a short-story writer and novelist whose work often plays with traditional literary conventions. She is known for the innovative use of structure in her stories. A visual component such as photographs or wood engravings frequently accompanies the text of her works. *Forms of Devotion* won the Governor General's Award for Fiction in 1998.

From Pride and Prejudice

Jane Austen

This silhouette, c. 1778, shows Jane Austen's father presenting his son Edward to Mr. and Mrs. Thomas Knight.

"I HOPE, MY DEAR," said Mr Bennet to his wife, as they were at breakfast the next morning, "that you have ordered a good dinner today, because I have reason to expect an addition to our family party."

"Who do you mean, my dear? I know of nobody that is coming, I am sure, unless Charlotte Lucas should happen to call in—and I hope *my* dinners are good enough for her. I do not believe she often sees such at home."

"The person of whom I speak is a gentleman and a stranger."

Mrs Bennet's eyes sparkled. "A gentleman and a stranger! It is Mr Bingley, I am sure. Why, Jane—you never dropt a word of this—you sly thing! Well, I am sure I shall be extremely glad to see Mr Bingley—. But—good lord! how unlucky! there is not a bit of fish to be got today. Lydia, my love, ring the bell. I must speak to Hill, this moment."

"It is *not* Mr Bingley," said her husband; "it is a person whom I never saw in the whole course of my life."

This roused a general astonishment; and he had the pleasure of being eagerly questioned by his wife and five daughters at once.

After amusing himself some time with their curiosity, he thus explained. "About a month ago I received this letter, and about a fortnight ago I answered it, for I thought it a case of some delicacy, and requiring early attention. It is from my cousin, Mr Collins, who, when I am dead, may turn you all out of this house as soon as he pleases."

"Oh! my dear," cried his wife. "I cannot bear to hear that mentioned. Pray do not talk of that odious man. I do think it is the hardest thing in the world, that your estate should be entailed away from your own children; and I am sure if I had been you, I should have tried long ago to do something or other about it."

Jane and Elizabeth attempted to explain to her the nature of an entail. They had often attempted it before, but it was a subject on which Mrs Bennet was beyond the reach of reason; and she continued to rail bitterly against the cruelty of settling an estate away from a family of five daughters, in favour of a man whom nobody cared anything about.

"It certainly is a most iniquitous affair," said Mr Bennet, "and nothing can clear Mr Collins from the guilt of inheriting Longbourn. But if you will listen to his letter, you may perhaps be a little softened by his manner of expressing himself."

"No, that I am sure I shall not; and I think it was very impertinent of him to write to you at all, and very hypocritical. I hate such false friends. Why could not he keep on quarrelling with you, as his father did before him?"

"Why indeed, he does seem to have had some filial scruples on that head, as you will hear."

Hunsford, near Westerham, Kent,
15th October

Dear Sir,

The disagreement subsisting between yourself and my late honoured father always gave me much uneasiness, and since I have had the misfortune to lose him, I have frequently wished to heal the breach; but for some time I was kept back by my own doubts, fearing lest it might seem disrespectful to his memory for me to be on good terms with anyone with whom it had always pleased him to be at variance.—"There, Mrs Bennet."—My mind however is now made up on the subject, for having received ordination at Easter, I have been so fortunate as to be distinguished by the patronage of the Right Honourable Lady Catherine de Bourgh, widow of Sir Lewis de Bourgh, whose bounty and beneficence has preferred me to the valuable rectory of this parish, where it shall be my earnest endeavour to demean myself with grateful respect towards her Ladyship, and be ever ready to perform those rites and ceremonies which are instituted by the Church of England. As a clergyman, moreover, I feel it my duty to promote and establish the blessing of peace in all families within the reach of my influence; and on these grounds I flatter myself that my present overtures of good-will are highly commendable, and that the circumstance of my being next in the entail of Longbourn estate, will be kindly overlooked on your side, and not lead you to reject the offered olive branch. I cannot be otherwise than concerned at being the means of injuring your amiable daughters, and beg leave to apologise for it, as well as to assure you of my readiness to make them every possible amends,— but of this hereafter. If you should have no objection to receive me into your house, I propose myself the satisfaction of waiting on you and your family, Monday, November 18th, by four o'clock, and shall probably trespass on your hospitality till the Saturday se'nnight following, which I can do without any inconvenience, as Lady Catherine is far from objecting to my occasional absence on a Sunday, provided that some other clergyman is engaged to do the duty of the day.—I remain, dear sir, with respectful compliments to your lady and daughters, your well-wisher and friend,

William Collins.

"At four o'clock, therefore, we may expect this peace-making gentleman," said Mr Bennet, as he folded up the letter. "He seems to be a most conscientious and polite young man, upon my word; and I doubt not will prove a valuable acquaintance, especially if Lady Catherine should be so indulgent as to let him come to us again."

"There is some sense in what he says about the girls, however; and if he is disposed to make them amends, I shall not be the person to discourage him."

"Though it is difficult," said Jane, "to guess in what way he can mean to make us the atonement he thinks our due, the wish is certainly to his credit."

Elizabeth was chiefly struck with his extraordinary deference for Lady Catherine, and his kind intention of christening, marrying, and burying his parishioners whenever it was required.

"He must be an oddity, I think," said she. "I cannot make him out.—There is something very pompous in his style.—And what can he mean by apologising for being next in the entail?—We cannot suppose that he would help it if he could.—Can he be a sensible man, sir?"

"No, my dear; I think not. I have great hopes of finding him quite the reverse. There is a mixture of servility and self-importance in his letter, which promises well. I am impatient to see him."

"In point of composition," said Mary, "his letter does not seem defective. The idea of the olive-branch perhaps is not wholly new, yet I think it is well expressed."

To Catherine and Lydia, neither the letter nor its writer were in any degree interesting. It was next to impossible that their cousin should come in a scarlet coat, and it was now some weeks since they had received pleasure from the society of a man in any other colour. As for their mother, Mr Collins's letter had done away much of her ill-will, and she was preparing to see him with a degree of composure which astonished her husband and daughters.

Mr Collins was punctual to his time, and was received with great politeness by the whole family. Mr Bennet indeed said little; but the ladies were ready enough to talk, and Mr Collins seemed neither in need of encouragement, nor inclined to be silent himself. He was a tall, heavy-looking young man of five and twenty. His air was grave and stately, and his manners were very formal. He had not been long seated before he complimented Mrs Bennet on having so fine a family of daughters; said he had heard much of their beauty, but that in this instance fame had fallen short of the truth; and added, that he did not doubt her seeing them all in due time well disposed of in marriage. The gallantry was not much to the taste of some of his hearers, but Mrs Bennet, who quarrelled with no compliments, answered most readily:

"You are very kind, sir, I am sure; and I wish with all my heart it may prove so; for else they will be destitute enough. Things are settled so oddly."

"You allude, perhaps, to the entail of this estate."

"Ah! sir, I do indeed. It is a grievous affair to my poor girls, you must confess. Not that I mean to find fault with you, for such things I know are all chance in this world. There is no knowing how estates will go when once they come to be entailed."

"I am very sensible, madam, of the hardship to my fair cousins,— and could say much on the subject, but that I am cautious of appearing forward and precipitate. But I can assure the young ladies that I come prepared to admire them. At present I will not say more; but, perhaps, when we are better acquainted—"

He was interrupted by a summons to dinner; and the girls smiled on each other. They were not the only objects of Mr Collins's admiration. The hall, the dining-room, and all its furniture, were examined and praised; and his commendation of everything would have touched Mrs Bennet's heart, but for the mortifying supposition of his viewing it all as his own future property. The dinner too in its turn was highly admired; and he begged to know to which of his fair cousins the excellence of its cooking was owing. But here he was set right by Mrs Bennet, who assured him with some asperity that they were very well able to keep a good cook, and that her daughters had nothing to do in the kitchen. He begged pardon for having displeased her. In a softened tone she declared herself not at all offended; but he continued to apologise for about a quarter of an hour.

Jane Austen (*Born 1775, Steventon, England; died 1817*), novelist, is known for her keen observation of social behaviour. A brilliant writer of the novel of manners, Austen drew on her world of the village and country town for characters and themes. *Pride and Prejudice* is one of the most enduringly popular novels in English.

Selection Activities, p. 374

Shinny Game Melted the Ice

Richard Wagamese

BACK HOME they still call me "the one who went away."

Whenever the Wagamese family gets together, my uncles refer to me that way. They're old bush men, those uncles of mine and, having never really become comfortable with English, they lean more toward the Ojibway when talking about family. So, for them, I'll always be "the one who went away."

When I was four I disappeared. I vanished into the maw of the Ontario child welfare system. For 20 years the little family I left behind wondered if I was alive and, if I was, where I was and what I was like. The man who walked back into their lives was vastly different from the fat-cheeked little boy who ran so carelessly through the bush.

It was hardest on my brother. My brother Charles, older, quieter, more refined than I, could never forget. It was he who, 20 years later, managed to track me down through Children's Aid Society records and bring me back home.

We don't get too much time to visit anymore. Jobs, geography, and our personal lives keep us apart like grown-up brothers everywhere. Telephones, the odd letter scribbled in the midst of the daily scurry, infrequent visits, and Christmas cards form the basis of our relationship these days.

I miss him. Despite the double decade absence, we managed to reconnect to each other, and there's a part of him that travels with me in everything.

One winter he hosted Christmas for the family. I travelled from out of the West, and the rest of the Wagamese clan headed from Ontario to Charles's home in Saskatoon, where he was a teacher in a Native cultural survival school.

I arrived a few days before the rest and we had a chance to spend hours and hours together. One morning stands out through the years.

It had snowed the night before and we were out early, standing in the frosty morning air, skates and sticks in hands, staring at the drifts that covered the neighbourhood rink. It was apparent that industry alone would enable us to skate, so we dug into the task of clearing the rink.

Once it was finished, breath coming in thick clouds from our lungs, we still had the energy to race each other getting into our gear. This would be the first time we'd ever skated with each other, despite several long discussions about our mutual love of hockey. I was 26 and Charles was 29.

At first it was tentative. Our passes were soft, unchallenging and our strides loose, casual, smooth. We didn't talk much except to mutter the usual low, appreciative "nice," "good one," "great shot," and perhaps the odd "ooh" and "ah" at something especially well done.

Nowadays I realize how very much it was like the development of our brotherhood.

Then someone—I don't recall which one of us it was—added a little hip as they swiped the puck from the other's stick. Soon the game became a frantic chase, complete with bone-jarring checks, elbows, trips, and over-the-shoulder taunts as we whirled around and around the rink, each other, and the unspoken effects of 20 years.

We must have kept it up for hours. Finally, we collapsed in a sweaty, exhausted heap at the blueline, arms slapped around each other in what was arguably a clean check, sticks strewn across the ice, and the puck a forgotten thing tucked away in the corner of the net.

We lay there for a long, long time laughing through our laboured breathing, staring away across the universe. Brothers. Friends and playmates joined by something far deeper than a simple game of shinny. This was blood, rekindled and renewed by the enthusiasm of a pair of boys disguised as men.

Neither of us cared what passersby might think of a pair of Native men hugging on the ice. Neither of us cared that the tears streaming down our cheeks might freeze, or that we'd have to walk home in wet blue jeans. All that mattered was that the disappeared years had finally melted down forever into this one hug between brothers who never had the chance to age together.

They call me "the one who went away." My family and I have had to work very hard at repairing the damage caused by the Children's Aid decision of 1959. A lot of Native families have. But the one who went away is home and those years have become a foundation for our future.

I believe we become immortal through the process of learning to love the ones with whom we share this planet. I believe that in the heart of everyone who takes the time to look, there's something like that rink where we've chased each others' dreams and lives around, only to collapse in the tears and laughter that will echo forever across the universe.

And in this, we are all Indians.

Richard Wagamese (*Born 1955, Minaki, Ontario*), newspaper journalist, novelist. Of Ojibway ancestry, he studied with traditional elders after finishing his formal education. He was a columnist with the *Calgary Herald* and has written for Aboriginal magazines. *That Terrible Summer* is a collection of his award-winning newspaper writings. He has also published two novels, *Keeper 'n Me* and *A Quality of Light*.

Selection Activities, p. 374

From Truth and Bright Water

Thomas King

ONE YEAR, when we were still all living together in Bright Water, my mother decided we should take a vacation. I voted for the West Edmonton Mall. I had seen brochures of the place, and Lucy Rabbit had even been there and said it was neat. But my mother wanted to go camping, to get into nature and see stuff like animals and scenery. I told her we saw that all the time, but she said the mountains were different. She wanted to go to Waterton Lake, hike around a little, and maybe rent a cabin on the water for a week or so.

My father didn't want to go anywhere. He had too much work to do, he said, and needed to get it done.

"Doesn't stop you from going to Prairie View when you want to go."

"That's business."

"So is this," my mother told him. "Family business."

In the end, my mother got her way, and we borrowed a tent and some sleeping bags from Lucy Rabbit's brother, Gorman, and a cookstove from Franklin, and we packed the truck up and headed for the Rockies.

"What am I going to do?" I asked my mother.

"You can fish."

"That's the second-to-last thing I want to do."

Waterton Lake looked like one of those postcards that Gabriel Tucker had in his sporting goods store for the tourists who stopped in for hunting licences and bullets. There was an old hotel on a hill overlooking the lake, and, of course, my mother had to stop just to see the place. It was old, and it smelled old, and the people who were sitting around in the lobby looked old. There were a couple of tour buses parked out front and everyone on the buses was over fifty at least. I saw a couple of kids, but they were dressed like their parents and moved around as if they had never been outdoors in their entire lives.

My father stayed outside and smoked a cigarette. "I'm going to watch the view," he told my mother. "And think about the money I'm losing."

The inside of the hotel was mostly logs and planks and big branches, and my mother dragged me back and forth, reading a bunch of boring junk out of one of the colour brochures that someone had left lying about on a table.

"Take a guess at how old this hotel is."

"Who cares?"

My mother went to the front desk to see how much a room would cost. She came back smiling and said that they had a few vacancies left, and that we could get a nice room for one hundred and fifty dollars.

"Is there a pool?"

"The lake's right there."

"That much for just a room?"

"It's a world-heritage resort."

My father stayed outside, smoking and looking at the lake, so he didn't get to hear about the price of the room until we were setting up our tent at the campsite. "How much?"

"That's what they said."

"Must be why this sorry-ass campsite is costing us twenty bucks."

"Why?"

"Because we get a view of the hotel."

My mother cooked up some rice and hot dogs and we got some soft drinks out of the cooler. After we had eaten, we sat on stumps and watched the sun settle into the lake. "What do you think now?" she asked me.

I should have told her that I was beginning to like Waterton Lake, just to make her happy, but I didn't. "Don't worry," she told me, "tomorrow's going to be a lot more fun."

It rained all the next day. We sat in the tent and played rummy and fish. The tent leaked a little at one side, and we had to keep shifting around because our legs would get cramped. Every so often, my father would unzip the flap and go out into the rain. We'd wait for him, look at our cards, and plan our strategies. After a while, he would come back in, wet, and we would begin again. I did most of the talking.

"They should put in a miniature golf course. I bet they could make a lot of money off that."

My mother didn't mind the rain. It was an adventure, she said. After each hand, she would carefully add up the scores and write them on the back of one of the brochures she had picked up at the Prince of Wales Hotel.

My mother was right, of course. The mountains were different from Truth and Bright Water. In the mountains, everything was bowed in and close. On the prairies, you could see forever. In the mountains, the air felt heavy and dark. On the prairies, the air was light and gold.

The next morning, the rain stopped and we went for a walk along the lakeshore. My father and I had a contest skipping stones across the lake. "So, what do you think?" he said.

"About what?"

"Your mother's vacation."

"It's okay."

"Pretty exciting playing rummy in a wet tent," he says. "And the mosquitoes are a lot of fun, too."

"Rain's stopped now."

"Your mother wants to hike to Crypt Lake." My father picked up a large, flat rock and threw it sidearm so hard I was sure it was going to bounce up and rattle off across the surface all the way to the far shore. Instead, it buried its nose in the water and sank immediately. "And she wants to take a boat ride up the lake and back."

"Great."

My father stood on the shore and watched the spot where the rock had disappeared, as if he expected it to come floating to the surface. "And that," he said, spitting into the lake, "is your lesson for today."

My mother walked behind us. Every so often, she would stop, bend over and pick up a small stone, and put it in her pocket. Sometimes my father would wander off ahead, looking for larger rocks to throw in the lake, and I would be left alone between them. Most of that day, we walked along the shore tossing rocks in the water until my shoulder started to ache, and then my mother got out the map she had picked up at the ranger's station and said we should climb a small hill called Bear Hump.

"It'll give us a view of the lake and the mountains and the prairies all at once."

"Got that already," said my father.

"If it's clear," my mother said, "we'll be able to see all the way into the United States."

Going up Bear Hump wasn't too hard, and I got to lead. We stopped twice on the climb so my father could have a cigarette. My mother was right. The view was great. And it kept changing. The sun would go in and out of the clouds, and when it went in, the lake turned deep green and grey, and when it came out, the lake flashed silver and black. My mother stood on the edge of the cliff with her arms wrapped around her. My father sat on the edge of a rock and swatted deer flies.

That evening, after we got back, my father told us that he had to go into town. "Forgot something," he said.

My mother was not happy about this. "Can't it wait?"

"It's business."

"What about our vacation?" said my mother.

"You mean your vacation."

"All right," my mother said, "what about my vacation?"

"I'll be back before you know it."

After my father left, the rain returned, gently this time, and my mother and I sat in the tent with the flap open and watched the clouds pour in over the lake.

I figured my father would show up the next morning, but he didn't, and by noon my mother gave up.

"Let's go for that boat ride," she said.

"What about dad?"

"He can catch up."

The cruise around the lake was interesting, and if I hadn't gone, I would never have known that the Canadian/United States border ran right through the middle of the lake. When the guy driving the boat told us that, I expected to see a floating fence or inner tubes with barbed wire and lights, something to keep people from straying from one country into the other. There was a cutline in the trees along with border posts on opposite sides of the shore, and a small border station to mark the line. We floated over to the station and the boat driver rang his bell and we all waved.

When we got back to camp, there was still no sign of my father. We had plenty of food, and we had the tent, and the townsite was right there, so we were in good shape.

"So, what do we do now?"

"Tomorrow," said my mother, "we go to Crypt Lake."

We didn't go to Crypt Lake. My mother slept in the next morning. I waited to see what was going to happen, but I finally gave up and walked over to the lake and practised skipping stones. I practised until I got hungry, and then I went back to the tent. The flap was open. The food was waiting for me in the cooler, but my mother had disappeared. I figured she had gone to the bathroom or something like that, but when she didn't come back, I went looking for her. I found her sitting in a chair in the lobby of the hotel. She was in a corner by herself in front of the windows that overlooked the lake.

"You okay?"

"This is what vacations are all about, you know."

"Sitting?"

"Relaxing," said my mother.

There were sailboats on the lake with bright white sails, and in the bay around the corner from the lake itself, a tour boat was just pulling away from the docks. "We could still go to Crypt Lake."

"No point in doing everything the first trip," she said. Her eyes were heavy and her hair was pulled straight back from her face and tied with a rubber band.

"So, what do you want to do?"

"Sit," she said. "I think I'd like to sit."

My mother sat in the hotel all day. In the evening, she came back to the tent and we had dinner. "There's a bus at seven," she told me, after we had cleaned up.

"What about Dad?"

We packed everything up and carried the tent and stove and the sleeping bags and the cooler into the townsite, and waited for the bus at the Petro-Can station.

"Maybe his truck broke down."

"Maybe it did."

As soon as we got settled in our seats, my mother closed her eyes. I don't think she was asleep, but she didn't talk and she didn't move the whole trip. I leaned against the glass and watched the road, just in case I spotted my father coming back to bring us home.

Thomas King (*Born 1943, Sacramento, California*), novelist, short-story writer, and poet, was born to a Cherokee father and a mother of Greek and German descent. Widely published, he uses a humorous and satiric style to address common misconceptions and stereotypes of Aboriginal people. He teaches Native Studies at the University of Guelph.

The Fly

Mai Vo-Dinh

EVERYONE IN THE VILLAGE knew the usurer, a rich and smart man. Having accumulated a fortune over the years, he settled down to a life of leisure in his big house surrounded by an immense garden and guarded by a pack of ferocious dogs. But still unsatisfied with what he had acquired, the man went on making money by lending it to people all over the country at exorbitant rates. The usurer reigned supreme in the area, for numerous were those who were in debt to him.

One day, the rich man set out for the house of one of his peasants. Despite repeated reminders, the poor labourer just could not manage to pay off his long-standing debt. Working himself to a shadow, the peasant barely succeeded in making ends meet. The moneylender was therefore determined that if he could not get his money back this time, he would proceed to confiscate some of his debtor's most valuable belongings. But the rich man found no one at the peasant's house but a small boy of eight or nine playing alone in the dirt yard.

"Child, are your parents home?" the rich man asked.

"No, sir," the boy replied, then went on playing with his sticks and stones, paying no attention whatever to the man.

"Then, where are they?" the rich man asked, somewhat irritated, but the little boy went on playing and did not answer.

When the rich man repeated his query, the boy looked up and answered, with deliberate slowness, "Well, sir, my father has gone to cut living trees and plant dead ones and my mother is at the market-place selling the wind and buying the moon."

"What? What in heaven are you talking about?" the rich man commanded. "Quick, tell me where they are, or you will see what this stick can do to you!" The bamboo walking stick in the big man's hand looked indeed menacing.

After repeated questioning, however, the boy only gave the same reply. Exasperated, the rich man told him, "All right, little devil, listen to me! I came here today to take the money your parents owe me. But if you tell me where they really are and what they are doing, I will forget all about the debt. Is that clear to you?"

"Oh, sir, why are you joking with a poor little boy? Do you expect me to believe what you are saying?" For the first time the boy looked interested.

"Well, there is heaven and there is earth to witness my promise," the rich man said, pointing up to the sky and down to the ground.

But the boy only laughed. "Sir, heaven and earth cannot talk and therefore cannot testify. I want some living thing to be our witness."

Catching sight of a fly alighting on a bamboo pole nearby, and laughing inside because he was fooling the boy, the rich man proposed, "There is a fly. He can be our witness. Now, hurry and tell me what you mean when you say that your father is out cutting living trees and planting dead ones, while your mother is at the market selling the wind and buying the moon."

Looking at the fly on the pole, the boy said, "A fly is a good enough witness for me. Well, here it is, sir. My father has simply gone to cut down bamboos and make a fence with them for a man near the river. And my mother . . . oh, sir, you'll keep your promise, won't you? You will free my parents of all their debts? You really mean it?"

"Yes, yes, I do solemnly swear in front of this fly here." The rich man urged the boy to go on.

"Well, my mother, she has gone to the market to sell fans so she can buy oil for our lamps. Isn't that what you would call selling the wind to buy the moon?"

Shaking his head, the rich man had to admit inwardly that the boy was a clever one. However, he thought, the little genius still had much to learn, believing as he did that a fly could be a witness for anybody. Bidding the boy goodbye, the man told him that he would soon return to make good his promise.

A few days had passed when the moneylender returned. This time he found the poor peasant couple at home, for it was late in the evening. A nasty scene ensued, the rich man claiming his money and the poor peasant apologizing and begging for another delay. Their argument awakened the little boy, who ran to his father and told him, "Father, Father, you don't have to pay your debt. This gentleman here has promised me that he would forget all about the money you owe him."

"Nonsense!" The rich man shook his walking stick at both father and son. "Nonsense! Are you going to stand there and listen to a child's inventions? I never spoke a word to this boy. Now, tell me, are you going to pay or are you not?"

The whole affair ended by being brought before the mandarin who governed the country. Not knowing what to believe, all the poor peasant and his wife could do was to bring their son with them when they went to court. The little boy's insistence about the rich man's promise was their only encouragement.

The mandarin began by asking the boy to relate exactly what had happened between himself and the moneylender. Happily, the boy hastened to tell about the explanations he gave the rich man in exchange for the debt.

"Well," the mandarin said to the boy, "if this man here has indeed made such a promise, we have only your word for it. How do we know that you have not invented the whole story yourself? In a case such as this, you need a witness to confirm it, and you have none." The boy remained calm and declared that naturally there was a witness to their conversation.

"Who is that, child?" the mandarin asked.

"A fly, Your Honour."

"A fly? What do you mean, a fly? Watch out, young man, fantasies are not to be tolerated in this place!" The mandarin's benevolent face suddenly became stern.

"Yes, Your Honour, a fly. A fly which was alighting on this gentleman's nose!" The boy leaped from his seat.

"Insolent little devil, that's a pack of lies!" The rich man roared indignantly, his face like a ripe tomato. "The fly was *not* on my nose; *he was on the housepole* ..." But he stopped dead. It was, however, too late.

The majestic mandarin himself could not help bursting out laughing. Then the audience burst out laughing. The boy's parents too, although timidly, laughed. And the boy, and the rich man himself, also laughed. With one hand on his stomach, the mandarin waved the other hand toward the rich man:

"Now, now, that's all settled. You have indeed made your promises, dear sir, to the child. Housepole or no housepole, your conversation did happen after all! The court says you must keep your promise."

And still chuckling, he dismissed all parties.

Mai Vo-Dinh (*Born Hue, Vietnam*), painter, printmaker, writer, and translator of Vietnamese folktales, was educated in Vietnam and Paris, before moving to the United States. Vo-Dinh's works have been exhibited in solo shows internationally, and his paintings and prints have appeared on UNICEF greeting cards.

The Cow-Tail Switch

a West African legend

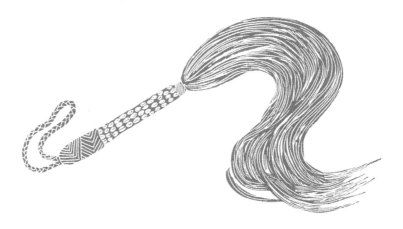

NEAR THE EDGE OF THE LIBERIAN RAIN FOREST, on a hill overlooking the Cavally river, was the village of Kundi. Its rice and cassava fields spread in all directions. Cattle grazed in the grassland near the river. Smoke from the fires in the round clay houses seeped through the palmleaf roofs, and from a distance these faint columns of smoke seemed to hover over the village. Men and boys fished in the river with nets, and women pounded grain in wooden mortars before the houses.

In this village, with his wife and many children, lived a hunter by the name of Ogaloussa.

One morning Ogaloussa took his weapons down from the wall of his house and went into the forest to hunt. His wife and his children went to tend their fields, and drove their cattle out to graze. The day passed, and they ate their evening meal of manioc and fish. Darkness came, but Ogaloussa didn't return.

Another day went by, and still Ogaloussa didn't come back. They talked about it and wondered what could have detained him. A week passed, then a month. Sometimes Ogaloussa's sons mentioned that he hadn't come home. The family cared for the crops, and the sons hunted for game, but after a while they no longer talked about Ogaloussa's disappearance.

Then, one day, another son was born to Ogaloussa's wife. His name was Puli. Puli grew older. He began to sit up and crawl. The time came when Puli began to talk, and the first thing he said was, "Where is my father?"

The other sons looked across the ricefields.

"Yes," one of them said. "Where is Father?"

"He should have returned long ago," another one said.

"Something must have happened. We ought to look for him," a third son said.

"He went into the forest, but where will we find him?" another one asked.

"I saw him go," one of them said. "He went that way, across the river. Let us follow the trail and search for him."

So the sons took their weapons and started out to look for Ogaloussa. When they were deep among the great trees and vines of the forest they lost the trail. They searched in the forest until one of them found the trail again. They followed it until they lost the way once more, and then another son found the trail. It was dark in the forest, and many times they became lost. Each time another son found the way. At last they came to a clearing among the trees, and there on the ground scattered about lay Ogaloussa's bones and his rusted weapons. They knew then that Ogaloussa had been killed in the hunt.

One of the sons stepped forward and said, "I know how to put a dead person's bones together." He gathered all of Ogaloussa's bones and put them together, each in its right place.

Another son said, "I have knowledge too. I know how to cover the skeleton with sinews and flesh." He went to work, and he covered Ogaloussa's bones with sinews and flesh.

A third son said, "I have the power to put blood into a body." He went forward and put blood into Ogaloussa's veins, and then he stepped aside.

Another of the sons said, "I can put breath into a body." He did his work, and when he was through they saw Ogaloussa's chest rise and fall.

"I can give the power of movement to a body," another of them said. He put the power of movement into his father's body, and Ogaloussa sat up and opened his eyes.

"I can give him the power of speech," another son said. He gave the body the power of speech, and then he stepped back.

Ogaloussa looked around him. He stood up.

"Where are my weapons?" he asked.

They picked up his rusted weapons from the grass where they lay and gave them to him. They then returned the way they had come, through the forest and the ricefields, until they had arrived once more in the village.

Ogaloussa went into his house. His wife prepared a bath for him and he bathed. She prepared food for him and he ate. Four days he remained in the house, and on the fifth day he came out and shaved his head, because this was what people did when they came back from the land of the dead.

Afterwards he killed a cow for a great feast. He took the cow's tail and braided it. He decorated it with beads and cowry shells and bits of shiny metal. It was a beautiful thing. Ogaloussa carried it with him to important affairs. When there was a dance or an important ceremony he always had it with him. The people of the village thought it was the most beautiful cow-tail switch they had ever seen.

Soon there was a celebration in the village because Ogaloussa had returned from the dead. The people dressed in their best clothes, the musicians brought out their instruments, and a big dance began. The drummers beat their drums and the women sang. The people drank much palm wine. Everyone was happy.

Ogaloussa carried his cow-tail switch, and everyone admired it. Some of the men grew bold and came forward to Ogaloussa and asked for the cow-tail switch, but Ogaloussa kept it in his hand. Now and then there was a clamor and much confusion as many people asked for it at once. The women and children begged for it too, but Ogaloussa refused them all.

Finally he stood up to talk. The dancing stopped and people came close to hear what Ogaloussa had to say.

Drawings by Madye Lee Chastain

"A long time ago I went into the forest," Ogaloussa said. "While I was hunting I was killed by a leopard. Then my sons came for me. They brought me back from the land of the dead to my village. I will give this cow-tail switch to one of my sons. All of them have done something to bring me back from the dead, but I have only one cow tail to give. I shall give it to the one who did the most to bring me home."

So an argument started.

"He will give it to me!" one of the sons said. "It was I who did the most, for I found the trail in the forest when it was lost!"

"No, he will give it to me!" another son said. "It was I who put his bones together!"

"It was I who covered his bones with sinews and flesh!" another said. "He will give it to me!"

"It was I who gave him the power of movement!" another son said. "I deserve it most!"

Another son said it was he who should have the switch, because he had put blood in Ogaloussa's veins. Another claimed it because he had put breath in the body. Each of the sons argued his right to possess the wonderful cow-tail switch.

Before long not only the sons but the other people of the village were talking. Some of them argued that the son who had put the blood in Ogaloussa's veins should get the switch, others that the one who had given Ogaloussa's breath should get it. Some of them believed that all of the sons had done equal things, and that they should share it. They argued back and forth this way until Ogaloussa asked them to be quiet.

"To this son I will give the cow-tail switch, for I owe the most to him," Ogaloussa said.

He came forward and bent low and handed it to Puli, the little boy who had been born while Ogaloussa was in the forest.

The people of the village remembered then that the child's first words had been, "Where is my father?" They knew that Ogaloussa was right.

For it was a saying among them that a man is not really dead until he is forgotten.

The Death of Balder

a Norse myth

BALDER WAS THE MOST BEAUTIFUL OF ALL THE GODS. He was so wise and kind and good that all heaven and earth adored him. Many considered him to be the light of the world.

But one night Balder had dark and terrible dreams. He dreamt that he was slain by an unknown enemy. In the morning he met with the gods in their council and told them about his dreams.

Everyone became frightened. They believed Balder's dark dreams were a warning that Balder would soon be harmed. "We must figure out how to protect my beloved son," said Odin.

Some recommended that Balder be guarded at all times. Others urged Odin to send him away. But Balder's mother, Frigg, had the best idea of all.

"I will go out in the nine worlds," the goddess said, "and secure a promise from all of nature that it will never bring harm to Balder."

The gods and goddesses applauded Frigg's plan, and she set out to make the world safe for her son.

Fire and water promised Frigg that they would never hurt Balder. Iron, metal, wood, stones, earth, disease, beasts, birds, and snakes— all assured Frigg that they would never bring harm to Balder.

Finally Frigg returned home, secure in the knowledge that her beloved son was safe.

The gods were so relieved that they played games, mocking fate. They shot arrows at Balder, only to watch their arrows miss their target. They threw stones at him, only to see their stones fall to the ground. They tried to stab Balder with their swords, but their swords bent in midair. They proved again and again that no harm could come to Balder.

All the gods celebrated Balder's invincible power, except for one. Loki, the trickster, grew jealous as he watched the gods at their play.

Loki's jealousy grew until he could bear it no longer. He disguised himself in woman's clothing and found Frigg in her palace.

When she saw Loki, Frigg mistook him for a servant-woman. "What is everyone doing outside?" she called from her spinning wheel. "Why are they laughing and clapping?"

"They're shooting arrows at Balder," said Loki in a high voice. "They're throwing stones at him to prove he cannot be harmed."

"Yes, of course," said Frigg. "That's because wood and stone promised me that they will never hurt him."

"Oh really?" said Loki. "So *all* of nature has promised not to harm your son?"

"Well, not quite all," said Frigg. "I did not bother with one small plant that grows on the eastern side of Valhalla—the mistletoe. It's too young and weak to ever hurt anyone."

"Ah, I see," said Loki. Smiling to himself, he slipped out of Frigg's hall and hurried into the woods east of Valhalla.

Loki searched the forest until he found a piece of mistletoe. He picked the sharp sprig, then rushed to the field where the gods were playing.

Hod, the blind twin of Balder, was standing outside the ring of players.

"Why do you not throw something at Balder?" asked Loki.

"Because I cannot see him," said Hod. "And because I have nothing to throw."

"Oh, but you must show honour to Balder the way the others do," said Loki. "I'll help you shoot him with this dart."

Loki placed the piece of mistletoe in Hod's hand. Then he directed Hod's aim and helped him send the mistletoe toward Balder.

The sharp sprig sailed through the air and lodged in Balder's heart. At once, Balder fell to the ground, dead.

The gods stared in disbelief at Balder's lifeless body. They knew that Loki had wrought this evil, but they could not take vengeance, for their pain and horror were too great.

None grieved more than Odin. With his deep wisdom and knowledge, he alone understood how disastrous was Balder's death. Odin knew that it meant that Ragnarok, the final battle of the world, was close at hand.

Frigg could not let go of her hope that Balder would return. She called the gods together and begged that one of them travel to the land of the dead to find her son and bring him back.

The god Hermod volunteered to go, and Odin gave him the magic horse Sleipnir for his journey.

The grieving gods carried Balder's body down to the seashore to Balder's dragon-ship, *Ringhorn.*

The gods planned to make Balder's funeral pyre on *Ringhorn.* But when they tried to push the ship into the sea, it would not budge. They sent for a giantess named Hyrrokin, and she arrived on the back of a wolf, snapping reins made of twisted snakes.

Hyrrokin leaned against the ship's prow, and with a single shove she pushed *Ringhorn* into the water.

All the inhabitants of the nine worlds paraded in Balder's funeral procession. First came Odin and Frigg, the Valkyries, and Odin's two ravens. Then came Frey in his chariot drawn by the golden boar, and Freya in her chariot drawn by cats. Then came Thor, Sif, Nanna, Tyr, Heimdall, Bragi, Idun, Njord, Skadi, Gerd, and all the light elves, dark elves, and dwarves. Even the mountain-giants and frost-giants came down from their icy mountains and marched in Balder's funeral procession.

The gods carried Balder onto the ship. When his wife, Nanna, saw the body laid on the pyre, she died of a broken heart and was laid to rest beside her husband.

Odin placed his magic gold ring upon Balder's body, and the funeral pyre was set aflame. Then the burning ship was pushed out to sea.

Meanwhile, the god Hermod was proceeding on his mission to the land of the dead. On the back of Sleipnir, he galloped for nine days and nine nights through deep valleys filled with shadows. Finally he came to a glittering golden bridge.

"Stop! Who are you? Are you dead?" cried a maiden guarding the bridge.

"Not yet," said Hermod. "But I seek one who is—Balder, the fairest of the gods. Have you seen him by chance?"

"Yes," said the maiden. "He and his wife came over this bridge only yesterday. You'll find him if you follow the road to the north."

Hermod crossed the bridge, then travelled until he came to the barred gates of the land of the dead. He spurred Sleipnir, and the horse leapt into the air—sailing over the gates without even touching them.

Hermod rode on to the palace. When he entered Hel's home, he found Balder and Nanna sitting in the hall's most honoured seats.

Hermod visited with his beloved brother all night. In the morning, he found Hel, the ruler of the dead, and begged her to let Balder and Nanna ride home with him. "The gods cannot stop mourning for this son of Odin," Hermod said.

Hearing these words, Hel's heart softened. "Return to the living," the monster said. "If you find that all beings weep for Balder, I will send him back to you. But if only one creature does not mourn this loss, I will keep him forever."

Before Hermod left, Balder placed Odin's magic ring in his hand. "Take this golden ring back to my father," Balder said. "Tell him I will see him soon."

"And please give this to Frigg," said Nanna, and she gave Hermod a beautiful woven rug.

Hermod said goodbye to Balder and Nanna. Then he rode night and day until he arrived back home.

When Hermod delivered the message from Hel, Odin and Frigg quickly sent messengers out from Asgard to bid the whole world to weep for the death of Balder. All creatures wept as they were asked: gods, goddesses, dwarves, light elves, dark elves, humans—even mountain-giants and frost-giants.

But as the messengers headed back to Asgard, convinced their mission had been successful, they came across a giantess sitting in a cave. She said her name was Thokk, though she was really Loki in disguise.

"Please weep for Balder," said a messenger. "The whole world must weep for him, so he can return from the land of the dead."

"Thokk will only weep with dry tears," Thokk said. "I loved him not. Let Hel keep him for as long as she likes."

And so Balder was not allowed to return to the land of the living. Thus the dark of winter was victorious over the light of the world.

The Death of Balder **109**

The Rebellion of the Magical Rabbits

Ariel Dorfman

WHEN THE WOLVES conquered the land of the rabbits, the first thing the leader of the pack did was to proclaim himself King. The second was to announce that the rabbits had ceased to exist. Now and forever it would be forbidden to even mention their name.

Just to be on the safe side, the new Wolf King went over every book in his realm with a big black pencil, crossing out words and tearing out pictures of cottontails until he was satisfied that not a trace of his enemies remained.

But an old grey fox who was his counsellor brought bad news.

"The birds, Your Wolfiness, insist that they have seen some ... some of those creatures. From on high."

"So how come I don't see anything from way up here, on my throne?" asked the Wolf.

"In times like these," answered the fox, "people have got to see to believe."

"Seeing is believing? Bring me that monkey who takes photos, the one who lives nearby. I'll teach those birds a lesson."

The monkey was old and weak.

"What can the Wolf of all Wolves want with me?" he asked, looking at his wife and daughter.

The little girl had an answer. "He must want you to take a picture of the rabbits, Dad."

"Quiet, quiet," said her mother. "Rabbits don't exist."

But the little monkey knew that rabbits did exist. It was true that, since the howling wolves had invaded the country, the rabbits no longer came to visit her as they had before. But in her dreams she continued hearing the green rain of their voices singing nearby, reflecting in her head as if she were a pond under the moonlight, and when she awoke there was always a small gift beside her bed. Walls and closed doors were like water for the rabbits.

"That's why I sleep well," said the little girl. "That's why that General Wolf must need the photo. To keep nightmares away. You'll bring me a picture of them someday, won't you, Dad?"

The monkey felt fear crawl up and down his fur. "Send this little girl to her room," he told his wife, "until she understands that there are certain things we just don't talk about."

The King of the Wolves was not in the best of moods when the monkey came in. "You're late. And I'm in a hurry. I need photographs of each important act in my life. And all my acts, let me tell you, are supremely important ... Can you guess what we're going to do with those pictures? You can't? We're going to put one on every street, inside every bush, in every home. I'll be there watching each citizen with my very own eyes. You'd better pity those who don't have the latest events of my life hung up on their walls. And you know who is going to distribute each picture? You don't know?"

The monkey was trembling so hard that no words came out.

"The birds, ugly monkey. Now they'll bite their own beaks before they twitter around with any nonsense about rabbits. And we'll tie an endless cord to their legs, so they can't escape. Understand?"

The monkey understood so well that his trembling paw immediately clicked the shutter of the camera, taking the first picture.

"Go," roared the Wolf, "and develop it. I want it on every wall in the kingdom."

But when the photographer returned some minutes later, he did not dare to enter the throne room, and asked one of the soldiers to call the counsellor. Without a word, the monkey passed him the picture he had just taken.

The fox blinked once, and then blinked again. In a corner of the photo, far from the muscular, ferocious figure of the King—who had both arms up in the air as if he had just won a boxing championship—appeared what was without any doubt the beginning of an ear, the ear of someone who had insolently come to spy on the whole ceremony.

"You blind monkey!" fumed the fox. "How come you didn't notice that this ... thing was there? Can't you focus that camera of yours?"

"If it could get into the picture," the monkey answered, "it was because you and your guards let it get close."

"It won't happen again," the counsellor promised. "Rub out that ... ear before His Wolfishness finds out."

From his bag, the monkey took out a special liquid that he used to erase any detail that might bother a client. The intruding ear began to disappear as if it had never existed.

The King of the Wolves was pleased with the portrait and ordered it sent all over the realm. Two hours later he personally went on an inspection tour to make sure that not a window was without a picture of his large, gleaming, dangerous grin. "Not bad," he said, "but this photo is already getting old. People should see my latest deeds. Take another. Quick. Show me scaring these pigeons—right away. And bring it to me immediately. You took too long last time."

But the monkey wasn't able to comply this time either. Once again he had the counsellor called secretly.

"Again?" asked the fox. "It happened again?"

Except that now it was worse than an indiscreet ear. A whole corner of the new picture was filled with the unmistakable face of ... yes, there was no denying it, of a rabbit winking an eye in open defiance of the nearby guards.

"We've got to tighten security," muttered the fox. "Meanwhile, erase that invader."

"Wonderful," shouted the King Wolf when finally he was given the picture. "Look at the frightened faces of the pigeons trying to escape. I want a million copies. I want them on milk cartons and on the coupons inside cereals ... Onward. Onward. Let's go and smash up a dam. Come on, monkey. Fame awaits us both."

The beavers had been working summer and winter for three years on a beautiful dam that would allow them to irrigate a distant valley.

The Wolf of Wolves climbed a tree. "I want you to shoot the precise moment when my feet crash into the middle of the dam, monkey. If you miss the shot, next time I'll fall on top of you and then I'll have to get myself another photographer. Are you ready?"

Not only was the monkey ready, so was the counsellor. The fox was breathing down the old monkey's back, peering over his shoulder, watching, listening. Nothing could escape those vigilant, darting eyes. Not a fuzzy ear would dare to make its appearance.

So neither the monkey nor the fox could believe it when, a bit later, they saw at the bottom of the picture a rabbit lolling on his side as if he were relaxing at a picnic. Next to him, another rabbit had raised her paw and was boldly thumbing her nose.

"This is an epidemic," said the fox, "and let me tell you, our lives are in danger."

"Let's start erasing," the monkey said wearily.

"You erase. I'll get a squadron of buzzards and hawks. They see all animals, even the quick and the small."

His Wolfhood the King yelped with pleasure when he saw the picture. It portrayed him at the exact moment he was breaking the backbone of the beavers' dam. In the distance, families of beavers could be seen fleeing. There was not a single shadow of a rabbit.

"Send it out! A strong country is an educated country, a country that always is tuned in to the latest news. What are we going to do now for some fun?"

"We could rest," the monkey suggested, his paws peeling from the harsh erasing fluid.

The Wolf looked at him as if he were a stone.

"And who asked you for an opinion? I'm in charge here. That's why I was born with these teeth, and you'd better pray you never have to feel them crunching your bones. Onward. We are the future, the morrow, the dawn! We'll go on until there's no more light."

But in each new photo, the rabbits became more plentiful, audacious, and saucy. His Wolfinity the King destroyed sugar mills, shook squirrels out of their trees and hid their nuts, stripped ducks of their feathers, drove sheep off cliffs, drilled holes in the road so that horses would break their legs, unveiled new cages and old dungeons ... and the more his frightening yellow eyes flickered, the more innumerable were the rabbits of every colour that frolicked in the margins of the photographs. Even the clouds seemed full of fur and whiskers and cottontails.

"Hey, birdie," jeered the Supreme Wolf, grabbing a swallow about to fly off with bag overflowing with pictures, "what tune are you singing now, featherhead? Who's that in the centre of the picture, huh? Who's the King?"

The bird held his beak tight, so that not even a peep could come out.

"Lights, camera, action, monkey!" the Monarch demanded. "Call this: WOLF KING RECEIVES HOMAGE FROM A MESSENGER."

The monkey obeyed, but could hardly hide his despair. Though nobody ever saw the rebels when the photos were taken, they were always there when it was time to show them, nibbling lettuce at the very feet of the biggest and baddest of wolves.

"Exterminate them," hissed the fox, who had ordered a stronger, more acid liquid. "Don't leave even a twitch of a nose."

But the pictures were beginning to look defective. There were blank spaces everywhere. The monkey knew that the only solution was to convince His Wolfishness to sit up high on an elevated throne. Since rabbits live underground, they wouldn't be able to wiggle their way into the frame of the photograph.

The king, fortunately, was delighted with the idea. "I'll look more impressive up here. And I can keep an eye on those birds. What a surprise for my subjects when they find a new picture at breakfast, right? So get here early, monkey, do you hear?"

When the exhausted monkey dragged himself home, his fingers hurting from the terrible liquid, the latest photograph of the King had just been plastered on the front door of his house. Just at that moment, a soldier was leaving.

"No cause for alarm, Mr. Monkey," the soldier laughed. "Just a routine inspection to see if anybody is sabotaging His Wolfhood's pictures."

The monkey rushed inside. "Our daughter? Is she all right? Did she say anything?"

"I'm fine, Dad," the little girl said. "Those wolves are gone, aren't they? And you brought me that special photo—you know, the one I asked you for?"

The monkey felt as if from all four walls, from all four pictures on the four walls, the eight eyes of the Biggest of Wolves were watching each word he might say.

"Let your father rest," said her mother. "The only pictures he's taken are the ones we've put up in the house, like good citizens."

But the next morning, the monkey was awakened by his child's kiss. She put her lips near his ears and whispered something so softly that only he could hear it: "Thank you. It's the best present you could ever give me. You're a magical dad."

"Thanks? Thanks for what?"

She motioned almost imperceptibly toward the wall from which the photo of the Wolf King ruled. Her father opened his eyes wide. In one of the corners of that picture, like the sun rising over the mountains, he could just glimpse, in the act of making their gradual but glorious appearance, a pair of, yes, of course, a pair of soft, pink, pointed ears.

The monkey jumped out of bed. The liquid he had applied did not work permanently. The rabbits had needed the whole night to sneak back into the pictures, but somehow they had managed it.

"I think they knew I was scared," the little girl murmured, "and came to see me while I slept."

Her father dressed in less time than it takes a chill to run up a spine and scurried to the palace without stopping for breakfast. Was this thing happening only at their house or could the same invasion have taken place everywhere in the kingdom? If so, how could the rabbits be removed from so many portraits?

His Wolfiness was still in bed, but the counsellor was already pacing about, biting the tip of his tail. "It's a plague," he said, "but, fortunately, it is already under control. The offending pictures have been burned. As for you ... "

"I swear that I—"

"Not a word from you," interrupted the fox. "It's lucky those creatures don't exist. Imagine the damage they'd cause if they really existed. But enough talk. What we need now is a new photo to replace the ones that are contaminated."

They rushed to the new throne, which was now set up on top of four colossal wooden legs, out of reach of the spreading virus of the mischievous ears.

"I want two shots," His Wolfhood demanded, "one of me ascending my throne and another of me sitting on it, enjoying the fresh air. And send them abroad too, so those silly foreign papers will stop attacking me."

This time, when the photos were developed, there was no trouble. Not so much as a carrot of a sign of a rabbit.

"Didn't I tell you? Didn't I tell you they don't exist?" the counsellor was jubilant. "It was just a matter of your focusing the camera properly."

For the next few days, there were no more unpleasant surprises. The Wolf of Wolves felt happy, high above the heads of the multitude. He let his lieutenants run things while he posed for pictures giving commands, delivering speeches, signing laws. He examined the shots carefully, however. "Congratulations," he said. "You're being more careful, monkey. It seems you're learning your trade just by being near me. I don't see any more of those whitish spots that spoiled my first pictures."

But one morning, the monkey was again awakened by his daughter's voice. "They're back, Dad," she whispered in his ears. "Those pictures you took sure are magical."

In one set of photos, at the foot of the towering throne, a small army of rabbits was biting, chewing, and splintering the wooden legs. Their teeth worked patiently, and they stopped their work only now and again to wave to the spectators.

The counsellor was waiting. The monkey could see his fur ruffling and swelling like a swarm of bees.

"How many this time?" the monkey asked.

"The photos are being taken care of," the fox said grimly. "But the birds have got wind of what happened, and now they're telling everyone that those ... those awful animals exist. And His Wolfinity is beginning to suspect something. 'Why are those birds so happy, so shrill?' he asks. I told him they're just a bunch of featherbrains, full of hot air."

"What did he answer?" asked the monkey.

The King had announced that balloons are full of hot air too and that they could be popped. If those birds didn't keep quiet, he would make them disappear.

But the counsellor had another idea: The Wolf of All Wolves should tie a recording of one of his latest speeches around the necks of the birds. They would have to carry not only the photos, but also the King's words, all over his kingdom. Nobody would be able to hear any of their songs.

"Hearing is believing," trumpeted His Wolfiness. "We'll give them a taste of some hymns, some military marches, some lessons in history, economics, and ethics."

The old monkey's life became unbearable. Not even the recorded howls of the King and his chorus of warlike beasts could stop the timid appearance, in the next photo, of an inquisitive nose, a pair of furry ears, some white whiskers, and something hungry gnawing away at the legs of the throne.

The fox replaced the chief officer of the royal guard with a boa constrictor straight from the jungle of a neighbouring country. He put small, hundred-eyed spiders in strategic places throughout the Wolfdom. One day he ordered half the population to shave off their shiny fur so that no spy could hide in it. To punish the cows, accused of uttering subversive moos, he commanded that their milk be soured. And finally, he raised the volume of the King's broadcasts. But in spite of these efforts, there began to be heard a persistent, rowdy, merry sound, the clicking of thousands of tiny teeth, the burbling of an underground stream.

The monkey felt dizzy.

The rhythm was maddening. During the night, the legs of the throne, spindlier by the minute, were reinforced grudgingly by woodpeckers who would have much preferred to take the throne apart. The monkey had to rely on every photographic trick of the trade, now erasing, now trimming with scissors, disguising ears so they looked like shadows and shadows so they looked like wallpaper. He even began using old portraits of the King, trying to make them seem like recent ones.

Until one night, when it was very late, the old monkey was awakened by an angry hand that shook him from his slumber. It was the counsellor, flanked by a fierce escort of soldiers. The Lord Wolf had sent for him.

The whole house was up by now. The little girl watched her father begin dressing.

"Say hello to His Foxcellency," said the monkey.

"Dad," she said, and it was astonishing that she did not speak in a low, fearful voice anymore, as if the armed guards were not even there, "today you've got to bring me that picture I asked for."

"A picture?" the counsellor showed interest. "A picture of what, of whom?"

The child continued to ignore him. "Today you'll bring me a photo of the rabbits, right, Dad? For my wall?"

The mother monkey touched the girl's head as if she had fever. "Hasn't your father told you that rabbits don't exist? Haven't we shut you up in your room for telling lies?"

"They exist," the girl announced. "Everybody knows they exist."

"Just as I suspected," said the counsellor. "Let's go."

The Wolfiest of Wolves was waiting for them atop his throne. Around each leg, hundreds of guards and snakes kept watch.

"Monkey, you are a traitor," thundered the King. "Your photos are being used by people who say that strange and malicious creatures— who are non-existent as everyone knows—are conspiring this very night to overthrow my rule. They say my throne trembles and my dynasty will topple. Is there any evidence that my throne trembles? Does anybody dare say so?" And he yowled like a hundred jet fighters in the air. "We'll start by making a recording of that sound. And you, you monkey, you're going to help me stamp out these rumours. Touching is believing. You are going to make me a wide-angle three-dimensional picture that will cover all walls. In colour. Because I am going to crown myself Emperor of the Wolves, the Supreme Wolferor. And if a single wretched rabbit shows its snout, I will make you eat the photos, one by one, a million of them, and then I'll eat you and not only you, but your wife and your daughter, and all the monkeys in this country. Now. Take that picture."

The monkey stuck his quaking head under the black cloth behind his camera and focused on the throne. He let out a little moan. Up till then, the rabbits had appeared only later, when the picture was developed. But here they were now, directly in front of his lens, ungovernable and carefree, gnawing away, biting not only the wood of the throne, but also the swords of the astonished guards and the very rattles of the rattlesnakes.

"What's the matter?" bellowed the future Wolferor, who was not looking downward so his profile would be perfect for posterity.

The monkey moved the camera nearer the throne, hoping the rabbit army would not come out in the picture. The rabbits moved faster than he did. They were clambering up the legs, one on top of the other as if they were monkeys or birds. The soldiers tried to frighten them away in silence, unwilling to attract the attention of the King, but the invaders were too agile. The Wolves kept bumping into one another and hitting each other over the head. The monkey realized that a contingent of birds had arrived from above, winging freely through the air, without a cord tied to them or a recording.

"Hurry up!" ordered the Wolf of all Wolves.

The monkey closed his eyes very tightly. It was better not to witness what was going to happen. At the very moment he clicked the shutter, he heard a deafening noise. He knew what he was going to see when he opened his eyes, but still could not believe it: Like an old elm tree rotten to the core, the throne had come crashing to the ground along with the King of Wolves, guards, snakes, counsellor, and all. The monkey blinked. There at the foot of his tripod lay the Biggest, Baddest, the Most Boastful Wolf in the Universe. His ribs were broken, his black fur was torn by the fall, his yellow eyes were reddened, and he was wailing in pain.

"Monkey," squeaked the would-be Wolferor of the World, "this picture ... you have my permission not to publish it."

At that moment, all the lights in the palace went out. The monkey was paralyzed. He did not know where to go. Then, as if someone in the darkness were suddenly shining a light on a pathway, he knew what he must do. He grabbed his camera and his bag, and clutching them to his chest like a treasure, he fled.

His daughter was waiting for him at the door of the house.

"Wait," he said to her. "Wait. I've brought you something." And without another word, he raced into his darkroom to develop the last picture as quickly as possible.

When he came out a few minutes later, his daughter and wife were standing on chairs, taking down the pictures of the Wolf King.

"Here," the old monkey said to his daughter, blinking in the bright light. "Here, this is the picture you've been asking for all this time. I've finally brought you your present."

"Thanks, Dad," the little girl said. "But I don't need it anymore."

She pointed around the room and toward the street and across the fields where the sun was beginning to rise.

The world was full of rabbits.

Ariel Dorfman (*Born 1942, Argentina*), author, journalist, playwright, and scholar, was exiled from Chile, his adopted country, in 1973, because of his outspoken resistance to the dictator, Augusto Pinochet. Since then he has taught at universities in France, the Netherlands, and the United States. His acclaimed play *Death and the Maiden* was adapted for film in 1994.

Nonfiction

NONFICTION

"Good reading is the only test of good writing."

–Robertson Davies

"Ideas won't keep; something must be done about them."

–Alfred North Whitehead

Nonfiction deals with actual people, places, ideas, and events in the present, the past, or the future. Because it covers so much territory, nonfiction includes a wide array of forms. Journals, biographies, magazine articles, interviews, speeches, newspaper columns, reviews, how-to manuals, encyclopedia entries, research reports, textbooks, letters to the editor, essays—all are forms of nonfiction. And, sometimes unexpectedly, all have the power to intrigue you.

Writers create nonfiction for many purposes and audiences. Journals and personal letters are meant for private reflection or to communicate with friends. Reviews and letters to the editor present a strong opinion to a wide audience. Encyclopedias, dictionaries, and almanacs are reference tools.

As you read each selection in this unit, pin down the writer's main idea, or thesis, usually found near the beginning. Look closely, as well, at the detailed information in each selection. Many nonfiction writers choose a structure, such as chronological order or comparison and contrast, to present these specific facts in a way that's convincing and appealing.

purpose: the main aim or goal of a piece of writing

reference tool: a text that provides background or source information

thesis: a central message or opinion in a text that the writer seeks to prove

structure: the overall organization or arrangement of the content in a text

Nonfiction

The Usual Things

Anita Rau Badami

AT SIX O'CLOCK in the morning on March 16, my mother phoned me from India. My first reaction was panic. Ma never called except in an emergency, unless someone in our family was ill, or dying. Otherwise she thought telephone conversations were a waste of time and money.

On this morning, however, she merely wanted to remind me about our New Year—Yugadi—the next day. I asked why she hadn't written, as she always did at the beginning of every year, with a list of all the feasts and festivals I was supposed to observe but never did—Shankranti in January, then Yugadi, followed by Ganesh Chatrurthi, Krishna Janamashtami, Diwali—a list that carried a trail of jasmine fragrance and memories of childhood with it. In the first few years after our arrival in Canada, I was so busy adapting to a new culture that I did not have the time or the energy to hold on to the old.

"What's the point writing to you when you always phone me a month after the festival saying that you lost the list?" my mother demanded. "This way you cannot possibly forget. Tomorrow is Yugadi. For your son at least you must do all the usual things. Promise you will?"

I promised.

The "usual things" included oil baths before sunrise, cleaning the small collection of silver gods sitting neglected at the back of a kitchen cupboard, prayers that echoed in my memory still, and an eight-course meal to be shared with friends. And I would need new mango leaves to string together and hang over the front door.

In Hindu mythology, the mango is supposed to be a wish-granting tree, and its foliage is a must for auspicious occasions. I would also need the foul-tasting leaves and buds of the neem tree, to be crushed with *jaggery* into a paste called *bevu bella*, and swallowed first thing in the morning, as a symbol of how life was to be lived—the bitter to be taken with the sweet, without a murmur.

Sweet thing

I looked out the window. Most of the trees I could see were bare, except for dark stands of pine. There were cherry blossoms trembling like ballerinas against the sodden sky, and golden broom lit up the moss-eaten walls of the house across the road. Mango and neem were definitely not part of the Vancouver landscape.

A friend suggested that I try the Indian grocers on Main Street.

When you walk down Main Street, it is easy to believe that you have left Vancouver and landed in Delhi. The air is spicy with cooking smells from half a dozen restaurants. Wild-eyed drivers hurtle toward the traffic lights as if they were truckers on the Grand Trunk Road in India. Women stroll along in *salwarkameez* suits and saris, stopping to greet friends or prod vegetables displayed in stalls on the pavement. The muted blare of Hindi film songs mingles with the voices of people speaking in several different languages. Travel agencies offer dirt-cheap fares to India.

First I tried a shop where I usually go to stock up my kitchen cupboards and get my monthly fix of deep-fried Punjabi samosas, even though it means tangling with the sour proprietor, a sixty-year-old woman with fraying hair dyed deep black. She is always dressed in bridal pink or red, her lips stained a matching shade, her scraggy neck layered with heavy gold jewellery, her wrists loaded with bracelets. For reasons I hadn't been able to fathom, she didn't like me. If I didn't keep an eye on her, she would slip one samosa fewer than I had ordered into the bag and forget (deliberately, I am sure) to include the small container of tamarind chutney she gave to her other customers.

When I asked if she had mango leaves, she looked at me as if I had demanded a rock from the moon.

"Why you want?"

"It's my New Year tomorrow. I need it for my front door."

"New Year? Where you are from?"

"From India."

"Me also, but we have New Year in April," she said. "Why yours is now?"

"I am from South India," I explained.

"Not all South Indians celebrate New Year tomorrow," argued a woman in the line behind me. "Tamil New Year is in April."

"I am not a Tamil," I said, my composure beginning to fray.

"What you are then?" asked the shop-lady, drumming her fingers impatiently on her cash register.

"It doesn't matter. Look, do you have mango leaves?"

"No."

"Do you have neem leaves then?"

"No," she said triumphantly.

I crossed the street to another store where the proprietor was far more polite. When he saw me carrying a bag with his rival's logo, however, he reproached me.

"You went there first. What you bought? Why you went there? They put stones in everything. To increase weight and cheat you."

"Only samosas," I said, opening the bag to show him the box.

He was appeased. His store did not carry samosas.

"I just need some leaves," I told him. "Mango and neem."

"Why for you need those leaves?" he asked. "They are not very good. I have others that are much tastier. Methi, coriander, two types of spinach. You buy those, I am advising you."

I explained that I followed a different calendar, according to which the year 2000 was actually 5102. I was born in September but my real birthday was in February, and my New Year began tomorrow.

He suggested that I try Chinatown. "Many funny-funny things they have," he offered. "Definitely you will find your leaves there. And just a month ago they celebrated Chinese New Year, so maybe ..."

Hours later, I staggered home, my bag full of supplies, but without the leaves I needed. My neighbour, a slender, chic, and somewhat inquisitive Romanian woman who always seemed to be smoking, waved when she saw me. She already knew of my quest.

"Did you find any?" she asked.

I confessed that I had not.

Why couldn't I use something else, she wondered, waving her cigarette in the air. Couldn't I be creative, make do, find another way? Wasn't life one long garland of improvisations? Surely my gods wouldn't mind if I used my imagination!

And so I did. At six the next morning, I hung a string of rhododendron leaves over my door. They looked a lot like mango leaves. A few sprigs of cherry blossom completed the decoration. Was it my fault that flowers appeared before leaves here? For the *bevu bella*, I substituted orange peel for neem and mashed it up with _jaggery_ from the Indian store. The result was suitably bittersweet, and at least half the recipe was as tradition demanded. Later, over steaming bowls of _saaru_, one of my friends reminded me how fortunate I was. Fifty years ago, she said, she had had to smuggle pickles and _papad_ and _asafetida_ past Canadian customs. What was I grouching about?

When I phoned my mother to tell her about my celebration, it was the second day of her New Year and the mango leaves were drying over her door.

"So," she demanded. "You did all the usual things?"

"Yes, Ma," I said. "All the usual things."

Anita Rau Badami (_Born 1961, Rourkela, India_), journalist and author, was educated in India. A writer since childhood, she sold her first story at the age of 18. She has worked as a scriptwriter for Indian national television and as a freelance newspaper writer. Rau Badami came to Canada in 1991, and published her first novel, _Tamarind Mem_, in 1996.

Bat Summer Reviewed

Erika Thornton and Diana Brebner

Sarah Withrow, *Bat Summer*, Groundwood Books/Douglas and McIntyre, Toronto, 1998, paperback, 174 pages, ISBN 0-88899-352-8.

REVIEW BY ERIKA THORNTON

In Sarah Withrow's *Bat Summer* there is a pearl of a novel built around a tried and true conflict theme, kept fresh by vibrant characters and inventive scenarios. At the simplest level, the story revolves around a twelve-year-old boy, Terence, who finds a new and very different friend in a girl, Lucy, who believes she is a bat. As bizarre and ludicrous as this may sound, Withrow doesn't allow the reader to dwell long on the strangeness here. Instead, she paints clear portraits of her characters. This is accomplished mainly through their actions and the opinions formed about them by the narrator, Terence.

The novel begins as Terence's long-time best friend is leaving for camp. While inwardly pondering the repercussions of his friend's departure, Terence makes several astute yet childlike observations about the world, and people. Often poignant and always witty, these remarks provide continuity and comic relief throughout the book. They are Terence's trademark, and they are perfect.

Facing what he feels will be a dull summer, Terence starts hanging out at the park with two other kids, Lucy and Rico. Lucy is our bat-girl, frighteningly intense and incredibly intelligent. Rico is everything people fear about teenage boys; a loud, cigarette-smoking, porn magazine–ogling hulk, with a sinister outlook. Also added, for what seems like no reason, are the two chess-playing cronies who sit in the shade at the park every afternoon. They crop up again in a somewhat ungainly subplot inserted toward the end of the book, but are largely useless to the reader. Here is a scuff mark on the shine of this book; "extras" like these "spare characters" and the plot they are involved with drag down the central plot. *Bat Summer* is built largely on strong characters and to a lesser degree on a plot which is inventive, but only slightly more than inconsequential here.

As Terence spends more and more time at the park, he delves more deeply into Lucy's "Bat World." He discovers that she is possibly the most complex person on the planet, with a whole big set of issues and some more to spare. Terence and Lucy compare notes on parents who ignore you, how to take care of yourself, and being a bat. Fluttering around them all the while like elegantly placed streamers are Terence's mother, Terence's cousin Elys, Rico, the chess-playing men, and the ghostly absence and neglect of Lucy's parents. While Withrow doesn't refer back to this constantly, it is always there, looming over the actions of the characters. As the story progresses, the reader becomes more and more aware of Lucy's deep unhappiness, and of some of the reasons behind it. All of this unhappiness culminates when Lucy, who has gone from quirky to crazy in the blink of an eye, runs away. The reader climbs once again into Terence's head to watch him piece things together.

The strength of this book, and to my mind the reason it was short-listed for a Governor General's Award, is the fresh narrating voice. Withrow has a perfect sense for how 12-year-olds talk, and seamlessly weaves these patterns into their thoughts and internal musings. This is too rare in fiction for young people. Also rare in such a book is the frankness with which Withrow presents disturbing issues. She uses powerful images to represent parental neglect and sacrifice in friendship. Her style is gutsy yet unobtrusive.

Now that I've wrested my copy of Sarah Withrow's *Bat Summer* from my younger daughter, I can begin the difficult task of containing my enthusiasm for this book within the confines of a short review. Yes, this is a book with a "bat" theme, following such successes as Jannell Cannon's exquisite *Stella Luna* and Canadian Kenneth Oppel's animal fantasy, *Silverwing*.

Cannon's and Oppel's bats take on charming human personalities and engage in anthropomorphized adventures. Withrow's twist on the theme is a story about the very human Lucy who has come to believe she is a bat, and fellow twelve-year-old Terence, who is drawn into her troubled world. Here's Lucy:

> *"Want to hear about the Midget Employment Stabilization Board?"* *she growls. Tom says Lucy is an embarrassment to humanity. She draws these magic marker tattoos on her face [...] And what's with that old blue sheet strung around her neck? It's like she's some kind of superhero. Plus she's got red hair, so she looks like a piece of red asparagus stuffed into a pillow case.*

We get the picture. This girl is weird. She has hung upside down with her feet in a noose with the bats in the rafters of her house. She eeps and cheeps in bat language with Terence. She is fierce, intelligent, intensely lonely, and neglected. Hers is a world where kids get head lice and parents don't notice, where kids steal shampoo and pasta to survive.

And yet, this is not a novel about toughness or streetwise kids. Ordinary is how Terence describes himself: "Being ordinary isn't exactly the same thing as being ugly but it's close." Ordinary meets extraordinary as Terence and Lucy manoeuvre their way through their "bat summer" with tenderness, loyalty, and the healing power of an absurd sense of humour.

Withrow's careful eye sees all: dog nails clicking on the hardwood floors, the pathway of a tear as it falls from cheek to running shoe, the thrill of kite-flying, the stomach-gnawing anxiety of protecting a runaway friend. Terence finds Lucy in a cave under a bridge in a Toronto ravine:

> *Lucy is bald. She's shaved her head. And I can tell she had a hard time doing it because there are a few nicks by her ear and at the base of her neck. She must have done it to get rid of the lice.*

Oh, Lucy. I can see her neck muscles tighten. I swear, I can see her brain thinking. She lets her face fall in her hands.

I can't catch my breath. I remember the colour of her hair. How I once thought it was spiky and stringy, and also how it burned like fire. And also, how I touched it.

It's not surprising that *Bat Summer* won the Groundwood Twentieth Anniversary First Novel for Children Contest and was nominated for the 1998 Governor General's Award. This is a jewel of a book. Let's hope this is the beginning of a long writing career for Sarah Withrow.

Erika Thornton was a teenager when she published this review.

Diana Brebner (*Born Kingston, Ontario*), poet. She studied philosophy at the University of Ottawa, and now lives in Ottawa. Her poetry has received numerous awards and has been published in several anthologies. She has also published several collections of poetry, including *Flora and Fauna*.

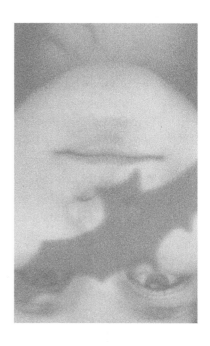

Selection Activities, p. 377

Reconnecting with the Earth

David Suzuki

LIKE THE ELECTRONIC "INFORMATION" we consume, the sphere of our activity and of the connections that make up the little world we live in have become a collection of disconnected fragments. We consume or use with little sense of the repercussions beyond our immediate surroundings.

Life in industrialized societies has become so complex that we need specialists of all kinds—plumbers, electronics experts, muffler and brake specialists, nurses, TV repairmen. Although I use a computer and drive a car, for example, I don't understand the intricacies of how they work or how to fix them when they don't.

And so we tend to see the world as a mosaic of disconnected bits and pieces rather than as an integrated whole in which we understand the relationship between cause and effect. We lose sight of the fact that we are biological beings who live in a finite world where matter is endlessly recycled through biological action in air, water, and soil. And not knowing where our consumer goods come from or where they end up, it's hard to relate how we live with the environmental consequences.

In cities we place our garbage at the curb in plastic bags, cans, or boxes, and like magic, it conveniently disappears from our view and our minds. I once spent a day at a waste disposal site near Toronto, looking at what was being discarded. There were all kinds of material that didn't have to be there: grass clippings (and leaves in the fall), wood that could be chipped, paper of every conceivable type, plastic containers, metal objects. Even with Toronto's vaunted blue box program, the output of unnecessary garbage is enormous.

I thought of that dump while flying in a tiny commuter plane from Montreal to Val d'Or. During the short flight, a continental breakfast was served in a plastic case. Inside were a plastic cup of yogurt, a plastic cup of orange juice, a plastic bag containing a plastic stirring rod, spoon, and fork as well as individually wrapped sugar, cream, and hand towel. Coffee was served in a foam cup. By the end of the meal, each passenger had a mound of packaging that was then swept into a plastic bag and deposited at the airport. This is repeated thousands of times daily all over the country. A visit to a dump makes you realize that we have to replace this unnecessary waste with reusable things.

A few years ago while filming an introduction to a report on the biological functions of different kinds of muscle, I used the light and dark meat of a chicken to illustrate. The lighting man exclaimed with surprise, "Is chicken meat a *muscle?*" When our food comes neatly packaged in plastic containers, the link between a piece of meat and a once-living animal becomes tenuous. But as animals ourselves, we are totally dependent on other living organisms for every bit of our nutrition. A visit to a slaughterhouse and a factory farm would be a powerful reminder of our biological roots and our need for other life forms.

It's the same with plants. Few of us have spent any time on a farm or understand the factors that propel farmers to rely on chemicals to ensure high yields while struggling against weather, pests, and disease, or the compromises that are made to enhance food's shelf life, transportability, and appearance. As soil and water accumulate pesticides, fungicides and preservatives, fruit and vegetables are bound to incorporate them. If young people spent time working on a farm, they would have a far different appreciation of the food they eat, not to mention the economic plight of farmers.

In cities and towns, we take our water and sewers for granted—just turn on the tap and out it flows. Flush the toilet or pour waste down the sink and we send it on its way without a thought about where it ends up. Yet often the water we consume is drawn downstream from someone else's effluent or from wells into which leachate from dumps is draining. Beaches that are no longer swimmable are directly related to the flushing of our toilets. Every responsible citizen should make an extensive tour of our sewer outlets and water treatment facilities to see how our activities are interconnected.

It's the same with energy. We turn our lights and machines on and off with little thought of where the energy comes from and its environmental cost. Only when there's a power failure are we aware of how dependent we are on electricity. Canadian folklore says that our great rivers and fossil fuel deposits provide a near limitless source of energy. But we are far less informed about the ecological destruction that accompanies huge hydroelectric dams or potential greenhouse warming from coal- and oil-fired plants. All we want is to be sure to have electricity at the flick of a switch.

We have to acquire a deeper understanding of the total costs of modern life in the context of a finite planet. Every benefit and convenience has hidden effects that we inflict on the environment. Children need to learn their lessons from firsthand experience at slaughterhouses, farms, factories, water sources, hydroelectric and nuclear power plants, sewage treatment facilities, garbage dumps, pulp mills, logging and reforestation areas, mining sites, et cetera. Even in the largest urban centres, we are still interconnected and dependent on our surroundings far beyond city limits.

David Suzuki (*Born 1936, Vancouver, British Columbia*) is an award-winning scientist, environmentalist, and broadcaster. During World War II, at age six, he was interned at a camp for Japanese Canadians in British Columbia. An author of 28 books, including ten books for children, Suzuki is known to television audiences as the host of a popular science documentary program, *The Nature of Things*.

Selection Activities, p. 378

After 27 years, he achieve

A Country Childhood

Nelson Mandela

Like these boys, the young Nelson Mandela herded sheep and cattle.

APART FROM LIFE, a strong constitution, and an abiding connection to the Thembu royal house, the only thing my father bestowed upon me at birth was a name, Rolihlahla. In Xhosa, Rolihlahla literally means "pulling the branch of a tree," but its colloquial meaning is "troublemaker." My more familiar English name was not given to me until my first day of school.

ancestry

I was born on 18 July 1918 at Mvezo, a tiny village on the banks of the Mbashe River in the district of Umtata, the capital of the Transkei. My father, Gadla Henry Mphakanyiswa, was a chief by both blood and custom. He was confirmed as chief of Mvezo by the king of the Thembu tribe, though under British rule his selection had to be ratified by the government.

According to tradition, the Thembu people migrated from the Drakensberg mountains in the sixteenth century, where they were incorporated into the Xhosa nation. Each Xhosa belongs to a clan that traces its descent back to a specific forefather. I am a member of the Madiba clan, named after a Thembu chief who ruled in the Transkei in the eighteenth century. Stories that I was in the line of succession to the Thembu throne are a myth. Although I was a member of the royal household, I was not among the privileged few who were trained for rule. Instead I was groomed, like my father before me, to counsel the rulers of the tribe.

In later years, I discovered that my father was not only an adviser to kings but a kingmaker. After the untimely death of Jongilizwe in the 1920s, a dispute arose as to who should be selected to succeed him. My father was consulted and recommended Jongintaba on the grounds that he was the best educated. In time, Jongintaba would return the favour.

My father had four wives, the third of whom was my mother, Nosekeni Fanny, the daughter of Nkedama from the amaMpemvu clan of the Xhosa. My father sired thirteen children in all, four boys and nine girls, and I am the youngest son. My father's heir as chief was Daligqili, the son of the Great House, who died in the early 1930s.

When I was an infant, my father was involved in a dispute that deprived him of his chieftainship. My father possessed a proud rebelliousness, a stubborn sense of fairness, that I recognize in myself. As a chief he was compelled to account not only to the Thembu king but to the local magistrate. One day, he asserted his traditional prerogative as a chief and challenged the authority of the magistrate over some tribal matter. Such behaviour was regarded as the height of insolence. The magistrate simply deposed my father, thus ending the Mandela family chieftainship. As a result, my father, who was a wealthy nobleman by the standards of his time, lost both his fortune and his title. My mother then moved to Qunu, north of Mvezo, where she would have the support of friends and relations.

The village of Qunu was situated in a narrow, grassy valley. It consisted of a few hundred people who lived in huts, grouped some distance away from the fields. There were no roads, only paths through the grass. Cattle, sheep, goats, and horses grazed together in common pastures.

The Transkei is a beautiful country of rolling hills, fertile valleys, and a thousand rivers and streams that keep the landscape green even in winter.

Our diet mostly consisted of maize (corn), sorghum, beans, and pumpkins, largely because people could not afford anything else. The water used for farming, cooking, and washing had to be fetched in buckets from streams and springs. This was women's work and, indeed, Qunu was a village of women and children: most of the men spent the greater part of the year working on farms or in the mines along the Reef. They returned perhaps twice a year, mainly to plow their fields. The hoeing, weeding, and harvesting were left to the women and children.

From an early age, I spent most of my free time in the veldt playing and fighting with the other boys of the village. We were

life in Qunu

in the field

mostly left to our own devices. We played with toys we made ourselves, moulding animals and birds out of clay and building ox-drawn sledges out of tree branches. At the end of the day, I would return to my mother's kraal where she was preparing supper. Whereas my father told stories of historic battles and heroic warriors, my mother would enchant us with Xhosa legends and fables that had come down from numberless generations. These tales stimulated my childish imagination, and usually contained some moral lesson.

The only rivalry between different clans or tribes at Qunu was that between the Xhosas and the amaMfengu. The amaMfengu were the most advanced section of the community, among the first to become Christians, to build better houses, and to use scientific methods of agriculture, and they were wealthier than the Xhosa.

My father befriended two amaMfengu brothers, George and Ben Mbekela, who were educated and Christian. While the faith of the Mbekela brothers did not rub off on my father, it did inspire my mother, who became a Christian. It was due to their influence that I was baptized into the Methodist Church and sent to school. One day, George Mbekela paid a visit to my mother. "Your son is a clever young fellow," he said. "He should go to school." No one in my family had ever attended school, but my father, despite his own lack of education, immediately decided that his youngest son should go to school.

On the first day of school my teacher, Miss Mdingane, gave each of us an English name. This was the custom among Africans in those days and was undoubtedly due to the British bias of our education. That day, Miss Mdingane told me that my new name was Nelson. Why this particular name I have no idea.

∞

When I was nine years old, my father died.

I do not remember experiencing great grief so much as feeling cut adrift. After a brief period of mourning, my mother informed me that I would be leaving Qunu. I did not ask her why, or where I was going.

I packed the few things that I possessed, and early one morning we set out westward. I mourned less for my father than for the world I was leaving behind. Qunu was all that I knew, and I loved it in the unconditional way that a child loves his first home. Before we disappeared behind the hills, I turned and looked for what I imagined was the last time at my village.

We travelled in silence until the sun was sinking slowly toward the horizon. It was an exhausting journey, along rocky dirt roads, up and down hills, past numerous villages, but we did not pause. Late in the afternoon, at the bottom of a shallow valley surrounded by trees, we came upon a village at the centre of which was a large and gracious home. It so far exceeded anything I had ever seen that all I could do was marvel at it. It consisted of two houses and seven stately rondavels (huts), surrounded by spacious gardens. Encircling the property was a herd of at least 50 cattle and perhaps 500 sheep. It was a vision of wealth and order beyond my imagination.

This was the Great Place, Mqhekezweni, the provisional capital of Thembuland, the royal residence of Chief Jongintaba Dalindyebo, acting regent of the Thembu people. As I contemplated all this grandeur an enormous motor car rumbled through the gate. Out of the car stepped a short, thickset man wearing a smart suit. He had the confidence and bearing of a man who was used to the exercise of authority. This was the regent, who was to become my guardian and benefactor for the next decade.

I learned later that, after my father's death, Jongintaba had offered to become my guardian. He would treat me as he treated his other children, and I would have the same advantages as they. My mother had no choice; one did not turn down such an offer. The regent had not forgotten that it was due to my father that he had become acting paramount chief.

My mother remained in Mqhekezweni for a day or two before returning to Qunu. Children are often the least sentimental of creatures, especially if they are absorbed in some new pleasure. Even as my mother was leaving, my head was swimming with the delights of my new home.

I was quickly caught up in the daily life of Mqhekezweni. When I was not in school, I was a plowboy, a wagon guide, a shepherd. I rode horses and shot birds with slingshots and found boys to joust with, and some nights I danced the evening away to the beautiful singing and clapping of Thembu maidens. Although I missed Qunu and my mother, I was completely absorbed in my new world.

I attended a one-room school next door to the palace and studied English, Xhosa, history and geography. We read *Chambers English Reader* and did our lessons on black slates. Our teachers took a special interest in me. I did well in school not so much through cleverness as through doggedness. My own self-discipline was reinforced by my aunt Phathiwe, who lived in the Great Place and scrutinized my homework every night.

If the world of Mqhekezweni revolved around the regent, my smaller world revolved around his two children. Justice, the elder, was his only son and heir to the Great Place, and Nomafu was the regent's daughter. I lived with them and was treated exactly as they were. We ate the same food, wore the same clothes, performed the same chores. We were later joined by Nxeko, the older brother to Sabata, the heir to the throne. The four of us formed a royal quartet.

Justice was four years older than me and became my first hero after my father. I looked up to him in every way. He was already at Clarkebury, a boarding school about a hundred kilometres away. Justice and I became the best of friends, though we were opposites in many ways: he was extroverted, I was introverted; he was lighthearted, I was serious. Things came easily to him; I had to drill myself.

At Qunu, the only time I had ever attended church was on the day that I was baptized. Religion was a ritual that I indulged in for my mother's sake and to which I attached no meaning. But at Mqhekezweni, religion was a part of the fabric of life and I attended church each Sunday along with the regent and his wife.

Because of the universal respect the regent enjoyed—from both black and white—and the seemingly untempered power that he wielded, I saw chieftaincy as being the very centre around which life revolved. My later notions of leadership were profoundly influenced by observing the regent and his court. I watched and learned from the tribal meetings that were regularly held at the Great Place. These were called to discuss national matters such as a drought, the culling of cattle, policies ordered by the magistrate, or new laws decreed by the government. All Thembus were free to come—and a great many did, on horseback or by foot.

On these occasions, the regent was surrounded by a group of councillors of high rank who functioned as parliament and judiciary.

They were wise men who retained the knowledge of tribal history and custom in their heads and whose opinions carried great weight.

Everyone who wanted to speak did so. It was democracy in its purest form. There may have been a hierarchy of importance among the speakers, but everyone was heard: chief and subject, warrior and medicine man, shopkeeper and farmer, landowner and labourer. The foundation of self-government was that all men were free to voice their opinions and were equal as citizens. (Women, I am afraid, were deemed second-class citizens.)

Only at the end of the meeting, as the sun was setting, would the regent speak. His purpose was to sum up what had been said and form some consensus among the diverse opinions. But no conclusion was forced on people who disagreed. If no agreement could be reached, another meeting would be held. At the very end of the council, a praise-singer or poet would deliver a panegyric to the ancient kings.

Nelson Mandela (*Born 1918, Transkei, South Africa*) is a lawyer and activist whose defiant campaign against the South African government's policy of apartheid led to his imprisonment in 1964. An international campaign resulted in his release in 1990. He was elected president of the African National Congress in 1991, shared the Nobel Prize for Peace in 1993, and became South Africa's first post-apartheid president.

Sunday Dinner for Tourists

as told to Barry Broadfoot

MY FATHER WAS FEROCIOUS ABOUT DEBT. Simply ferocious. One of my brothers wanted a bicycle once and another boy wanted it and my brother had $5 coming to him for haying that summer from a farmer and was going to be paid in a week but father said no, he had to hand over the money when he took the bike. That's how the other boy got the bike.

We had this house, living room and dining room in one, a big kitchen, yes, a big kitchen, and three tiny bedrooms upstairs which weren't enough because my father and mother had one, my grandfather and his big dog had another and there were six kids so the three boys slept in a lean-to by the house, winter and summer. No matter how cold, that's where they slept. Kids grew up tough in Nova Scotia.

Dad came home from Pictou one morning and he looked upset and he told us kids to clear out, do your chores. I was hidden in the pantry off the kitchen and heard him say to my mother that the banker had said there was no loans left, especially for shore people, us, with no fish markets, and on and on and on. Dad was really ferocious about that banker, let me tell you, and he called him a "damn Canadian." He meant the man was from Ontario, an Upper Canadian, and that was not good. He wasn't from Nova Scotia. He didn't understand our ways.

I recall Father saying, "Lorna, there isn't a cent in the bank and there isn't a sou in my pocket." I think it was the first time I'd seen him lose his self-confidence. He was low as a flounder. He just walked around the kitchen saying, "Damn that man. Damn him." That was bad, because Father was Presbyterian. No cursing, ever. Scots. Old family. We were an old Nova Scotia family.

Mother asked what was the trouble, didn't we own the house and farm, about seven acres, and the bank couldn't take that away, and Dad said, "Eat, woman, eat. How will we eat? Shoes. Dresses. Gas for the boat."

Mother said, "Dinna fash yerself," and then she started to talk low and fast, and every time she said something Dad didn't like he'd take a swing at the sticky fly catcher hanging from the ceiling. They didn't see me, of course. When mother had finished, Dad said, "You've done considerable pondering about this, haven't ye, Lorna?" and she said, "Father and me." That was grandfather, the permanent guest with the permanent guest-dog.

That's how we got into the restaurant business. Everybody pitched in. Except Dad, of course. I've heard this kind of story about the Thirties over and over, how the women took over. It must have made the men feel lowly, but the women took over.

The idea was sound. Dinners Sunday afternoon and evening. Nova Scotia dinners. Fish. All you could eat, and this was before we ever heard of the smorgasbord. We just called it McGregor's Seafood Dinner. Underneath that was the word, Home-cooked. I scrounged a four by four foot Coca-Cola sign and painted it white and my brother did the actual printing with green paint we used on the boat, and mother had us move everything but the table and chairs and big buffet out of the dining room and we all decided— even Dad, because he was starting to come around—we decided what to serve and finally Dad said, "We'll give them a feast from the sea and the land."

Now how much was the price to be? In Pictou or over at Inverness or down at Halifax you could get a meal for twenty-five cents but funny, even today, those places don't serve much fish and the water's full of them. My oldest brother, Rod, said we didn't want local people, they'd just criticize, and besides, they were too cheap and would eat at home. But what we wanted was those American tourists from Boston and New England and the rich people from Montreal and Ontario. There were no wealthy people in the Maritimes. Everyone was poor. If you wanted a good job you went to the States or Upper Canada, Ontario. We decided fifty cents. We'd go on that.

We gave them fish chowder soup. I'm just remembering that table now. They got fresh herring when they were running, and boiled salt herring. Fresh cod. Cod stewed for hours in milk, and our milk was like everybody's else's cream. They could have crabs and mussels in a garlic gravy. Mackerel. Smelts by the bucket if they wanted. Flatfish. There was always a big pot of steaming-hot potatoes, just as delicious as the fish, and there was a cold potato salad with boiled eggs sliced up and all spicy. Mother had a way with herbs. There was her own buns and thick bread and our own white butter, no colouring. We had three of the best little Jersey cows in the county, thanks to grandfather because he bought them. There was a rice and raisin pudding. That was all for fifty cents, and I never saw a man, even the biggest, not eat his fill.

Lobsters weren't considered much down our way then, and in fact, even today a lot of shore people don't consider them all that much even though they fetch about two dollars a pound, landed. That is something fierce. But some people asked for lobsters. Why, they were out there pretty well for the taking so we added lobsters too, and they got to be so popular that mother had me write on the sign outside, Fresh Lobster.

How did we do? We cleaned up. That table, which sat 16 with three extra leaves in it, was jammed from one in the afternoon until eight at night. Then *we* ate, if we hadn't grabbed something in the kitchen. Dad and the boys did the fishing Thursday and Friday and, I forgot to mention, we began serving on Saturday too. The boys brought in the vegetables too, potatoes, dandelions, Swiss chard, turnips, and carrots, and Mom and us three girls, we worked hours at a time. I do mean hours at a time. Grandfather set himself up just outside the front door and took fifty cents from each person.

A thing like this spreads, you know. People would say they heard about the dinner in Boston and had made a detour, and others would ask the tourist people, the ladies who ran guest houses, and they'd point down the highway toward our place. We had more than we could really handle and we just kept plugging away.

Fifty cents was just the right price, and while a Scotsman is thrifty you don't see too many greedy ones. I guess seventy-five cents would have done, but we felt fifty cents was fair and square. It was a dull Sunday when we didn't feed a hundred people and nearly that, about eighty or so, on Saturday. We didn't make out too badly.

I remember a man from Providence, Rhode Island, who was in the hotel business. He had an inn. He said we could never make any money at fifty cents. He asked mother before he left how she did it, and she didn't know beans about the business so she said we just went ahead and did things. He asked what her inventory was and then he had to explain what that was and she pointed to the ocean and the garden and the cow pasture and he shook his head and then he asked what her overhead was, how much it cost to operate, and she looked at him with a funny kind of smile and said, "Soap to wash the dishes and pans and salt and pepper for the table." He just shook his head and told her she'd make a million easily.

When the war came, and especially when the Americans went into it, things dropped off. Rod and the next oldest joined the army and there wasn't enough gas and Dad went fishing under contract on a big boat and we just couldn't keep it going. Like the lady said, it was fun while it lasted.

Barry Broadfoot (*Born 1926, Winnipeg, Manitoba*), journalist, author, and oral historian, has been a reporter and columnist for 30 years. Broadfoot is known best for his oral history books that present the stories of Canadian men and women who lived through the Depression and the First and Second World Wars. In 1998 Broadfoot received the Order of Canada.

Publishing Anne

Lucy Maud Montgomery

Friday, Aug. 16, 1907
Cavendish, P.E.I.

[Recently] there has not been much to write about and I've been very busy and contented. Since spring came I haven't been dismal and life has been endurable and—by spells—pleasant.

One really important thing *has* come my way since my last entry. On April 15th I received a letter from the L. C. Page Co. of Boston accepting the MS of a book I had sent them and offering to publish it on a royalty basis!

All my life it has been my aim to write a book—a "real live" book. Of late years I have been thinking of it seriously but somehow it seemed such a big task I hadn't the courage to begin it. I have always hated *beginning* a story. When I get the first paragraph written I feel as though it were half done. To begin a *book* therefore seemed a quite enormous undertaking. Besides, I did not see just how I could get time for it. I could not afford to take time from my regular work to write it.

I have always kept a notebook in which I jotted down, as they occurred to me, ideas for plots, incidents, characters, and descriptions. Two years ago in the spring of 1905 I was looking over this notebook in search of some suitable idea for a short serial I wanted to write for a certain Sunday School paper and I found a faded entry, written ten years before:—"Elderly couple apply to orphan asylum for a boy. By mistake a girl is sent them." I thought this would do. I began to block out chapters, devise incidents and brood up my heroine. Somehow or other she seemed very real to me and took possession of me to an unusual extent. Her personality appealed to me and I thought it rather a shame to waste her on an ephemeral little serial. Then the thought came, "Write a book about her. You have the central idea and character. All you have to do is to spread it out over enough chapters to amount to a book."

The result of this was "Anne of Green Gables".

I began the actual writing of it one evening in May and wrote most of it in the evenings after my regular work was done, through that summer and autumn, finishing it, I think, sometime in January 1906. It was a labor of love. Nothing I have ever written gave me so much pleasure to write. I cast "moral" and "Sunday School" ideals to the winds and made my "Anne" a real human girl. Many of my own childhood experiences and dreams were worked up into its chapters. Cavendish scenery supplied the background and *Lover's Lane* figures very prominently. There is plenty of incident in it but after all it must stand or fall by "Anne". *She* is the book.

I typewrote it out on my old second-hand typewriter that never makes the capitals plain and won't print "w" at all. The next thing was to find a publisher. I sent it to the Bobbs-Merrill firm of Indianapolis. This was a new firm that had recently come to the front with several "best sellers." I thought I might stand a better chance with a new firm than with an old established one which had already a preferred list of writers. Bobbs-Merrill very promptly sent it back with a formal printed slip of rejection. I had a cry of disappointment. Then I went to the other extreme and sent it to the MacMillan Co. of New York, arguing that perhaps an "old established firm" might be more inclined to take a chance with a new writer. The MacMillan Co. likewise sent it back. I did not cry this time but sent it to Lothrop, Lee and Shepard of Boston, a sort of "betwixt and between" firm. They sent it back. Then I sent it to the Henry Holt Co. of New York. *They* rejected it, but not with the formal printed slip of the others. They sent a typewritten screed stating that their readers had found "some merit" in the story but "not enough to warrant its acceptance." This "damning with faint praise" flattened me out as not even the printed slips could do. I put "Anne" away in an old hat box in the clothes room, resolving that some day when I had time I would cut her down to the seven chapters of my original idea and send her to the aforesaid Sunday School paper.

The MS lay in the hat box until one day last winter when I came across it during a rummage. I began turning over the sheets, reading a page here and there. Somehow, I found it rather interesting. Why shouldn't other people find it so? "I'll try once more," I said, and I sent it to the L. C. Page Co.

They took it and asked me to write a sequel to it. The book may or may not sell well. I wrote it for love, not money—but very often such books are the most successful—just as everything in life that is born of true love is better than something constructed for mercenary ends.

I don't know what kind of a publisher I've got. I know absolutely nothing of the Page Co. They have given me a royalty of ten percent on the *wholesale* price, which is not generous even for a new writer, and they have bound me to give them all my books on the same terms for five years. I didn't altogether like this but I was afraid to protest, lest they might not take the book, and I am so anxious to get it before the public. It will be a start, even if it is no great success.

Well, I've written my book. The dream dreamed years ago in that old brown desk in school has come true at last after years of toil and struggle. And the realization is sweet—almost as sweet as the dream!

Lucy Maud Montgomery (*Born 1874, Clifton—now New London—Prince Edward Island; died 1942*), novelist and short-story writer, began writing for Canadian and American children's magazines after a brief career as a teacher. Her first book, *Anne of Green Gables*, attracted international recognition and led to seven sequels. Montgomery's work remains extremely popular around the world, and has been adapted theatrically and for the screen.

 Selection Activities, p. 379

Sowing the Wind

Lake Sagaris

They have sown the wind, and they shall reap the whirlwind.
— *The Bible*

YOU'RE BORN IN WASHINGTON ON JANUARY 7, 1961. You grow up engrossed in the scores of Senators and Redskins baseball games. At Easter you hunt for eggs; on Memorial Day you run in competitions organized by the neighbours. You spend weekends with your family in the Shenandoah Valley. Lots of families live between two cultures in Washington. You do too. Your father's away a lot. Your mother teaches Spanish. You learn Spanish and behind your first country there's a second, the shadowy presence of sunny Christmases, cousins' laughter, mischief, horseback riding on the beach.

Your father's strict. He wants all four sons to go to the military academy, as he did. You and your brothers don't eat dinner with your parents. Sometimes, public reality tears the private fabric of your days: the day Robert Kennedy was shot, McGovern launched his candidacy, or Nixon won. You discuss these events with friends, but most of your life runs a smooth course between school (private and Catholic), holidays on the east coast, visits to Atlantic beaches. You watch the anti-war movement, civil rights marchers, hippies. Neighbours go to war, return. You ask a lot of questions. Your hair grows. Your father complains. You fight. Your mother teaches you songs by Peter, Paul and Mary, The Beatles, Pete Seeger. You learn to play the guitar. You think it's good that people don't want to go to war.

One day, the holiday country, the family country, jolts closer. Your father's become ambassador in Washington. Now you know you're different from your friends. It's not common for nine-year-olds to meet presidents. You ask more questions. Your father's away a lot.

Then, one piece of the family after another climbs onto a plane and heads off into an unknown future. One day, you climb onto one yourself, leave Washington's spring and step into Santiago's fall. You miss your friends, eighth grade, the girls you liked, the girls you thought liked you. But the marches are exciting. Gradually, you feel at home. When the trees outside your new apartment bud lush and pale, your father arrives. It's September—fall in Washington, spring in Santiago. The family is whole again, surrounded by unpacked crates, the fragments of transition.

The next day your father leaves early. An aunt arrives. The radio's always on. No one knows where your father is. Suddenly, this matters. Days pass, then weeks, months. You learn new rules. You speak about some things to some people. You don't speak to others. You keep a lot to yourself. The Air Force takes over your school and wants to expel you. You fight to finish the year. Your father's imprisoned, your mother under house arrest. Your father, the newspapers tell you, is a thief. You're furious. And helpless. You see a corpse pulled from the river as you cross a bridge on your way to school. Your father's moved to the Air Force Academy. You pass it every day on your way to a new school. One day, you, your brothers, your mother, an aunt, your grandmother enter the Academy. Your father is pale, thin. Your father is alive. You have learned to be grateful for this.

Beyond the greetings, your parents must talk. This means sometimes you and your brothers must be very quiet. Sometimes you must make a big fuss. When he's transferred to a camp, visits become rituals. Your father is moved to an island in southern Chile. Your father's friend and fellow prisoner dies of unnatural causes. You remember his death. You remember the funeral. What you miss most about Washington is the feeling you were safe.

The family breaks into pieces. First, your father's expelled, then a brother; then your mother, another brother, you. The whole family meets again in Venezuela. From there, "home" to the States. But now you are in exile. This is hard to explain. "Oh Chile, that's in Mexico?" your new friends ask. You think they live safe in the empire's heart, oblivious to anything beyond it.

You've always assumed there's an invisible wall between your two worlds. You've gone back and forth, but not much else has. In Santiago, you were a bright, observant boy. In Washington, you're a typical east-coast teenager.

This begins to break down, but you don't see that at first. At the most you're aware that encouragement, interference, has travelled from Washington to there, but nothing's come back. Washington remains immune. The stately white buildings still stand majestically on their immaculate green lawns. They still promise safety, security, a place where normal can't be turned upside down from one day to the next, where people's insides aren't suddenly spilled out. Life keeps death in place here, neatly shelved away in cemetery rows. Cemeteries are relentlessly kept out of the picture.

But now you realize something's changed. Your two lives, two languages, no longer co-exist. Something unspoken shoots back and forth, silent and tense between them, it won't leave you in peace. You're still technically an American citizen. You go back to school. Find a girlfriend. But her parents don't like you. Still, you go steady. You fight with your mother and your father, you go to proms, to high school. Then it's September again, spring in Santiago, fall in Washington. One day you're called out of class. You rush to the hospital. Your mother hugs you and says: "I don't want you to come out of this hating."

Your two separate independent worlds, with their separate words and separate rules and separate values, have collided in the shape of a car that explodes, blowing your father's legs off, cutting the throat of a young American woman he was driving to work. Her new husband was left staggering through smoke and dust, the sharp stench of explosives.

The men who had spent money, written articles, and held conversations in low voices with military officers in a country their fellow citizens had barely heard of did not expect the bombs they'd encouraged in one land to echo so lethally in their own. And the men who gave the orders, seated in plush offices in safe and solid white buildings surrounded by neatly manicured lawns, the men who had held their silence through bombings and deaths in other countries, will react to this one. But you don't know this yet. What you know is that your girlfriend's parents won't let her attend your father's funeral.

Lake Sagaris (*Born 1956, Montreal, Quebec*), poet, journalist. She has lived in Chile since 1981 and is bilingual in Spanish and English. Her work has appeared in print and on radio and television in Canada and around the world. Her book *After the First Death* was shortlisted for the 1996 Governor General's Award for Nonfiction.

From Into Thin Air

Jon Krakauer

OUR ROUTE TO THE SUMMIT would follow the Khumbu Glacier up the lower half of the mountain. From the *bergschrund* at 23,000 feet that marked its upper end, this great river of ice flowed two and a half miles down a relatively gentle valley called the Western Cwm. As the glacier inched over humps and dips in the Cwm's underlying strata, it fractured into countless vertical fissures—crevasses. Some of these crevasses were narrow enough to step across; others were eighty feet wide, several hundred feet deep, and ran half a mile from end to end. The big ones were apt to be vexing obstacles to our ascent, and when hidden beneath a crust of snow they would pose a serious hazard, but the challenges presented by the crevasses in the Cwm had proven over the years to be predictable and manageable.

The Icefall was a different story. No part of the South Col route was feared more by climbers. At around 20,000 feet, where the glacier emerged from the lower end of the Cwm, it pitched abruptly over a precipitous drop. This was the infamous Khumbu Icefall, the most technically demanding section on the entire route. The movement of the glacier in the Icefall has been measured at between three and four feet a day. As it skids down the steep, irregular terrain in fits and starts, the mass of ice splinters into a jumble of huge, tottering blocks called *seracs*, some as large as office buildings. Because the climbing route wove under, around, and between hundreds of these unstable towers, each trip through the Icefall was a little like playing a round of Russian roulette: sooner or later any given serac was going to fall over without warning, and you could only hope you weren't beneath it when it toppled. Since 1963, when a teammate of Hornbein and Unsoeld's named Jake Breitenbach was crushed by an avalanching serac to become the Icefall's first victim, eighteen other climbers had died here. ...

So it came to pass that at 4:45 a.m. on Saturday, April 13, I found myself at the foot of the fabled Icefall, strapping on my crampons in the frigid predawn gloom.

Crusty old alpinists who've survived a lifetime of close scrapes like to counsel young protégés that staying alive hinges on listening carefully to one's "inner voice." Tales abound of one or another climber who decided to remain in his or her sleeping bag after detecting some inauspicious vibe in the ether and thereby survived a catastrophe that wiped out others who failed to heed the portents.

I didn't doubt the potential value of paying attention to subconscious cues. As I waited for Rob to lead the way, the ice underfoot emitted a series of loud cracking noises, like small trees being snapped in two, and I felt myself wince with each pop and rumble from the glacier's shifting depths. Problem was, my inner voice resembled Chicken Little: it was screaming that I was about to die, but it did that almost every time I laced up my climbing boots. I therefore did my damnedest to ignore my histrionic imagination and grimly followed Rob into the eerie blue labyrinth.

Although I'd never been in an icefall as frightening as the Khumbu, I'd climbed many other icefalls. They typically have vertical or even overhanging passages that demand considerable expertise with ice axe and crampons. There was certainly no lack of steep ice in the Khumbu Icefall, but all of it had been rigged with ladders or ropes or both, rendering the conventional tools and techniques of ice climbing largely superfluous.

I soon learned that on Everest not even the rope—the quintessential climber's accoutrement—was to be utilized in the time-honoured manner. Ordinarily, one climber is tied to one or two partners with a 150-foot length of rope, making each person directly responsible for the life of the others; roping up in this fashion is a serious and very intimate act. In the Icefall, though, expediency dictated that each of us climb independently, without being physically connected to one another in any way.

Mal Duff's Sherpas had anchored a static line of rope that extended from the bottom of the Icefall to its top. Attached to my waist was a three-foot-long safety tether with a carabiner, or snaplink, at the distal end. Security was achieved not by roping myself to a teammate but rather by clipping my safety tether to the fixed line and sliding it up the rope as I ascended. Climbing in this fashion, we would be able to move as quickly as possible through the most dangerous parts of the Icefall, and we wouldn't have to entrust our lives to teammates whose skill and experience were unknown. As it turned out, not once during the entire expedition would I ever have reason to rope myself to another climber.

If the Icefall required few orthodox climbing techniques, it demanded a whole new repertoire of skills in their stead—for instance, the ability to tiptoe in mountaineering boots and crampons across three wobbly ladders lashed end to end, bridging a sphincter-clenching chasm. There were many such crossings, and I never got used to them.

At one point I was balanced on an unsteady ladder in the predawn gloaming, stepping tenuously from one bent rung to the next, when the ice supporting the ladder on either end began to quiver as if an earthquake had struck. A moment later came an explosive roar as a large serac somewhere close above came crashing down. I froze, my heart in my throat, but the avalanching ice passed fifty yards to the left, out of sight, without doing any damage. After waiting a few minutes to regain my composure I resumed my herky-jerky passage to the far side of the ladder.

The glacier's continual and often violent state of flux added an element of uncertainty to every ladder crossing. As the glacier moved, crevasses would sometimes compress, buckling ladders like toothpicks; other times a crevasse might expand, leaving a ladder dangling in the air, only tenuously supported, with neither end mounted on solid ice. Anchors securing the ladders and lines routinely melted out when the afternoon sun warmed the surrounding ice and snow. Despite daily maintenance, there was a very real danger that any given rope might pull loose under body weight.

But if the Icefall was strenuous and terrifying, it had a surprising allure as well. As dawn washed the darkness from the sky, the shattered glacier was revealed to be a three-dimensional landscape of phantasmal beauty. The temperature was six degrees Fahrenheit. My crampons crunched reassuringly into the glacier's rind. Following the fixed line, I meandered through a vertical maze of crystalline blue stalagmites. Sheer rock buttresses seamed with ice pressed in from both edges of the glacier, rising like the shoulders of a malevolent god. Absorbed by my surroundings and the gravity of the labour, I lost myself in the unfettered pleasures of ascent, and for an hour or two actually forgot to be afraid.

Three-quarters of the way to Camp One, Hall remarked at a rest stop that the Icefall was in better shape than he'd ever seen it: "The route's a bloody freeway this season." But only slightly higher, at 19,000 feet, the ropes brought us to the base of a gargantuan, perilously balanced serac. As massive as a twelve-storey building, it loomed over our heads, leaning 30 degrees past vertical. The route followed a natural catwalk that angled sharply up the overhanging face: we would have to climb up and over the entire off-kilter tower to escape its threatening tonnage.

Safety, I understood, hinged on speed. I huffed toward the relative security of the serac's crest with all the haste I could muster, but since

I wasn't acclimatized my fastest pace was no better than a crawl. Every four or five steps I'd have to stop, lean against the rope, and suck desperately at the thin, bitter air, searing my lungs in the process.

I reached the top of the serac without it collapsing and flopped breathless onto its flat summit, my heart pounding like a jackhammer. A little later, around 8:30 a.m., I arrived at the top of the Icefall itself, just beyond the last of the seracs. The safety of Camp One didn't supply much peace of mind, however: I couldn't stop thinking about the ominously tilted slab a short distance below, and the fact that I would have to pass beneath its faltering bulk at least seven more times if I was going to make it to the summit of Everest. Climbers who snidely denigrate this as the Yak Route, I decided, had obviously never been through the Khumbu Icefall.

Jon Krakauer, American author, magazine writer, and adventurer, climbed his first mountain when he was eight years old. He financed his first major climbing expeditions by working as a carpenter, and later as a magazine writer. In March 1996, Krakauer joined a commercial expedition up Mount Everest, covering the climb for *Outside* magazine. The journey ended in tragedy as several climbers died in a sudden blizzard.

From The New Ice Age

Stephen Brunt

Joey Kocur of the Red Wings took the Stanley Cup fishing as part of the trophy's wild ride after Detroit's 1996–97 victory.

IT HAS BEEN FONDLED AND KISSED and filled with beer. It has served as a cradle for babies; a vase for flowers; an ornament on a bar; a passenger in trains, planes, automobiles, and boats. It was once drop-kicked into the Rideau canal. It is venerated like a religious relic, and it is used like a party favour. It is an ungainly hunk of silverware, the bowl a replica of the humble mug Lord Stanley bought for $50 and donated to the hockey champions of the Dominion in 1893, the collar a place to commemorate every person who can lay claim to it, 1600 names in all. During the Stanley Cup finals, crowds have lined up all night just for a moment in its presence: in New York where it was so long coming; in Denver where it arrived all but instantaneously; in Canada, anywhere, where the Shroud of Turin wouldn't draw a bigger or more devout gathering. Children are held aloft to gaze at it and told to remember what they're seeing. Those at the other end of life's spectrum strain failing eyes for a glimpse to hold in memory. For any hockey fan, to see it sparkling from a distance is to imagine what it must be like to touch it, to hold it, to bear it aloft around the ice as the crowd stands and roars, to see your name inscribed among so many others.

Forget the comparisons. There is nothing else like it in all of sport. The Stanley Cup, to Canadians and others who have fallen under the spell of hockey, is more than just a trophy. It has come to symbolize the pure, perfect mesh of culture and sport. It's not just a prize, but an icon. For a player, to touch it is to touch the entire history of the game, to put your hand where Howie Morenz put his, to feel what Gordie Howe felt, or Rocket Richard, or Wayne Gretzky, to be connected to every childhood fantasy, every dream dreamed at dawn on the way to the local rink.

It says something about the game, about the passion of the athletes who play it, and about their innocence, their lack of cynicism, that the members of the winning team are still given the opportunity to take the Cup home. Just try to imagine that in baseball, in basketball, in football. Whereas the championship trophies in other sports are locked safely away before and after the presentation, the Stanley Cup goes on the road. Anyone who deals with professional athletes will tell you that none have a stronger bond with their sport than hockey players. None seem more grateful just to have the chance to be part of it. None retain so much joy of childhood, of play. What could be more fulfilling, then, than to take the Cup back to the place whence you came, back to family and friends and the people who watched you learn the sport. Each member of the winning team takes a turn doing just that.

The trophy is delivered to each member of the winning team in turn by its handlers from the Hockey Hall of Fame. It is removed from the special casket in which it travels. After that, it's up to the player where it goes. In the summer of 1997, members of the Detroit Red Wings took it on a long, wild ride to points in Canada, in the United States and, for the first time, to Russia, where curious onlookers were at first perplexed and then dazzled. Whatever the place, the faces look the same when the Cup comes into view: joy, awe, wonder, seeing in the glittering a reflection of ourselves.

Stephen Brunt, journalist and author, was born in Hamilton and studied journalism at the University of Western Ontario. He started working at the *Globe and Mail* in 1982 as an arts intern, and went on to work in news and then sports. In 1988 Brunt won the Michener Award for public service journalism, for his series on corruption and negligence in boxing. A sports columnist since 1989, he is also the author of three books.

The Art of Genius: Eight Ways to Think Like Einstein

Michael Michalko

How do geniuses come up with ideas? What links the thinking style that produced the *Mona Lisa* with the one that spawned the theory of relativity? What can we learn from the thinking strategies of the Galileos, Edisons, and Mozarts of history?

For years, scholars tried to study genius by analyzing statistics. In 1904, Havelock Ellis noted that most geniuses were fathered by men older than 30, had mothers younger than 25, and usually were sickly children. Other researchers reported that many were celibate (Descartes), fatherless (Dickens), or motherless (Darwin). In the end, the data illuminated nothing.

Academics also tried to measure the links between intelligence and genius. But they found that run-of-the-mill physicists had IQs much higher than that of Nobel Prize-winner and extraordinary genius Richard Feynman, whose IQ was a merely respectable 122. Genius is not about scoring 1600 on your SATs, mastering 14 languages at the age of 7, or even being especially smart. As psychologist Joy P. Guilford and others have demonstrated, creativity is not the same as intelligence.

Most people of average intelligence can figure out the expected conventional response to a given problem. For example, when asked "What is one-half of 13?" most of us immediately answer six-and-one-half. That's because we tend to think *reproductively*. When confronted with a problem, we sift through what we've been taught and what has worked for us in the past, select the most promising approach, and work within a clearly defined direction toward the solution.

Geniuses, on the other hand, think *productively*. They ask "How many different ways can I look at this problem?" and "How many ways can I solve it?" A productive thinker, for example, would find a number of ways to "halve 13":

$$6.5$$

$$1/3 = 1 \text{ and } 3$$

$$\text{THIR TEEN} = 4$$

$$\text{XI/II} = 11 \text{ and } 2$$

$$\cancel{\text{XIII}} = 8$$

The mark of genius is the willingness to explore *all* the alternatives, not just the most likely solution. Asked to describe the difference between himself and an average person, Albert Einstein explained that the average person faced with the problem of finding a needle in a haystack would stop when he or she located a needle. But Einstein would tear through the entire haystack looking for all possible needles.

Reproductive thinking fosters rigidity. This is why we so often fail when we're confronted with a new problem that appears on the surface to be similar to others we've solved, but is, in fact, significantly different in its deep structure. Interpreting such a problem through the prism of past experience will inevitably lead you astray. If you think the way you've always thought, you'll get what you've always gotten.

For centuries the Swiss dominated the watch industry. But in 1968, when a U.S. inventor unveiled a battery-powered watch with no bearings or mainspring at the World Watch Congress, every Swiss watch manufacturer rejected it because it didn't fit their limited paradigm. Meanwhile, Seiko, a Japanese electronics company, took one look at the invention and proceeded to change the future of the world watch market.

Biologists have long known that a gene pool lacking in variation will sooner or later be unable to adapt to changing circumstances. In time, the genetically encoded wisdom will convert to foolishness, with consequences fatal to the species. Similarly, we all have a rich repertoire of ideas and concepts based on past experiences that enables us to survive and prosper. But without any provision for variation, they become stagnant and ineffectual.

When Charles Darwin returned to England after his famous trip to the Galapagos Islands, he showed the finch specimens he found there to distinguished zoologist John Gould. But Gould didn't know how to interpret them. Thinking the way he had been conditioned to think, he assumed that, since God made one set of birds when he created the world, the specimens from different locations would be identical. As a result, he thought Darwin's finches, which looked quite different from the English variety, represented a distinct species—and missed the textbook case of evolution right in front of him. As it turned out, Darwin didn't even know the birds were finches, but because of his unorthodox way of thinking, he came up with an idea that would reshape the way we see the world.

By studying the notebooks, correspondence, and conversations of some of the world's great thinkers in science, art, and industry, scholars have identified eight thinking strategies that enable geniuses to generate original ideas:

1 Geniuses look at problems from all angles

Einstein's theory of relativity is, in essence, a description of the interaction between different perspectives. Sigmund Freud's analytical methods were designed to find details that didn't fit traditional paradigms in order to come up with a completely new point of view. To solve a problem creatively, you must abandon the first approach that comes to mind, which usually stems from past experience, and reconceptualize the problem. Thus geniuses do not merely solve existing problems, they identify new ones.

2 Geniuses make their thought visible

Once geniuses have a certain minimal verbal facility, they develop visual and spatial abilities that allow them to display information in new ways. The explosion of creativity in the Renaissance was intimately tied to the development of graphic illustration during that period, notably the scientific diagrams of Leonardo da Vinci and Galileo Galilei. Galileo revolutionized science by making his thought graphically visible while his contemporaries used more conventional means. Similarly, Einstein thought in terms of spatial forms, rather than along purely mathematical or verbal lines. In fact, he believed that words and numbers, as they are written or spoken, did not play a significant role in his thinking process.

3 Geniuses produce

Thomas Edison held 1093 patents, still the record. He guaranteed a high level of productivity by giving himself idea quotas: one minor invention every 10 days and a major invention every six months. Johann Sebastian Bach wrote a cantata every week, even when he was sick or exhausted. Wolfgang Mozart produced more than 600 pieces of music. In a study of 2036 scientists, Dean Keith Simonton of the University of California at Davis found that the most respected scientists produced more "bad" works than their less successful peers.

4 Geniuses make novel combinations

Like playful children with buckets of building blocks, geniuses constantly combine and recombine ideas, images, and thoughts. Einstein didn't invent the concepts of energy, mass, or speed of light; he simply combined them in a novel way. The laws of heredity were developed by Gregor Mendel, who combined mathematics and biology to create a new science of genetics.

5 Geniuses force relationships

Their ability to connect the unconnected enables geniuses to see things others miss. Da Vinci noticed the similarity between the sound of a bell and the ripples from a stone hitting water—and concluded that sound travels in waves. Organic chemist F. A. Kekule intuited the shape of the ringlike benzene molecule by dreaming of a snake biting its tail. When Samuel Morse was trying to figure out how to produce a telegraphic signal strong enough to transmit coast to coast, he observed teams of horses being exchanged at a relay station. His solution? Give the travelling signal periodic boosts of power.

6 Geniuses think in opposites

Geniuses, according to physicist David Bohm, are able to think differently because they can tolerate ambivalence between two incompatible subjects. Another physicist, Niels Bohr, argued that if you hold opposites together in your mind, you will suspend your normal thinking process and allow an intelligence beyond rational thought to create a new form. Example: Bohr's ability to imagine light as both a particle and a wave led to his conception of the principle of complementarity.

7 Geniuses think metaphorically

Aristotle believed that the ability to perceive resemblances between two separate areas of existence—to think metaphorically, in other words—is a special gift. Alexander Graham Bell compared the inner workings of the ear to a stout piece of membrane moving steel—and, in the process, conceptualized the telephone. Einstein made some of his most stunning discoveries by drawing analogies between abstract principles and everyday occurrences such as rowing a boat or standing on a platform watching a train pass by.

8 Geniuses prepare themselves for chance

Whenever we attempt to do something and fail, we end up doing something else. That's the first principle of creative accident. We may ask ourselves why we have failed to do what we intended, which is a reasonable question. But the creative accident leads to the question: What have we done? Answering that one in a novel, unexpected way is the essential creative act. It is not luck, but creative insight of the highest order.

Alexander Fleming was not the first physician studying deadly bacteria to notice that mould formed on an exposed culture. A less gifted physician would have dismissed this seemingly irrelevant event, but Fleming thought it was "interesting" and wondered if it had potential. It did: penicillin. One day, when Edison was pondering how to make a carbon filament, he found himself mindlessly twisting a piece of putty in his fingers. He looked down at his hands and found the answer to his problem: Twist the carbon like rope.

This may be the most important lesson of all: When you find something interesting, drop everything and go with it. Too many talented people fail to make significant leaps of imagination because they've become fixated on their preconceived plan. But not the truly great minds. They don't wait for gifts of chance; they make them happen.

Michael Michalko, an American writer and self-described "creativity expert," began his career as a military officer working with NATO intelligence specialists. His first book was the best-selling *Thinkertoys (A Handbook of Business Creativity),* which was highly acclaimed by reviewers and the business community.

·

Preventing Conflict in the New Century

Kofi Annan

introduction give main idea.

IN THE PAST 20 YEARS we have understood the need for military intervention where governments grossly violate human rights and the international order. In the next 20 years we must learn how to prevent conflicts as well as how to intervene in them. Even the costliest policy of prevention is far cheaper, in lives and in resources, than the least expensive intervention.

This is why we have been pressing the international community to take prevention more seriously. In cost-benefit terms the case for doing this is compelling. A recent study by the Carnegie Commission on Preventing Deadly Conflict estimated that the cost to the international community of the seven major wars in the 1990s, not including Kosovo and East Timor, was US$199 billion. Add in these two conflicts and US$230 billion seems a likely figure.

Effective prevention could have saved most of this huge sum. More important, it could have saved hundreds of thousands of lives.

Time and again, differences are allowed to develop into disputes and disputes allowed to develop into deadly conflicts. Time and again, warning signs are ignored and pleas for help overlooked. Only after the deaths and the destruction do we intervene at a far higher human and material cost, by which time there are fewer lives left to save. Only when it is too late, it seems, do we value prevention.

There are, in my view, three main reasons for the failure of prevention, when prevention is so clearly possible. First, the reluctance of one or more of the parties to a conflict to accept external intervention of any kind. Second, the lack of political will at the highest levels of the international community. Third, a lack of integrated conflict-prevention strategies within the UN system and the international community. Of all these, the will to act is the most important. Without the political will to act when action is needed, no amount of improved co-ordination or early warning will translate awareness into action.

The founders of the UN drew up its charter with a sober view of human nature. They had witnessed the ability of humanity to wage a war of unparalleled brutality and unprecedented cruelty. They had witnessed, above all, the failure of prevention, when prevention was, throughout the 1930s, still possible and every signal pointed to war.

Of course, as realists we must also recognize that in some cases the sheer intractability of conflicts and the obduracy of the warring parties will make intervention unlikely to succeed. But even wars that cannot be stopped once started might well have been avoided with effective prevention policies.

We are under no illusion that preventive strategies will be easy to implement. For a start, the costs of prevention have to be paid in the present, while its benefits lie in the distant future. And the benefits are not tangible—when prevention succeeds, nothing happens. Taking such a political risk when there are few obvious rewards requires conviction and considerable vision.

Second, there are real institutional barriers to the institutional co-operation that prevention requires. In national governments and international agencies, departments responsible for security tend to know little about development or governance; those responsible for the latter rarely think of them in security terms. Identifying such constraints is not a counsel of despair. It is a necessary, if not sufficient, condition for progress.

The UN has long argued that good governance, democratization, respect for human rights, and policies for equitable and sustainable development are the best form of long-term conflict prevention. The changing patterns of global conflict and governance in recent years, particularly with respect to democratization, provide ample evidence to support our conviction.

More Votes, Less War

During the 1990s there was a remarkable and little-noticed reduction in global warfare. More old wars ended than new ones began. Between 1989 and 1992 on average eight new ethnic wars began each

more democracy, conflict fewer ↓

We have
democracy
We not
War

year; by the late 1990s the average had fallen to two a year. Between 1992 and 1998 the scope and intensity of armed conflict around the world declined by about a third. The number of democratically elected governments increased by about the same proportion.

We cannot leap to the conclusion that the increase in the number of democracies has caused the decrease in warfare. Other factors, such as the end of the Cold War, surely also played a role (although the two are obviously related). But the evidence is in line with the well-established, if little publicized, finding that democracies have far lower levels of internal violence than non-democracies. This is not really surprising. The non-violent management of conflict is the very essence of democracy. In an era when more than 90% of wars take place within, not between, states, the import of this finding for conflict prevention should be obvious.

Prevention is no panacea. It requires that governments act in good faith and place the welfare of citizens above narrow sectional interests. But we know that some conflict-prone governments see prevention policies, particularly those which stress democratization and good governance, as a threat to their own power and privilege. For that reason, they are likely to reject them.

The fact that prevention will not work everywhere is an argument against naive optimism, but not against actively supporting democratization, good governance, and other preventive policies. These are not only important goods in their own right. They are also among the most potent and cost-effective antidotes to the scourge of war.

Kofi Annan (*Born 1938, Kumasi, Ghana*) is the seventh Secretary-General of the United Nations. Annan joined the UN in 1962 as an officer with the World Health Organization in Geneva. His work with the UN has included negotiating the release of Western hostages during the Persian Gulf crisis of 1990–91, and helping implement a peace agreement in the former Yugoslavia in 1995–96. He was elected Secretary-General in 1997.

Canada's Aboriginal Languages

Mary Jane Norris

CANADA'S ABORIGINAL LANGUAGES *are many and diverse, and their importance to indigenous people immense. Language is one of the most tangible symbols of culture and group identity. It is not only a means of communication, but a link that connects people with their past and grounds their social, emotional, and spiritual vitality. Although loss of language doesn't necessarily lead to the death of a culture, it can severely handicap transmission of that culture. For Aboriginal people, great losses have already occurred. During the past 100 years or more, nearly ten once-flourishing languages have become extinct; at least a dozen are on the brink of extinction. When these languages vanish, they take with them unique ways of looking at the world, explaining the unknown, and making sense of life.*

Societal factors often contribute to the decline of languages. Without doubt, the forces of dominant languages and modernization exert a strong influence on any minority language. In the case of Aboriginal languages, historical events such as the prohibition of indigenous language use in residential schools have also contributed to this process. In addition, the fact that most Aboriginal languages were predominantly oral may also have diminished, in an already difficult environment, their chances of survival.

As of 1996, only 3 out of Canada's 50 Aboriginal languages had large enough populations to be considered truly secure from the threat of extinction in the long run. This is not surprising in light of the fact that only a small proportion of the Aboriginal population speaks an Aboriginal language. Of some 800 000 persons who claimed an Aboriginal identity in 1996, only 26% said an Aboriginal language was their mother tongue, and even fewer spoke it at home. This article explores which of Canada's Aboriginal languages are flourishing and which are in danger of disappearing. It also examines the factors that differentiate viable languages from endangered ones. Finally, it compares language use and maintenance patterns between 1981 and 1996 to understand what happened to Aboriginal languages over the years and what the future may hold for them.

Some Languages Large, Others Tiny

The current 50 languages of Canada's indigenous peoples belong to 11 major language families—10 First Nations and Inuktitut. Most families consist of separate but related member languages, and each member language may include several dialects. Exceptions are the Haida, Tlingit, and Kutenai families—known as the isolates—which cannot be further broken down into individual languages.

Some language families are large and strong, others small and vulnerable. The three largest families, which together represent 93% of persons with an Aboriginal mother tongue, are Algonquian (with 147 000 people whose mother tongue is Algonquian), Inuktitut (with 28 000) and Athapaskan (with 20 000). The other eight account for the remaining 7%, an indication of their relative size. Tlingit, one of the smallest families, has a mere 145 people in Canada whose mother tongue is that language. Similar variations apply to individual languages—Cree, with a mother tongue population of 88 000, appears immense when compared with Malecite, at 660.

Geography Influences Size and Diversity of Languages

Geography is an important contributor to the diversity, size, and distribution of Aboriginal languages across Canada's regions. Open plains and hilly woodlands, for example, are ideal for accommodating large groups of people. Because of the terrain, groups in these locations can travel and communicate with each other relatively easily and often tend to spread over larger areas. On the other hand, soaring mountains and deep gorges tend to restrict settlements to small pockets of isolated groups. British Columbia's mountainous landscape with its numerous physical barriers was likely an important factor in the evolution of the province's many separate, now mostly small, languages. Divided by terrain, languages such as Salish, Tsimshian, Wakashan, Haida, Tlingit, and Kutenai could not develop as large a population base as the widely dispersed Algonquian (particularly Cree and Ojibway) and Athapaskan languages, whose homes are the more open central plains and eastern woodlands.

In some instances, geography can also influence the likelihood of a language's survival. Groups located in relatively isolated regions, away from the dominant culture, face fewer pressures to abandon their language. They tend to use their own language in schooling, broadcasting, and other communication services and, as a result, are likely to stay more self-sufficient. Communities living in the northern regions of Quebec, Nunavut, the Northwest Territories, and Labrador—the Inuit, Attikamek, and Montagnais-Naskapi—are examples of such groups.

Because of their large, widely dispersed populations, the Algonquian languages account for the highest share of Aboriginal languages in all provinces except British Columbia and the territories, ranging from 72% in Newfoundland to practically 100% in the other Atlantic provinces. In both British Columbia and the Yukon, the Athapaskan languages make up the largest share (26% and 80% respectively), while Inuktitut is the most prominent language in the Northwest Territories (77%) and practically the only one in Nunavut (virtually 100%). British Columbia, home to about half of all individual languages, is the most diverse in Aboriginal language composition. However, because of the small size of these language groups, the province accounts for only 7% of people with an Aboriginal mother tongue.

Large Languages More Likely to Flourish

There are a number of factors which contribute to a language's ability to survive. First and foremost is the size of the population with an Aboriginal mother tongue or home language. Since a large base of speakers is essential to ensure long-term viability, the more speakers a language has, the better its chances of survival.

Indeed, Inuktitut, Cree, and Ojibway—the three most flourishing languages—all boast over 20 000 people with an Aboriginal mother tongue. In contrast, endangered languages rarely have more than a few thousand speakers; often they have only a few hundred. For instance, the two smallest and weakest language groups, Kutenai and Tlingit, have mother tongue populations of 120 and 145 respectively.

Passing on Language Critical for Survival

To survive, a language must be passed on from one generation to the next. The most effective way of making this happen is to speak it in the

Mother tongue population (MT): those people whose first language learned at home and still understood is an Aboriginal language.

Home language population (HL): those people whose language spoken most often at home is an Aboriginal language.

Knowledge or ability population (Kn): those people who speak an Aboriginal language well enough to conduct a conversation.

Index of continuity (HL/MT): measures language continuity or vitality by comparing the number of those who speak a given language at home to the number of those who learned that language as their mother tongue. A ratio less than 100 indicates some decline in the strength of the language (i.e., for every 100 people with an Aboriginal mother tongue, there are fewer than 100 in the overall population who use it at home). The lower the score, the greater the decline or erosion.

Index of ability (Kn/MT): compares the number of people who report being able to speak the language with the number who have that Aboriginal language as a mother tongue. If for every 100 people with a specific Aboriginal mother tongue, more than 100 persons in the overall population are able to speak that language, some clearly learned it as a second language, either in school or later in life. This may suggest some degree of language revival.

home, where children will learn it as their mother tongue. Spoken in the home, language is used as the working tool of everyday life. In contrast, when learned as a second language, it is often used in potentially limited situations only, as may be the case, for example, in immersion programs. There is, therefore, no equivalent to learning a language as a mother tongue.[1] Because, unlike other minority language groups, Aboriginals cannot rely on new immigrants to maintain or increase their population of speakers, passing on the language from parents to children is critical for all indigenous languages' survival.[2]

Language Vitality Declines Between 1981 and 1996

Between 1981 and 1996, the index of continuity has declined for all Aboriginal languages. Although the number of people reporting an Aboriginal mother tongue increased by nearly 24% between 1981 and 1996,[3] the number of those who spoke an Aboriginal language at home grew by only 6%. As a result, for every 100 people with an Aboriginal mother tongue, the number who used an indigenous language most often at home declined from 76 to 65 between 1981 and 1996.

Although most languages experienced a steady erosion in linguistic vitality during these years, endangered ones suffered the most. For example, the index of continuity for Salish languages fell from 35 in 1981 to only 12 by 1996. Tlingit and Kutenai, as languages most often spoken at home, had practically disappeared by the 1990s. Given that in 1996 there were only 120 people with a Kutenai mother tongue, it is not hard to see why there is serious concern for the survival of this language. In contrast, although the continuity index dipped for the relatively strong Cree as well, it did so by considerably less, from 78 to 65. Although Inukitut did experience a slight erosion in the early 1980s, the past decade has seen the index stabilize at 84.

By 1996, these rates of language erosion resulted in strikingly different continuity levels for viable and endangered languages as a whole. For every 100 speakers with an Aboriginal mother tongue, an average of about 70 used an indigenous home language among viable groups, compared with 30 or fewer among endangered groups.

The Younger the Speakers, the Healthier the Language

Age also plays an important role in how healthy languages are and what the future may hold for them. The average age of those who speak an Aboriginal language or have it for a mother tongue reveals the extent to which language transmission has been successful. The higher the average age, the fewer young people have learned or still understand the language, and the older the people who still speak it. When these older people die, so may the languages.

For indigenous language groups as a whole, average ages are getting higher. Two main factors are responsible for this trend. First, although fertility rates are still high they are declining, translating into relatively fewer children. And second, the proportion of the Aboriginal population with an indigenous mother tongue is decreasing with younger generations. In fact, in 1996 only 20% of children under 5 had an indigenous mother tongue.[4] Overall, between 1981 and 1996, the average age of the population with an Aboriginal mother tongue rose by three years, to reach 31 years in 1996. Similarly— although to a lesser extent—the average age of Aboriginal home language speakers increased by nearly two years, to 27 years in 1996.

LANGUAGE CLASSIFICATION: "VIABLE" AND "ENDANGERED"

This article's classification of language survival is based on M. Dale Kinkade's 1991 study, "The Decline of Native Languages in Canada." Other classification schemes exist, but there is general agreement as to which languages are viable and which endangered. Kinkade divides Aboriginal languages into five groups: already extinct, near extinction, endangered, viable but with a small population base, and viable with a large population.

- Languages near extinction are considered to be beyond the possibility of revival, since generally only a few elderly people know them. (These languages are not discussed in this study because reliable Census data are not available.)
- Languages considered endangered are still spoken by enough people to make survival an outside possibility, given sufficient community interest and educational programs.
- Languages that are viable but small tend to have more than 1000 speakers and are spoken in isolated or well-organized communities with strong self-awareness. In these communities, language is considered one of the important marks of identity.
- Viable languages have large enough population bases that long-term survival is relatively assured. In this article, the terms "healthy," "strong," and "flourishing" are used alternatively to describe viable languages.

For discussions on viable and endangered Aboriginal languages, see UNESCO. 1996. *Atlas of the World's Languages in Danger of Disappearing*. Edited by Stephen A. Wurm. Paris: Unesco Publishing; Report on the Royal Commission on Aboriginal Peoples. 1996. *Gathering Strength*. Vol. 3. Ottawa: Minister of Supply and Services Canada; Indian and Northern Affairs Canada. 1990. *Indians and Inuit of Canada*, Ottawa: Minister of Supply and Services Canada.

Aboriginal Languages	Mother Tongue Populations	Index of Continuity	Index of Ability	Average Age of Population			Status of Language
				Knowledge	Mother Tongue	Home Language	
Total	208 610	70	117	30.4	31.0	28.3	mix of viable and endangered
Algonquian Family	146 635	70	117	30.5	30.9	28.8	mostly viable
Cree	87 555	72	117	29.9	30.2	27.9	viable large
Ojibway	25 885	55	122	34.9	36.2	34.4	viable large
Montagnais-Naskapi	9 070	94	104	25.1	25.2	24.8	viable small
Micmac	7 310	72	111	29.5	29.9	29.2	viable small
OjiüCree	5 400	80	114	25.7	26.3	26.8	viable small
Attikamek	3 995	97	103	21.8	21.9	21.5	viable small
Blackfoot	4 145	61	135	36.4	39.7	40.6	viable small
Algonquin	2 275	58	119	29.8	30.7	31.4	viable small
Malecite	655	37	148	40.5	44.0	44.8	viable small
Algonquian	350	40	159	47.2	52.2	46.7	uncertain
Inuktitut Family	27 780	86	109	23.9	23.9	23.3	viable large
Athapaskan Family	20 090	68	117	31.4	32.5	30.0	mostly viable
Dene	9 000	86	107	24.4	24.8	24.1	viable small
South Slave	2 620	55	124	35.6	37.8	38.4	viable small
Dogrib	2 085	72	118	28.3	29.8	30.6	viable small
Carrier	2 190	51	130	37.5	41.4	40.5	viable small
Chipewyan	1 455	44	128	39.4	40.2	40.7	viable small
Athapaskan	1 310	37	129	41.6	44.7	44.2	uncertain
Chilcotin	705	65	130	32.2	37.0	36.9	viable small
Kutchin-Gwich'in (Loucheux)	430	24	114	53.0	53.1	56.8	endangered
North Slave (Hare)	290	60	116	38.3	39.1	39.8	endangered
(Dakota) Siouan Family	4 295	67	111	31.0	31.9	28.0	viable small
Salish Family	3 200	25	132	42.0	48.7	47.2	endangered
Salish	1 850	24	130	43.0	49.7	48.5	endangered
Shuswap	745	25	134	38.7	46.3	42.9	endangered
Thompson	595	31	135	43.1	48.6	48.3	endangered
Tsimshian Family	2 460	31	132	43.2	48.0	49.6	endangered
Gitksan	1 200	39	123	41.4	45.2	45.7	viable small
Nishga	795	23	146	41.8	47.5	57.6	endangered
Tsimshian	465	24	132	50.5	55.9	52.7	endangered
Wakashan Family	1 650	27	118	47.3	51.3	51.1	endangered
Wakashan	1 070	24	129	47.7	53.0	53.2	endangered
Nootka	590	31	99	46.5	48.1	48.4	endangered
Iroquoian Family	590	13	160	36.4	46.5	52.0	uncertain
Mohawk	350	10	184	36.6	46.1	60.5	uncertain
Iroquoian	235	13	128	35.8	47.0	41.4	uncertain
Haida Family	240	6	144	46.7	50.4	64.6	endangered
Tlingit Family	145	21	128	45.5	49.3	41.6	endangered
Kutenai Family	120	17	200	37.1	52.3	41.2	endangered

Average ages and rates of population aging do, however, vary by language. Not only do viable languages have younger populations, but the average age of these groups rises more slowly than that of endangered groups. For example, the average age of the Inuktitut mother tongue population—young by any standard—increased only slightly from 23 to 24 years between 1981 and 1996. The rise was somewhat higher, but still relatively modest for the Cree, from 26 to 30. In comparison, the average age of the much older Kutenai mother tongue group increased from 44 in 1981 to 52 in 1996; for the Tlingit, from 47 to 58. The pattern, then, repeats: as with language erosion, population aging affects endangered languages more, thus accelerating their slide toward extinction.

Language Loss Most Pronounced During Family Formation Years

Examining the rate at which a specific group of people shifts from one language to another provides a way of understanding language use and decline in relation to lifestyle changes. Language maintenance seems very much to depend on the stage of life people are going through.

Young children, for example, have not yet had time or reason to shift from their mother tongue to another language, and for most of them their mother tongue is, therefore, the same as their home language. As a result, for every 100 children who were under five in 1981, 91 spoke their mother tongue at home. However, in 1996, when these children were in their mid- to late teens, only 76 still used their mother tongue as their home language. While this indicates a serious loss in home language usage, the decline does not stop here.

As youth move out of the original family home, marriage, entry into the labour force, and a different, often large, urban environment can further accelerate their language decline. Without the support of a closely knit community, and immersed in the language and culture of the dominant society, language erosion becomes difficult to resist. Indeed, the data show that language loss is most pronounced during the labour force years. While this holds for both men and women, it is particularly notable for women. Why this should be so is not clear, but contributing factors may include the fact that women are more likely than men to leave their reserves and move to other locations where the chances of marrying non-Aboriginals are higher. Indeed, the index of continuity declines from 74 for women between the ages of 20 and 24, to 45 by the time these women reach the ages of 35 to 39. Because these are the very years during which women tend to bring up young children, their shift from an Aboriginal to another home language is all the more serious for the transmission of these indigenous languages.

With the older cohorts nearing the end of their working lives and moving into their retirement years, the loss in home language is less pronounced. Their language use still declines, but more slowly than before. For example, language continuity for the cohort aged 50 to 54 in 1981 declines from a ratio of about 64 in 1981 to 61 by 1996. A similarly slow erosion occurs among the older seniors.

Registered Indians Account for Majority of Aboriginal Speakers

Groups that live in remote communities or in settlements with concentrated populations of indigenous speakers appear to find it easier to retain their language. Indeed, two such groups, on-reserve Registered Indians and the Inuit, show the highest indexes of language continuity among all groups: 80 and 85, respectively.[5] In contrast, non-status Indians and Métis, who tend to live off-reserve, as well as off-reserve Registered Indians, have home language— mother tongue indexes of 58, 50, and 40 respectively, pointing to a more pronounced state of language decline. Clearly, the off-reserve environment poses major threats to Aboriginal languages.

Signs of Hope for Endangered Languages

Despite the grim prospects facing many small languages, there are some signs which give rise to hope. The Kutenai language family, for example, has the smallest mother tongue population, one of the lowest indexes of continuity, and some of the oldest populations. However, for every person with a Kutenai mother tongue, there are two people (generally younger) who are able to speak it, suggesting that younger generations may be more likely to learn Kutenai as a second language than as a mother tongue. Similar second-language patterns are showing up for other endangered languages. A growing awareness of Aboriginal cultural identity may be partly responsible for this resurgence in language.[6]

Other positive signs are also apparent. According to the 1991 Aboriginal Peoples' Survey, about 9 in 10 adults would like to relearn an Aboriginal language they once spoke. In addition, the great majority of adults who never spoke an Aboriginal language reported that they would like to learn one.[7]

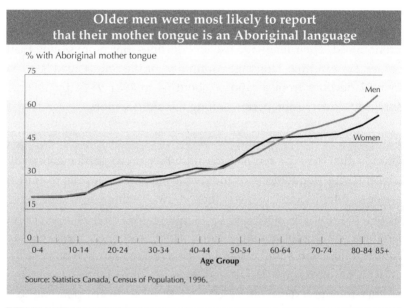

Older men were most likely to report that their mother tongue is an Aboriginal language

% with Aboriginal mother tongue

Source: Statistics Canada, Census of Population, 1996.

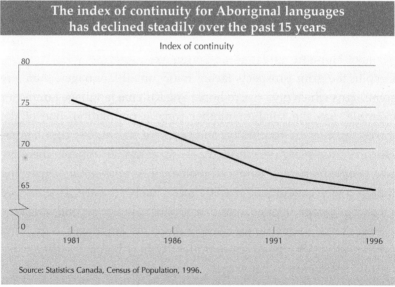

The index of continuity for Aboriginal languages has declined steadily over the past 15 years

Index of continuity

Source: Statistics Canada, Census of Population, 1996.

Summary

Canada's Aboriginal languages are among the most endangered in the world.[8] Significant numbers of languages have either already disappeared or are close to extinction, and among those spoken today, only 3 of some 50 are viable with a large population base. Large or small, viable languages tend to have relatively young speakers, are successfully passed on between generations, and are spoken in isolated or well-organized communities. In contrast, endangered languages are characterized by small population groups, older speakers, and lower rates of language transmission.

Aboriginal elders, teachers, and other leaders are well aware of the gravity of the linguistic situation and are taking steps to preserve indigenous languages. These include such measures as language instruction programs, Aboriginal media programming, and the recording of elders' stories, songs, and accounts of history in the Aboriginal language.[9] Perhaps as a result, the number of people who can speak and understand an Aboriginal language has been on the rise.

The Royal Commission on Aboriginal Peoples (RCAP) has studied Aboriginal language use and retention extensively. Its recommendations aimed at saving these languages from extinction echo some of the steps taken by Aboriginal elders. In addition, RCAP also recommends granting special status to Aboriginal languages and guaranteeing their extended use in the public domain, at least within the confines of Aboriginal communities; providing formal education in the Aboriginal language; and conducting research on these languages. The Commission emphasizes that everyday language use in the home and in the community is critical for intergenerational transmission and for acquiring Aboriginal languages as a mother tongue.

Notes

1. Some 75% of those who have learned the language at home are fair to excellent speakers, compared with 23% of those who have learned it at school only. Yukon Executive Council Office. 1991. *A profile of Aboriginal languages in the Yukon.*

2. For example, immigration spurred the growth of the Chinese mother tongue group from 95 000 in 1971 to 517 000 in 1991. B. R. Harrison. 1997. "Language integration: Results of an

intergenerational analysis." *Statistical Journal of the United Nations ECE* 14: 292.

3. The growth in Aboriginal mother tongue populations is attributed to the high fertility rates of the Aboriginal population. To a lesser extent, adults relearning their mother tongue and more people reporting their Aboriginal mother tongue may also have contributed to the growth.

4. In comparison, 60% of those 85 years and over, and 30% of 40- to 44-year-olds reported an Aboriginal mother tongue in 1996.

5. However, significant variations exist between Inuit communities depending on location. While the Eastern group of dialects have high indexes of continuity, the Western groups have much lower ones.

6. For example, the off-reserve Aboriginal Head Start Program, designed primarily for preschoolers, incorporates language as one of its components.

7. Ponting, J. R. 1997. *First Nations in Canada: Perspectives on Opportunity, Empowerment and Self-determination.* Toronto: McGraw-Hill Ryerson.

8. UNESCO. 1996. *Atlas of the World's Languages in Danger of Disappearing.* Edited by Stephen A. Wurm. Paris: Unesco Publishing, p. 23.

9. Ponting, *First Nations in Canada*, p. 252.

Mary Jane Norris is a senior analyst with the Demography Division of Statistics Canada.

The Internet and Global Human Rights

Lloyd Axworthy

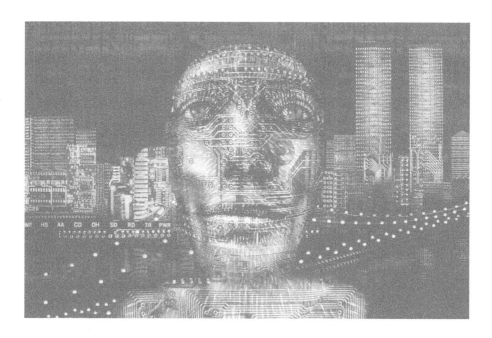

LAST WEEK, GRAND CHIEF PHIL FONTAINE, the head of Canada's Assembly of First Nations, gave me a wonderful gift: a talking stick. It is a technology that goes back thousands of years, and when handed to a speaker it is supposed to imbue that person's words with courage, honesty, and wisdom. Of course, it's not always guaranteed to work because much depends on the person holding the stick. For our First Nations people it carries great significance and responsibility: when the stick is in your hand you have the power to speak straight, to communicate what is good, and to help in the search for truth.

I thought that bringing the talking stick to the opening of this conference made some sense and would perhaps carry the right message. After all, we are here to discuss how today's electronic, wired cyberspace technology can also be a talking stick, bringing with it the capacity to speak straight, to contribute to the common good, and to advance the cause of human rights and commitment to that cause.

We are here to examine how we can maximize the Internet's potential for good as a tool to promote and protect human rights— its use for human rights education, as a means of organizing human rights defenders, and getting information on human rights violations out to the world. We are here to talk about a technology that is revolutionizing the world—changing the equations of power, challenging the conventional channels of communication, distributing and disseminating influence in the broadest possible fashion, to the point of democratizing the channels and getting rid of the gatekeepers.

The question posed is, to what end and for what purpose will the Internet be used? As with most technologies there is the potential for evil as well as good. For all the opportunity it represents, there is a dark side. Just this past week, an international operation led by Interpol arrested over 100 people in 12 countries involved in a child pornography ring. Racist and extremists use the Net to incite hatred. The drug dealers and the crime rings turn the Internet to their own advantage, using it to help overturn governments and corrode society. So part of the human rights and Internet issue is the question of how to prevent the abuse of this technology.

The information superhighway can transport the best, but it can also transport the worst. Hate speech, child pornography, and child prostitution have moved onto the Net and they have to be dislodged. The aim is not to control the Internet per se, but to take aim at those who would misuse it for criminal and other illegal activities that can hurt or harm. The Internet should not be a law-free zone. We are working with other governments, through the Organization for Economic Cooperation and Development, the Group of Eight leading industrialized nations, the United Nations and other international organizations to prevent the Internet from becoming a safe haven for conduct that threatens human rights. Canadian courts and legislatures have done groundbreaking work in defining when freedom of expression must give way to criminal law sanctions to control obscenity, hate propaganda, and child pornography. Our experience in the real world could guide us in addressing similar challenges in the cyberworld, where the consequences of hurtful actions are no less destructive.

In addition to better enforcement of domestic and international criminal laws, other means are being developed to address harmful and illegal content on the Net; these include self-regulation, software filtering, voluntary codes of conduct, and various forms of Internet watch activities to protect consumers and children. Next January in Paris, UNESCO will convene an international meeting of officials and experts on child pornography to coordinate a worldwide offensive against pedophile materials on the Internet.

The newly minted International Criminal Court [ICC] has helped give definition to a range of international crimes and a mechanism to enforce the international rule of law. The Internet offers a potentially powerful way to make the most of this new instrument. It can disseminate information on the court's objectives and offer a channel to gain support for the court's work. It can provide access and links to sites with key documents, such as the International Law web site. It could perhaps provide a cyberforum where experts can assist the ICC from their own desktops. In these ways the Internet can extend the reach and ensure the effectiveness of the court.

Yet we should not be overly preoccupied with the dark side of the Internet because the technology has a mind-boggling potential to break through barriers and overcome political obstacles—to educate, inform, and be an agent of political change. Putting information and communication technologies at the service of human needs means developing ways to deal with harmful and illegal uses, but we must take care that in doing so we do not destroy the very attributes that make these technologies such powerful tools for human rights advocacy in the first place.

The revolution in communications and information technology is taking place at the same time as two other global trends: increasing democratization and the growing importance of global governance. One of the key questions for this conference is how we can link all these three trends. Information technology is reorganizing international politics, giving power and influence to the disenfranchised, empowering new groups and reshaping the constellation of international players. The Internet is an unparalleled tool in a complex world where soft power—influencing events by using attractive ideas, promoting shared values and partnership—is emerging as a way of pursuing our goals. I have seen firsthand the power of the new communications in the landmines campaign, where the Internet gave international civil society a new say in pushing forward shared objectives. Clearly, the new information and communications technologies are instruments for change. Our concern here is how to use them to achieve our goals of more democratic societies and better governance, with respect for the rule of human rights law.

Democratization does not happen simply by holding elections. Democratization requires an active, effective civil society. It requires citizens who are ready, willing, and able to participate in the political life of their country, and who are not only permitted but encouraged to do so. The Internet has the potential to shelter and nourish opposition groups who are seeking democratic change under repressive regimes. It can help overcome the monopolies of state-controlled media. Governments are still coming to grips with this new phenomenon. Some have not fully comprehended it. Some are reacting out of fear, trying to seal off their populations from the connection and influence of the Net—an effort that frankly is futile. Others are realizing that in new democracies the Net can increase democratic awareness and popular participation.

There is thus a need for a serious agenda of potential actions to ensure that today's talking stick is not used to foment hatred and exploitation but is used instead to support those working against such evils.

Lloyd Axworthy (*Born 1939, North Battleford, Saskatchewan*), Minister of Foreign Affairs for Canada, is a graduate of Princeton University. Axworthy was a professor of political science at the University of Winnipeg for more than ten years, before being elected to Parliament in 1969. He was appointed to his current office in 1996.

Selection Activities, p. 382

Spinning Facts into Fiction: Talking with Timothy Findley

Timothy Findley's novels are meticulously researched. Even his publisher's lawyers admit to having difficulty determining where fact ends and fiction begins.

Famous Last Words, Findley's fourth and most exhaustively prepared book, required four years of research. A gripping account of fascism during the Second World War, the novel probes an international cabal whose members include the Duke and Duchess of Windsor, prominent Nazis, and other well-known figures. The narrator is Hugh Mauberley, a fictitious figure borrowed from one of Ezra Pound's poems. Mauberley is an American expatriate writer who is a confidant of members of the cabal. He knows too much, flees the Nazis, hides in an Austrian hotel, and scrawls everything he knows in silver pencil along the walls of the hotel. He is murdered while doing this, and the story really unfolds by flashing back to his handwritten account.

In the following interview, Findley reveals how relatively simple the research was for this complex novel.

At a writer's conference, I had a wonderful talk with the author E. L. Doctorow. He wrote what I would call the definitive metafiction book, *Ragtime*. When I asked him how he did his research, he answered this way: "I discovered that once I had really stated my subject, I became a magnet." That is a very good definition of what happens when you have staked out your territory. Doctorow's territory was pre–First World War. My territory was 1943 back to wherever it was going to lead as far as the Duke and Duchess of Windsor were concerned.

The magnet phenomenon works as follows: you pick up a book of basic history, you read, and you discover a sequence of names. Let us pretend that Doctorow and I have picked up the same book.

Doctorow does not write or think like me, and I do not write or think like him; therefore, he and I are not going to follow the same line in reading this book. As Doctorow reads—and this is the magnet at work—his eye hits on a particular sequence, and he follows it. He picks up on names, personality traits, the recurrence of links between people and events. A whole other set of magnetic episodes are going to happen with me.

My subject dictated a sequence that followed fascist thinking from one set of people to another. I had to begin with something basic, so I used W. L. Shirer's *Rise and Fall of the Third Reich*—an invaluable guide to fascism and the Second World War. Where did it take me? For one thing, its bibliography gave me a reading list. I discovered an alarming consistency in the cast of characters from one piece of reading to another. Here's a good example: in one book I discovered that the wedding of the Duke and Duchess of Windsor had taken place at the Château du Conde in France, which was owned by a man named Charles Eugène Bedaux. The information was a mere mention of the wedding—just a sentence—but I had never heard of Bedaux and was intrigued. In another book, however, I had read that prior to the wedding the Duchess was staying with friends in their villa in the south of France and the Duke was with friends at a castle in Austria. That led to the question, "Why did they get married at Bedaux's villa—seemingly, the home of a stranger—when they could have been married where they already had friends whom they knew were willing to perform the ceremony?"

Reading newspaper accounts of the wedding, I learned that Bedaux had offered the Windsors his villa absolutely out of the blue—he did not even know them. And I still knew very little about him; he was a mystery and a challenge. What helped me understand this man was a series of columns written by Janet Flanner in the *New Yorker.* Sure enough, my instinct had been correct. I had made the right connection, and Bedaux had been worth tracking, because it turned out that he had been pivotal to the Windsors' fascist connections.

Bedaux was the inventor of the concept of time study. He would walk into factories and say, "Get rid of those people—they're stopping you. Bring in other people and make use of them." He worked out a system that to me is highly fascist: he would extract the most from labourers, making them work very hard for four minutes, then relax for one minute. In other words, he advocated turning people into machines to make them more productive. The carrot to reward them was the one minute of rest. He made a fortune. And, not incidentally, some Canadian firms adopted his methods.

I read through all the books I could find on the Windsors to discover any further connections with Bedaux. I had to do a lot of scrutinizing, because some books were very sympathetic and others were overly damning. A good researcher has to learn to recognize an author's bias.

The real starting point for me was to determine what was to be the circle of events and who were to be the people involved in this cabal I was imagining—and then to discover what might have been real. By reading through material I had borrowed from libraries and purchased at bookstores, I discovered that, at its widest, the circle included people like Ezra Pound, the Duke and Duchess of Windsor, Bedaux, Walter Schellenberg (who was the top SS counterintelligence officer), Ribbentrop, and Rudolf Hess. The magnet in me took over once I had that overview. As soon as I saw any of those names, I would mentally reach out to collect data. I could be walking down the street and out of the corner of my eye see Hess's face staring out of a bookstore window from the dust jacket of a book. It's an eclectic process.

I also read the bibliographies of every book I used and followed them up, ultimately reading nearly everything written about some of these key figures. By reading and rereading material I acquired, over time, a deeper understanding of the characters I had found.

Another thing that paid off for me was to tell friends what I was writing about. One of these friends, the writer Charles Taylor, was especially helpful. His father, E. P. Taylor, lived in Nassau, and the Taylors inevitably got to know some of the people in the circle around the Duke of Windsor during his tenure there as governor during the Second World War. This connection turned out to be invaluable for me. In my novel I used a real-life incident involving Sydney Oakes and his father, Sir Harry Oakes, but I gave my own interpretation of the circumstances in which it had taken place. It is a pertinent scene that develops the character of Sir Harry and, I think, forms a part, however small, of the explanation of why he was murdered.

When I had finished *Famous Last Words*, the lawyers for my publisher, Clarke Irwin, were worried that Sydney might still be alive and sue. My memory had told me he had died in a car accident. Charles Taylor helped me confirm this by telephoning his father's secretary in Nassau. The secretary made a few calls to relatives of the Oakeses, who confirmed that, indeed, he was dead.

There were other areas where Charles Taylor helped me. A number of places mentioned in my book—Spain, Vienna, Rome, Venice, and Nassau—were places I had never been. Quite deliberately, I avoided visiting them, because I wanted to maintain a kind of mythic view of them, so that they would be "written" places, not real. I read a lot about them and asked a lot of questions. For instance, I mentioned to Charles Taylor that I had placed the governor's mansion in Nassau at the top of the hill. He remarked, "Yes, it's at the top of a sort of hill. It's actually just a slight rise in the land." He was greatly amused. I also asked him other questions: "What do the trees smell like?" "What does the land smell like at night?" By researching the setting in this way, I was getting a mythic, distanced, very "writerly" interpretation of the place. Don't forget: the book was being written by a writer, Mauberley, who was a failed romantic. I had to serve his style.

I also studied maps in the library to get the geography and street connections right. Studying the photographs was also helpful to make sure I was correctly describing the clothing, cars, and things like that. These were the kinds of details Mauberley thrived on: dress, appearance, atmosphere.

This process is, of course, different from a journalistic reportage of a place. This is a valid type of approach, but it would destroy a book like mine, which requires a different kind of shape to make it succeed.

Selection Activities, p. 382

Family Matters: Sometimes the Perfect Mate Is Someone You Hardly Know

From Utne Reader

ASLAM ABDULLAH *was 23 years old when he married 21-year-old Amtul Aziz in Delhi, India. It was 1979, and the couple had met just a few times before their marriage, which was arranged by their families, according to tradition. Aslam and Amtul had two children in India and then moved to Los Angeles where they had two more children. Aslam, now editor of two national Muslim magazines,* Minaret *and* Observer, *says he expects that his older, Indian-born children, ages 18 and 15, will someday consult him in arranging a marriage match. He's not so certain about the wishes of his younger, American-born children, ages 9 and 5.*

"While I am very happy with my marriage," he told Utne Reader, *"I am aware that, even in India, the cultural acceptance of arranged marriage has changed. So my children will make up their own minds, and hopefully they will allow us, their family, to play at least a small role."*

How was your marriage arranged?
First, my sisters and my mother and other family members talked to me. They asked what I was looking for in a wife. Then they looked around, found a family they felt was suitable, and sent a formal proposal to the parents. Through the parents, the proposal went to the girl. But I think that she learned about the proposal before her parents told her, through other girls.

Did Amtul know who you were before she accepted your proposal?
In a way, yes. I was involved in the student movement in India, so my photo had appeared in newspapers, and I had been interviewed on television. Also, my family was well known in India. So she knew this, and I think she agreed to marry me after she was briefed by her friends and family. Usually you trust the judgment of your parents and other members of your family because you trust they are acting in your best interest.

At the time of your betrothal, arranged marriage was already on the decline in India. What did your friends think when you told them your match would be arranged?
At my university, almost everyone was getting married in the modern style. I was really one of the only people I knew who chose to follow the old marriage traditions. My friends were mostly following the mood of the age, the way they felt modern romance should develop: dating or talking with one another, falling in love, deciding to marry, and then at last involving their parents and family.

My friends asked me, "Why, when you are living in such a modern age, would you want to do something like this?" I said, "I believe in traditional values. Families ought to have a say in these things. Marriage is not just a union of two individuals. It is a union of two families."

You saw your bride just a few times before you married. What was your state of mind at your wedding?
I was excited and quite nervous. This is the kind of moment that most of us would feel excited about. Here you are meeting a new person, and you have the opportunity to win over that person. If you are successful, together you will embark on a wonderful journey that will last a lifetime. It is both thrilling and romantic.

What advantages do arranged marriages have over those based entirely on love?
In an arranged marriage, you start with the presumption that you will live your entire life with this person. Because of this, you accept that you have to change and adjust yourself according to the mood and the character of your spouse, because you expect that this partnership will certainly continue until your death.

Other kinds of marriages can be like shopping at a market, where you go by yourself and try on the clothes and select whatever fits you best at that moment. Maybe the next day you pick up what you've bought and realize that you've gained weight overnight. Then you throw that garment out and buy a new one. In an arranged marriage, your family has selected your mate according to your interests, and you accept that they know your heart the same way as you do.

Why do Westerners discount arranged marriage?

I'm not certain, because if you look at Western civilization you find that until the 20th century, arranged marriages of a fashion were quite common in Europe. Then came the First World War and the Second World War, when people went far away from home and a different standard of family involvement in romantic relationships came to be accepted. Even now in the West, marriages are still somewhat arranged in certain social classes. Families make connections between their children, and parents may try to influence their children's decisions. They'll say, "Look at that girl. She's compatible to you." So it's the same, only less blatant.

Will you expect to play the same role in your children's marriages as your parents played in yours?

We live in modern times, so I cannot force this sort of decision on my children. Because my older children were born in India, they are still more influenced by Indian culture. The younger ones are much more American.

When it comes time for our children to marry, we will help identify people for them—if they ask us for help. We would like to be part of their decision-making process, not because we've forced them to comply with our wishes, but because we have that kind of relationship with our children. This culture is very different from the one my wife and I were raised in. As long as they respect the values of their faith, their decisions will be fine.

Zen and the Art of Stand-Up Comedy

Jay Sankey

Writing

Ultimately, the success of a stand-up comic is often determined by his material.

—Woody Allen

To write effective stand-up material, you need three primary skills. First, the ability to develop the "comic ear," to be able to hear (and see) "the funny" in the things around you. Second, the determination to write a large quantity of jokes, the more the better. Many seasoned comics say you have to write a thousand jokes before you start to really become proficient. And third, the ability to be able to separate the good jokes from the bad. It's like panning for gold—but as a writer not only do you have to do all the panning, you also have to write the river of material! It's an awful lot of hard work, but many have done it before you. So there's no reason why you can't do it too. Just take it one joke at a time.

Where Do You Get Your Ideas?

The best way to get a good idea is to get a lot of ideas.

—Roger von Oech

The question above is probably the one writers are asked more than any other. My answer is: From everywhere. Every day each of us moves through a world lush with possibilities. We are virtually surrounded by possible sparks for inspiration. But it's *seeing* them that's the hard part. What I try to do is force myself to think about stand-up as much as possible. About being onstage, about delivering my material. I also often ask myself, "What do people care about?"—a question I believe to be one of the real keys to this craft.

Good ideas sometimes just come to you, but more often than not they are the result of hard work. By "work" I mean putting energy toward putting yourself in a fertile frame of mind and giving your natural Muse the time, and the reason, to do its thing. Every successful artist has his or her own way of wooing creativity. For some, it's getting up first thing in the morning with a hot cup of coffee and a notepad, and just spending some time writing whatever comes to mind. For others, it's about always keeping a pad of paper handy when they are exercising. Find what works for you. Remember, it's not going to come to you, at least not on a regular basis. You have to go to it.

The Power of Ideas

Writer's block is for amateurs.

—Charles M. Schulz

Write down every joke idea you ever have. Seriously, every single one. And don't just keep them in several different drawers all over the house (not to mention the glove compartment of your car). Go through them on a regular basis, edit them down, polish them, and even go so far as to file them, perhaps by subject, in a file system or on computer disk. Treat them like they're gold, because that's exactly what they are.

You see, unlike a comic, who is pretty much restricted to either a live performance or a television taping, a good joke idea is *raw potential* and can be used in an almost unlimited number of contexts: commercials, album covers, posters, cartoons, radio shows, television sitcoms, plays. Ideas can freely flow from medium to medium in a way very few performers can.

Lenny Bruce kept absolutely everything, and comics who saw him perform a few years before his death say that, in his sets, they saw ideas he'd been playing with for years that had by then become much more sanded and polished. One of the really wonderful things about writing all your own ideas down, and keeping them in a safe place, is that when you go over some of them several years later you'll see brand-new ways of making them work onstage. If you're funny, there's probably a decent idea behind most funny thoughts you will ever have. It's just a matter of finding the right context and the right way of doing it.

So treat your ideas well. In fact, I believe ideas are not unlike customers in a store. The better service they receive, the more likely they are to return. Remember, your ideas are precious—literally, the lifeblood of your craft.

The Stand-Up Ear

With any luck (and a lot of hard work!) after performing on a few dozen amateur nights and watching many professional stand-up shows, you will begin to develop a "stand-up ear." You'll be talking with a friend on the phone and suddenly you'll hear yourself say something that sounds like a joke. Or you'll be sitting on the subway, listening to two kids talk, and again you'll hear something that sounds like a joke. With a great deal of thought and practice, both on

IF A TREE FALLS IN THE FOREST
AND IT LANDS ON A MIME...

and off stage, you will begin to hear, think, and even talk in a stand-up sensitive fashion.

Remember, stand-up tends to focus on

1. simple ideas that can be
2. commonly understood, and
3. verbally expressed.

Subtle puns about nuclear chemistry, and party stunts that have to be performed with the lights off do not make for strong stand-up.

Expressing vs. Communicating

To me, this is one of the most important distinctions in the entire craft of stand-up comedy. When you take the stage, are you going to be a true communicator, or merely an "expresser"? Almost anyone can vent, blurt out thoughts and feelings, express themselves in one form or another. But to *communicate* is a whole other thing, because to be a communicator you have to care, not just about speaking, but also about *being heard*. That involves taking into account your audience. Their expectations, their perspectives, everything. All of which cannot help but influence material and your choice of subject, vocabulary, and speed of delivery. To be a communicator is to desire connection. Unlike the self-absorbed expresser, the communicator not only wants his audience to understand what he is trying to say, but he's willing to work to make it happen.

Clever vs. Funny

If clever is a performer balancing a pie on a stick, funny is the pie falling off and landing on the performer. I have seen some decidedly unclever comics do very well in a comedy club, and I have seen some very clever comics bomb again and again. That's because, even though most effective stand-up material has clever, witty moments, it doesn't mean people are going to think it's funny.

The difference between wit that gets belly laughs and wit that gets bored silence is not only a matter of the style the material is both written and delivered in, but also a matter of the *degree to which the audience cares about the subject*. An extremely clever comment about quilting is simply not going to get as many laughs as a slightly witty comment about fast food.

Now, some comics say that, compared to jokes about quilting, jokes about fast food are "easy," but I think this is a misguided attitude. Trying to sharpen a knife with a whet stone is certainly going to be "easier" than trying to sharpen it with a handful of butterscotch pudding. That's because, when it comes to sharpening a knife, a whet stone suits the job. In much the same way, when it comes to stand-up comedy, talking about stuff that people care about also suits the job.

Why Should an Audience Care?

If the audience doesn't care about what you are talking about, they will not laugh. It's really that simple. No emotional investment, no fuel for laughter. Fortunately, there are several ways to coax people to become truly involved with what you are saying.

Direct Involvement

People will only emotionally invest in something they care about. So if they are going to care about a stand-up performance, usually they have to care about either *what* is being said, or *who* is saying it. It's you or your material, ideally both. Getting crowds to care about you, night after night, city after city, usually requires years of experience, performing for thousands of different audiences. But fortunately, getting people to care about your material is a fair bit easier. In fact, if you want to have a pretty good idea of what people care about, just open a newspaper ... crime, drugs, violence, money, sports, education, movie stars, fitness, etc. These are the things most people care about. If you stick closely to them, you can't go too far wrong.

Ideally, you want material that *both you and the audience find funny*. If they don't find it funny, they aren't going to laugh. But if you didn't find your material funny, you probably aren't going to be able to deliver with full commitment and conviction. And remember, the more deeply both you and the audience care about a topic, the more likely it will be to get a big laugh.

But as I've mentioned before, originality is an important ingredient when it comes to success as a stand-up comic. Which is why the thing you are ideally searching for is material that is not only funny to you and funny to audiences but also fresh and original.

Jay Sankey, stand-up comic, writer, and cartoonist, has published two collections of sleight-of-hand routines, and his book *Zen and the Art of Stand-Up Comedy* is an insider's look at working as a stand-up comic. He has performed around the world for over 20 years, made numerous television appearances, and recorded a CD. He lives in Toronto.

Shapes of Cities

Vanessa Baird

FROM TORONTO TO TIMBUKTU the shapes of cities vary quite dramatically. But why? Here are some attempts to explain and categorize the differences.

The cosmic (or holy) city

This city reflects beliefs about the universal and social order. Characteristic design features are a monumental axis (a temple, cathedral, or citadel, for example), some dominant landmarks, and reliance on a regular grid. Baroque ideal city plans tend to fit this model.

The practical city

The design of colonial and company towns and the grid cities of the U.S.A. are motivated by practicality. A city, according to this model, is made up of small autonomous parts linked together into a great machine which has clearly differentiated functions and motions.

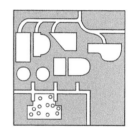

The organic (or walking) city

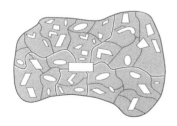

This city is a living thing, evolving in a natural way to fit the landscape. It has a definite boundary, an optimum size, and a cohesive individual internal structure. All destinations can be reached by foot in 30 minutes, and it is rarely more than five kilometres wide. This model is typical of medieval towns and can still be found in the centres of older European and North African and Asian cities.

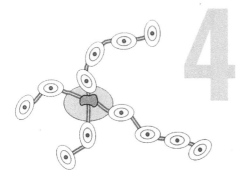

4 The transit city

At the end of the nineteenth century, trains and trams allowed cities to expand outward. Trains create subcentres at train stations, and trams generate development along their routes. The transit city tends to be a medium-density, mixed-use city, with a dominant focus at the city core. These cities now spread 20 to 30 kilometres across.

5 The automobile city

The growth of car use after 1945 made it possible to expand in all directions. Low-density suburbs house commuters, with separate zones for industry and commerce created by planners. The city is decentralized and dispersed and is typically 50 kilometres or more wide. This model is very dominant in the world today.

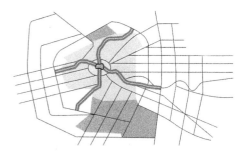

Future city?

This could be more compact in nature, with mixed use—residential, commercial, and small-scale industrial. Apart from the city centre, there would be subcentres or nuclei, linked by an extensive and efficient network of public transit, reducing the need for car ownership and freeing up space for green amenities.

6

Selection Activities, p. 384

Food Facts: What Doesn't Kill You Will Make You Stronger

From Shift *magazine*

- Number of genetically altered crops currently being field-tested, including tomatoes spliced with fish genes — **678**

- Number of the 300 English test fields of bioengineered crops that have been sabotaged by environmentalists — **40**

- Percentage of the public that wants labels on genetically altered food — **93**

- Percentage of genetically altered foods that are labelled as such in North America — **0**

- Ratio of livestock to humans on Earth — **3 to 1**

- Percentage of all land that is used for livestock breeding and grazing — **50**

- Number of people who could be fed if North Americans consumed 10 percent less meat — **100 Million**

- Number of people who die annually from malnutrition and starvation — **18 Million**

• Percentage of Africans who are malnourished	**75**
• Percentage increase over the past 20 years in the amount of money North Americans spend on fast food	**1567**
• Chance that a North American has worked at McDonald's	**1 in 8**
• Average number of pounds a North American gains between Thanksgiving and New Year's Day	**6**
• Percentage of 10-year-old girls who fear becoming fat	**81**
• Percentage of teenage girls who diet .	**50**
• Percentage of all antibiotics consumed in the U.S.A. that are fed to animals	**55**
• Percentage of food sales composed of organic produce	**1**
• Percentage of North Americans who would buy organic food if prices were comparable to non-organic alternatives	**90**
• Percentage of men who would eat a piece of food after a fly had landed on it	**70**
• Percentage of women who would	**41**

POETRY

Poetry

"Poetry is a very concentrated form, and therefore the explosiveness of each word becomes much greater."

– Margaret Atwood

"Poetry is the shape and shade and size of words as they hum, strum, jig, and gallop along."

– Dylan Thomas

When poets craft their work, they choose words carefully. To appreciate poems, you need to read them slowly, paying attention to the way the poet appeals to your imagination through your senses.

Like painters, poets create **images**, but with words. Some images are formed when the poet describes an object. Others are created through **figurative language**. That's when a concrete image is used to symbolize an abstract concept, such as love or loyalty.

Poetry is often meant to be read aloud, and so poets carefully listen to the sound of each line. They use **auditory devices**, such as **rhythm** and **rhyme**, to appeal to your sense of hearing. Poets also care about the way a poem looks on the page. Some poems have stanzas of equal length. Others vary the shapes and length of lines. In concrete and shape poems, poets invent layouts that reflect their themes.

Read poems. Listen to poems. Imagine them into being.

image: a vivid or graphic description of something created by the poet

figurative language: the way in which poets link one thing to another through such devices as similes, metaphors, and personification

auditory devices: devices, including alliteration, assonance, and onomatopoeia, which enhance meaning when the poem is read aloud

rhythm: the flow and beat of the words and lines of a poem, created by the pattern of stressed and unstressed syllables

rhyme: the repetition of similar sounds at the ends of words

Poetry

Chance Encounter

Alden Nowlan

There is something odd in the road ahead.
A man in a black coat walking a dog,
a tall man in a long black coat walking a big red dog,
or is it a black mare with a red colt.
                              God
don't let me hit them.
                    I don't like
to be splashed by death.
                      The car stops in time
and I roll down the window.
                            There is a cow moose
standing not ten feet away
and her calf a little farther off,
neither of them knowing what to make of the headlights,
bright as lightning, solid as the light
of a full moon on a cloudless night.
Then the cow crosses over, very slowly,
not looking back
until she reaches
the edge of the woods
on the other side
and finds the calf has not followed her,
                              but gone back
and they look at one another
across the light that separates them
and perhaps she makes little coaxing sounds I can't hear,
while I will him
not to run away where they might never find each other
but to be brave enough
to walk into the light
I don't dare turn off
for fear of humans like myself
—and at last he begins to walk

toward the road
              and after a moment's pause
enters the light
             and crosses it
in about thirty seconds,
             a long time
when you're holding your breath,
             and the instant
he's safely over, she runs and he
      runs behind her,
          and I drive on,
             happy about it all,
bursting to tell someone about the great sight I've seen,
yet not even sure why it should seem so important.

Alden Nowlan (*Born 1933, Windsor, Nova Scotia; died 1983*), poet, short-story writer, novelist, and playwright, moved to New Brunswick at 18, where he worked as a newspaper editor. He began publishing poetry in the 1950s, and then began writing in other genres. His poems chiefly describe life in small-town New Brunswick.

Sarajevo Bear

Walter Pavlich

The last animal
   in the Sarajevo Zoo

a bear
   died of starvation

because the leaves
    had fallen

from the trees
   because

the air was
    getting colder

so the snipers
    could more easily see

the few remaining people
     who were trying to

feed it.

Walter Pavlich (*Born 1955, U.S.A.*) has published a number of poetry collections, and many of his poems have appeared in American magazines and literary journals. He has won several awards for his poetry. Pavlich has taught in various settings, including universities and state prisons, and has also worked as a firefighter.

 Selection Activities, p. 385

La Belle Dame sans Merci

John Keats

La Belle Dame sans Merci, Sir Frank Dicksee

"O what can ail thee, knight-at-arms,
    Alone and palely loitering?
The sedge is withered from the lake,
    And no birds sing.

"O what can ail thee, knight-at-arms,
    So haggard and so woe-begone?
The squirrel's granary is full,
    And the harvest's done.

"I see a lily on thy brow
        With anguish moist and fever dew;
And on thy cheek a fading rose
        Fast withereth too."

"I met a lady in the meads,
        Full beautiful—a faery's child,
Her hair was long, her foot was light,
        And her eyes were wild.

"I made a garland for her head,
        And bracelets too, and fragrant zone;
She looked at me as she did love,
        And made sweet moan.

"I set her on my pacing steed
        And nothing else saw all day long.
For sideways would she lean, and sing
        A faery's song.

"She found me roots of relish sweet,
        And honey wild and manna dew,
And sure in language strange she said,
        'I love thee true!'

"She took me to her elfin grot,
        And there she wept and sighed full sore;
And there I shut her wild wild eyes
        With kisses four.

"And there she lullèd me asleep,
        And there I dreamed—Ah! woe betide!
The latest dream I ever dreamed
        On the cold hill side.

"I saw pale kings and princes too,
        Pale warriors, death-pale were they all;
Who cried—'La Belle Dame sans Merci
        Hath thee in thrall!'

"I saw their starved lips in the gloom
        With horrid warning gapèd wide,
And I awoke and found me here
        On the cold hill side.

"And this is why I sojourn here
        Alone and palely loitering,
Though the sedge is withered from the lake,
        And no birds sing."

John Keats (*Born 1795, England; died 1821*) was the son of a livery stable manager. He studied medicine, but chose to support himself as a writer, publishing his first volume of poems in 1817. He is considered one of the principal Romantic poets. His best-known works include "Ode to a Nightingale" and "La Belle Dame sans Merci."

To My Son

Helen Fogwill Porter

When you were small
you used to climb
in our bed
when lightning ripped the sky.
We'd hold you tight
between us
while your father said:
"That storm is miles away"
a second before the room
was lit
with fearsome light.

Now when lightning strikes
you stay in your own
narrow bed
trying to think of other
safer things
and we in our wide bed
sigh separate sighs
because we no longer know how
to comfort you.

Helen Fogwill Porter (*Born 1930, St. John's, Newfoundland*), writer of short stories, novels, plays, poetry and nonfiction, has had works appear in many Canadian publications. Her 1991 novel *A Long and Lonely Ride* is set in her birthplace. Several of her plays have been produced on stage and for CBC radio.

Selection Activities, p. 386

Africville

Maxine Tynes

We are Africville
we are the dispossessed Black of the land
creeping with shadows
with life
with pride
with memories
into the place made for us
creeping with pain away from our home
carrying, always carrying
Africville on our backs
in our hearts
in the face of our child and our anger.

I am Africville
says a woman, child, man at the homestead site.
This park is green; but
Black, so Black with community.
I talk Africville
to you
and to you
until it is both you and me
till it stands and lives again
till you face and see and stand
on its life and its forever
Black past.

No house is Africville.
No road, no tree, no well.
Africville is man/woman/child
in the street and heart Black Halifax,
the Prestons, Toronto.

Wherever we are, Africville,
you and we are that Blackpast homeground.
We mourn for the burial of our houses, our church, our roads;
but we wear Our Africville face and skin and heart.
For all the world.
For Africville.

Maxine Tynes (*Born 1949, Dartmouth, Nova Scotia*), poet and playwright, is a descendant of Black Loyalists who settled in Nova Scotia. Her poems have been published in numerous literary anthologies and in collections of her own work. She has co-written and performed in a CBC radio docudrama, and is known for her lively poetry readings.

 Selection Activities, p. 386

Fifty Below

Richard Van Camp

I remember one time in Fort Rae
I was walking with my cousins,
four girls, who were walking with me
they were laughing at me those girls
and I was wearing my father's boots
two sizes too big for me
and these four girls
these four cousins
they laughed at me as I dragged my boots

   "You girls," I said, "what's so funny?"

One girl
one cousin
stopped me and pointed to my feet

   "Auntie told us, if you're going to marry a man,
   listen to his feet when you walk with him
   if he drags his feet when he walks
   you must not marry him;
   he is lazy
   no good
   he won't be a good father
   he won't be a good husband."

And those four girls
those four cousins
they ran far ahead of me laughing
and this time
when I ran after them
I lifted my feet as high as I could.

Richard Van Camp (*Born 1971, Northwest Territories*), poet, novelist, short-story writer, and radio dramatist, is a member of the Dogrib nation. His poems and short stories appear in many anthologies. His first novel, *The Lesser Blessed*, was published in 1996.

Selection Activities, p. 387

Hunger

Kingmerut

Fear hung over me.
I dared not try
to hold out in my hut.

Hungry and chilled,
I stumbled inland,
tripping, falling constantly.

At Little Musk Ox Lake
the trout made fun of me;
they wouldn't bite.

On I crawled,
and reached the Young Man's River
where I caught salmon once.

I prayed
for fish or reindeer
swimming in the lake.

My thought
reeled into nothingness,
like run-out fish-line.

Would I ever find firm ground?
I staggered on,
muttering spells as I went.

Kingmerut was a member of the Copper nation from Ellis River, Queen Maud's Sea, in the Eastern Arctic. His poems were recorded by Knud Rasmussen, who collected oral poetry in Canada and Greenland during the first decades of the 1900s.

  Selection Activities, p. 387

The Charge of the Light Brigade

Alfred, Lord Tennyson

Half a league, half a league,
Half a league onward,
All in the valley of Death
   Rode the six hundred.
"Forward, the Light Brigade!
Charge for the guns!" he said.
Into the valley of Death
   Rode the six hundred.

"Forward, the Light Brigade!"
Was there a man dismayed?
Not tho' the soldier knew
    Some one had blundered.
Theirs not to make reply,
Theirs not to reason why,
Theirs but to do and die.
Into the valley of Death
    Rode the six hundred.

Cannon to right of them,
Cannon to left of them,
Cannon in front of them
    Volleyed and thundered;
Stormed at with shot and shell,
Boldly they rode and well,
Into the jaws of Death,
Into the mouth of Hell
    Rode the six hundred.

Flashed all their sabres bare,
Flashed as they turned in air
Sabring the gunners there,
Charging an army, while
    All the world wondered.
Plunged in the battery-smoke
Right thro' the line they broke;
Cossack and Russian
Reeled from the sabre-stroke
    Shattered and sundered.
Then they rode back, but not,
    Not the six hundred.

Cannon to right of them,
Cannon to left of them,
Cannon behind them
    Volleyed and thundered;
Stormed at with shot and shell,
While horse and hero fell,
They that had fought so well
Came thro' the jaws of Death
Back from the mouth of Hell,
All that was left of them,
    Left of six hundred.

When can their glory fade?
O the wild charge they made!
    All the world wondered.
Honour the charge they made!
Honour the Light Brigade,
    Noble six hundred!

Alfred, Lord Tennyson (*Born 1809, Somersby, England; died 1892*) remains one of the most popular Victorian poets. His most ambitious work was *Idylls of the King*, a series of twelve narrative poems telling the legends of King Arthur and his knights. Tennyson succeeded William Wordsworth as poet laureate of Great Britain in 1850.

Without Hands

Lorna Crozier

*In memory of Victor Jara, the Chilean musician whose hands were smashed
by the military to stop him from playing his guitar and singing for his fellow
prisoners in the Santiago stadium. Along with thousands of others, he was
tortured and finally killed there in September 1973.*

All the machines in the world
stop. The textile machines, the paper machines,
the machines in the mines turning stones to fire.
Without hands to touch them, spoons, forks and knives
forget their names and uses, the baby is not bathed,
bread rises on the stove, overflows the bowl.
Without hands, the looms
stop, the music
          stops.
The plums turn sweet and sticky and gather flies.

Without hands
          without those beautiful conjunctions
those translators of skin, bone, hair
two eyes go blind
two pale hounds sniffing ahead and doubling back
to tell us
          of hot and cold or the silk of roses after rain
are lost
          two terns feeling the air in every feather
are shot down.

Without hands my father doesn't plant potatoes
row on row, build a house for wrens,
or carry me
from the car to bed
when I pretend I'm sleeping.
On wash-days my mother doesn't hang clothes
on the line, she doesn't turn the pages of a book
and read out loud,
or teach me how to lace my shoes.

Without hands my small grandmother
doesn't pluck the chicken for our Sunday meal
or every evening, before she goes to sleep,
brush and brush her long white hair.

Lorna Crozier (*Born 1948, Swift Current, Saskatchewan*) attended the University of Saskatchewan and the University of Alberta. Many of her poems are filled with images of the prairie landscape. Her work includes ten collections of poetry, and in 1992 she won the Governor General's Award for *Inventing the Hawk*.

Young

A thousand doors ago
when I was a lonely kid
in a big house with four
garages and it was summer
as long as I could remember,
I lay on the lawn at night
clover wrinkling under me,
my mother's window a funnel
of yellow heat running out,
my father's window, half shut,
an eye where sleepers pass,
and the boards of the house
were smooth and white as wax
and probably a million leaves
sailed on their strange stalks
as the crickets ticked together,
and I, in my brand new body,
which was not a woman's yet,
told the stars my questions
and thought God could really see
the heat and the painted light,
elbows, knees, dreams, goodnight.

Anne Sexton (*Born 1928, Newton, Massachusetts; died 1974*) focused much of her poetry on her personal experience with depression. Between 1960 and 1974, she published eight volumes of poems, winning many awards, including the Pulitzer Prize in 1967 for *Live or Die*. Several more collections of her work were published after her death.

Selection Activities, p. 388

In the Almost Evening

Joy Kogawa

In the almost evening loneliest time of day
I looked out the window and could see sky
and I said "Sky, what can you give me?"
and sky said, "I can give you sunset." So I
looked at sunset with moon and star
and said "Sunset, what can you give me?"
and sunset said, "We can give you skyline."
And I looked at skyline with bright lights
and I said "What can you give me" and
skyline said "We'll give you people" and
I said to people, "People, give me love."
And people said, "Too busy."
So in the almost evening loneliest time of day
I took to listening feverishly.

Joy Kogawa (*Born 1935, Vancouver, British Columbia*), poet and novelist, is best known for her 1981 novel *Obasan* about a Japanese-Canadian girl's experience of being sent to an internment camp during World War II. Kogawa published her first poetry collection, *The Splintered Moon*, in 1967.

Justice

Rita Joe

Justice seems to have many faces
It does not want to play if my skin is not the right hue,
Or correct the wrong we long for,
Action hanging off-balance
Justice is like an open field
We observe, but are afraid to approach.
We have been burned before
Hence the broken stride
And the lingering doubt
We often hide

Justice may want to play
If we have an open smile
And offer the hand of communication
To make it worthwhile

Justice has to make me see
Hear, feel.
Then I will know the truth is like a toy
To be enjoyed or broken

Rita Joe (*Born 1932, Cape Breton, Nova Scotia*), Mi'kmaq nation poet and author, spent her early life in foster homes and residential schools, an experience she explores in her work. In 1990 she received the Order of Canada, and in 1997 the National Aboriginal Achievement Award.

Three Strangest Words

Wislawa Szymborska

As I speak the word Future,
the first syllable is already entering the past.

As I speak the word Silence,
I destroy it.

As I speak the word Nothing,
I create something not contained in any nothingness.

Wislawa Szymborska (*Born 1923, Prowent-Bnin, Poland*) gained international attention in 1996 after receiving the Nobel Prize for Literature. Her first volume of poetry, *Dlatego Zyjemy (That's Why We Are Alive)*, appeared in 1952, and she has published more than a dozen collections since. Her work has been translated into many languages.

First Ice

Andrei Voznesensky

A girl freezes in a telephone booth.
In her draughty overcoat she hides
A face all smeared
In tears and lipstick.

She breathes on her thin palms.
Her fingers are icy. She wears earrings.

She'll have to go home alone, alone,
Along the icy street.

First ice. It is the first time.
The first ice of telephone phrases.

Frozen tears glitter on her cheeks—
The first ice of human hurt.

Andrei Voznesensky (*Born 1933, Moscow, U.S.S.R., now Russia*) is a poet who rose to international prominence in the 1960s, while under constant pressure from Soviet officials. Voznesensky is a member of International PEN and has served as the vice-president of the Russian branch.

Selection Activities, p. 389

Younger Sister, Going Swimming

Margaret Atwood

Beside this lake
where there are no other people

my sister in bathing suit continues
her short desolate
parade to the end of the dock:

against the boards
her feet make sad statements
she thinks no one can hear;

(I sit in a deckchair
not counting, invisible:
the sun wavers on
this page as on a pool.)

She moves the raft out
past the sandy point:
no one comes by in a motorboat.

She would like to fill the lake
with other swimmers, with answers.
She calls her name. The sun encloses
rocks, trees, her feet in the water, the circling
bays and hills as before.

She poises, raises her arms
as though signalling, then disappears.
The lake heals itself quietly
of the wound left by the diver.
The air quakes and is still.

(Under my hand the paper
closes over these
marks I am making on it.

The words ripple, subside,
move outwards toward the shore.)

Margaret Atwood (*Born 1939, Ottawa, Ontario*), poet, novelist, and critic, studied at the University of Toronto, Radcliffe College, and Harvard University. She has published many poetry collections, novels, plays, and works of nonfiction, and has received numerous awards, including the 1996 Giller Prize for her novel *Alias Grace*.

  Selection Activities, p. 390

Sonnet XXIX: When in disgrace ...

William Shakespeare

Detail from a lithograph by Eugene Delacroix, 1843

When in disgrace with Fortune and men's eyes
I all alone beweep my outcast state,
And trouble deaf heaven with my bootless cries,
And look upon myself and curse my fate,
Wishing me like to one more rich in hope,
Featur'd like him, like him with friends possess'd,
Desiring this man's art, and that man's scope,
With what I most enjoy contented least;
Yet in these thoughts myself almost despising,
Haply I think on thee, and then my state
(Like to the lark at break of day arising
From sullen earth) sings hymns at heaven's gate,
    For thy sweet love rememb'red such wealth brings,
    That then I scorn to change my state with kings.

William Shakespeare (*Born 1564, Stratford-upon-Avon, England; died 1616*), poet and playwright, is universally recognized as one of the greatest writers in the English language. He wrote most of his best-known plays during the 1590s and early 1600s, and published his sequence of 154 sonnets in 1609. Today his works are performed and studied all over the world.

Gurl

Mary Blalock

From Adam's rib
it's prophesied
I came,
but that's his story

I'm walking on my own
down these streets
with a stop sign on every corner,
takin' my time.
I've got no place to go 'cept forward.

Down these highways without a
road map,
down these sidewalks,
where the cracks want to
break my mother's back,
where the city is crowded.
I'm walking on my own.

I'm not on a Stairmaster,
and I won't wait for an elevator.
I'm taking the fire escape
to the top floor.

If I want to,
I'll walk all around the world,
taking the long way
or the shortcuts,
'cross countries and through
oceans.
I won't be swimming.
I'll walk
on my own.

Mary Blalock was a high school student in Portland, Oregon, when she wrote this
poem.

Warrior Woman

Maria Jastrzebska

Lying propped up
on a large cushion
in my woolly pink
dressing gown
is probably not
how you imagined her.

To be honest
I didn't either.
I rather fancied myself
dancing over hilltops
swirling swords in the air
all yells and flying kicks
or even leading
a mass protest rally
at least strutting my stuff
in trendy denim or leather
anything but like this.

Nevertheless
here I am
a warrior woman
in my pink dressing gown
dozing
or staring into space
watching the trees
through my window.

Imperceptibly
at first
ever so slowly
I am fighting back.

With every act of kindness
towards myself
every refusal
to blame
or despise myself
I strike back
against the men
in grey suits
who don't think
I'm cost effective
the ones in white coats
who don't even believe
I exist
all those too busy
or in too much of a hurry
to notice who I am.

From behind
my drooping eyelids
I am watching
with the stillness
of a lizard or snake.

I have learnt
the languor
and stealth
of a tiger
lying in wait
ready to pounce.

So next time
you come across
a woman like me
tired looking
in a pink dressing gown
just because
I'm lying low
don't imagine
I take anything
lying down.
Watch out
I have never been
as slow
or as deadly before.

Maria Jastrzebska (*Born 1953, Warsaw, Poland*), poet, author, and editor, is best known to English-speaking readers as the author of *Postcards from Poland*. She is also the co-editor of a Polish women's anthology.

Selection Activities, p. 391

Kidnap Poem

ever been kidnapped
by a poet
if i were a poet
i'd kidnap you

put you in my phrases
and meter you to jones beach
or maybe coney island
or maybe just to my house

lyric you in lilacs
dash you in the rain
alliterate the beach
to complement my sea

play the lyre for you
ode you with my love song
anything to win you
wrap you in the red Black green
show you off to mama

yeah if i were
a poet i'd kid
nap you

Nikki Giovanni (*Born 1943, Knoxville, Tennessee*), poet, writer, lecturer, and educator, is one of the most prominent poets to emerge from the Black literary movement of the 1960s. Giovanni is known for her strongly voiced poems that explore the struggles of Black women in America. She received the Langston Hughes Award in 1996.

And I Remember

Afua Cooper

And I remember
standing
in the churchyard on Wesleyan hill
standing and looking down on the plains
that stretched before me
like a wide green carpet
the plains full with sugar cane and rice
the plains that lead to the sea

And I remember
walking
as a little girl to school
on the savannas of Westmoreland
walking from our hillbound village
along steep hillsides
walking carefully so as not to trip and plunge
walking into the valley

And I remember
running
to school on the road that cuts into the green carpet
running past laughing waters
running past miles of sugar cane and paddies of rice
running to school that rose like a concrete castle
running with a golden Westmoreland breeze

And I remember
breathing
the smell of the earth plowed by rain and tractors
breathing the scent of freshly cut cane
breathing the scent of rice plants as they send
their roots into the soft mud

and I remember
thinking
this is mine   this is mine
this sweetness of mountains
valleys
rivers
and plains
is mine
mine
mine

Afua Cooper (*Born 1958, Jamaica*), now living in Toronto, Ontario, has published three collections of poetry. She has also recorded poems on the album *Womantalk*, and on several independent cassette releases. Co-author of *Essays in African-Canadian Women's History*, Cooper is pursuing a doctorate in history.

Selection Activities, p. 391

My Father

On the land where he was born
my father built his house.

Beside the roads he travelled
and under the mountains he climbed
the house stands singing
where dragonflies dwell
and bears eat crab apples.

My father always at table's head
beside windows watching
the sun and clouds
through green fields rush by.

All the sky long
among eagles and owls
and coyote's dreams borne on the dust
my father walks heaven's trail on snowshoes
made by his hands.

On the land where he was born
now cut by poles, roads and rail
the crab apples still grow sweet.

Russell Wallace, decended from the Lil'Wat Nation of British Columbia, has been active in Aboriginal media, including theatre and film, in the Vancouver area since 1982. He has composed and produced music and sound for *Hands of History* for the National Film Board.

*P*oint Scored

C. Cardenas Dwyer

up against the backboard ... almost ... lolling ... leaning ... looping

i

n

Charlotte Cardenas Dwyer, whose poetry has been anthologized for over two decades, frequently writes poetry with sports themes.

Peter Park

HISTORY

          Y

IS

I T

HIS

STORY

Peter Park (*Born 1972, Suwon, South Korea*) immigrated to Canada as a child in 1974. In his final year of high school he wrote the poem "History" for an English course. Park graduated from the University of Toronto in 1995 and now works as a computer programmer in Toronto.

Selection Activities, p. 392

Blues

bp Nichol

Barrie Phillip (bp) Nichol (*Born 1944, Vancouver, British Columbia; died 1988*) was a Canadian poet at the forefront of experimental poetry in the 1960s. In his prose, as well as his concrete and sound poetry, Nichol stretched the boundaries of writing. Long before his work became known in Canada, he was part of an international subculture of concrete poetry.

e.e. cummings

l(a

le

af

fa

ll

s)

one

l

iness

Edward Estlin Cummings (e.e. cummings) (*Born 1894, Cambridge, Massachusetts; died 1962*), poet, novelist, and playwright, was best known for his unconventional use of punctuation and capitalization, and his experimentation with typography. Some of his best known works are *The Enormous Room, The Balloon Man*, and *Fifty Poems*.

*L*ast Ride

Andrea Holtslander

We watch in horror as
the booster rockets twist
crazily through the sky
like balloons
whipped free
from a child's grasp.

The horror is the reality on the screen.

"On this day of tragedy … we watch in horror
as …"
       And for the benefit of those who
missed the live show
            we will run the
               fireworks once again.

   The spotlight moves to the grief-stricken
families and we can have our
                 heart-strings pulled
    with 20 million others
as we watch their
tears fall,
       LIVE.

Having wrung all the tears from his
audience the ringmaster can now turn to sports
            as seven families try to put
      together their lives
            scattered over the Atlantic
                Ocean.

Andrea Holtslander was a high school student in Saskatoon, Saskatchewan when she wrote this poem.

Selection Activities, p. 394

Perfect

Alanis Morissette

Sometimes is never quite enough
If you're flawless, then you'll win my love
Don't forget to win first place
Don't forget to keep that smile on your face

Be a good boy
Try a little harder
You've got to measure up
And make me prouder

How long before you screw it up
How many times do I have to tell you to hurry up
With everything I do for you
The least you can do is keep quiet

Be a good girl
You've gotta try a little harder
That simply wasn't good enough
To make us proud

I'll live through you
I'll make you what I never was
If you're the best, then maybe so am I
Compared to him compared to her
I'm doing this for your own damn good
You'll make up for what I blew
What's the problem ... why are you crying

Be a good boy
Push a little farther now
That wasn't fast enough
To make us happy
We'll love you just the way you are if you're perfect

Alanis Morissette (*Born 1974, Ottawa, Ontario*), songwriter, performer, and recording artist, appeared on a children's television show at the age of 10, and released her first album at the age of 16. Her subsequent release, *Jagged Little Pill*, became the top-selling album by a female artist. Her awards include six Junos and six Grammys.

Selection Activities, p. 394

The Songs of the Birds

Indian folk songs

What is that mournful song
The bird sings on the tree?
Is your heart heavy too?
Are you as sad as me?

The bird will find its mate
But I must suffer pain
I see you in my dreams
You're gone when I awake.

The breezes gently blow
The blossom is in bloom
The dancing butterfly
Sucks nectar from the flowers.

These sweet perfumes, this shining sun
These birdsongs fill the countryside
This day seems made for love.

The night has just arrived
A bird begins to sing
Her plaintive song reflects
The pain of being apart.

Within my heart I feel
Sad echoes of her song
I too lie here apart
Quite helpless and quite lost.

Northwest Passage

Stan Rogers

Chorus:
Ah, for just one time I would take the Northwest Passage
To find the hand of Franklin reaching for the Beaufort Sea;
Tracing one warm line through a land so wide and savage
And make a Northwest Passage to the sea.

Westward from the Davis Strait 'tis there 'twas said to lie
The sea route to the Orient for which so many died;
Seeking gold and glory, leaving weathered, broken bones
And a long-forgotten lonely cairn of stones.

Three centuries thereafter, I take passage overland
In the footsteps of brave Kelso, where his "sea of flowers" began
Watching cities rise before me, then behind me sink again
This tardiest explorer, driving hard across the plain.

And through the night, behind the wheel, the mileage clicking west
I think upon Mackenzie, David Thompson and the rest
Who cracked the mountain ramparts and did show a path for me
To race the roaring Fraser to the sea.

How then am I so different from the first men through this way?
Like them, I left a settled life, I threw it all away.
To seek a Northwest Passage at the call of many men
To find there but the road back home again.

Stan Rogers (*Born 1949, Hamilton, Ontario; died 1983*), songwriter, singer, and recording artist, spent his childhood summers in Nova Scotia. He made his first recording, a collection of songs about the Maritimes called *Fogarty's Cove*, in 1969. Like his later albums, it reflects and celebrates the lives of those who work on land or sea.

Selection Activities, p. 395

Vincent

Don McLean

Starry, starry night
Paint your palette blue and grey
Look out on a summer's day
With eyes that know the darkness in my soul.
Shadows on the hills
Sketch the trees and the daffodils
Catch the breeze and the winter chills
In colours on the snowy linen land.
Now I understand
What you tried to say to me
And how you suffered for your sanity
And how you tried to set them free:
They would not listen; they did not know how—
Perhaps they'll listen now.

Starry, starry night
Flaming flowers that brightly blaze
Swirling clouds in violet haze
Reflect in Vincent's eyes of china blue
Colours changing hue
Morning fields of amber grain
Weathered faces lined in pain
Are soothed beneath the artist's loving hand.

Now I understand
What you tried to say to me
And how you suffered for your sanity
And how you tried to set them free:
They would not listen; they did not know how—
Perhaps they'll listen now.

For they could not love you
But still, your love was true
And when no hope was left inside
On that starry, starry night
You took your life as lovers often do—
But I could've told you, Vincent:
This world was never meant
For one as beautiful as you.

Starry, starry night
Portraits hung in empty halls
Frameless heads on nameless walls
With eyes that watch the world and can't forget
Like the strangers that you've met
The ragged men in ragged clothes
The silver thorn, a bloody rose
Lie crushed and broken on the virgin snow.

Now I think I know
What you tried to say to me
And how you suffered for your sanity
And how you tried to set them free:
They would not listen; they're not listening still—
Perhaps they never will.

Don McLean (*Born 1945, New Rochelle, New York*), singer and songwriter, is best known for his 1971 ballad "American Pie". During the late 1960s and early 1970s, he was a well-known environmentalist who performed concerts to raise awareness of water pollution. McLean has more than a dozen gold records.

Selection Activities, p. 395

DRAMA

"People don't always understand that there is incredible theatricality and passion in everyday life."

– Judith Thompson

"Let the audience look to their eyes."

– William Shakespeare

Drama is literature meant to be performed for an audience. Traditionally, the most common form of drama has been the stage play presented in front of a live audience, but modern technology has expanded the range, as you'll see in the Media section. Drama shares many of the key elements of fiction. Like fiction, a play has a plot that is triggered by a conflict which the characters in the drama struggle with and try to resolve. In a dramatic work, these characters are known as the cast. Some modern plays are written for a single actor.

Drama uses dialogue to develop plot and reveal character. The characters' words reveal what they are like and what they are thinking. How other characters in the drama respond to these words reveals their personalities and thoughts, and pushes the action forward.

Dramatists provide settings for their works. These settings are enhanced by the set design, by the arrangement of scenery and props, and by lighting, music, and sound effects.

audience: those people who view, listen to, or read a dramatic work

plot: the pattern of events, or action, in a narrative or drama

character: a person portrayed in an artistic piece, such as a novel or a dramatic work

dialogue: conversation between characters in a drama or narrative

setting: the time, place, and circumstances in which a drama or narrative takes place

Drama

Treads

Bill Dempster

On June 5, 1989, a man stood in front of a line of tanks heading east on Beijing's Cangan Boulevard in Tiananmen Square. The man was calling for an end to violence against pro-democracy demonstrators.

CHARACTERS / cast

TANK COMMANDER
TANK DRIVER
TANK NAVIGATOR

TIME   setting = time / place
June 1989

SETTING
In a tank on a road to Tiananmen Square

NAVIGATOR: (*binoculars on advance area*) Five minutes to target area, sir.

DRIVER: Sir, there is someone in our way.

NAVIGATOR: It appears to be a revolutionary, sir.

COMMANDER: How far away is he?

NAVIGATOR: About half a click, sir.

COMMANDER: Straight ahead. Let him make the first move.

DRIVER: (*concerned*) He's very young, sir.

COMMANDER: Blasted student rebellion!

DRIVER: He's carrying his books.

NAVIGATOR: Probably has a Molotov cocktail behind his back!

DRIVER: No, sir, his hands are outstretched, pleading.

COMMANDER: Straight ahead! Bloody revolt. Run him over!

DRIVER: Sir?!

COMMANDER: Give me the binoculars. (*He grabs them from the* NAVIGATOR *and looks straight ahead. Silence. His eyes widen and his face turns pale.*) Halt procedures!

DRIVER: Sir, isn't that—

COMMANDER: Yes ... my son.

Bill Dempster (*Born 1974, Toronto, Ontario*) studied law at Queen's University and articled at a Toronto law firm. In 1999 he travelled to Thailand as part of a United Nations regional study. He wrote *Treads* while still in high school.

A One-Act True Story

David G. McLeod

CHARACTERS

ALLAN, a government employee, not First Nations
DAVID, a First Nations man
SECURITY GUARD

TIME
May 1993
SETTING
A federal government building in Winnipeg, Manitoba

ALLAN has invited his long-time friend DAVID to visit the office he works at. They enter the building together and join a small crowd of people waiting at the elevator doors.

ALLAN: I'm sure glad you were able to come down this weekend.
DAVID: It's sure worth it. I needed a break in a big way.
   (*The elevator door opens and all enter. A guard appears.*)
SECURITY GUARD: (*authoritative*) Where do you think you're going?
DAVID: (*look of confusion*)
ALLAN: You mean him?
SECURITY GUARD: Is he with you?
ALLAN: Yeah, he's with me.
SECURITY GUARD: Okay, then go ahead.

Curtain

I felt stunned, humiliated. These kinds of acts I can live without.

David G. McLeod, playwright, lives in Thompson, Manitoba. His heritage is Métis, a combination of Saulteaux, French, and Scottish.

 Selection Activities, p. 396

Whale Watch

Colleen Curran

CHARACTERS

TED, a newspaper photographer
MAURA, an environmental activist

SETTING
Inside the stomach of a whale

Darkness. The sounds of the ocean, then of whale song. Lights come up to reveal what appears to be a cave with ribs. It is half-filled with water and two people, a woman and a man, are bobbing in small outboard motorboats side by side. It is pitch dark and they cannot see each other.

MAURA: (*calling*) Hellllllllooooooo? Is anybody in here with me?
   (*She searches through her army pants pockets.*)
   Ohhhh, I hope I brought it. I did. I did.
   (*She pulls out a flashlight.*)
   Please let it work.
   (*It does. She uses it to get a better view of her surroundings until it illuminates the man in the next boat.*)
   Ohh. Hi. Have you been there the whole time?
TED: Yes.
MAURA: Why didn't you say anything?
TED: I recognized your voice.
MAURA: You did?
TED: And I thought: all this and her, too.
MAURA: How come you know my voice?
TED: Because it carries so much over your bullhorn. I was also at your rally.
MAURA: (*smiles*) Yeah? You were?
TED: By assignment, not association.
   (*He shows her his camera case.*)
MAURA: Did you get any good pictures?
TED: It doesn't matter now.

MAURA: Yes it does. You must have gotten some great stuff.

TED: My last one was of the bull whale opening his mouth.

MAURA: That'll win you a few awards.

TED: If I can beam it out by satellite. We are not getting out of this one.

MAURA: We are so. Lots of people know where we are.

TED: So will the rest of the world pretty soon.

MAURA: Yes. So somebody will rescue us pretty soon.

TED: How are they going to find us?

MAURA: There aren't that many sperm whales left in the world. He'll have to surface for air.

TED: Then what? Is somebody from Sea World gonna coax him into giving us up peacefully?

MAURA: Maybe. If they found the *Titanic*, they can find us.

TED: That only took seventy-three years. And it stayed in one place.

MAURA: They've probably called out the navy. The subs. Scuba divers.

TED: I'm sure they'll want to conduct a million-dollar search and rescue for a woman whose friends spend their free weekends dodging harpoons and sabotaging ships. They'd love to save a bunch of rich, old hippies whose hobby is environmental terrorism.

MAURA: Who are you calling terrorists? What about those butchers out there? They don't care that these animals are protected by international agreements. They don't care about quotas or size limits or extinction. All they care about is harvesting the most incredible creatures on this planet for fertilizer and cosmetics and animal feed!

TED: Save it, sweetheart. I heard it all back on shore.

MAURA: How can you not care?

TED: The only thing I care about is the fact that I am someplace nobody will ever find me. I'm not in a landslide or a cave-in or lost in space even.

MAURA: They will find us. (*smiles*) Pinocchio found Gepetto.

TED: Pinocchio?

MAURA: Somebody will find us. Stop complaining and being so sarcastic. We're lucky we're still alive and in one piece.

TED: Oh we're real lucky. Moby Dick spared us this time.

MAURA: Don't drag Moby Dick into this. He's the cause of whale hate and distrust in the world. They're friendly mammals.

TED: Our guy was super friendly. He tried to eat the whaling ship.

MAURA: After it attacked his friends.

TED: Then he swallowed us. And probably broke my finger.

MAURA: It's bleeding.

TED: A bit.

MAURA: (*She takes a small first-aid kit from her pants.*) Let me fix it.

TED: What's the point?

MAURA: Don't get pessimistic with me. You've got more reason to get out of this than I do.

TED: Why's that?

MAURA: (*She bandages his hand.*) Think of the photo opportunities in here. You'll get a *National Geographic* cover out of this.

TED: How can you be so up? So cheery?

MAURA: I'm not going to let myself get depressed about this.

TED: How do you plan to manage that? Large doses of Seconal?

MAURA: I look on the bright side. I did what I set out to do. What happened to me probably stopped the whale hunt. And the one we're inside of, got away. (*pause*) I think your finger might be broken.

TED: So what? How long is your flashlight good for?

MAURA: Hours. It has those last-and-last batteries.

(*TED takes out a package of cigarettes.*)

TED: Want one?

MAURA: No! And neither do you.

TED: Don't start telling me they're bad for my health.

MAURA: They're bad for his.

(*She points to whale.*)

TED: I'd have to smoke sixteen cartons a day for three years.

MAURA: This isn't a bus or an airplane or an elevator. This is a living organism.

TED: So is this.

(*TED takes out his Bic lighter, lights it, and MAURA flicks the cigarette out of his mouth into the water. He stares at her, calmly takes out another cigarette, and this time MAURA tosses the entire package in the water.*)

That was deliberate. The first time could have been a mistake.

MAURA: It wasn't.

TED: You animal rights activists make me sick. What about human rights? You Greenpeacers and Save the Whales and Sea Shepherds, you're all nuts. Fanatics. Maniacs. Know what I did to one of your kind last winter? A big blizzard and one of your Greenpeaceniks is at my door canvassing to Save the Seals. Know what I did? I slammed the door in his face. That's what I did!

MAURA: Are you finished?

TED: No! When we get out of here, I'm going to sue you.

MAURA: I'm glad my act inspired hope.

TED: Do sperm whales beach themselves?

MAURA: They'd need a very large beach.

TED: My luck this type doesn't go in for mass suicide. Come on, please, be the exception.

MAURA: Then it would die.

TED: But we'd have a chance of getting out alive.

MAURA: At what cost?

TED: At what cost! I'm right. You *are* crazy.

MAURA: You're probably hoping the hunters catch him.

TED: Yes! I don't know why. I have this weird life wish. It's our only hope unless you think he's gonna spit us out like Ol' Noah when he feels like it.

MAURA: Like who?

TED: Noah.

MAURA: Noah had the ark. Jonah was swallowed by the whale. Don't you know that?

TED: Sure, sure. Look, I made a mistake.

MAURA: It's a pretty big mistake. Jonah and Noah were pretty different people.

TED: Gabriel blew his horn and Daniel was in the lion's den. Satisfied?

MAURA: Who cut off Samson's hair?

TED: Leave the Bible quiz for somebody else, okay?

MAURA: You know, this is rather biblical.
(*pause*)

TED: Yeah, hell gets mentioned quite a bit in the Bible.

MAURA: (*pause*) Do you think we might be dead?

TED: Oh, that makes me feel real good.

MAURA: This sure is impossible. And quite fantastic. Maybe we're in some celestial waiting station. Maybe we are dead.

TED: Not if I'm still hungry.
(*She hands him some cookies still in their wrapper.*)

MAURA: Here.

TED: You wouldn't have a walkie-talkie in there, would you?

MAURA: Sorry. (*She takes articles out of her pants.*) Compass. Penknife—Swiss Army.

TED: Of course.

MAURA: With can-opener attachment. Beans. My Jacques Cousteau book. Needle and thread.

TED: How come you're so well prepared? You a Girl Guide? (*He laughs.*)

MAURA: A Brown Owl.

TED: Brown Owl?

MAURA: I'm the leader of Troop 144. Every Tuesday night at six-thirty. They're the nicest little girls. What a great, open age. They recycled newspapers so they could adopt a whale.

TED: Why are you a Brown Owl?

MAURA: It's something to do. Something I enjoy.

TED: Any of the Brownies yours?

MAURA: No.

TED: I've got two girls. They might be Brownies.

MAURA: You don't know?

TED: They live with their mother. You're sure a surprise. I didn't think your kind did things for people.

MAURA: What's that supposed to mean?

TED: You're so busy crying out for animals you forget about people.

MAURA: Is that true?

TED: The Brownies are probably a cover. I'll bet you have lots of stuffed animals and calendars with cats on them.

MAURA: No. Whales.

TED: Of course. And you probably work in a pet store.

MAURA: A hospital.

TED: Aha. An animal hospital.

MAURA: A people hospital. I'm a nurse.

TED: Oh, okay so I'm wrong, you do care about people.

MAURA: Do you?

TED: I guess so. When I have to. (*The flashlight goes out.*)

MAURA: Oh no.

TED: You said it was good for hours and hours.

MAURA: Yes. They're the batteries in the toy that out-drums all the other toys.

TED: How long have they been in there?

MAURA: Three ... or four years.

TED: You're supposed to take batteries out when you're not using them.

MAURA: Ohhhhh. I hate this.

TED: (*He uses his lighter for some light.*) Lucky for you I have filthy habits.

MAURA: Oh thank goodness. I hate total darkness. I was in a cave tour once and when the guide had us at the very end of it he said, "We are now two kilometres from the mouth of the cave. Above us rises two-and-a-half kilometres of mountain and rock." And then he turned off the lights and said, "This is total darkness. Your eyes will never adjust, it will always be this pitch black. Imagine if I left you here." And then he didn't talk anymore. Finally somebody said, *"Please the lights, the lights!"*

TED: Was that somebody you?

MAURA: I don't remember.

TED: Scared of the dark, eh?

MAURA: *Yes!*

TED: It doesn't bother me that much.

MAURA: That's why you flicked your Bic so quick.

TED: Okay, okay, so I don't like the dark either. It doesn't cast much light, does it?

MAURA: It casts something. (*sings*) "This little Brownie light of mine, I'm gonna let it shine."

TED: *Please.*

MAURA: It makes me feel better.

TED: It doesn't help me. I don't know it. I can't sing along.

MAURA: I'll teach it to you.

TED: No. It's too little girlie for me.

MAURA: How about this one? It's a spiritual. Now you sing: *Who did? Who did?* Everytime I sing: *Who did swallow Jonah?* Ready, everybody. Here we go. *Who did swallow Jonah, Jonah, who did swallow Jonah, Jonah.* You're not singing.

TED: I know.

MAURA: (*sings*) *Swallow Jonah, Jonah, who did swallow Jonah uuuuuupppppp!*

TED: Did you have to pick that song?

MAURA: It's simple to learn.

TED: Little too close to home, don't you think?

MAURA: It came to mind, that's all.

TED: It must be one of your Greenpeace ditties.

MAURA: Yes. We sing it on bus trips. It's kind of our ninety-nine-bottles-of-beer-on-the-wall song. We keep changing the species of whale for the second verse. We'll go, "Whale did, whale did" then, "beluga did, beluga did" and, "humpback did, humpback did" and—

TED: I get the picture. It makes it an even stupider song. And I won't sing it.

(*His Bic goes out.*)

MAURA: Oh no oh no.

TED: You got any matches in those Israeli army pants?

MAURA: Yes. But they got wet.

TED: This is it then?

MAURA: Yesss.

TED: It's so dark.

MAURA: So dark.

(*Pause. Then TED sings*)

TED: *Who did? Who did? Who did swallow Noah, Noah.*

MAURA: *Jonah, Jonah.*

TED: (*still singing*) *Whoever you say, just keep singing. Who did? Who did?*

MAURA: *Who did swallow Jonah, Jonah?*

TED: *Who did, who did ...*

MAURA: *Who did swallow Jonah, Jonah?*

TED: *Who did, who did ...*

(*As they sing on in the darkness the whale joins in their song. The end.*)

Colleen Curran (Born in Montreal, Quebec) worked as a radio copywriter, school teacher, magazine writer, and researcher before becoming a playwright. She was playwright-in-residence at the Centaur Theatre in Montreal from 1984 to 1985. Her forte is comedy writing, and her work has been produced across Canada and in the United States. *Whale Watch* was published in 1994.

The Odyssey

adapted from Homer

This painting, on a vase dated about 450 B.C., shows Penelope with her son Telemachus. In the background is her loom with the unfinished cloth.

CHARACTERS

PALLAS ATHENA, goddess of wisdom and warfare
ODYSSEUS, hero of the Trojan war
PENELOPE, wife of Odysseus
TELEMACHUS, son of Odysseus
KTESSIPOS, EURYMACHUS, LEODES, ANTINOUS, Penelope's suitors
OLD MAN
EURYLOCHUS, PEREMIDES, PERITES, POLITES, HYLAX, sailors
CYCLOPS, a one-eyed giant, son of the sea god Poseidon
POSEIDON, god of the sea
KING AEOLUS, keeper of the winds
CIRCE, a sorceress
HERMES, messenger of the gods
ANTICLEA, mother of Odysseus
TEIRESIAS, a blind prophet
APOLLO, the sun god
ZEUS, king of the gods
SIRENS, sea nymphs, whose singing lured sailors to their deaths
Attendants
Dead souls

Long ago

SETTING
Ancient Greece

A loud steady bass drumbeat accompanies a parade of the masks of
HERMES, POSEIDON, ZEUS, APOLLO, *and* ATHENA *across the stage. All the*
masks except that of ATHENA *exit.* ATHENA *enters, introduced with music.*
One actor supports her mask behind her, then hangs it on the back wall.
After each god appears in the play, his mask, too, is hung on the back wall,
so that the gods appear to watch the proceedings.

PALLAS ATHENA: I, Pallas Athena, speak of Odysseus
    Whom the whole world knows
    Because of his famous journey.
    (*Each character or group of characters, except* ZEUS, *enters when*
    mentioned by ATHENA, *forming a tableau.*)
    I tell the story of resplendent Penelope   (*tinkle*)
    And of the many young suitors   (*clacker*)
    Who demand that she marry.

    I tell the story of wandering Odysseus   (*three wood bells*)
    Whom Father Zeus calls the cleverest man alive.

    Ten years of war against the mighty Trojans
    Nine years of wandering and captivity
    Even to the point of despair
    Until I, Pallas Athena, lead him home.
    Home to Ithaca, to his wife Penelope,
    to his son Telemachus   (*wood bells*)
    to wreak vengeance on the spoilers.   (*wood bells*)
    (*Exit* ODYSSEUS.)

    Even now, I go there myself, disguised
    As an old poet, singing my songs and begging food,
    While Odysseus struggles in vain
    to sail back to his home.
    (*Exit* PALLAS ATHENA.)

(*laughter as the tableau activates*)

KTESSIPOS: More wine! I die of thirst. Would you like some wine, Eurymachus?

EURYMACHUS: You die of drink, not thirst, Ktessipos.

KTESSIPOS: I die of waiting for the lady to make up her mind which of us she will marry.

LEODES: Fair Penelope, we know this weaving is only a trick to put us off.

PENELOPE: Young princes, I tell you again, I cannot think of marriage until I have finished this winding sheet for my husband's father. He is very old and near death.

EURYMACHUS: You do not fool us anymore. We have discovered that while you weave cloth by day, you unravel it by night.

ALL: Yes!

ANTINOUS: It is only a way to avoid choosing one of us to be your husband.

PENELOPE: I see.

ALL: Choose!

(*The suitors all press around* PENELOPE *at the loom as* OLD MAN *enters, masked.*)

OLD MAN: Peace! To all travellers in this land.

PENELOPE: Telemachus, take this cup and give it to the stranger who now enters our door. Tell him not to be shy, for he may freely beg from these suitors.

TELEMACHUS: Old stranger.

OLD MAN: May Lord Zeus make you a happy man.

TELEMACHUS: You are welcome here. My mother makes you this gift: go round and beg at your pleasure.

ANTINOUS: Penelope, may I ask why you let this old beggar in to pester us?

PENELOPE: Zeus forbid that we should not welcome a stranger to our house.

KTESSIPOS: He stinks so he will ruin my exquisite sense of taste!

ANTINOUS: Telemachus, don't you already have enough guests eating up your father's wealth?

TELEMACHUS: I appreciate your fatherly concern, Antinous, but he is welcome here. Give him something yourself.

OLD MAN: A small coin, sir; you look to be a king and can afford a generous gift. There was a time when I, too, was lucky, and rich, lived in a house, had many servants, and went ...

ANTINOUS: What god has inflicted this talking plague upon us, to spoil our dinner. Stand off, you leech!

(ANTINOUS *kicks him away.*)

OLD MAN: Ah ... I was wrong about you. You eat freely from another man's table and yet you will not give even a crust to a beggar!

EURYMACHUS: Watch your tongue, Old Man, and get out of here. Next time I will drag you out of here by the leg. Ha!

(EURYMACHUS *grabs the* OLD MAN's *arm and flings him out.*)

TELEMACHUS: Gentlemen! This is not a public inn, but Odysseus' palace. Though I am young, I know right from wrong ... You are many and strong, and so I must ... but if ...

(SUITORS *threaten* TELEMACHUS.)

KTESSIPOS: My friends, my friends! Let us not bully Telemachus. I feel that he speaks prudent ... prudent ... hic ... URRRRP!

(*Suitors laugh.*)

LEODES: Then I shall speak prudently, and to fairest Penelope.

PENELOPE: Speak, Leodes, I shall listen.

LEODES: As long as there was any hope that your husband would return, none of us could blame you for waiting.

EURYMACHUS: Daughter of Icarus, the time for waiting is over. Odysseus is gone forever. All the men in Argos will fill this house, for in beauty there is no one to match you.

PENELOPE: Alas, all beauty that I had was destroyed when Odysseus embarked for Troy. Now I am alone and my house cursed with strangers.

ANTINOUS: Madam, your husband has been gone for nineteen years. Some wave has washed him into the sea. He is either dead or lost forever. Therefore, you must pick the best, most generous of your suitors, marry him, and go live in his house. Then Telemachus can enjoy his natural inheritance.

KTESSIPOS: It is the custom, fair Penelope.

PENELOPE: The custom? None of you observe the custom! Surely it is the oldest of customs for suitors to entertain the lady, bring her gifts, not carouse at her expense.

ANTINOUS: You speak true. That is our custom, but we shall not leave your palace until you agree to choose a husband.

SUITORS: Aye ... Aye .,. We shall not ... (*etc.*)

PENELOPE: I see. Very well, you have driven me to this moment. Antinous, we must both observe the custom. If all the suitors will bring their traditional matrimonial gifts to the palace, I shall select one to be my husband. Will you accept my choice?

ANTINOUS: I will! Do you all agree with the lady?

SUITORS: We do! Come ... a fine proposal ... (*etc.*)

(*Suitors exit, ANTINOUS last, bowing graciously to PENELOPE and nodding to TELEMACHUS.*)

PENELOPE: If I had my way, there's not a man among them who would see tomorrow's dawn.

TELEMACHUS: I hate them all ... especially Antinous, who is the most treacherous.

PENELOPE: May Apollo strike him, even as he did that old man. Go, my good son, ask the old man to come here that I may greet him and ask if he has any news of Odysseus.

(*TELEMACHUS exits.*)

Unless my husband returns soon and purges our house of these terrible men, I must bid farewell to it forever, although in my dreams I shall never forget it.

(*TELEMACHUS enters with Old Man.*)

TELEMACHUS: And so, if you speak the truth, she will give you a warm cloak to protect you from the cold.

OLD MAN: Royal madam.

PENELOPE: Peace, old man! Where is your home? Have you any news of Odysseus?

OLD MAN: I have, fair Queen. I am from the land in the dark blue sea called Crete, a mighty island. My grandfather, King Minos, once reigned there, and long ago, nine years ago, Odysseus himself touched our shores. It happened thus.

(*Seven notes sound as PENELOPE and TELEMACHUS exit. ODYSSEUS and his men, EURYLOCHUS, PEREMIDES, PERITES, POLITES AND HYLAX, push the prow of a ship on stage, set a mast, and kneel with their oars in a ready position, with ODYSSEUS at the helm. The sailors are wearing cloaks with cowls.*)

After the burning of Troy, all the finest Greeks set sail for their homes, carrying their rich booty. All reached their homes safely, except Odysseus. A mighty gale blew his ship off its course to my island Crete.

I took him to my home and made him welcome for thirteen days, until the winds fell and he bade us thanks and farewell. (*ODYSSEUS waves goodbye to the OLD MAN, a bass drumbeat begins, and the men start to row.*)

And so he left my country, his sailors raising their sails and pulling their oars. I have heard that he sailed into unknown seas, even to the land of the giant Cyclops. (*OLD MAN exits. Rowing stops, the ship lands, and ODYSSEUS leaps to the shore.*)

ODYSSEUS: Good sailors, we must go onto this shore. Make fast the ship. (*Ship prow and mast are pushed aside.*) Well, we shall soon see whether these Cyclops are lawless savages, or a god-fearing people who are bound by Zeus' laws. (*The sailors step ashore and begin exploring the island, accompanied by jungle sounds.*)

EURYLOCHUS: Although I am no coward, I have a foreboding about this place.

PEREMIDES: Watch carefully then. Be ready.

PERITES: Look!

EURYLOCHUS: Where?

PERITES: Here, a cave. And look at the size of the opening.

PEREMIDES: Why, it's large enough for a giant.

POLITES: He's a shepherd. Look at all these lamb and goat pens.

ODYSSEUS: Come, let's go in the cave and see. (*They mime entering and exploring the cave.*)

POLITES: Oh, look, cheese! Goat cheese!

PERITES: Polites, I have never seen a wedge of cheese as large as this.

(*sheep bells*)

PEREMIDES: What's that? (*sheep sounds*)

ODYSSEUS: Quiet. The shepherd is coming back. He may be friendly but we'd better be careful. Let's hide. (*While the men hide, the CYCLOPS enters, herding his sheep into the cave and rolling a big stone across the opening. He is gigantic and wears a mask with only one eye in the centre of his forehead.*)

CYCLOPS: In goats ... in rams, in sheep for the night ... there, in sheep. Now I roll the big stone in front of the mouth of the cave so you can sleep safely until the morning. There ... over there, big ram, sheep. Wait! Who else is here? Strangers? And who may you be?

ODYSSEUS: We are Greeks. A contrary wind has driven us to your island.

CYCLOPS: Are you not roving pirates come to rob me of my sheep?

ODYSSEUS: No. We are Greek soldiers returning home from our great victory over Troy. We hope for hospitality from you, remembering Zeus' great edict binding all to give hospitality to travellers.

CYCLOPS: Ha, ha, ha! Strangers, you are either fools, or have come very far afield. We Cyclops care not a jot for Zeus' law nor any of the gods. But, tell me where you have moored your ships.

EURYLOCHUS: (*whispering*) Captain, he is trying to trick us.

ODYSSEUS: Softly ... I know. Cyclops—

CYCLOPS: My name is Polyphemus.

ODYSSEUS: Polyphemus, our ship is wrecked upon your shore. We desperately need food.

CYCLOPS: So do I! I am hungry too, so I think I shall eat you, pirate sailor! (*POLYPHEMUS reaches out and grabs POLITES by the neck.*)

PEREMIDES: Look out! He's got Polites!

ODYSSEUS AND EURYLOCHUS: Help us!

(*Several sailors combine to pull POLITES away from the strong CYCLOPS. This leads to a chase accompanied by drums, clackers, and other noises. Eventually the CYCLOPS catches POLITES. The Sailors rush the CYCLOPS. During the struggle, POLITES puts his cloth cowl partially in the CYCLOPS' mouth. With a mighty movement, the CYCLOPS throws the sailors to the side of the stage. The actor playing POLITES goes with them and exits unnoticed. The CYCLOPS puts his hand to mouth as he goes upstage to sit and eat POLITES.*)

EURYLOCHUS: He's eating him! He is eating him! We must kill him before he eats us all.

PERITES: I'll stab him with my sword.

EURYLOCHUS: No, wait. Let's all rush him together. Ready? Now.

ODYSSEUS: Hold, hold fast. If we kill him now, we may be trapped inside this cave forever. That is a heavy stone across the door. Eurylochus, men, come help me try to move it. (*They mime trying to move the great stone, even using an oar as a lever, but they cannot budge it.)*

EURYLOCHUS: It's no use. We can't move it, and he is not likely to move it for us. I would rather die killing this monster than be eaten.

ODYSSEUS: Maybe he would do it for us! I have a plan. Give me that wineskin.

(*ODYSSEUS takes wineskin and goes to the CYCLOPS.*)

Cyclops! Polyphemus, here, have some Greek wine to wash down your meal of human flesh. Come, take it in your hands. It will be the finest wine you ever tasted.

(*He places the wineskin between the two hands of the CYCLOPS, who drinks the wine.*)

CYCLOPS: Hmmm. Ahh. This wine is delicious. A pleasure to drink ... Tell me your name, sailor, and I will reward you for giving me this good wine, it tastes like nectar and ambrosia. What is your name?

ODYSSEUS: My name is "Nobody."

CYCLOPS: (*little tipsy now*) Whatsch that?

ODYSSEUS: "Nobody." That is the name my father gave me: "Nobody."

CYCLOPS: (*yawning now*) Ahhhhh ... Well, then, Nobody, your reward shall be this: I shall eat you last. Ahhhh ... Eat all the others first. I am getting schleeepy from this good wine ... so very schleepy ...

(*Now drunk, the CYCLOPS sits down and sleeps as his eye closes.*)

ODYSSEUS: Success. The wine's made him sleepy. Peremides, take that staff. Perites, sharpen it with your sword. Now put it in that fire to harden it. Good, now lift it up and aim for his eye. Now drive it home. Take that, you cannibal!

(*The sailors mime the action described by ODYSSEUS, using an oar for the staff, a red cloth for the fire. Then they take the staff and start toward the sleeping CYCLOPS. He almost wakes but then mumbles and lays his head on his other hand. The sailors guide the staff to the eye and, with a big push, force the eye into the mask, leaving only the eyehole showing. They scramble to one side as the CYCLOPS roars and stands up.*)

CYCLOPS: Help, neighbours! Cyclops, neighbour Cyclops! I am being attacked!

VOICES: (*off-stage*) Who is attacking you, Polyphemus?

CYCLOPS: Nobody!

VOICES: If nobody is attacking you, you must be dreaming. Leave us alone. We must drive our sheep out to pasture. It is morning already. (*sheep noises and bells*)

CYCLOPS: Oh ... Oh ... it is morning already. I must let my sheep out to graze. I must roll away this big stone. Out, sheep!

(*The CYCLOPS rolls the stone aside and ODYSSEUS' men try to sneak out. But the CYCLOPS blocks the entrance with his hands, and mimes feeling the backs of his sheep as they pass through the opening. Enter the OLD MAN.*)

But I must not let those men escape.

OLD MAN: And he passed his hand over the back of each sheep as it went through to make sure that none of Odysseus' men escaped. But clever Odysseus tied his men to the bellies of the largest sheep, and he himself clung to the belly of the largest ram.

(*ODYSSEUS puts a sheepskin on the back of each of his men, who crawl past the CYCLOPS as he feels the wool on their backs. ODYSSEUS is the last to start crawling out, but the CYCLOPS stops him.*)

CYCLOPS: Ho! Big Ram, why are you last? You who never lagged before, are you grieved for your master's eye, blinded by these wicked men?

(*The CYCLOPS lets ODYSSEUS through. Meanwhile the men have reassembled at the ship so that when ODYSSEUS escapes, they are ready to sail away.*)

ODYSSEUS: Cyclops!

CYCLOPS: They have escaped.

ODYSSEUS: We men are not as weak as you thought. For your great crime of eating your guests, Zeus has punished you! If anyone should ask, tell them Odysseus of Ithaca put out your eye.

OLD MAN: So angry was the Cyclops that he seized a mountaintop and hurled it at Odysseus' ship.

PEREMIDES: Look out!

OLD MAN: It fell right in front of the ship and almost drove it back to shore.

(*The CYCLOPS mimes throwing a huge stone that goes over the top of the boat and lands just ahead, almost swamping it.*)

(*whistle, drum, cymbals*)

CYCLOPS: Father Poseidon, Father Poseidon, if I am your son, grant that Odysseus never reaches his home in Ithaca.

POSEIDON: (*entering*) I hear your prayer, my son. I will never let this impudent Odysseus go unpunished. Rise, great sea, buffet them, toss them about. They shall not escape my vengeance.

(storm noises)

(*A storm rises and rocks the ship mightily as* POSEIDON *and the* CYCLOPS *exit.*)

OLD MAN: And the seas raged. Poseidon's mighty waves tossed Odysseus' ship to and fro, almost drowning the sailors. At last the sea began to calm and Odysseus cried out.

ODYSSEUS: Landfall! At last some relief from these angry seas.

(Storm noises fade)

(*He leaps ashore and finds it spongy, like walking on rubber.*)
What's this? This island is floating on the water! Now I know where we are. This is the floating island of King Aeolus who is the keeper of all the winds. These wild winds have blown us here to their master. And he can tame them.

(KING AEOLUS *and two* ATTENDANTS *enter, singing to an airy tune played on a recorder. He is masked and the* ATTENDANTS *each carry a flag made of many coloured ribbons which flutter in the wind when they are moved.*)

KING AEOLUS: Clever Odysseus, your black-prowed ship survived Poseidon's rough sea. You are welcome here with me and my children. Come, tell us of your adventures. We long to hear them.

OLD MAN: And Odysseus stayed with his kind host for a month, and he told him of the Greeks' great victory over the walled city of Troy, and all things else that had transpired.

(ODYSSEUS *mimes the battles of Troy.*)

KING AEOLUS: What exciting news, Odysseus. Now, in recompense, what may we do for you?

ODYSSEUS: King Aeolus, my men and I have been away from our homes in Ithaca these nineteen years and more. Despite all we have suffered, the winds and the seas thwart our return. Can you help us?

KING AEOLUS: I can. I will. Come with me. Here, take this large pouch. In it I have imprisoned all the rough winds and gales so they cannot bother you any more. Keep this strong cord tightly around the pouch because these winds are so powerful they could blow your ship apart.

(KING AEOLUS *gives* ODYSSEUS *a large round bag, which seems to float in the air. It is tied with a cord.* ODYSSEUS *stows it on his ship and waves goodbye.*)

Farewell now. To drive you safely home, here is a gentle west wind.

(KING AEOLUS *opens a small bag and one of the* ATTENDANTS *imitates a gentle wind with her flag, taking the wind so it strikes* ODYSSEUS' *sails gently and he sails away.* KING *and* ATTENDANT *fade to side of the stage.*)

OLD MAN: King Aeolus' west wind blew them kindly on the seas, toward Ithaca. Along the way they stopped at many ports, where Odysseus was welcomed, as became his reputation, and he was given many costly gifts. (ODYSSEUS *mimes greeting people at various ports and then lies down to rest and sleep.*) In a short time, the ship hove in sight of land. (HYLAX *rushes to prow and stares ahead.*)

HYLAX: Land ahead! Ithaca!

PERITES: Is it?

HYLAX: Rocky Ithaca! We're home! We're home!

(*They dance for joy.*)

HYLAX: I'll wake Odysseus.

EURYLOCHUS: No, don't wake him yet. It will be at least an hour before we reach shore.

HYLAX: I can't wait.

EURYLOCHUS: Then start bringing our cargo on deck.

PERITES: Well, this is the biggest pouch.

(*He has the large bag* KING AEOLUS *gave them.*)

PEREMIDES: Wherever we go they always gave him costly treasures, but they never gave anything to us. We ought to have a share in all these treasures.

HYLAX: If we want any of this we had better take it for ourselves— and now!

(*They all open the sack, which begins to tremble and make an increasingly loud humming sound until it whirls them all about, waking* ODYSSEUS. *They are in a terrible storm, all clinging to the mast, which almost blows over. At the same time,* KING AEOLUS *and the* ATTENDANT *each take up a larger flag of ribbons that they use to lash the sailors and the ship. They exit as the storm subsides.)*

OLD MAN: Out blew all those terrible, wild winds, raging into a mad tempest, driving them farther and farther away from Ithaca. Six days, six nights! Driving them into seas unknown, even to the strange enchanted Island of Aeaea, home of the strange goddess, Circe.

ODYSSEUS: Hear my words, men. We are fortunate to escape from those winds but they have blown us I know not where. We are lost. I cannot even tell which is east and which is west.

EURYLOCHUS: Well, the land may look inviting but ...

ODYSSEUS: Look! There's smoke rising from that dense wood. There must be inhabitants here. Maybe they can help us.

PEREMIDES: They might be Cyclops, too. Maybe they could eat us!

ODYSSEUS: Peremides, we have no choice. We must divide into two groups, one to explore that dense wood and seek help, the other to secure the beach.

PEREMIDES: Oh, great Odysseus, let us take our chances on the sea with Poseidon.

ODYSSEUS: Which way would we sail? We are lost and would soon starve to death at sea. Come now, bravely. Half with Eurylochus, and half with me. Draw, Eurylochus, to see which group must explore and which guard the beach. (ODYSSEUS *holds straws for* EURYLOCHUS *to draw, who loses.*) Come Perites, we'll go this way.

PERITES: Peremides, good luck.

(ODYSSEUS *exits with* PERITES.)

(PEREMIDES, EURYLOCHUS, *and* HYLAX *start to explore with drawn swords. Strange music begins, like the rustling of the wind in the trees, reflecting the enchantment of the island and the spirits there.)*

(tinkle and small drum sounds)

PEREMIDES: Why am I the one who always has to go on these expeditions?

(*Wind voices off-stage echo and fade "Aeaeaeae ..."*)

EURYLOCHUS: Quiet, listen ...

HYLAX: It's only the leaves rustling.

WINDS: (*off-stage voices*) Beware ... Beware ...

EURYLOCHUS: I hear words! It is as if the wind is speaking ...

HYLAX: No, the whole forest is quiet as death. Ooooh, why did I have to mention death?

WINDS: (*echoing*) Death ... Death ... Death ...

PEREMIDES: Oh, there! What do I see?

WINDS: See, see, see.

HYLAX: Ah! A huge wolf came right at me!

PEREMIDES: Ah! Lions! Oh, help us Athena, goddess with the bright eyes.

HYLAX: Trapped. Wolves and lions.

(*Off stage, CIRCE begins to sing her song accompanied by enchantment music and sounds.*)

EURYLOCHUS: No, wait, shipmates, look. Look at them carefully. They are not attacking. They are wagging their tails.

HYLAX: Like dogs ...

PEREMIDES: I don't like this ...

HYLAX: Neither do I, but what a wonder. They fawn at our feet like dogs.

EURYLOCHUS: Strange how gentle they are.

(*CIRCE enters.*)   (*Finger cymbals*)

CIRCE: (*singing*)

Sweetly, sweet, let darkness come,
Sad night sings in hollow tones,
Rest is near and sorrow gone.
Lay thy swords upon the earth,
Voyager, whose weeping wakes
The forest with thy human tale.

(*During the scene, whenever she moves her hands close to their faces they follow her movements in a hypnotic trance until she stops or snaps her finger cymbals. EURYLOCHUS, who was farthest from her, breaks her spell and hides, watching what happens.*)

PEREMIDES: Have mercy upon us, goddess or woman, whichever you are.

CIRCE: Strangers, you are welcome to the Island of Aeaea.

(*Echo: "Aeaeaeaeae ..."*)

HYLAX: Thank you, lovely lady. We are Greeks searching our way home to Ithaca. And I ask, who are you?

CIRCE: I am Circe. My father is the Sun who lights the earth and my mother is Perse, daughter of the Ocean. You are welcome, refresh yourselves from your journey with this honey-wine in its golden bowl.

HYLAX: Hmmm. What a splendid taste. Oink, oink.

PEREMIDES: (*giggling and drifting into oinks*) This is delicious. Hylax, your nose. It's beginning to look just like an oink—I mean a pig's!

HYLAX: Well, oink yourself, you old oink, oink, oink, oink.

(*As the sailors drink, they are transformed into pigs. This can be done by concealing cloth pig masks in their cowls. As they begin to change, they pull them up as hoods. Then CIRCE touches them with her wand, they drop on all fours, and appear to be men with pig heads.*)

(*EURYLOCHUS exits.*)

CIRCE: And now, sailors, my powerful drug steals away your memory of home in Ithaca. You are pigs! You grunt like pigs, but your minds are human. You eat like pigs, some acorns, eat, acorns. Come piggies, follow me ...

(*They follow her off, squealing like pigs as the enchantment music rises, then stops. EURYLOCHUS enters with ODYSSEUS.*)

EURYLOCHUS: And then they all followed her to the pigsty. They were crying like men, but grunting and rooting like pigs. Both of them!

ODYSSEUS: Quick, we must go help them! This way.

EURYLOCHUS: (*falling to his knees*) My king, leave me here. Don't force me to go back there. You will never return yourself, nor save a single man. This island is bewitched! We must escape now while we have the chance and with what men we have left.

ODYSSEUS: Eurylochus, I am their leader. I must go to them. You stay here and guard the ship.

(*EURYLOCHUS exits while ODYSSEUS draws his sword and begins warily to hunt for his men. HERMES and his mask enter. They follow ODYSSEUS, who senses something is wrong, but HERMES, the trickster, never lets himself be seen until he has had some fun with ODYSSEUS.*)

ODYSSEUS: (*whirling and drawing his sword*) Ha! Who are you?

HERMES: Wouldn't you like to know!

ODYSSEUS: Watch your tongue, man. (*HERMES sticks out his tongue to "watch" it.*) I do not like your insolence either. I have killed men for less.

HERMES: To kill me you would have to catch me. To catch me, you'd have to run to Mount Olympus and back as fast as this!

(*HERMES makes as though he leaps into space at incredible speed.*

ODYSSEUS' *eyes follow this imagined journey with amazement. Finally,* HERMES *taps him on the shoulder.*) Hello, there. I'm back.

ODYSSEUS: I know who you are. You must be Hermes.

HERMES: (*simultaneously with him*) Hermes! Son of Zeus and his messenger on earth to you silly mortals.

ODYSSEUS: I heard you were something of a trickster.

HERMES: Ah, well, you need a master trickster, Odysseus. Circe will turn you into a pig, too.

ODYSSEUS: Please help me, Hermes. Help me rescue my men.

HERMES: That is the reason Pallas Athena asked me to come to you. Well, all right, with this.

(*He magically produces a flower.*)

Take this flowering herb, called Moly, with its white flower and black root. It is the antidote to the drug Circe will give you.

(*Circe begins singing off-stage.*)

Come closer, even the leaves in the forest have Circe's ears.

(HERMES *mimes whispering to* ODYSSEUS *that he must put the Moly into the goblet before drinking it or else he will be changed into a pig. Enchanted music sounds.*)

Now, do what I have told you and no harm will come to you.

ODYSSEUS: Hermes, guardian of the wayfarer, I thank you.

HERMES: Thank the goddess Pallas Athena, she sent me, and now, farewell.

(HERMES *again makes as though to leap off rapidly into space; again* ODYSSEUS *follows with his eyes.* HERMES *shrugs, grins, and trots off stage.* CIRCE'S *song continues as she enters.*)

CIRCE: (*singing*)

Sweetly, sweet let darkness come,
Sad night sings in hollow tones.
Give up thy shield and helmet strong,
As life grows old thy dreams grow young.
Welcome stranger. You are welcome to the enchanted island of Aeaea. (*Echoes off-stage:* "Aeaeae ... ")
Refresh yourself from your journey with this honey-wine in its golden bowl.

(*She begins to hypnotize* ODYSSEUS *as she did the sailors with her hands and movements. He takes the goblet, but when she moves behind him, he drops the Moly flower into the goblet and drinks.*)

And now, my powerful drug turns you into a pig. Go and join
the other swine in the sty!

(*She taps him with her wand. ODYSSEUS has a terrible struggle because
her drug tries to pull him onto all fours. At last, he overcomes it, draws
his sword, and threatens her with it. She falls to her knees.*)

ODYSSEUS: No, terrible sorceress. You shall die on my sword!

CIRCE: No man has ever resisted my potion before! Who are you?
What parents bred you? What city claims you?

ODYSSEUS: I am the son of Laertes, from rocky Ithaca.

CIRCE: Ah, then, you must be Odysseus, the man whom nothing
defeats! It has long been prophesied that you would come to me.
Stay and live with me in my palace.

(*OLD MAN enters. A drum begins.*)

OLD MAN: And she had rich rugs laid, and a silver basin for him to
wash himself with sweetly perfumed water. And she entertained
him with dancing.

(*An ATTENDANT enters with a silver basin and cloth so ODYSSEUS can
wash his hands. Then he sits and CIRCE dances for him.*)

So, Odysseus trusted Circe and stayed in her enchanted palace
for a year. But he did not forget his friends, or his wife and son in
faraway Ithaca.

CIRCE: Why do you sit there, speechless, neither eating nor
drinking?

ODYSSEUS: Can any man eat and drink while his friends grunt and
root in the ground like pigs?

CIRCE: I will restore them to you. Come, pigs.

(*They enter. She taps them with her wand and they transform back into
men by removing their pig masks.*)

HYLAX: What's happening?

PEREMIDES: My snout, the bristles are falling off …

HYLAX: We are changing back into humans!

PEREMIDES: Now I remember, we were pigs! Odysseus, what has
happened?

ODYSSEUS: Circe has released you from her secret drug. You are free
to return to our ship.

HYLAX: Thank you, Odysseus! You have saved us!

PEREMIDES: Oh, great leader, if we ever are to escape this magic
place, it must be now.

ODYSSEUS: You're right. I will ask Circe to free us all. Go make our ship ready.

(*They go.*)

Circe, I beseech you, let us leave this place in peace.

CIRCE: My beloved Odysseus, I cannot keep you here against your will. You are free. But, royal son of Laertes, hear this: before you reach your home you must take a strange and difficult journey.

(*Music: a drum heartbeat begins.*)

ODYSSEUS: A strange and difficult journey? Where?

CIRCE: You must go to the dread kingdom of Hades.

ODYSSEUS: How can I leave this earth? How descend into hell? No man has ever sailed there and lived!

CIRCE: Have courage, my love. Go now. Do not fret about a pilot to guide you. Set your mast and sail. The north wind will blow you to the waters of the River Styx, then to the great rock pinnacle at the confluence of the River of Flaming Fire and the River of Lamentation. There dig a pit and pour in it a drink offering of milk mixed with honey. Then, take a cup of red blood—life-giving blood of an all-black ram—and draw your sword, because a multitude of dead souls and wraiths will come to you, begging to drink the life-sustaining blood. But you must seek out the blind prophet, Teiresias. He alone can tell you where you must go, how long it will take, and thus direct you home across Poseidon's seas.

(*Using only the prow of the ship for the voyage, ODYSSEUS quickly mimes the voyage CIRCE has described. He leaps off the ship, and goes downstage centre and mimes the sacrifice. He ends on his knees with a cup in one hand and his sword in the other. Music changes to strong drum and cymbal beats. Enter four wraiths, each completely covered with flowing black cloth. One carries a mobile of death masks on a long stick that floats over ODYSSEUS' head while the others swirl like black clouds.*)

VOICES OF THE DEAD: Brave Odysseus, give us a drink ... blood is life, only a drop.

ODYSSEUS: Keep back!

VOICES OF THE DEAD: Don't hurt me with your sword ... one sip of blood ... blood ... blood.

ODYSSEUS: No. I seek the blind prophet, Teiresias.

(*ANTICLEA, dressed as a wraith, enters swirling, the other wraiths drop*) *to the ground like pools of black water. She floats to and fro, approaching Odysseus.*)

ANTICLEA: Noble son ... Odysseus, my boy ...

ODYSSEUS: Who is it that calls my name?

ANTICLEA: I am your mother, Anticlea. Give me but one drink that I may speak with you.

ODYSSEUS: Alas, dear mother! Here, drink one sip and tell me what has brought you to this horrible place.
(*She drinks a sip and when she lowers her cloth-covered head, the cloth slides down revealing her death mask.*)

ANTICLEA: My son, it was no disease that brought me to this place of darkness. It was my longing for you to return from Troy that brought my life to an end.

ODYSSEUS: We are now reunited. Let me embrace you once more. Why do you avoid me? May I not hold you in my arms once more?

ANTICLEA: You can't. I am only a spirit now. It is the fate of mankind. I have no flesh, no bones. You must fly from this black place. It is no place for you, the living. Go back ... go back ... go back to the lighted world.
(*She exits, whirling out like a wisp of black fog.*)

ODYSSEUS: I cannot go until I see Teiresias. Oh, mother, please return. What a terrible place this is. Lord Hades, I beseech you send the blind prophet Teiresias, that I may speak with him.
(*Loud drum. Enter TEIRESIAS, also covered with black cloths and wearing a blind death mask. Then, low drumbeats under the scene. The other wraiths whirl, then drop.*)

TEIRESIAS: I come. I come, great Odysseus, I come. Hold your sword aside so I can drink the blood and prophesy the truth to you.
(*ODYSSEUS holds the cup so TEIRESIAS can drink from it.*)

ODYSSEUS: Tell me, blind prophet, how I may get home to Ithaca?

TEIRESIAS: You must sail past the Isle of Thrinacia, where the Sun God, Apollo, pastures his golden cattle. If you do not harm them, you *may* reach your home. But if you do them harm, you and all your men may be drowned at sea! I have told you the truth.

ODYSSEUS: Thank you, blind prophet.

TEIRESIAS: One final warning: You must sail past the rocks of the Twin Sirens. Beware! Now I must return, return, return to the darkness ... return ...

VOICES OF THE DEAD: Give me life ... drink ... Odysseus, help us ... return ... return ... Blood ... help us ... life ... !

(*As TEIRESIAS leaves the sounds grow louder. The wraiths rise again from the floor and swirl even stronger. Then all the wraiths leave except one who three times tries to take the goblet from him. At last the wraith seizes it from him, drinks the blood and floats off. Crescendo of music and sounds.*)

ODYSSEUS: This is no place for the living! I must fly out of here. Ho, Sailors!

(*The sailors enter, set the prow and the mast.*)

Raise the mast! Man the long oars, we fly out of Hades! Away, away! We are bound for Apollo's golden island of Thrinacia. We are going home to Ithaca!

SAILORS: Hooray! Yea!

(*They begin to sail away as EURYLOCHUS mans the tiller and ODYSSEUS joins him.*)

EURYLOCHUS: What an adventure, Odysseus! To descend alive into Hades and return safely! One death is enough for every man, but now you will have two.

HYLAX: Reefs ahead! Beware, helmsman.

PEREMIDES: Rocks on this side, steer carefully.

(*Using their oars the sailors guide the ship off the reefs on both sides.*)

PERITES: Reefs off there!

ODYSSEUS: Good sailors, hear me. We must sail through these treacherous rocks. But beware, the Sirens who live here sing so beautifully that every sailor is drawn to them, hypnotized, and their ship is smashed on the rocks. Put this wax in your ears so that you cannot hear them.

(*He gives them wax, which they put in their ears and then man their oars in a ready position.*)

Eurylochus, come quickly! Tie me to the mast, for I shall hear the Sirens' song and live! And do not loose the bonds no matter how I beg until we are safely past. Do you promise?

EURYLOCHUS: I promise, Odysseus.

(*EURYLOCHUS ties ODYSSEUS to the mast.*)

ODYSSEUS: Good. Now I am ready for them.

(EURYLOCHUS *puts wax in his ears and takes the tiller. The men begin to row; they neither see nor hear the* SIRENS, *who enter and begin singing, while the men sing a low counterpart of "row, row" to the rhythm of their rowing. The* SIRENS *move from the prow to the helm trying to catch the attention of the sailors.*)

SIRENS: (*singing*)

Come here, come here,

Sailor so long on the sea.

ODYSSEUS: What a beautiful song ... I hear you, I will come!

SIRENS: (*singing*)

Come here, come near,

Following my song, come to me.

ODYSSEUS: Eurylochus, steer to the left. No, steer to the right. Do as I tell you!

SIRENS: (*singing*)

Sail here, don't fear.

Come here and rest close to me.

ODYSSEUS: Over there, please go over—I am trying, please, please ... I am coming to you, ohhhhh ...

SIRENS: (*singing*)

Come near, come near,

Follow my song and be free.

(*As they exit,* ODYSSEUS *tries to reach out to them and faints.*)

EURYLOCHUS: Are we past them yet? Odysseus? He has fainted from the strain. I wonder if I can take the wax out of my ears yet.

(*He does so.*)

Rowers, you can take the wax out of your ears now!

(*They don't hear, he speaks louder.*)

Take the wax out of your ears!!!!

(*They still do not hear him. He shows them in mime to take the wax out of their ears, while saying it softly. This time they understand.*)

Take the wax out of your ears.

HYLAX: Those were terrible rocks ... and the current ... almost too strong ... What a horrible ordeal.

PERITES: Six days and nights of rowing! We have never rowed so hard and travelled so far without rest. And we have had no food for three days.

PEREMIDES: Wait! Look there, land! Steer in toward the shore.

PERITES: We can put ashore and find food. It's shallow. Ease her in.

HYLAX: (*leaping ashore*) I am not staying on this ship tonight. I shall sleep on land.

PERITES: (*leaping ashore, followed by* PEREMIDES) Come on.

PEREMIDES: We can forage for food. What ... look there, or is it a mirage? (*cow bell*)

PERITES: No, it is cattle grazing.

HYLAX: Beautiful—golden in the sunlight, with long horns.

EURYLOCHUS: Wait, men. Don't touch those golden cows, they're sacred to the god Apollo.

HYLAX: We intend to kill and eat one of these cattle while we still have the strength. Join us—or, at least, don't try to stop us!
(*EURYLOCHUS attempts to draw his sword but they prevent him and threaten him with their weapons.*)

EURYLOCHUS: All right ... in another minute we'll be killing each other. Apollo forgive us: we starve.

HYLAX: Come on! Take that one! Haaa! (*Cow bells sound.*)
(*They mime killing a cow. The mask of* APOLLO *comes forward and they freeze in a tableau.*)

APOLLO: No! Father Zeus, I, Apollo, call upon you to punish these wicked followers of Odysseus. They are killing my golden cattle. If you let them go unpunished, I will take my golden sun down into Hades to shine among the dead and leave this earth dark and cold forever.

ODYSSEUS: Oh, my friends, what are you doing? Oh no! A golden cow! Oh gods who live forever, why have you lulled me into a sleep while my men offended Apollo? He will surely punish us. Come, we must leave this island quickly, although I fear it is already too late.
(*They enter the ship, apprehensive of the danger they feel around them. The ship is configured so that the prow faces downstage and the ship is sailing directly at the audience.* ZEUS *is on one side,* APOLLO *on the other.*)

ZEUS: Apollo, continue to shine your sun upon the earth. I, Zeus, Lord of Olympus, will soon strike them with my thunderbolt, and scatter them on the wine-dark sea. Now rise great waves! Rock their boat from side to side!
(*With mime and manipulation of the prow, mast and tiller, the actors make*

the ship pitch up and down, then roll from side to side—even tossing a
man overboard, who saves himself by clinging to the prow at water level.)

HYLAX: Man overboard!

ZEUS: Now, omnipotent thunderbolt, strike!

(*The ship breaks apart; the prow tumbles off stage, as does the tiller, the*
mast holder, and all the sailors, leaving ODYSSEUS *clinging to the mast,*
awash in the sea.)

ODYSSEUS: Swim, men, swim! Pallas Athena, help us! We are
drowning!

(*He, like the men, is then tumbled off stage. Drums and sounds*
throughout the scene. After the ship's breakup, the two gods pass each
other and go upstage, bow to each other and their masks are hung on
the wall. A gong sounds.)

ANTINOUS: (*entering with all the suitors*) It is true! Odysseus was
drowned in the sea by Zeus' great thunderbolt. He is dead.
Now, Penelope, we have brought you our matrimonial offerings
as is the custom. Now you must choose which one of us you
will marry.

PENELOPE: (*entering with* TELEMACHUS) I shall choose, Antinous.
Telemachus, fetch your father's bow from its accustomed place.
I shall choose by challenge. He among you who can string
Odysseus' great bow and shoot an arrow through those twelve axes
as he did, shall have my consent. Will you accept the challenge?

EURYMACHUS: A fair challenge. He who can string the bow and shoot
through the axes wins Penelope's hand.

ANTINOUS: Are we agreed then to take up this challenge?

SUITORS: Agreed!

(TELEMACHUS *returns with the bow.*)

TELEMACHUS: Here is the bow. Try it if you dare.

SUITORS: (*laughter*) If we dare, ... (*etc.*)

ANTINOUS: Come, young princes, we shall go even as the wine is
passed: from left to right.

KTESSIPOS: (*tipsy*) Me? Am I first? Give me the bow.

ANTINOUS: Ktessipos.

KTESSIPOS: Fair Penelope.

(KTESSIPOS *tries to string the bow but fumbles with it and hits himself*
on the nose.)

This is a strong bow ...

EURYMACHUS: Did you say a strong drink, Ktessipos?

KTESSIPOS: Yes, I'll have one! I may not be able to string this bow, but I can drink these two goblets of wine in only one breath.

(*He drinks two goblets of wine simultaneously.*)

ANTINOUS: Leodes, son of Oenos. You are next.

(*He tries but cannot string it.*)

LEODES: Generous Queen, I have tried the strength of this bow and I shall never string it. Believe me, this bow will break the heart and be the death of many a champion here today!

EURYMACHUS: What a preposterous thing to say, Leodes. Surely there be men—or at least one—here today who can string this bow. Like this!

(*With great strength, EURYMACHUS almost strings the bow, but cannot.*)

ANTINOUS: Lo, mighty Eurymachus cannot even string Odysseus' bow! Then how can he shoot an arrow?

(*laughter and taunts from the suitors*)

EURYMACHUS: Here, Antinous, take this bow. This humiliates me and the disgrace sticks to my name.

ANTINOUS: There is no disgrace here today. Today should be a holiday—in preparation for a princely wedding! We shall call today a festival and tomorrow we can take up the challenge of this bow once again.

EURYMACHUS: No Antinous, you will try today.

SUITORS: (*general ad lib*) No—today! You must try now!

(*tinkle sound*)

(*Enter the OLD MAN.*)

OLD MAN: Young princes, let me try the strength of these old arms and hands on that great bow.

ANTINOUS: Miserable old beggar, are you out of your senses? Are you not content to eat with your betters and be quiet? Now I warn you, you will come to harm. Stand off!

PENELOPE: Antinous, it is not common courtesy to be so rude to a guest in my house.

EURYMACHUS: And it is not proper behaviour for you to let a miserable beggar compete for your hand in marriage.

TELEMACHUS: Peace, I say. (*Takes the bow from ANTINOUS.*) No man in Ithaca has more right than I to give this bow. Though I am young, I am still master of this house. I shall decide. Try it, Old Man.

SUITORS: (*laughter, ad lib*)

EURYMACHUS: Oh, the too young and the too old!

(*The OLD MAN strings and mimes shooting an arrow past the suitors, whose eyes and heads follow its flight. Drum roll and beat for arrow shot and hit.*)

KTESSIPOS: A hit!

OLD MAN: And now I shall conclude my story of Odysseus: He returned to his home, disguised as an old beggar (*he takes off the mask and hat*) to meet again his beloved wife and his brave son. (*He embraces PENELOPE and grasps TELEMACHUS' hand, then turns to the suitors.*)

And to find his home filled with corrupt men who would steal his wife, murder his son, and dishonour the immortal gods. So the match is played and won. Odysseus is home!

ANTINOUS: It's Odysseus!

ODYSSEUS: Yes! And who is to say he should not rid his house of the vermin that infest it?

EURYMACHUS: Get your weapons! Attack him, everyone!

(*The slaughter of the suitors is in slow motion. With PENELOPE on one side of ODYSSEUS and TELEMACHUS on the other, the family make a fortress. TELEMACHUS mimes handing arrows to ODYSSEUS, who then shoots each suitor: ANTINOUS, KTESSIPOS, LEODES and EURYMACHUS. As each is hit by an arrow, he brings a red silken handkerchief to the place of the wound and falls to the ground.*)

ODYSSEUS: It is not yet finished! I have purged my house, but I fear the families of these dead will rise up in arms for revenge.

(*Humming begins and grows.*)

PENELOPE: Is there to be still more slaughtering?

ODYSSEUS: Fair Penelope, only the gods of Olympus know. Telemachus, when we are in the heat of battle, I know you will not bring disgrace to our house.

TELEMACHUS: Father, I shall stand at your side, and you will see!

ODYSSEUS: I hear them coming even now. Ready!

(*The suitors begin an increasing hum and slowly rise, placing their red handkerchiefs over their heads and raising their swords. ODYSSEUS,*

PENELOPE, *and* TELEMACHUS *take up a siege position.* ATHENA *enters between them.*)

ATHENA: Stop, you Greeks! Lay down your weapons! (*They do.*) I, Pallas Athena, tell you! There will be no more bloodshed. Odysseus: you shall make a treaty of mutual friendship with these noble families. You, Ithacan nobles, will make peace with his family. Salute each other, so that peace and prosperity will return to my beloved Greece. Now, let us all join hands as we celebrate the end of this Odyssey.
(*They shake hands, then turn and bow.*)
(*The suitors remove the red cloths and lay them down with their swords. One of them shakes hands with* ODYSSEUS, *then all join hands with* PALLAS ATHENA *in the centre and, facing the audience, bow to them.*)
(*Curtain*)

Homer is said to be the ancient Greek poet who wrote the *Iliad* and the *Odyssey*. There is some controversy about Homer's very existence, and some scholars believe the epic poems were written by two different authors. Most scholars do agree that the poems were written between 800 and 700 B.C., judging by their references to social conditions during that period.

From *Fashion, Power, Guilt, and the Charity of Families*

Carol Shields and Catherine Shields

CHARACTERS

FATHER
MOTHER
MICHAEL, their son, about 12 years old
SALLY, their daughter, about 15 years old
MAN

SETTING
A living room

The lights come up on the living room where the family has gathered.
The following scene has a tone of gaiety—the family is at its best.

FATHER: (*pushing the couch*) Come on. We need all hands on deck.
MICHAEL: We're moving the table? We've never moved the table
   before.
FATHER: Come on. Just two more feet.
MOTHER: That looks good. And now—bing! (*idea!*)—The lamp table.
   Next to the rug. There.
SALLY: (*to the furniture*) Hey, you two were meant for each other.
FATHER: (*to* MICHAEL) Lamp! (*He runs off to get lamp.*)
MICHAEL: Hey, dust balls.
SALLY: You can add them to your collection, Michael. (*considering the
   changes*) It's off-balance. Definitely off-balance. But, you know,
   there's something kind of—
MOTHER: —thrilling about an off-centre room?

MICHAEL: I like it. It's got the movers-and-shakers look. Hey, my basketball. (*He starts to dribble it.*)

FATHER: (*removing a picture from the wall*) Much brighter.

MOTHER: Why, it looks brand new.

FATHER: But not too new.

SALLY: It's just—different!

FATHER: (*glancing at the TV*) Look. Quiet everyone. It's coming on TV. The report on the nuclear family.

(*They all sit and watch the TV screen flicker. The theme from W5 plays.*)

VOICE-OVER: This evening, direct from the capital, we have the chairperson of the Royal Commission on the family. Our story tonight: "Family on the Fault Line." (*more theme music*)

FATHER: "Family on the Fault Line."

SALLY: The fault line?

MICHAEL: (*wearily, ready to explain*) That means—

FATHER: (*Half-speaking, half-singing, he steps to front of the stage.*) Your fault—

MOTHER: (*stepping*) My fault?

FATHER: Our fault—

MOTHER: Their fault—

(*They freeze. MICHAEL and SALLY step to the front of the stage, facing each other, and chant in rounds.*)

MICHAEL: His fault, her fault—

SALLY: Her fault, his fault.

MICHAEL: Our fault?

SALLY: Their fault.

(*MAN enters wearing a black derby, and carrying a laptop computer which he places on the coffee table. The family sing the following, while MAN interjects with comments.*)

ALL:
Family at the fault line,
Family at the fault line,
Shaking, quaking,
Sleeping, waking
Famil-ee-hee—

(*They freeze as MAN's watch alarm beeps. He turns it off and clears his throat.*)

MAN: Time please. Please come to order. Is everyone present ready to review the transcripts of the family project to date?

ALL: (*singing again*) Family at the fault line, one, two—

MAN: Order please!

MOTHER: All unhappy families are unhappy in the same way ...

FATHER: No, no, you've got it wrong, honey. All unhappy families are unhappy in different ways, or something or other—How does it go?

MAN: Wait a minute, wait a minute. I'm trying to get this all down.

ALL: (*singing again*)
Family at the fault line,
My fault, your fault, our fault,
Family at the fault—

MICHAEL: A family is just a random scattering of genetic chips.

SALLY: A family is the basic building block of society and its most conserving agent. A family's whatever you want it to be.

MICHAEL: The trouble is, people are always trying to climb out of their families ... then falling back in—

SALLY: A family gives you your primary wounds.

ALL: (*crooning*) Fam-i-ly, fam-i-lee-hee—

MAN: (*speaking as he writes*) A family gives you your primary wounds? Have I got that right? Can I quote you?

FATHER: A family is the crucible of ... of ... of ... I dunno—the crucible of ... hmmmm ... whatever. And another thing ... Now what was that other thing?

SALLY: Even an intact family can be pretty ... tacky.

MOTHER: Every tacky family is tacky in its own way.

ALL: (*singing, clapping, including* MAN)
Family at the fault line,
Our fault, their fault,
One, two, three, four.
Salvation at the family door.
Family at the fault line—

FATHER: Now I remember what I was going to say. A family heals, protects its members—

SALLY: A family is like these people, you know? With nothing in common? Who sort of like live together, under the same roof kind of thing, even though—

ALL: (*singing*)
  Family at the fault line.
  Fitting in, fitting out,
  Making up, making do.
  Family at the fault line—
MOTHER: (*speaking directly to* MAN) A family—I hope you're getting this down—helps you grow out of your silences—
FATHER: Or else freezes you in them.
MICHAEL: Families like to sit around and play ... y'know, games and stuff. Good games. And bad games.
FATHER: Talking to each other. Or not talking.
ALL: (*crooning*) Fam-i-ly. Fam-i-le-hee.
MOTHER: Families have a way of pretending everything is just fine, and sometimes—
SALLY: Sometimes it really is. Just fine. Oh, God, when that happens, it's heaven. It's like it's the only place you want to be.
FATHER: And ... I don't know why but, and this is what worries me, there're always these funny little pieces of family history that go ... missing.
MICHAEL: Maybe, sometimes, not all the time, but sometimes that's ... okay?
MAN: (*speaking as he types on keyboard*) Hold on, I can't input that fast. I've got to get all this in the official report. You're saying that—
ALL: (*singing*)
  Family on the fault line,
  Their fault, our fault.
  One, two, three, four,
  Making up, making do,
  Family on the fault line.
MAN: What the subcommittee for the report on the Commission wants is—
MICHAEL: Wait a minute, wait a minute. I've got something to say.
MOTHER: Go ahead, no one's stopping you—
MICHAEL: You keep interrupting.
FATHER: Your turn, go ahead.
MICHAEL: I just want to say that a family—
ALL: (*singing*)
  Family on the fault line,

Family on the fault line—

MOTHER: Shhhhh. Let this young person speak. Give him his moment.

MICHAEL: It's just that, well, with a family you have to take it or leave it, except you can't.

SALLY: Can't what?

MOTHER: Take it.

FATHER: (*slight pause*) Or leave it.

MAN: The committee is expecting our conclusions today. Do we go with opinion A, B, or C, or all of the above?

FATHER: How 'bout none of the above.

SALLY: There doesn't seem to be any formula.

MICHAEL: Just say—

FATHER: Say we want to table it. Until the next century?

MOTHER: (*hesitantly*) We could, you know, just carry on and sort of see-what-happens kind of thing?

MAN: (*as he types*) How's this? "In closing, we continue to watch, with interest—"

MOTHER: Eyes on the future ...

SALLY: And the past ...

MICHAEL: Let's remember to write it down—

SALLY: Listen! What's that noise?

(*A dog howls in the distance as the family freezes for a moment, listening, then carry on. After a long pause, they sing softly as the lights fade. Music has segued into gospel rhythm.*)

ALL:

Family on the fault line,
One two three four,
Trouble always at the door.

Family on the fault line,

On the fault line,
On the line, on the line,
Looking for a recipe.

Fami-l-ee, fami-l-ee.
Right there, right there,

On the line, on the line, on the line, line, line
Line, line, line, line, fault line,
Fam-i-leee-hee-heeee-ee.
Fam-i-lee-ee.
Carryin' on,
Carryin' on,
Carryiiiin' oooooonnn.
(*Music and singing fades to silence as brilliant sunlight floods the stage. It slowly fades as a single dog barks. The end.*)

Carol Shields (*Born 1935, Chicago, Illinois*), professor, author, and playwright, has lived in Canada all her adult life. She has taught at a number of Canadian universities, most recently at the University of Manitoba. Her novels include *Larry's Party*, *The Republic of Love*, and *The Stone Diaries*, for which she won the Governor General's Award and the Pulitzer Prize.

Catherine Shields (*Born 1962*), researcher, playwright, and librarian, has collaborated on a number of plays with Carol Shields, including *Thirteen Hands*, *Departures and Arrivals*, and *Fashion, Power, Guilt, and the Charity of Families*.

Selection Activities, p. 397

Beatrice = Alberta

Geraldine Farrell

The Silencer

The best thing in the whole world was when Mummy would walk to school and wait for us to break for lunch, so she could walk us home. Kathleen and I. (*shrugging*) Maybe she did it twice.

    Beat

I look out of the window and there she is with the dog. My God, she is so exquisite. I like to hug her very hard. Why is that? I just want to melt into her or have her melt into me. I do the same thing to the dog. You want to hug them so tightly, so that they'll vanish and you won't have to hug them anymore.

She loved clothes, my mother.

She bought everything on sale. She was always well put together. She loved hats. She had this one outfit: black and white striped dress, black and white leather shoes with small polka dots. Accentuated with a wide-brimmed black hat. My heart swelling with love at her put-togetherness. One time she came home from the hairdresser's with a new hairdo. She was quite taken with this new look. She asked me.

"So, what do you think?"

"It's very nice."

I was taught tact at an early age.

    Beat — pause — dramatic

I hated it. What was wrong with the way you looked before?

One day a few years later I stayed home from school, to take my mother for her radiation treatment at St. Mary's Hospital. She tried to put herself together with her usual flair. It was a warm day but she wore a wool dress—solid navy, straight lines, no belt—a yellow and blue tie wrapped around her throat trying to conceal the scars of former radium treatments. Blue leather pumps.

No hat today. She wore a short wig. No hair today.

The navy wool dress had fit her snugly a few months ago, now it hung awkwardly from her shoulders. A skeleton swimming in a sea of blue wool. Her wig refused to sit properly on her head. When she bought it she had had a full head of hair to pin it to. Now nothing but a few undyed strands. She used to get me to curl that leftover hair. We rode home from St. Mary's in the back seat of a cab.

Silence

I looked out the window, not seeing the passing city.

Silence

My mother staring straight ahead, eyes glazed.

Silence

Something had entered our lives that drove a wedge of terrible silence between us. I was no longer able to ask Mummy questions or come to her with my everyday problems. Some enormous, unforeseen catastrophe was hovering over our lives, forcing us to look at …

Forcing us to look at … What?

I had never known pain before. Now it became a familiar companion. For her. For me. For all of us.

"Roberta, where are you going?"

"Aw, ma, I've gotta go. I've gotta!"

"But I asked you to make me breakfast."

"I know. I started it. Can't you finish the rest? I got library duty."

"I'm sick."

"I know you're sick. Why don't you ever get better?"

"I've got cancer. I'm never getting better."

She looks at me. I grab my stuff and run out, slamming the door behind me.

My God, no, no, that's not true! Please dear God tell me it's not true! I see her in the front door window, looking at me.

She waves. (*Roberta waving*)

I run up the street as fast as I can.

The Wake

Party sounds

At my mother's wake, my brothers and sisters congregated in the smoking room, in the basement of the funeral parlour. Here we'd gather and we'd laugh. We spent those three days telling jokes, laughing in the smoking room. Laughter was anaesthetic for our hurting hearts. My Aunt Mary who was my father's sister kept saying to me, "Well, Roberta, you're the lady of the house now. You'll have to take care of your father, brothers, and Kathleen."

If she said this once, she said it twenty times. As if my mother's death wasn't enough.

She was there that morning just before the coffin was to be sealed. She knelt down before the coffin. Said a prayer. Got up. Leaned over and kissed the corpse. She looked at me and said,
"Kiss your mother one last time."

I look at her. Then kissed my mother's cold, hard, embalmed lips. Nothing about that body resembled my mother. Though I had heard from several people that she looked good. Or, she looked just like she was asleep. I would agree, nodding my head. But I thought—Nobody looks good as a corpse. I had seen my mother asleep many times. No she didn't look like she was asleep. Her soul was gone. I understood what a soul was by the absence of one.

I walked down the church aisle following the coffin. My classmates and my homeroom teacher looking at me. Looking for some sign of emotion. Sadness, grief. But I looked ahead, nothing exposed. When I returned to school, Rita, who sat beside me, said,
"How can you stand it?"
"Rita, my mother was very sick. It's better for her that she died."

Fragments

I lie in bed one night, waiting to hear her come in. Waiting to hear those welcome, familiar footsteps. The door opens, I hear her walk up the stairs. Heels clicking against the linoleum. She's home now, I can go to sleep knowing she's home now. Safe. Then I remember, she's been dead for months. Her clothes still hanging in the closet. Her drawers still filled with her clothing, undergarments, scarves, jewellery ... The junk drawer still filled with JUNK—false teeth, gallbladder stones, costume jewellery. Stuff kids like to look at—Junk. She kept her gallbladder stones in a jar. She said she wanted them made into a bracelet. I wear some of her clothes. The tray with her cotton swabs and her medication remains on the TV tray in the hall beside the bathroom. My father still wears his black tie. We don't sent Christmas cards this year. Kathleen and I go to school. Her presence is so real. We don't talk about her.

   "Dites-moi" is heard softly.
I was thinking that if I ever have a child, well, first of all I'll have a girl. I'll name her Beatrice after my mother.
Bea.

Geraldine Farrell, actor, author, and playwright, grew up in Montreal and studied theatre at Concordia University. She currently lives in Los Angeles, California. She has performed *Beatrice* at the Los Angeles Women's Theatre, at the Minnesota and Winnipeg Fringe Festivals, at Toronto's New Works, and Theatre Lac Brome in Quebec. The production was aired across Canada on CBC Radio's *Morningside*.

Selection Activities, p. 397

MEDIA

"Once there was only the world, directly lived. Now there is the representation— the re-presentation—of the world."

– Julian Barnes

"Viewing or listening to television, radio, or videos is shared experience carried out in private."

– Ursula Franklin

When you rent a video, browse the *Internet*, listen to a CD, skim a magazine, or channel-surf through commercials, you are one of millions of people receiving media messages. As technology has developed, so have the ways we can send and receive these messages. In fact, these new media partially shape the messages they deliver. The **mass media** now have almost unimaginable power to reach people instantaneously.

Different kinds of media texts can be found in **cyberspace**, and also in print, audio, and visual forms. These texts need to be examined with the same sharp attention that you give poems, short stories, essays, and plays. By taking a **media text** apart, you can interpret its message and analyze its stylistic techniques. And as you create your own media texts, you can take an insider's look at the media world.

You already know a lot about media, but you can increase your expertise. Greater understanding of media messages will add to your enjoyment of them and at the same time defend you from manipulation.

Internet: a worldwide network of interconnected computers that allows the movement of electronic data from point to point

mass media: modern means of communication—such as television, film, radio, newspapers, magazines, on-line publications, and web sites—that appeal to and reach vast audiences

cyberspace: an online environment or virtual space created by a software application or computer network such as the Internet

media text: a media message or product such as a film, advertisement, web site, television program, or newspaper article

Media

Birth *of a*

Matt Kelley's brave new magazine targets a mixed-race world. Andy Steiner

Matt Kelley doesn't speak much Korean, and his grandmother, Jin Hyang Lee, doesn't speak much English. Still, they eat dinner together in her tiny Seattle apartment four times a week. Lee, 82, cooks, and Kelley, 20, eats (and eats).

"If you don't eat a lot of what she makes, she gets mad," he says, gesturing toward his grandmother, who's busy deep-frying pieces of battered squid. "She always makes a lot, too, so usually after a meal I'm all bloated and full." He rubs his stomach, rolls his eyes, and mock-groans. "It's a test of my loyalty, I think."

Not that any test is needed. Since he left Wesleyan University and moved home a little over a year ago,

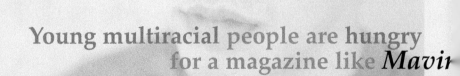

Young multiracial people are hungry for a magazine like *Mavin*

Mavin

Kelley has been a regular grandma's boy. He rented an apartment just blocks away from Lee's place, and the two have spent hours together, eating, watching TV (the PBS series *Nature* is one of her favourites), and talking—after a fashion.

But Kelley didn't leave college just to know his grandmother better. He came home to start *Mavin,* a magazine for young people from mixed-race backgrounds. Spending more time with his *halmuhnee* (Korean for mother's mother) is a fringe benefit, one that's helped him understand why he wanted to start a magazine in the first place.

"All my life, I've straddled two cultures," says Kelley, who grew up on nearby Bainbridge Island with his Korean-born mother and Midwestern American father. "For a long time when I was younger, I didn't think about it, but as I got older I realized I was different, and that being *different* is a big part of who I am. I'm still trying to sort it all out, but knowing that I'm not alone is important. The magazine does that for me and for the people who read it, and also for our families."

In magazine-speak, those people are a big, untapped market. While the concept of *race* is difficult to quantify using traditional survey methods, and *mixed race* even harder, statisticians have been working to define the demographic trend. The number of mixed-race marriages in the United States today has been estimated at more than 1.6 million—a tenfold increase since 1960. About one in 25 married couples today is interracial, and there are more than 3 million children of mixed-race parentage living in the United States.

No matter how you look at it, that's a lot of people. Even at such a young age, Kelley's got natural business savvy. He understands that the audience for his magazine is booming. And if reader response is any measure, he knows that young multiracial people are hungry for a magazine like *Mavin*, which speaks to their experience without sounding preachy, parental, or whiny. A typical issue of *Mavin*, whose name comes from the Hebrew word for "one who understands our experience," includes newsy articles about issues affecting mixed-race people around the world, interviews with multiracial celebrities, humour pieces, fashion spreads featuring mixed-race models, and updates on campus activities and conferences.

"*Mavin* is not a support group," Kelley says. "We've done that. It's about celebrating who we are, plain and simple. We get so many e-mails and letters each day from people who are so passionate in their response [that we] almost take it for granted. Then, every once in a while, you actually realize what a profound impact it is already having. It's amazing."

It's especially amazing when you consider that *Mavin* is all of two issues old. Kelley has paid for the 7000-circulation, four-colour, nationally distributed magazine through a combination of ad sales, subscription revenues, and gifts from friends and relatives. He's also dumped about $10 000 of his own savings, money he earned mostly from part-time jobs, into the endeavour. A third issue is due out in the fall, and he hopes the gathering buzz will soon start to pay off—in increased ad revenues and news-stand sales. If not, *Mavin*'s future may be in question.

"We're at a crossroads," Kelley says. "The market is there. The niche needs to be filled. I'd hate to miss [that opportunity]."

Going for broke may mean forgoing college a little while longer. Kelley originally planned to take a one-year leave to start the magazine and then return to Wesleyan and work on *Mavin* part-time from Connecticut. But it's become an all-consuming passion, and Kelley's not sure just when he'll go back to the academic life.

"Maybe because I want to go back to school isn't a good enough reason to stop," he says. "There are a lot of people who say they really need this magazine, and I feel like I have a responsibility to them. Besides, I've found out that putting *Mavin* together is a full-time job. I'm not sure I could go to school and produce a magazine at the same time. So I still have to weigh my options.'"

"*Mavin* world headquarters" is what Kelley likes to call his tidy one-bedroom apartment in Seattle's First Hill neighbourhood. He used to be crammed into a nearby first-floor studio, complete with a fold-down Murphy bed. But after three attempted break-ins, he packed up and moved to his current address, where he can spread out his computer, printer, and scanner—and

programs, and answering the ever-ringing telephone. "I probably have a slight case of ADD," he says, sheepishly, wiping his hands on his baggy khakis. But he's actually remarkably focused, especially for a young man busy juggling the details of a fledgling publishing business.

Mavin is, to a large degree, a one-man band. Kelley is founder, editor-in-chief, publisher, public relations executive, staff writer, and, for the first two issues, chief production designer.

> "It finally seems like recognizing and identifying with our mixed-ness is **Legitimate** in the eyes of society."

still have a place to sleep. The walls are decorated with large, shadowy paintings by Kelley's 24-year-old sister, Joanna Lee Kelley, and the sound track is generally hip-hop or jazz. It's a relaxed place, and Kelley makes his visitors feel at home, serving up refreshments (cookies and spring water in plastic squirt bottles) and rapid-fire conversation.

On a deadline, Kelley lopes around the office, distractedly running his hands over his close-cropped black hair, fussing over touchy computer

His sister, Joanna, a fashion designer based in Brooklyn, New York, directs the magazine's creative side, organizing fashion shoots, recruiting models, and, for the upcoming issue, coaxing a graphic designer friend to help develop a more professional look. There's also Kelley's college friend Risë Nelson, who serves as *Mavin*'s long-distance assistant editor, and Mariko Kawabori, *Mavin*'s on-site intern and associate editor.

The magazine is nearly all Kelley thinks about these days. In fact, he says, he has "no social life. I never see anybody except for my grandma and my mom." Kawabori comes into the office three days a week to help out with mailings, answer the phone, and respond to subscriber inquiries. The two have an easy, joking relationship, sharing their multiracial heritage (Kawabori, adopted at birth by a Japanese American family, is half Japanese, half Filipino), their love of music, and their tongue-in-cheek fascination with biracial pop star Mariah Carey.

"For mixed folk, Mariah's a big bonding point," Kelley says, eyebrows raised but voice serious, and Kawabori nods her agreement, laughing. "Mariah and Tiger [Woods] identified themselves as multiracial way before that was accepted by society. They paved the way for us ... When my sister and I drove out to Wesleyan, we listened to Mariah all the way. She's singing *our* song."

Well, maybe. But it seems that Kelley's humming his own tune just fine. He's done so many interviews about the magazine that he's got his message down pat—he can tell the same stories over and over without sounding rehearsed. He's a man on a mission, and he speaks with the conviction of a person who's seen the future and knows that he—and other young people like him—will play a key role in it.

"We're on the verge of a national, collective mixed-race consciousness," Kelley wrote in *Mavin*'s Spring/Summer 1999 issue. "It finally seems like recognizing and identifying with our mixed-ness is legitimate in the eyes of greater society."

It's not clear whether Jin Hyang Lee sees her grandson as such a change agent. During dinner, she proudly pulls out a worn copy of an article about *Mavin* that appeared in the local newspaper. It's written in English, so she can't read it, Kelley explains, but she still took it to church to show her friends. When the local Korean paper published a story about him written in Korean, she was bursting with pride, Kelley says, and showed it to everybody she knew.

Before we leave, Lee takes a carefully wrapped package of home-made beanpaste cakes and presses it on her visitor.

"She wants you to take this," Kelley explains, interpreting his grandmother's gestures and heavily accented English. "So you'll remember the meal. It's a gift."

Just like *Mavin*, maybe.

Andy Steiner (*Born 1968, Minneapolis, Minnesota*), senior editor of *Utne Reader*, has written for numerous publications, including *Ms.*, *Glamour*, and *Mademoiselle*. She is the author of two books about girls and sports.

Selection Activities, p. 398

COMING
OF AGE

James MacKinnon

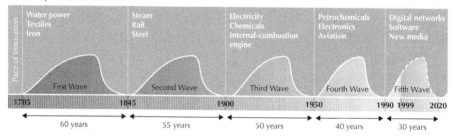

Surf's up
Schumpeter's waves accelerate

Water power Textiles Iron	Steam Rail Steel	Electricity Chemicals Internal-combustion engine	Petrochemicals Electronics Aviation	Digital networks Software New media

Pace of Innovation

First Wave — Second Wave — Third Wave — Fourth Wave — Fifth Wave

1785 — 1845 — 1900 — 1950 — 1990 1999 — 2020

60 years — 55 years — 50 years — 40 years — 30 years

IT WAS THE FIRST TECHNOLOGICAL FRONTLINE. The perfection of the steam engine and the spinning jenny launched the Industrial Revolution—"the conquest of nature"—loosely set between 1785 and 1845. By 1811, the revolution's internal resistance had boiled over: a series of workshop raids in central England launched the movement remembered as "The Luddites." In their first week of action, 1000 followers of the mythical King Ludd destroyed at least 70 of the weaving frames and looms that had sparked a crisis of unemployment, poverty, and community dislocation.

Before the Luddites faded four years later, over 1150 frames would be ruined, 40 factories attacked, 30 Luddites killed, and over 16 000 soldiers called into battle.

With the second wave of steam—worldwide industrialization—came the spread of communism, socialism, unionism, anarchism, and other movements that aimed to redistribute the productive wealth. But these movements, too, contained a doubt of technological advance. In 1905, the Industrial Workers of the World foresaw the age of the global market and braced with a global union, yet their most enduring symbol is a black cat, arched and hissing—the symbol of industrial sabotage.

As an age of electricity and chemicals turned to an age of nuclear power and fossil fuels, each step was followed by resistance: environmentalists, anti-nuclear activists, the drop-out culture of the hippies, the situationists and their warning that the conquest of nature was being replaced by the commercialization of life itself.

Joseph Schumpeter was dead by the time situationists were hurling cobblestones at police in the streets of Paris in 1968. But it was this Austrian economist who first showed that technology came and passed like swells on the horizons of time, wave after wave of industrial revolution. Schumpeter also saw that those waves were accelerating. His first industrial wave—the age of steam, textiles, and iron—lasted 60 years. Schumpeter died in 1950, the year *The Economist* marks as the beginning of the fourth wave, an age of petro-chemicals, electronics, and aviation that would last just 40 years.

Our age, the Information Age, began in 1990 with the flood of digital network, software, and new media technology. It is set to end by 2020, if not sooner.

Schumpeter measured techno-logical advance, yet the waves of human resistance, too, have accelerated. Today, biotechnology emerges into a world that confronts it with a new complexity ethic; hackers evolve as fast as digital networks. Now the Information Age has hardened into a virtual era of brands and symbols, an industrial battle for our psychogeography. But this time, the troops and the resistance—the corporate designer and the culture jammer—have emerged at the same moment to occupy the same historical space.

All that remains is for one to fall from the balance.

James MacKinnon, journalist, is a regular contributor to *The Economist* magazine.

Selection Activities, p. 398

How *Seventeen* Undermines Young Women

Kimberly Phillips

Harvard professor Carol Gilligan, studying the psychological development of teenage girls in 1988, found that they experience a major drop in self-esteem as they reach adolescence. Only 29 percent of teenage girls said that they "felt happy the way I am," as opposed to 60 percent of nine-year-old girls. Gilligan suggests that this adolescent crisis in confidence is due to the conflict between the image that a girl has of herself and what society tells her a woman should be like.

Seventeen, the most widely read magazine among teenage girls in North America, claims to "encourage independence" and help each reader "become this wonderful person that she dreams she will be." But far from encouraging independence, *Seventeen* only reinforces the cultural expectations that an adolescent woman should be more concerned with her appearance, her relations with other people, and her ability to win approval from men than with her own ideas or her expectations for herself.

An average issue of *Seventeen* contains about 8 to 12 fashion and beauty features, taking up two-thirds of the magazine's editorial content. There is usually one story about a new exercise or fitness regime, one story in which an "average-looking" girl gets a make-over, numerous pages of make-up tricks and techniques, mini-stories on what's new in the fashion world, and the feature fashion spreads, which are usually four to six pages long.

For a magazine aimed at an audience of teenage girls, *Seventeen* does a lot of reporting on men. In a recent year, 61 of the celebrities profiled in *Seventeen*'s "Talent" section were men, while only 20 were women. Every issue of *Seventeen* has a column called "Guy Talk," in which a columnist named Robert Love expounds upon the male view of relationships and women. One of only two articles in one year about featured a blonde, blue-eyed model wearing stylish clothing trying to "find Monsieur Right in France," which, according to the captions that accompany the story, is "all about flair—looking très cute—and searching like crazy!" That April, a fashion spread featuring young women in short bloomers and cowboy boots was captioned "How to Rustle Up a Ranchero." The August issue ran a fashion spread called

For a magazine aimed at an audience of teenage girls, *Seventeen* does a lot of reporting on men.

eating disorders among teenage girls was written by a man, giving his perceptions of "My Sister's Battle with Anorexia." The whole of one July issue was devoted to describing "One Hundred Guys We Love." (Perhaps as a follow-up, the August issue ran an article called "Hello, I Love You: How to Write a Knockout Fan Letter.")

Even the fashion and beauty stories are centred around men. A fashion spread in a February issue called "A Little Romance" "Romance 101," which had photographs of a young woman gazing adoringly at her boyfriend. A caption read, "Making the honour roll can have some hidden perks—like John begging me to cram for the English midterm with him ..."

In keeping with this trivialization of intellectual pursuits, an average issue of *Seventeen* has only two or three full-length articles on non-beauty topics. These articles almost invariably deal with a teenage girl's relations with other people, rather than ways for her to be happy with her own life. There are articles about how to find the right boyfriend, whether it's by taking a special *Seventeen* quiz ("What's Your Guy Style?") or by consulting the horoscopes ("The Love Scope"). Then there are articles about how to fit into the social structure at school ("Popularity: What's the Secret?"). The fiction stories that *Seventeen* publishes usually deal with the same kinds of topics.

In the Year of the Woman, there was not one article about the abortion debate. There were also no full-length articles about the Year of the Woman. Aside from one full-length article about sexual harassment, political issues were minimized and crammed into a three-paragraph column, which frequently shared the page with another column about makeup or trendy clothing. Even environmental issues were turned into beauty issues, as in the opening line of an article on ozone depletion: "The environment's in trouble—and the more it suffers, the tougher it is on your skin."

By assuming that skin care is the first thing on their minds, magazines like *Seventeen* are telling young women that their minds are unimportant. By teaching young women that the most important things in a woman's life should be her looks and her relationships to men, they only serve to reinforce the drop in self-esteem reported in Gilligan's study.

Kimberly Phillips (*Born 1976*) was just seventeen years old and working as an intern at FAIR, an American media-watch group, when this article was published in 1994.

Who's on First?

Bud Abbott and Lou Costello

ABBOTT: You know, strange as it may seem, they give ball players nowadays very peculiar names. Now, on the Cooperstown team we have Who's on first, What's on second, I Don't Know is on third ...

COSTELLO: That's what I want to find out. I want you to tell me the names of the fellows on the Cooperstown team.

ABBOTT: I'm telling you. Who's on first, What's on second. I Don't Know is on third ...

COSTELLO: You know the fellows' names?

ABBOTT: Yes.

COSTELLO: Well then, who's playing first?

ABBOTT: Yes.

COSTELLO: I mean the fellow's name on first base.

ABBOTT: Who.

COSTELLO: The fellow's name on first base for Cooperstown.

ABBOTT: Who.

COSTELLO: The guy on first base.

ABBOTT: Who is on first base.

COSTELLO: Who is on first base?

ABBOTT: Who is on the first base.

COSTELLO: Well, what are you asking me for?

ABBOTT: I'm not asking you, I'm telling you Who is on first.

COSTELLO: I'm asking you—Who's on first?

ABBOTT: That's the man's name.

COSTELLO: That's whose name?

ABBOTT: Yes.

COSTELLO: Well, go ahead, tell me!

ABBOTT: Who.

COSTELLO: The guy on first.

ABBOTT: Who.

COSTELLO: The first baseman.

ABBOTT: Who is on first.

COSTELLO: Have you got a first baseman on first?

ABBOTT: Certainly.

COSTELLO: Well, all I'm trying to do is find out what's the guy's name on first base.

ABBOTT: Oh, no, no. What is on second base.

COSTELLO: I'm not asking you who's on second.

ABBOTT: Who's on first.

COSTELLO: That's what I'm trying to find out.

ABBOTT: Well, don't change the players around.

COSTELLO: I'm not changing anybody.

ABBOTT: Now take it easy.

COSTELLO: What's the guy's name on first base?

ABBOTT: What's the guy's name on second base.

COSTELLO: I'm not asking ya who's on second.

ABBOTT: Who's on first.

COSTELLO: I don't know.

ABBOTT: He's on third. We're not talking about him.

COSTELLO: How could I get on third base?

ABBOTT: You mentioned his name.

COSTELLO: If I mentioned the third baseman's name, who did I say is playing third?

ABBOTT: No. Who's playing first.

COSTELLO: Stay offa first, will you?

ABBOTT: Please. Now what is it you want to know?

COSTELLO: What is the fellow's name on third base?

ABBOTT: What is the fellow's name on second base.

COSTELLO: I'm not askin' ya who's on second.

ABBOTT: Who's on first.

COSTELLO: I don't know. (*makes noises*) You got an outfield?

ABBOTT: Oh, sure.

COSTELLO: Cooperstown has got a good outfield?

ABBOTT: Oh, absolutely.

COSTELLO: The left fielder's name?

ABBOTT: Why.

COSTELLO: I don't know. I just thought I'd ask.

ABBOTT: Well, I just thought I'd tell you.

COSTELLO: Then tell me who's playing left field.

ABBOTT: Who's playing first.

COSTELLO: Stay out of the infield.

ABBOTT: Don't mention any names out here.

COSTELLO: I want to know what's the fellow's name in left field.

ABBOTT: What is on second.

COSTELLO: I'm not asking you who's on second.

ABBOTT: Who is on first.

COSTELLO: I don't know. (*makes noises*)

ABBOTT: Now take it easy, man.

COSTELLO: And the left fielder's name?

ABBOTT: Why.

COSTELLO: Because.

ABBOTT: Oh, he's centre field.

COSTELLO: Wait a minute. You got a pitcher on the team?

ABBOTT: Wouldn't this be a fine team without a pitcher?

COSTELLO: I don't know. Tell me the pitcher's name.

ABBOTT: Tomorrow.

COSTELLO: You don't want to tell me today?

ABBOTT: I'm telling you, man.

COSTELLO: Then go ahead.

ABBOTT: Tomorrow.

COSTELLO: What time?

ABBOTT: What time what?

COSTELLO: What time tomorrow are you gonna tell me who's pitching?

ABBOTT: Now listen. For the last time, Who is not pitching. Who is on—

COSTELLO: I'll break your arm if you say who's on first.

ABBOTT: Then why come up here and ask?

COSTELLO: I want to know what's the pitcher's name.

ABBOTT: What's on second.

COSTELLO: I don't know. Ya got a catcher?

ABBOTT: Yes.

COSTELLO: The catcher's name?

ABBOTT: Today.

COSTELLO: Today, and Tomorrow is pitching.

ABBOTT: Now you've got it.

COSTELLO: That's all? Cooperstown's got a couple of days on their team. That's all?

ABBOTT: Well, I can't help that.

(*Costello makes noises.*)

ABBOTT: All right. What do you want me to do?

COSTELLO: Gotta catcher?

ABBOTT: Yes.

COSTELLO: I'm a good catcher too, you know.

ABBOTT: I know that.

COSTELLO: I would like to play for the Cooperstown team.

ABBOTT: Well, I might arrange that.

COSTELLO: I would like to catch. Now I'm being a good catcher. Tomorrow's pitching on the team and I'm catching.

ABBOTT: Yes.

COSTELLO: Tomorrow throws the ball, and the guy up bunts the ball.

ABBOTT: Yes.

COSTELLO: Now, when he bunts the ball—me being a good catcher—I want to throw the guy out at first base, so I pick up the ball and throw it to who?

ABBOTT: Now, that's the first thing you've said right.

COSTELLO: I DON'T EVEN KNOW WHAT I'M TALKING ABOUT!

ABBOTT: Well, that's all you have to do.

COSTELLO: I throw it to first base?

ABBOTT: Yes.

COSTELLO: Now, who's got it?

ABBOTT: Naturally.

COSTELLO: Who has it?

ABBOTT: Naturally.

COSTELLO: Naturally.

ABBOTT: Naturally.

COSTELLO: I throw the ball to Naturally?

ABBOTT: You throw the ball to Who.

COSTELLO: Naturally.

ABBOTT: Naturally. Well, say it that way.

COSTELLO: That's what I'm saying!

ABBOTT: Now don't get excited. Now don't get excited.

COSTELLO: I throw the ball to first base.

ABBOTT: Then Who gets it.

COSTELLO: He better get it.

ABBOTT: That's it. All right now, don't get excited. Take it easy.

COSTELLO: Hmmmmmph.

ABBOTT: Hmmmmmph.

COSTELLO: Now I throw the ball to first base, who grabs it, so the guy runs to second.

ABBOTT: Uh-huh.

COSTELLO: Who picks up the ball and throws it to what. What throws it to I don't know. I don't know throws it back to tomorrow—a triple play.

ABBOTT: Yeah. It could be.

COSTELLO: Another batter gets up and it's a long fly ball to centre. Why? I don't know. And I don't care.

ABBOTT: What was that?

COSTELLO: I said, I don't care.

ABBOTT: Oh, that's our shortstop.

(*Costello makes noises, throws bat angrily, steps closer to Abbott, and they glare.*)

Bud Abbott (*Born 1897, Asbury Park, New Jersey; died 1974*) and **Lou Costello** (*Born 1906, Paterson, New Jersey; died 1959*), comedians, teamed up in 1936 and became instant celebrities as regular guests on the *Kate Smith Radio Hour*. Their signature skit "Who's On First?" is still one of the best-known comedy routines ever performed.

Selection Activities, p. 399

DO NOT DISTURB

Sometimes you have to wonder what it is that scientists do, research scientists especially. I haven't talked to a great many and I guess there is an obvious reason for that. Often their fields are beyond my comprehension. Not so with Jane Goodall. It doesn't matter if we don't understand all the implications and intricate details of a primatologist's work, because we all love stories about chimpanzees. Jane Goodall is a science star, which is dandy for her, because she has been able to raise funds for continued work at her encampment at Gombe in Tanzania. Mind you, there can never be enough money, and there is a foundation that works full-time to keep her projects going, the Jane Goodall Institute in San Francisco. I enjoyed speaking to her in person.

VG: Your last *National Geographic* special had an outrageous number of people viewing it.

JG: It was 17.9 million. Isn't that staggering?

VG: People don't seem to be able to get enough of it.

JG: It is interesting, isn't it? I sometimes wonder why it is. I think it's partly because chimps are so like us, and I also think that there is a strange myth around me because I was the first person to do this sort of thing.

VG: At a time when it was odd for a young girl to do such a thing. Did you have this life in mind from childhood, that you would eventually rush off to the jungle?

JG: Apparently, when I was two I began watching animals and when I was four I disappeared. I was staying with my mother's family in the English countryside and I was gone so long that my mother called the police. After four and a half hours I appeared and I was so happy. I can still remember the moment. I'd been hiding in a hot, stuffy, little, dark henhouse because I could not understand where there was a hole big enough in the chicken for the egg to come out. So I waited. I waited for the chicken to come in and settle down in her nest and I can still see that egg coming out.

VG: Well, there's the basis of all your research—great patience.

JG: Exactly.

VG: The patience has been the key. You actually sat in that jungle for nearly two years before you could really get next to those chimps.

JG: That's right, it did take patience. But as I loved the life and I loved the forest—and I just loved being there—it didn't require as much patience as you might think. I didn't have to rush out and get a Ph.D. and earn my living, you know.

VG: But how did you keep up your enthusiasm and interest when there appeared to be no breakthroughs?

JG: Well, there were, because all the time I was sitting there I could see those chimps from a distance and little pieces of the puzzle began to fit together. But I've always liked being alone. It doesn't mean I'm antisocial; I'm not. I love being with people, too.

VG: How alone were you?

JG: All day, from the time I got up to the time I got back to the camp in the evening, when the authorities said I had to be with somebody. But even then I would climb up to some point and say, "You wait here, and I'll go over there."

VG: You are a rare breed, aren't you? Not too many do this kind of thing.

JG: There are far more now, let me tell you. I get so many letters from children and young people saying, "What do I do to get to do what you do?" This is a big responsibility, because these days it's getting very difficult to do what I did. The economic situation has changed and the political situation, too. More and more field stations are being closed down.

VG: You said that the Tanzanian officials didn't want you to be alone out there. Were they scratching their heads about you?

JG: They surely thought it was peculiar. Louis Leakey, who got the money for me to start off, was accused of being amoral. Sending a young girl off into the bush like that, it just wasn't done in those days.

VG: How did you get to Leakey in the first place? You didn't just march up to him, a legendary anthropologist and all.

JG: It wasn't quite that easy. I think when I was about eighteen my desire to be with animals really crystallized and I wanted to go to Africa. Eventually I began to save enough money; in fact, I worked as a waitress to save up my fare. I had to get a return fare, you see. Finally I got to Africa. I had a temporary job, so I wasn't dependent on anyone. And I had heard about Dr. Leakey. People told me, "If you are interested in animals, you should go to see him." So I did.

VG: Was he thrilled to meet you or did he think you a bit odd?

JG: Oh, no. Almost immediately he offered me a job as his assistant. While I was working with him at the Olduvai Gorge where *Zinjanthropus* [the ancient human skeleton] was found, he started to talk to me about this little group of chimps on a wild lakeshore. I thought he was teasing, but one day he said, "Why do you think I'm talking to you about this? That is what I want you to do, to study those chimps there." It really was fantastic. But then he had to wait a whole year before he could find any money for me to go. Because it was so unique, nobody wanted to give any money, and I had no qualifications. At least no academic qualifications.

VG: Did he want you to have or get a degree?

JG: No, he didn't want me to. He wanted me to have an unbiased mind. He wanted me to go because I wanted to find out.

VG: Do you remember the arrival at your camp in the bush?

JG: I certainly remember the moment I arrived and looked up at that rugged country, thinking, "It is going to be difficult, but how exciting. And I'm jolly well going to do it."

VG: Who was with you?

JG: My mother. This was the amazing thing. She is fantastic and an adventuress and she wanted to come. She lives in England, but when I was working with Dr. Leakey in Nairobi she came for a short visit. When it came time for me to go in, and I told you I had to be with somebody, I chose her. She stayed for three months and she set up this clinic with the local fishermen, which put me in such a good position with them.

VG: Is she a doctor or nurse?

JG: No, neither, but we have a medical family and my uncle was a

surgeon. He gave us masses of medicine and instructions as to how to use it. Do you know it is nearly a quarter of a century ago?

VG: And I suppose some of the chimps that you encountered originally are still alive?

JG: Oh, sure they are; they live till they are fifty. And I am still working and now I have ten Tanzanian field assistants and they are there all the time collecting data, even as I talk to you.

VG: Throughout your studies there, it seems to me that the only encroachment you made upon them was the institution of the banana station. Apart from that, you introduced nothing into the chimps' lives that would be foreign to them.

JG: That's right. But we did it very badly at one time, right at the beginning before I had any idea that this research could carry on in the way it has been. I wanted to find out as much as I could. I kept thinking, "Golly, this is the end, I have to go back and write my thesis and write my degree." So we gave bananas every day and this had the most dramatic effect on the social structure, on the levels of aggression. When I realized that I could continue the study and have students, then we had to change the feeding altogether.

VG: From bananas to what?

JG: We still feed bananas, but, say, six every ten days, whereas a chimp can eat fifty at one sitting. So six is a very tiny amount. We only give bananas if a chimp comes by himself or in a small group.

VG: So as to not create a party atmosphere?

JG: Just enough so that if they're in the neighbourhood, they'll drop by to see if there's anything going.

VG: At the local pub?

JG: That's right.

VG: Are they gluttonous? Will they eat till they burst?

JG: They'll eat till they really can't eat any more. They will stuff themselves. They do enjoy their food, and they make these lovely oo-oo-ah chimp noises. They're happy when they get food.

VG: It must be a temptation to try and communicate, but you don't?

JG: Oh, I don't. It is very important not to try and interact. One could. You could be right in there, part of the group. But we specifically don't.

VG: What is your reaction to people who do the reverse to what you do—make attempts to communicate through sign language or whatever?

JG: It certainly doesn't upset me. It's not so much another world as it is the other side of the coin. It is an attempt to find out about the chimp intellect in a way that I can't do in the wild. It could make for a very good collaborative attempt to understand this very complex creature. In fact, I was just visiting the original chimp who learned sign language. That chimp has now adopted a baby and she's teaching the baby sign language, in the lab.

VG: Isn't that a remarkable thing, that what she learned, she is now teaching?

JG: In the wild, although a young one learns from the mother by observing and imitating and practising, we now find that if a chimp is taught by humans, then she is capable of teaching. That is fascinating.

VG: Has any one of them ever become aggressive with you?

JG: Yes. The worst are the adolescent males, because they are out to intimidate the females of the community. And they can "sex" humans into males and females, too. These adolescent males will treat me rather as they treat the females of the community. In other words, I must be intimidated. I don't think they'd ever really hurt one, but they jump up and they pound on you and hit you, and it does hurt. But once they've intimidated all the females, they work their way through the male hierarchy. Then they finally sort of grow up, as it were. They don't bother the females any more, and they don't bother with me.

VG: In your opinion, do you think that they think about you in any way?

JG: I don't think I could ever answer that. They basically pay very little attention to us, which is nice. It is the young ones who watch more carefully, though. The most intelligent female there today once watched me drinking a cup of coffee, and then I set it down. I didn't even know what she was doing, but she came over and picked up that cup and tried to drink it as we would. But of course it was hot, and she didn't put her lip touching the cup, but she poured it just as we would. That is pretty incredible for a wild animal. And that is the only example I have ever seen of a chimp trying to imitate something we've done. They imitate each other, but not us, fortunately. Otherwise we would really have trouble.

VG: What are your living circumstances in Gombe?

JG: Well, in 1975 I had a large research station with many foreign students, that is, non-Tanzanian students, mostly Americans. I lived there all the year round with my son, except when I was teaching over here. Then four of those students were kidnapped by a rebel group from Zaire. And although they were safely returned to their families in the end, unharmed, this area was then considered a sensitive one and it was deemed not wise to have foreign students there any more. So today I actually live in Dar es Salaam, the capital of Tanzania, and I visit Gombe for about three weeks every two months.

VG: Would you say you are living a city life?

JG: I wouldn't exactly call it that. I am outside the city, and the house is on the beach. I seldom see people. It is a beautiful place for working, and I have so much analysis to do, so much writing.

VG: And on occasion the *National Geographic* specials. It must be wonderful to have all those photos and the film footage of you romping around with these creatures.

JG: Yes, it is a bit like watching your family grow up, isn't it?

VG: Do the chimps rejoice in any way when you visit?

JG: No, thank goodness. But sometimes you feel a bit hurt. After all, I am so pleased to see them. Fifi, let's say, doesn't even look at me. But that is what I have been striving for, that is what I wanted, and that's what I've got.

VG: And what of your son? He goes to school in England. Does he have a similar passion to yours?

JG: No, he dislikes chimps intensely. And it is not really surprising, because chimps are hunters, and most of their prey is other primates, and this does include human infants. So when he was very tiny we had a cage made so that he'd be really safe. I think he probably resents the time that I've spent with the chimps, even though until he was nine he had one-half of every single day of my life, and when he was smaller he had the whole day virtually. But anyway, it turns out that very quietly, and unknown to anyone, he's been observing the behaviour of the boys at his school. And he has come up with some shrewd insights. So, to answer your question: sort of. I think he may share a passion, but it will be human psychology.

VG: What are his observations?

JG: They are to do with why boys are aggressive to each other, and why some of them can turn the aggression off more easily than others, and why some are picked on and others are not. I've only just learned about this in the last few weeks and I think they are super insights. I would love it if he went into human psychology. If you are interested in the chimp because it's the most complex of creatures, then there is only one creature that is more fascinating, and that is us.

Vicki Gabereau (*Born 1946*), broadcaster, began her career at a small radio station in Brampton, Ontario, where she worked as a researcher and story editor. She has hosted a number of CBC Radio talk shows, and began hosting her own television program, *Gabereau*, for VTV in 1997. Gabereau has won three ACTRA awards for best host-interviewer, and is the author of *This Won't Hurt a Bit* and *Cooking Without Looking*.

Eggs

We open on a fridge. A young woman's head enters the frame and opens the fridge door with her mouth. The light from the fridge suddenly bathes her in brightness and for the first time we see she has no arms. The girl sucks up an egg from the fridge, walks to a nearby table and sets it down. Then she returns to the fridge for another.

Cut to the young woman as she drops an egg into a mixing bowl. The egg breaks and the liquid and shell mix together. She lowers her head into the bowl and delicately lifts out the shell with a fork held in her mouth. Then she repeats the process with the second egg.

Next she beats the eggs with a fork held between her teeth. We linger on the shot until her head movement makes us dizzy, then watch her pour the contents into a second bowl. She opens the microwave by pressing the door with her head and places the eggs inside. The girl unwraps a loaf of bread using her teeth and puts two slices in the toaster.

Cut to the girl who is now wrapping a tea towel around the handle of the kettle which has just boiled. With some difficulty she lifts the kettle with her mouth. It takes a few attempts before she pours hot water into a mug. She pours a little at a time, twice putting down the kettle to check how full the mug is.

Finally, her meal is ready. She sets down the plate of scrambled eggs on toast for the camera and steps back to admire her handiwork with satisfaction.

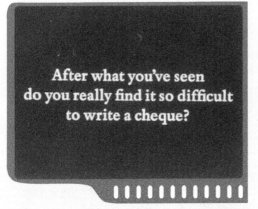

After what you've seen, do you really find it so difficult to write a cheque?

The Queen Elizabeth Foundation for Disabled People.

Retraining to rebuild shattered lives.

BBC films children hoping for adoption

Monthly program to feature youngsters appealing for homes

By Carl Honoré

LONDON – Brushing aside charges of cheap sensationalism, the British Broadcasting Corp. has begun filming a program that will feature children appealing straight to the camera for adoptive parents.

Though not due on British TV screens until next year, *A Family of My Own* has sparked a national debate. While the BBC defends the show as a public service, critics accuse the state broadcaster of exploiting children and pandering to voyeurism.

Gerald Howarth, a Conservative member of Parliament, suggested yesterday the show would amount to an auction of available children.

"[The children] are going to be placed in the shop window on a daily basis. I think the risk here is that it's going to be some kind of a circus."

A Family of My Own will run every day for a month in the new year.

Each episode will have three segments: one on parenting, another on adoption and a third featuring parentless children.

The children will be showcased in various ways, with some appealing directly to the camera, and others using voice-overs to accompany video footage of themselves.

Despite fears, the program will not offer the instant gratification of TV shopping. Viewers who see a child they like cannot have him or her delivered to their doorstep. Prospective parents will have to go through the slow and rigorous screening process prescribed for any adoption.

Jane Lush, the BBC's head of daytime programs, spent

yesterday trying to calm the storm the show has provoked by underlining the altruistic aims of the show.

With more than 10 000 British children looking for new families, she said the show will debunk the myths about adoption and encourage more people to try it.

"This is a great example of the public service broadcasting we aim to provide," said Ms. Lush. "All the experts in the field agree that children in care and fostering arrangements will benefit from the program."

Most adoption experts have expressed cautious support, arguing that anything that helps children find secure homes should be welcomed.

Yet the prospect of a TV program in which children peddle themselves to invisible viewers has raised awkward questions.

Will less attractive children really be given as much airtime as more telegenic ones? What will the effect be on children if they're rejected despite making a national, televised plea?

The BBC insists the show is working with adoption agencies to ensure that a range of children are chosen for broadcast.

Carl Honoré, journalist, is based in London, England, as a foreign correspondent for the *National Post*.

Selection Activities, p. 400

From *The Making of*
Pride &
Prejudice

Sue Birtwistle and Susie Conklin

The Script

Writing a six-part television serial is difficult and time-consuming work, but for Andrew Davies adapting *Pride and Prejudice* was a particularly enjoyable experience: "The novel itself is actually my favourite novel and has been for ages. I've reread it simply for pleasure so many times, and I think I like it better than any other Jane Austen novel, largely because, like everybody else, I'm in love with Elizabeth. I find her kind of joyful energy and sassiness just so beguiling. Later on Jane Austen tried to do rather more complex things with her heroines. For me just this book, just Elizabeth, has these qualities, which are really very modern. She's fiercely moral, she's got a terrific sense of humour, she makes fun of people, she doesn't take herself seriously, but she doesn't put herself down either. She needs to marry money but she's determined she's going to love the man she marries. She is a great character."

Before Andrew could sit down and enjoy the process of writing the scripts, he had to determine the length of the adaptation. "Of course, *Pride and Prejudice* has been done as quite a short movie, but you leave out some very important things doing it at that length. Because the book is so tight—her plot works just like a Swiss clock and doesn't have any flabby bits in it—everything counts. Originally I thought I could do it in five episodes but, because the needs of television scheduling make four, six, or seven episodes a much more convenient thing, this was not a popular idea at all!

"So I looked again and found that if we did it in six episodes, we'd be able to be really filmic with the letters, and show those events that Jane Austen alludes to as little flashback or invented scenes. And I found that it fitted very neatly into six episodes. I say 'very neatly' in comparison with *Middlemarch*, which was like trying to get an elephant into a suitcase in some ways. One would have liked more, and it was a struggle deciding what to leave out. With *Pride and Prejudice* I was jolly pleased we were able to get it all in."

At this stage there was much discussion to ensure that each episode opened as vibrantly as possible and ended as strongly as possible—ideally at a key turning point in the story. Overall the first three episodes lead us to Darcy's arrogant first marriage proposal, which Elizabeth rejects; the last three episodes lead up to his heartfelt second proposal, which a chastened Elizabeth joyfully accepts.

The process of adapting a book for television is not as straight-forward as some might assume. All too easily an adaptation can lovingly copy a book scene by scene only to find that the final product is too literary and undramatic. Important scenes in the book suddenly don't seem to make sense on screen, or time-jumps, which are explained beautifully in prose, make for a fragmented narrative in the film, or memorable dialogue on the page turns to lead in the actor's mouth. This can happen for a number of reasons.

Usually there is no central narrator (or voice-over) who can point out the intricate state of mind of a particular character, or describe a new character when he or she appears, or relate the back history of a character's life for the audience. And though occasionally a voice-over is used in an adaptation, it tends to work best when the original book is written in the first person—*Brideshead Revisited,* for example. The narration then becomes an integral part of a known character in the story rather than an omniscient presence that can distance the audience and prevent it from getting fully involved.

Andrew Davies taught literature for many years and has a thorough understanding of the structure of the novel but, when it comes to television and film, he is a full advocate of the "show, don't tell" approach to scriptwriting. In other words, the camera can tell you a great deal that a narrator would, but in a different and quicker way. Of course, dialogue is terribly important—and Jane Austen has written some of the most delightful dialogue in literature—but good visual storytelling is at the heart of a memorable film. The goal therefore was clear—to remain true to the tone and spirit of *Pride and Prejudice* but to exploit the possibilities of visual storytelling to make it as vivid and lively a drama as possible.

"The advantage of writing for film [as opposed to traditional studio drama on videotape] is that it just frees it up tremendously. For example, I wrote in a little opening sequence, which isn't in the book at all. It shows Bingley and Darcy riding their horses, and Bingley deciding to take Netherfield. It then moves to Elizabeth seeing them from perhaps half a mile away, and thinking, 'Oh, there are two chaps on horses!' Of course, she doesn't know who they are but, almost as if inspired by the galloping of their horses, she turns and runs downhill toward Longbourn. So right at the beginning one's trying to express some of this vitality. That's something you couldn't possibly do in a studio.

"With scenes I've included in the dramatization which aren't in the novel, people sometimes ask, 'What is the justification for that?' and I would have to say, what is the justification of spending money if you're just going to produce a series of pictures alongside the dialogue of the novel? You have to offer an interpretation of the novel. There's this nonsense which some people say about adaptations that you've 'destroyed' the book if it's not identical scene by scene. The novel is still there for anybody to read—and everybody has their own 'adaptation' in a sense when they're reading it.

"In something like that opening scene, part of the justification for showing Bingley and Darcy at that moment when Bingley decides to take Netherfield is to show them as two physical young men. They are young animals on their big horses; that's one of the things they are. We also see in that brief exchange that Bingley, as he's described in the novel later on, is impulsive because he makes a quick decision, and that Darcy views life with a rather critical eye and is a little contemptuous of country manners. Of course, very importantly, you also get the sense of the kind of income level we're dealing with. We see Netherfield, which is a seriously big house and so anyone thinking of renting it must have a lot of money. And almost immediately afterward you see Elizabeth walking up to her own house, which most of us nowadays would consider very desirable, but it's about a twentieth of the size of Netherfield. That indicates that the income of the Bennet family is about a twentieth of the income of the guys they hope to marry. And you can convey all of that without any ponderous dialogue."

On Learning the Dialogue

Jennifer Ehle (Elizabeth Bennet): "It's the hardest dialogue I've ever had to learn. Shakespeare is a doddle compared to Jane Austen. I think this is essentially because the sense of the line comes at the end of it and also the lines are much longer. When I get to the end of a sentence I usually say, 'Oh, I see!' and then I have to go back and read it again. Sometimes the thoughts are quite convoluted—you do all these hair-pin bends—so it takes some getting used to. But it's like anything—by the end I found it much easier to learn. It's like learning another language."

Alison Steadman (Mrs. Bennet): "I haven't done a lot of period drama, so at first I found the language very difficult. You think you've learned it and then, when you come to run it, odd lines and phrases are completely wrong. Because we speak in a completely different way I kept wanting to put in modern phrases. It was a nightmare at first. I thought, 'I'll never get on top of this; I'll never get the hang of it.' And what was worse was that I imagined I was the only one who was having problems. But then I found everyone was finding it extremely difficult to learn. Then I felt better and once you get over that feeling, you get into the rhythm of it and the speech patterns suddenly all begin to make sense."

Visual Effects

For *Pride and Prejudice* the visual effects team provided a range of effects from candles and gas fires through to changing weather conditions, including rain, snow, and frost. Candles required the most attention to detail, as many of the locations had chandeliers and other light fittings incorporating modern features. Most of the time it was impossible, and sometimes forbidden, to remove these, so we had metal tubes manufactured, in a variety of sizes, to cover all manner of light fittings so that they would appear to be candles. A recess was built in at the top to allow us to light a stub of candle, and a drip tray was added to the bottom. The whole thing was painted in heat-resistant paint of approximately the right colour, and then dipped in genuine beeswax to make a perfect match with the candles of the period. During a day's filming, these

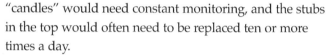

"candles" would need constant monitoring, and the stubs in the top would often need to be replaced ten or more times a day.

We were also involved in simulating flambeaux and Argand lamps, which were the other methods of lighting used during the period. The latter was a predecessor of the modern paraffin lamp and burned an oil that is very similar to modern cooking oil.

Traditionally, snow has been made using either fire-fighting foam or, even more harmful to the environment, salt. Both of these options would have been out of the question at most of the locations, so the alternative we chose was paper. To get the snow effect, one needs reasonably coarse fragments of paper, but for the frost, which we used in the final wedding sequence, one needs a very fine, almost dust-like grade of paper. The whole location is sprayed with a fine mist of water where the frost is required, and the paper dust is blown on top of this. The water then holds it in position. Clearing the area after filming is not so bad as it might sound, as the whole location can simply be hosed down, and the paper disintegrates in the soil without doing any damage.

Most young women in Jane Austen's period had short hair at the front (see the painting used as a source). Susannah Harker (Jane Bennet) agreed to have her long hair cut in this fashion.

From *The Making of Pride and Prejudice*   **327**

Diary of a Filming Day
Friday, 14 October 1994

Overnight

The previous day's filming is developed and the sound rushes
are transferred.

7:30 a.m.

Sam (location manager) phones RAF base and Bristol airport for
weather check for our area.

Alan in Ranks Lab looks at previous day's rushes (picture only) at high
speed to check if the exposure is correct, if there are scratches on the
negative, and if it's in focus. He then sends developed rushes on a van
to the cutting room.

8:00 a.m.

The catering manager goes to the market to buy fresh supplies for 110
people. The first horses start their journey to the location.

Editor and assistant look at yesterday's rushes without sound. They
realize that in the long Steadicam shot of Lizzy and Wickham film
lamps can clearly be seen in the windows along the street. They check
all the material to see if they can edit the sequence to avoid seeing
these. They can't. This is a big problem.

Art Dept is re-laying part of ground cover on the village street. Item
about our filming is broadcast on local radio.

9:00 a.m.

Editor phones film unit and tells them that part of sequence will have
to be reshot. This means remounting this scene in addition to the
scheduled day's filming. The Steadicam operator left yesterday for
another job, so we can't reshoot the entire sequence. Editor suggests
linking shot. We need to see the material to know exactly what is to be
shot. Assistant editor transfers rushes to a VHS cassette and sends it on
courier bike to Wiltshire.

Paul (production manager) starts to change the schedule to include
new shot. We need to call back three actors who have been released.
Roger Barclay is in London, and Adrian Lukis is about to leave

Malmesbury for Cornwall. The co-ordinator phones Roger Barclay in London and asks him to go to Paddington Station immediately. He is due to rehearse at his drama school. Co-ordinator promises to ring his drama school to excuse him from rehearsals.

Catering team is peeling potatoes in preparation for lunch. Wayne and his transport team are cleaning out costume, make-up, and actors' rest-room caravans, toilets, and mobile office.

9:30 a.m.

Paul contacts all departments with new schedule for the day. All call times are adjusted. The 2nd AD calls the actors and organizes transport.

In the cutting room, the editing assistant links the sound and picture of yesterday's material. All the shots are logged. Jennifer Ehle and Julia Sawalha are collected from hotel by 3rd AD.

Roger Barclay leaves London by train.

Rest of horses start journey to location.

Art Department dresses shop front.

10:00 a.m. ...

Later that day:

9:30 p.m.

One of supporting artists is allergic to horses and has a very bad asthma attack. Paul Brodrick administers first aid and she is sent for medical treatment.

10:00 p.m.

Filming continues until 11:30 p.m., still watched by crowds of spectators.

Sam delivers flowers to each house on the main street to thank them for their co-operation.

11:30 p.m.

Filming finishes.

Actors get out of costume and make-up.

Hot snacks and drinks are served as people work.

From *The Making of Pride and Prejudice* **329**

Horses are loaded into boxes for return journeys.

Carriages start journey home.

The lights are derigged. The rostrum is taken apart.

Camera equipment is checked and packed.

The rushes are packaged and collected by courier to go to labs.

Call sheets are handed out for the next filming day.

Anything fragile is moved by Art Department, small props are packed, false doors are removed from cottages.

Dogs return to kennels.

Preparation for large trucks to clear road cover next morning.

12:00 midnight

Caterers do final washing up, and all the day's rubbish is packaged and driven to the tip.

Make-up and costume pack up and store everything for next filming day.

Wayne and team lock all vehicles in preparation for large unit move the following morning back to main location.

Night security takes over.

Sue Birtwistle is director of the Royal Lyceum Theatre in Education Company, in Edinburgh. She has produced many television programs and has written two plays for children.

Susie Conklin, script associate at Granada Television, grew up in the American Southwest. She has worked as a production trainee, publications editor, and freelance writer.

Selection Activities, p. 400

by Ophira Edut

Buffy's New Gigabyte

There's a low, mysterious hum rising from the corner of Buffy Sainte-Marie's hotel room. I hear it, like faint singing, as she directs me to a table draped in hand-stitched Native American fabric, on which there are musical instruments neatly arranged around a long white box. It looks ceremonial, like an altar. The humming falters. I glance around the room nervously— what is that noise?—then I see it. My breath quickens. I can't stop staring.

It's a Macintosh PowerBook G3 laptop. Latest edition. The kind I lust after in computer showrooms and catalogues. The expensive, large-screen model with turbo-charged processing that makes Mac lovers toy with the notion of bank robbery.

It's powered on, buzzing as it loads the special software that's stored in the white box. And for Sainte-Marie—

artist, composer, singer, actor, activist, and educator—it's the instrument she can't live without.

When I told people I was interviewing Buffy Sainte-Marie, reactions varied according to age. Older women fondly recalled a fierce protest singer of the 1960s, famous for anti-war and cultural-resistance anthems like "Universal

Soldier" and "Now That the Buffalo's Gone." Gen-Xers vaguely remembered a *Sesame Street* guest star who appeared with her son and her acoustic guitar during the late 1970s to tell kids "Indians exist." And

Sainte-Marie's non-profit Nihewan Foundation for American Indian Education, Cradleboard aims to "put Native American educators in the driver's seat of delivering their cultures" to students and teachers.

Mainstream kids can now partner with a distant Native class, and both study Indian culture together.

everyone knew "Up Where We Belong," the 1982 Oscar-winning song that she co-wrote for the soundtrack of *An Officer and a Gentleman.*

But it's Sainte-Marie's less well known life as a computer geek—and an adjunct professor of digital art, Native American studies, and philosophy at several universities—that brings her to midtown Manhattan today. Sainte-Marie has lived what she calls a "digital lifestyle" for the last 30 years, using computers to paint, teach, record music, and re-educate the masses about Aboriginal history. She's flown in from her Hawaiian home base to promote her Cradleboard Teaching Project, a multimedia, Native American–centred curriculum for third grade through college. Sponsored by

Using cutting-edge video and computer technology, the project places mainstream schools in year-long distance-learning partnerships with indigenous schools nationwide. Classes exchange "goody" boxes of local information and "self-identity videos" (kids get 30 seconds each to introduce themselves), then begin corresponding through e-mail, phone calls, and Internet chats. Meanwhile, everyone studies Cradleboard's geography and science packets, a collection of materials written by Native educators and edited by Sainte-Marie.

Cradleboard counters the typical approach to Indian Studies, which treats Native peoples as a monolithic unit rather than as a network of diverse tribes, languages, and traditions. "Instead of studying dead text, handed down by generations of non-Indian educators," explains Sainte-Marie on the Cradleboard web site <www.cradleboard.org>, "mainstream kids can now partner with a distant Native class, and both study Indian culture together."

A large W. K. Kellogg Foundation grant funded Cradleboard's 1996 pilot, which set up ten schools with compatible technology. Sainte-Marie also used funds to design and produce an elaborate companion CD-ROM, *Science: Through Native American Eyes*, targeting grades five and up. Non-Indian participants came from public, independent, and parochial schools; Aboriginal students were from Mohawk, Apache, Navajo, Coeur d'Alene, Cree, Quinault, Lakota, Hawaiian, and Ojibway community-based schools. Eighteen classes from 13 states were on board this past school year, and three groups even travelled cross-country to meet their partners. Sandra Tedder, Cradleboard's site co-ordinator, says she's received applications from teachers as far away as Egypt and New Zealand. For now, the modest staff of four has its hands full, but sells the CD-ROM worldwide and directs on-line visitors to her indigenous resources.

"Shall we look at the CD?" Sainte-Marie asks, as she hands me her laptop, sweeping her long black hair off the shoulders of her tailored blazer. We surf through video clips (narrated by Sainte-Marie and other Native American educators), music, an extensive image library, a glossary, interactive games, and quizzes. The software runs smoothly, and it's easy to follow. The colourful menu and navigation buttons are elaborate Indian bead compositions, which Sainte-Marie scanned onto her computer and arranged using graphics software. I take an entry quiz and cringe at my own ignorance. "People usually flunk, then do well on the exit quiz," Sainte-Marie kindly reassures me. Sure enough, she's right. The CD is the kind of "edutainment" that pleases a short-attention-span learner like me—it's easy to follow, and too interactive to evoke memories of boring old school.

I'm also impressed by Cradleboard's user-friendly teacher's edition. The software automatically evaluates student performances and downloads a report to a floppy disk. Teachers can then mail the disk to

Cradleboard for feedback on how the program is working for their students. "Pretty cool, huh?" says Sainte-Marie.

At close to 60 years old, Sainte-Marie is actualizing a dream she first had as a young adoptee in Maine. At her all-white school, she felt alienated and invisible as the lone Aboriginal student. In her teens, Sainte-Marie was reunited with her biological family on Saskatchewan's Piapat Reservation. Later, as a college student at the University of Massachusetts at Amherst, she became a political

issues, and founded several Native American arts, education, and women's groups.

The Cradleboard Project's roots extend back 15 years, to when Sainte-Marie's son, Dakota Wolfchild, was in fifth grade in Hawaii. His teacher asked Sainte-Marie to help rewrite the school's Indian studies unit. "I looked at the available materials and was appalled that they weren't any better than when I was getting my teaching degree 15 years before," recalls Sainte-Marie.

She continued adding to the

Mr. Man doesn't control things anymore. Artists, creative people, people with new ideas are much more empowered now.

activist. When music executives spotted Sainte-Marie's spirited performances at a Greenwich Village coffeehouse in 1963, her recording career took off, and she used her international tours to connect with indigenous people as far away as Australia and Lapland. She has since recorded some 17 albums, earned a teaching certificate and a Ph.D. in fine arts, scored and acted in films, established a career as a visual artist, published widely on Native

curriculum each year, and after a decade, she struck on the idea of arranging a pen-pal program with the Starblanket Reserve School in Saskatchewan, where Sainte-Marie's cousin was a teacher. In 1991, the two classes began using e-mail and live chat to correspond, and "the entire curriculum came alive," says Sainte-Marie. Five years later, Kellogg's funding helped make Cradleboard official.

Meanwhile, Sainte-Marie was experimenting with technology in her personal and artistic ventures. "I got my Mac before they really came on the scene," she says proudly. "It was wonderful, because all of a sudden, as an artist, I had a little machine that would remember my artwork and my writing. Since that time, I've created a digital studio in my home."

As a pioneer in projects that combined technology and the arts, Sainte-Marie made the first quadrophonic (surround-sound) vocal album in the 1960s, long before electronic music became a widely used format. In 1992, she recorded her album *Coincidence and Likely Stories* in her home, wowing producers by sending the tunes to them in London via modem. She's also recorded a live album in a teepee, broadcast worldwide by CBC television. An internationally recognized visual artist, Sainte-Marie exhibits her "digital paintings"—two-foot to seven-foot (1 to 2 m) tall computer images printed on giant sheets of photo paper—across North America and Europe. And she designed the Cradleboard CD-ROM in her home studio, using state-of-the-art software to animate graphics, edit sound, and digitize video.

"It used to be that Mr. Man and his brother and his cousin owned everything—the publishing houses, the recording companies, the political scene," says Sainte-Marie. "In order to do something as an artist, or as an outsider, you had to go stand in that line until you got the stamp of approval. Technology is changing that. Mr. Man doesn't control it anymore. The cat's out of the bag—and having kittens! You can publish on-line, you can have digital paintings that you can work on forever. Artists, creative people, people with new ideas—individuals are much more empowered now."

And the surprise to many is that Native peoples, often assumed to be left out of the high-speed, high-tech culture, have been at the forefront of the Internet's evolution. "We are not all dead and stuffed in some museum with the dinosaurs," Sainte-Marie quips in "Cyberskins," her eloquent on-line manifesto at <www.aloha. net/~bsm/cybersk.htm>. "We are Here in this digital age."

Ophira Edut, American writer, editor, graphic artist, Web designer, and cartoonist, is the founding publisher of *Hear Us Emerging Sisters*, a multicultural women's magazine, and the author of *Adios, Barbie: Young Women Write About Body Image and Identity.*

Selection Activities, p. 401

Welcome to Alpine Racing … With a Difference!

Web Site of the Canadian Disabled Alpine Ski Team

1998 Winter Paralympic Games

Photo by Kazuji Shimizu

Daniel Wesley, 1998 Nagano Paralympics	
Downhill	Bronze Medal
Super Giant Slalom	Gold Medal

 1998 Nagano Paralympic Games

 Nagano Daily Updates

 About Disabled Skiing …

Disabled skiing got its start initially as a unique form of physical therapy for veterans, and has evolved into an enjoyable recreational pursuit for people of all ages and disabilities. Inevitably recreation gave birth to sport and the Winter Paralympics (for the physically disabled—not to be confused with the Special Olympics), held at the same venues and time as the Winter Olympics, as well as periodic World Championships, have been held for over twenty years throughout the world.

About the Canadian Association for Disabled Skiing …

The Canadian Association for Disabled Skiing (CADS) was started by Jerry Johnston, a visionary ski-school owner in Banff, Alberta. CADS today has a membership of about 4000 with divisions in every Canadian province and ties to disabled skiing organizations around the world. Whether you're interested in volunteering, are disabled and want to give it a try, or simply want to learn—read on!

Recreational Programs • Our Sponsors • Alpine Racing • Contact Us
Recent Results & Upcoming Events • X-Country Racing
CDAST Member Profiles • CDAST Sponsorship Opportunities • Other Links
Photo Gallery • What's New? • European Tour '98

http://www.canuck.com/cads/

Researchers
Find Sad, Lonely World in
Cyberspace

BY AMY HARMON

In the first concentrated study of the social psychological effects of Internet use at home, researchers at Carnegie-Mellon University have found that people who spend even a few hours a week on-line experience higher levels of depression and loneliness than they would have if they used the computer network less frequently.

Those participants who were lonelier and more depressed at the start of the two-year study, as determined by a standard questionnaire administered to all the subjects, were not more likely to use the Internet. Instead, Internet use itself appeared to cause a decline in psychological well-being, the researchers said.

The results of the $1.5 million project ran completely contrary to expectations of the social scientists who designed it and of many of the organizations that financed the study. These included technology companies like Intel Corp., Hewlett-Packard, AT&T Research, and Apple Computer, as well as the National Science Foundation.

"We were shocked by the findings, because they are counter-intuitive to what we know about how socially the Internet is being used," said Robert Kraut, a social psychology professor at Carnegie-Mellon's Human–Computer Interaction Institute.

"We are not talking here about the extremes. These were normal adults and their families, and on average, for those who used the Internet most, things got worse."

The Internet has been praised as superior to television and other "passive" media because it allows users to choose the kind of information they want to receive and, often, to respond actively to it in the form of e-mail exchanges with other users, chat rooms, or electronic bulletin board postings.

Research on the effects of watching television indicates that it tends to reduce social involvement. But the new study, titled "HomeNet," suggests that the interactive medium may be no more socially healthy than older mass media. It also raises troubling questions about the nature of "virtual" communication and the disembodied relationships that are often formed in the vacuum of cyberspace.

Participants in the study used inherently social features like e-mail and Internet chat more than they used passive information gathering like reading or watching videos. But they reported a decline in interaction with family members and a reduction in their circles of friends that directly corresponded to the amount of time they spent on-line.

At the beginning and end of the two-year study, the subjects were asked to agree or disagree with statements like "I felt everything I did was an effort," and "I enjoyed life" and "I can

The interactive no more socially older mass media

find companionship when I want it." They were also asked to estimate how many minutes each day they spent with each member of their family and to quantify their social circle. Many of these are standard questions in tests used to determine psychological health.

For the duration of the study, the subjects' use of the Internet was recorded. For the purposes of this study, depression and loneliness were measured independently, and each subject was rated on a subjective scale. In measuring depression, the responses were plotted on a scale of 0 to 3, with 0 being the least depressed and 3 being the most depressed. Loneliness was plotted on a scale of 1 to 5.

By the end of the study, the researchers found that one hour a week on the Internet led, on average, to an increase of .03, or 1 percent, on the depression scale, a loss of 2.7 members of

medium may be healthy than

the subject's social circle, which averaged 66 people, and an increase of .02, or four-tenths of 1 percent, on the loneliness scale.

The subjects exhibited wide variations in all three measured effects, and while the net effects were not large, they were statistically significant in demonstrating deterioration of social and psychological life, Kraut said.

Based on these data, the researchers hypothesize that relationships maintained over long distances without face-to-face contact ultimately do not provide the kind of support and reciprocity that typically contribute to a sense of psycho-

logical security and happiness, like being available to baby-sit in 'a pinch for a friend, or to grab a cup of coffee.

"Our hypothesis is there are more cases where you're building shallow relationships, leading to an overall decline in feeling of connection to other people," Kraut said.

The study tracked the behaviour of 169 participants in the Pittsburgh area who were selected from four schools and community groups. Half the group was measured through two years of Internet use, and the other half for one year. The findings were published by *The American Psychologist,* the peer-reviewed monthly journal of the American Psychological Association.

Because the study participants were not randomly selected, it is unclear how the findings apply to the general population. It is also conceivable that some unmeasured factor caused simultaneous increases in use of the Internet and decline in normal levels of social involvement. Moreover, the effect of Internet use varied depending on an individual's life patterns and type of use. Researchers said that people who were isolated because of their geography or work shifts might have benefited socially from Internet use.

Even so, several social scientists familiar with the study vouched for its credibility and predicted that the findings would probably touch off national debate over how public policy on the Internet should evolve and how the technology itself might be shaped to yield more beneficial effects.

federal government provide e-mail access to all Americans.

"It's not clear what the underlying psychological explanation is," Ms. Bikson said of the study. "Is it because people give up day-to-day contact and then find themselves depressed? Or are they exposed to the broader world of Internet and then wonder, 'What am I doing here in Pittsburgh?' Maybe your comparison

"You said I should spend more time with our children, so I turned their faces into icons."

"They did an extremely careful scientific study, and it's not a result that's easily ignored," said Tora Bikson, a senior scientist at Rand, the research institution. Based in part on previous studies that focused on how local communities like Santa Monica, California used computer networks to enhance civic participation, Rand has recommended that the

standard changes. I'd like to see this replicated on a larger scale. Then I'd really worry."

Christine Riley, a psychologist at Intel Corp., the giant chip manufacturer that was among the sponsors of the study, said she was surprised by the results but did not consider the research definitive.

"For us, the point is there was really no information on this before," Ms. Riley said. "But it's important to remember this is not about the technology per se; it's about how it is used. It really points to the need for considering social factors in terms of how you design applications and services for technology."

The Carnegie-Mellon team—which included Sara Kiesler, a social psychologist who helped pioneer the study of human interaction over computer networks; Tridas Mukophadhyay, a professor at the graduate business school who has examined computer-mediated communication in the workplace; and William Scherlis, a research scientist in computer science—stressed that the negative effects of Internet use that they found were not inevitable.

For example, the main focus of Internet use in schools has been gathering information and getting in touch with people from faraway places. But the research suggests that maintaining social ties with people in close physical proximity could be more psychologically healthy.

"More intense development and deployment of services that support pre-existing communities and strong relationships should be encouraged," the researchers write in their forthcoming article.

Government efforts to wire the nation's schools, for example, should consider on-line homework sessions for students rather than just on-line reference works."

At a time when Internet use is expanding rapidly, social critics say the technology could exacerbate the fragmentation of society or help to fuse it, depending on how it is used.

"There are two things the Internet can turn out to be, and we don't know yet which it's going to be," said Robert Putnam, a political scientist at Harvard University and author of *Bowling Alone*, a book that chronicles the alienation of Americans from each other since the 1960s. "The fact that I'm able to communicate daily with my collaborators in Germany and Japan makes me more efficient, but there are a lot of things it can't do, like bring me chicken soup."

Putnam added, "The question is how can you push computer-mediated communication in a direction that would make it more community friendly."

Perhaps paradoxically, several participants in the Internet study expressed surprise when they were informed by a reporter of the study's conclusions.

"For me it's been the opposite of depression; it's been a way of being connected," said Rabbi Alvin Berkun, who used the Internet for a few hours a week to read *The Jerusalem Post* and communicate with other rabbis across the country.

But Berkun said his wife did not share his enthusiasm for the

provide a self-correcting mechanism to the technology that tries to cross it.

The rabbi's daughter, Rebecca, 17, said she spent a fair amount of time in teenage chat rooms at the beginning of the survey in 1995.

> "There are two things the Internet can turn out to be, and we don't know yet which it's going to be."

medium. "She does sometimes resent it when I go and hook up," he said, adding after a pause, "I guess I am away from where my family is while I'm on the computer."

Another possibility is that the natural human preference for face-to-face communication may

"I can see how people would get depressed," Ms. Berkun said. "When we first got it, I would be on for an hour a day or more. But I found it was the same type of people, the same type of things being said. It got kind of old."

Selection Activities, p. 402

A VIRTUAL night out on the town

From dance-club music to live baseball games, webcasting is bringing entertainment programming to the home PCs of those who can't get to the actual events themselves.

by Grant Buckler

Tuesday, November 30, 1999

Ben Sargent is a Calgary student and disc jockey who likes underground dance music. But because he gets little opportunity to hear it live locally and recordings are difficult to find, he spends many hours on the Internet, especially on a web site called Groovetech.

Seattle-based Groovetech broadcasts live performances and "DJ sets" of new recordings. So, while working at his computer or just relaxing, Mr. Sargent can enjoy a six-hour DJ set live from a U.S. nightclub that is made up mostly of new music and has no repetition.

When he hears something he especially likes, he often can order it on-line. Besides offering live music, Groovetech is an on-line retailer and "you can listen to specific tracks right off the [CD] before you buy it."

Mr. Sargent, who was introduced to the site by a friend about two years ago, is one of a growing number of people tuning in to music from on-line disc jockeys or from nightclubs around the world—often accompanied by live video from the clubs themselves. Other Web users find sports events and movies more attractive. The common bond is the Internet's role in giving them access to entertainment they cannot find locally or on television. Revenue for these sites comes mostly from ads, but some (including Groovetech) also sell CDs on their sites.

Digital Club Network Inc. of New York broadcasts on the Web—or "webcasts" in the popular jargon—live from nightclubs, mostly in New York but also in other U.S. cities. The company evolved from a series of annual week-long festivals in which bands played at New York clubs while their performances were webcast into a full-time web site. "The response so far has been great," chief operating officer Ted Werth says.

Similar operations such as The Womb, Betalounge, and Raveworld broadcast music—largely recordings played by DJs—from dance clubs, mostly in the United States. A recent performance by singer Melanie C.—formerly with the Spice Girls—was webcast live from the London Astoria on Nov. 1.

Sports fans may prefer sites where live audio from baseball games is available along with video clips of game highlights and live coverage of pre-game news conferences. Webcasting, which can be defined as transmitting audio and video over the Internet, has been quite widely used in business, but there is a growing consumer market for the technology, too. Shaun McIver, general manager in Toronto of the Canadian branch of Activate.net, a Seattle-based webcasting firm, says Activate began diversifying into the entertainment field in the past year. Music and sports are

the most promising types of entertainment programming, he says.

Mr. Werth says one major audience for services such as his are teenagers, who are interested in music but cannot go to the clubs because most serve alcohol. Still, they are not the only audience. Adults also often find it hard to have a night on the town—perhaps because they have young children—and many live far from the major cities where live-music venues are concentrated.

Mr. McIver says most home Internet users today do not have fast enough modems to provide the quality that will keep them sitting in front of their computers for long webcasts, but that is changing. Mr. Sargent has a cable modem at home, which gives him a high-speed connection that provides fairly good sound quality. Another Groovetech user, Martin Apps of Thornhill, Ontario, says the audio he hears over his 56-kilobit-a-second modem is not as good as a compact disc played in his computer's CD-ROM drive, but it's good enough when you consider he can hear music on Groovetech before he can find it locally.

However, the video component is less satisfactory. Although a 56K modem will provide decent audio quality,

Mr. Werth acknowledges, for video you really need a very high-speed connection such as an Integrated Services Digital Network (ISDN) line.

Good speakers or headphones—or a connection to the home stereo system—are essential to get the most from on-line audio. As for video, Mr. Werth says most computer monitors sold today will do justice to the best video signal most people can receive via the Internet.

create some interesting challenges for traditional networks."

The on-line medium has some possibilities that television and radio lack, too. Some sites, including Digital Club Network, pair webcasts with on-line chat areas to let visitors simulate going to a club together, even though they may be far apart. Mr. Werth says this is popular with recent university graduates who "meet" on the site and chat while

> Some sites pair **WEBCASTS** with **ON-LINE CHAT AREAS** to let visitors simulate going to a club together.

Over time, Mr. Werth expects computers and home-entertainment systems to be increasingly interlinked, so consumers will receive entertainment programming over the Internet and watch it on their television sets. As that happens, Mr. McIver says, "down the road it's going to

listening to music, almost as if they were spending Friday evening at the school coffee house. Of course, it's not quite the same as being there, he says. "We're never really going to be able to duplicate it completely until we can transmit cappuccino through the computer."

***

Grant Buckler (*Born 1959, Nova Scotia*), journalist, studied computer science and journalism before joining the staff of *Computing Canada* in 1980. Now freelance, he has written articles—mostly about technology—for many publications, including the *Globe and Mail* and *Financial Post*.

Selection Activities, p. 402   *A Virtual Night Out on the Town*

Back   Forward   Reload   Home   Search   Images   Print   Security   Shop   Stop

site: http://www.talkcity.com/   What's R

WebMail   Radio   People   Yellow Pages   Download   Calendar

TALK CITY

Click Here Now

KEEN.com   Win a Digital Camera

eFriends   Chat   Discussion Boards   Home Pages   Live Events   Email   JoinNow!   Store

Santa's Workshop
Visit Santa and his friends at Santa's Workshop - there's lots of fun stuff to see and do!

shopping

CheckOut.com

MUSIC MOVIES GAMES

CheckOut.com

Visit Now
CheckOut the best in music, movies, and games!

What Interests You?

Arts & Books	Collectibles	Movies, TV, Radio
Autos	Computing	Music
Business & Finance	Games	News & Sports
Cities & Travel	Health & Wellness	Teen
College	Home & Family	Women

eFriends
Create your own club! Invite your friends to join.

Chat Now!

Members enter here   **View list of chats**

○ Visitor Centre   ○ Current Event
○ General Chat   ○ Health Chat

[   ] Chat

[   ] Go!

Join or create a room!
Room name:

Join Talk City today! It's Free!
Free email! Free home pages! Start a club!

Search
☑ chats   ☐ Talk City

[   ] Find

Search the Web
Browse Best of the Web

[Choose a category... ⬦]

Speak Up Poll
Topic: How soon do you start your holiday shopping?

○ A year in advance!
○ A month prior to the occasion
○ Starting the day after Thanksgiving!
○ One week prior to the occasion
○ I don't shop for the holidays
○ None of the above

[Vote Now!]

What's hot at Talk City
Friends don't let friends lose touch
Find out what's up with friends and family at any time with Talk City eFriends. Discussion boards, group announcements and a private photo gallery are at your disposal. Check it out! Find out more!

Come join the shopping fun!
... at the Talk City Shopping Network, the first live interactive shopping program on the Internet. The only thing better than the prices are the products! Find out more!

4:00PM PT - Dec. 18
Take a trip to Santa's Village for a virtual visit with Santa Claus and Company.

TCSN

6:00PM PT - Dec. 18
Get all your holiday shopping done as EnoCCCh presents gifts for the season.

Sweepstakes
TALK CITY's
$10,000 GRAND PRIZE VACATION

Play Now!
Win an instant prize or a Grand Prize Vacation in Talk City's Reindeer Games Sweepstakes.

SmarterKids.com
SmarterKids.com
EDUCATIONAL GAMES, BOOKS & SOFTWARE

Visit Now
SmarterKids.com - The World's Smartest Learning Store

Back Forward Reload Home Search   Images Print Security Shop Stop

site: http://www.talkcity.com/   What's Related

WebMail   Radio   People   Yellow Pages   Download   Calendar

Talk City special programs

Earn Points at MyPoints® by Talk City
- Earn More Points
- Spend Points
- Check Account Balance

Come join the shopping fun!
At the Talk City Shopping Network, the first live interactive shopping program on the Internet, the only thing better than the prices are the products! click here.

You Have Mail!
If you are a Talk City member, you already have an email account with us. click here.

Give Power Point Presentations Online!
Guide any number of people through an online presentation made directly from your PowerPoint slides. Your audience can be anywhere in the world—all they need is access to the 'Net and a standard web browser. click here.

Get an Instant Store for your Site!
In minutes, add a unique store to your site. FREE! With Affinia, feature products from over 1,000 merchants and turn your traffic into profit. click here.

Talk City Now Supports FrontPage® 2000!
Now Talk Citizens can use the extra features of the leading web site creation and management tool from Microsoft. You can create your pages using FrontPage® 2000 and upload them to your Talk City site. You can even include your MS Office documents on your site without having to convert them to a different format first! For more information, click here.

Football
GO TO
TALK CITY
FOOTBALL

Check It Out!
Join the huddle and see what's new on Talk City's Football site.

Sweepstakes
OnNow's

Big... BIG...
B I G!

Play Now
Brand New Vacation Sweepstakes! Meet Hepcat and win a $10,000 trip to the Bahamas!

MSN
msn.
eShop at MSN.com

Try It Now
The easiest way to find the right gift.
eShop at MSN.com™

Products and Advertising | Feedback

out Talk City | Code of Conduct | Advertising and Products | Business Services | Feedback | Jobs | Help | Press

Kipp Cheng

Setting Their Sites on Generation Y

Should Marketers Hop on the Teen Bandwagon?

There's a youthquake trembling across North America and the seismic tremors rumbling through the corridors of pop culture and the economy are affecting everything from movies and television programming to spending habits and purchasing trends. Little wonder, then, that advertisers have finally caught on to the country's current obsession with all things Teen by aggressively chasing the mindshare and dollars of the "it" market of the moment, Generation Y, a.k.a. teens age 12 to 19.

According to U.S. Census projections, Gen Y is 30 million strong and growing, nearly three times the size of the aging and passé twenty- and thirty-something Generation X. Add to Gen Y's enormous cultural influence the expendable cash burning holes in their $150 designer-label jeans and they become a big-time target indeed.

"The demographic of Generation Y, growing rapidly as it is, and the emergence of the Internet really highlight the importance of Gen Y in the entire economy," says Jim Johnson, chief operating officer at Alloy, the New York–based off-line girlz-and-boyz-gear catazine that boasts 2.5 million members on its e-commerce site.

While Hollywood and trend-watchers have already

jumped on the teeny-bop band-wagon, it was only recently that web companies finally began addressing this lucrative audience with web sites featuring teen-oriented content and compelling e-commerce offerings.

So what's taking big-name advertisers so long to identify and serve this highly prized audience on the web?

The somewhat stealthy nature of web enterprises aimed at teens to know about Generation Y is that they're a generation of multimedia, multitasking people," says Susan Mernit, director of new media at react.com, the New York–based Gen Y e-zine. "Teens are typically on the phone, with the computer on, surfing the web, instant messaging or chatting, and either listening to music or watching the television, all at the same time. That's just standard operating procedure for them."

If a marketer is being dishonest, it will ring false to teens. They know when they're being lied to.

is perhaps due to all of the bad press and negative media attention focused on the many minefields teens must navigate through while they're on-line. Pundits were often quick to point out the evils of this thing called the Internet and equally quick to vilify teen users for spending more time on-line in unproductive or potentially harmful ways.

In reality, though, adults may not have given teens enough credit for their ability to discern what's good and what's bad content on-line.

"I think the thing adults need So while the exact same attention-dividing activity was termed "slacking off" a half-generation ago, the born-with-a-mouse-in-hands Gen Y-ers have cleverly recast their split-focus endeavours as "multitasking."

Marketers also believe that teens, despite their overall cynicism, are still receptive to marketing messages, as long as those messages are pertinent and enticing.

"I think teens today are more jaded, a bit more sceptical than we were at that age," says Brad

Mehl, vice-president of marketing at Bolt.com. "Teens readily reject false images. If a marketer is being dishonest, it will ring false to them. They know when they're being lied to."

Card-carrying members of Generation X may look at their savvy unlike previous generations of teens.

"It's very difficult to reach teens through traditional media outlets," says Dan Pelson, CEO of Bolt.com. "They're in school all day and then they're hanging out with their friends. They're

**"We need more customers. By the year 2010,
our goal is to teach every dog and cat
in North America how to spend money!"**

upstart rivals with a bit of envy or scorn, but the reality is that Gen Y-ers simply spend more than their predecessors, and they are flexing their collective purchasing muscle to the tune of $141 billion annually, according to Mediamark, New York.

While advertisers may have found in Gen Y the new marketing Holy Grail, the young group has proven to be both elusive and fickle, possessing a media not in a dormant situation where they're going to be sitting in front of a television a lot."

Nielsen Research has found that younger teens today watch less television than 18- to 49-year-olds but spend more time on-line than any other demographic. Marketing to teens on the web therefore gets them where they live, or at least where they surf.

"Traditional media products for teenagers, by and large, are dumbed down," says Margaret Gould Stewart, general manager at community site Tripod. "They don't treat teenagers, generally speaking, like they are smart young adults who are capable of absorbing complex concepts."

For advertisers, it's a matter of whether or not teens will buy what they're selling. "Teens, I think, tend to be as brand-loyal as anyone out here," says Pelson. "People tend to say that they are brand-disloyal, but if they trust the brand, they are extraordinarily brand-loyal. If they don't trust the brand, they run away screaming. There's no middle ground."

Mernit agrees, with a condition. "They can be very loyal—but loyalty in their world represents six to eight months. During that six to eight months,

they will only listen to that radio station, they'll buy that brand of jeans, and then they'll move on to the next brand. This is not a generation that's shopping on price. It's completely the opposite. They want style and they want what they think is quality."

Still, the marriage of teens and the Internet looks like one that will last, at least until the next fad (can we say broadband?) rolls along.

"Teens are unquestionably the drivers of this medium," says Pelson. "They've made the Internet absolutely part of the fabric of their culture today. It's their rock and roll. In the '50s, my parents were focused on being in a band. Today it's being an Internet developer or doing your own web site."

Kipp Cheng (*Born 1968, Taipei, Taiwan*), journalist, is a news editor at IQ News, the weekly technology news section appearing in *Adweek, Brandweek*, and *Mediaweek* magazines. He also publishes plays and short stories.

The Arts *and* Media Images

Oopik Pitsiulak *(Born 1946, Lake Harbour, NWT, now Nunavut)*, sculptor. She lived in Lake Harbour, a settlement near the Hudson's Bay Company trading post where her father and uncles worked, until she was nine. She began carving in the 1960s, while working with her relative, sculptor Peter Pitseolak. Her first sculpture was of a woman carrying a baby on her back; her work continues to focus on the daily lives of women.

Vincent van Gogh *(Born 1853, Groot-Zundert, the Netherlands; died 1890)*, artist. His enormous fame came only after his death; he sold only one painting during his lifetime. His early works were sombre still lifes and peasant scenes. In 1886 he visited his brother Theo in Paris and was inspired by the work of Pissarro, Seurat, and others. He moved to Arles in southern France and his work became more expressive, characterized by swirling brushstrokes and brilliant colours.

Courtney Milne *(Born 1943, Saskatoon, Saskatchewan)*, photographer. An award-winning freelance photographer since 1975, Milne's academic background is in psychology, journalism, and mass communication. He has written many articles for photographic magazines and has published several books, including three featuring the Canadian Prairies. He has travelled extensively, photographing landscapes and nature scenes throughout Canada, the USA, and around the world.

Andrew Wyeth *(Born 1917, Chadds Ford, Pennsylvania)*, painter. Noted for his portraits and rural landscapes, he received his art training from his father, N. C. Wyeth, an illustrator and muralist. His works demonstrate a technical mastery and affection for his subjects.

Molly Lamb Bobak *(Born 1922, Vancouver, British Columbia)*, artist, writer, teacher. As a student at the Vancouver School of Art, she was profoundly influenced by her teacher, Jack L. Shadbolt. In 1942 she joined the Canadian Women's Army Corps, and in 1945 became the only woman appointed as a war artist. She is best known for her colourful, lively paintings, which often depict public celebrations and leisure activities.

Maud Lewis *(Born 1903, South Ohio, Nova Scotia; died 1970)*, folk artist. Lewis lived with her husband in a one-room cottage only one hour's drive from her birthplace for over 30 years. Her colourful and lively naive paintings were made with marine or house paint on pieces of board. A shy, private woman, she observed and recorded the rural life around her, painting farm and village life, animals, boats, and ocean scenes.

Oopik Fetching Water, Oopik Pitsiulak, 1990

Selection Activities, p. 403

The Starry Night, Vincent van Gogh, 1889

                                   Selection Activities, p. 404

Life's Highway, Courtney Milne, 1993

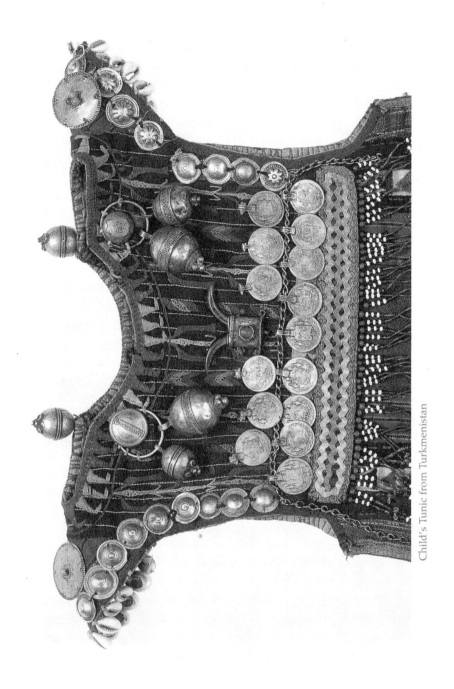

Child's Tunic from Turkmenistan

Selection Activities, p. 404

Christina's World, Andrew Wyeth, 1948

Skaters on the Rideau, Molly Lamb Bobak, 1980

Selection Activities, p. 405

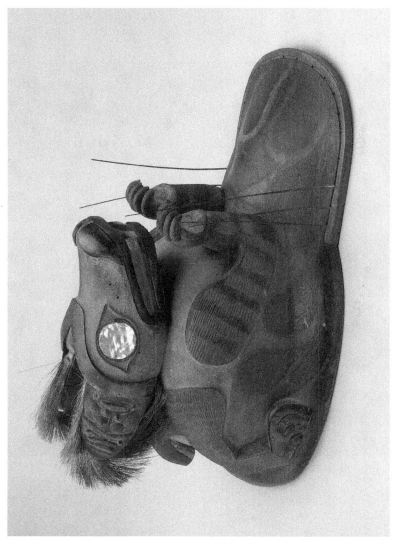

Tlingit Clan-Emblem Hat, 1830–60

Springtime, Maud Lewis, undated

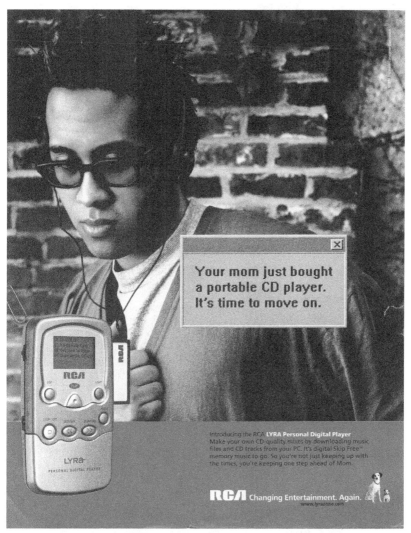

Lyra Personal Digital Player, print advertisement

swept on
face
running

Without Limits, movie poster 1

it shows fantastic movie

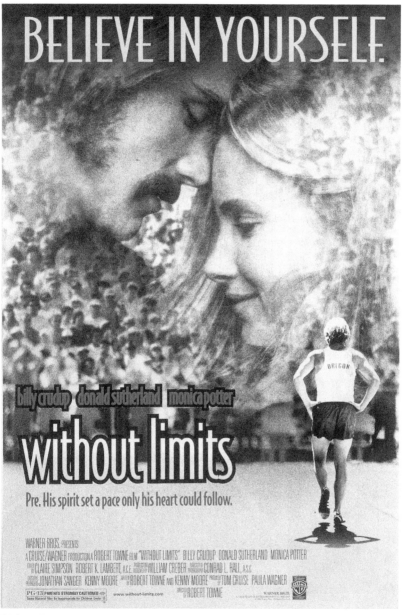

Without Limits, movie poster 2

CAB RIDE

VIDEO	AUDIO
Open on exterior busy airport terminal. Richard and David emerge through the glass doors. Richard carries the Toshiba Notebook under his arm. He wears a big, relieved smile on his face.	SUPER: Toshiba logo. SFX: AMBIANCE OF A BUSY TERMINAL, CARS HONKING, ETC.
A cabbie approaches Richard and David.	CABBIE: Where to?
Richard doesn't know. He places the notebook on the trunk of a cab. The cab has a luggage rack.	RICHARD: I'll check my notebook.
To Richard's horror, suddenly the cab pulls away. They all jump into the second cab.	RICHARD: Follow that cab!
Cut to inside Richard's cab. Richard sits forward looking tense and anxious.	RICHARD: I thought that was your cab. I'm not worried ... I'm not worried ...
Cut to Richard leaning out of the cab.	RICHARD (Shouting): Stop that cab! DAVID: Look on the bright side ... RICHARD: Oh, thank you!
Cut to notebook sliding around on the back of the cab's luggage rack.	DAVID: Boy, that thing's really taking a beating.

VIDEO	AUDIO
	CABBIE: Look at that baby go!
Richard grabs the cabbie.	RICHARD: Can we please catch up to that cab? CABBIE: Yeah.
Richard's cab pulls up beside the cab with his notebook on the back. Richard leans out, attempting to grab it.	RICHARD: I can get it ...
There is a "Y" in the road. Each cab takes a different route.	RICHARD: You lost it, you bad cabbie you!
Down the street, David sees the cab with the notebook.	DAVID (Matter-of-factly): There it is.
The cab hits a bump. The notebook flies into the air. Richard jumps out of his cab.	RICHARD: No ... my notebook!
The notebook lands on the street. Distraught, Richard kneels beside it and taps a few keys. It still works. Richard is ecstatic.	ANNOUNCER: Toshiba notebook computers. Tough enough for today's world. RICHARD (Laughing hysterically): Yes!
SUPER: Toshiba logo.	

Creative Direction
BILL KEENAN

Copyrighting
BILL KEENAN

Art Direction
MICHAEL CROSS

Production Company
IMPORTED ARTISTS

Producer
SHARON KOSOKOWSKI

Director
RICHARD D'ALESSIO

Film Editor
PANIC & BOB

Music/Sound
EINSTEIN BROTHERS

Agency
PROMANAD COMMUNICATIONS INC., TORONTO, ON
(416) 869-3800

Client
TOSHIBA ISG

Cab Ride, television advertisement storyboard and script

Selection Activities, p. 407

Trix/Crunch 'n Munch, product packaging

they sell sexual adult

different color ; toy access → gender . adventie—what they are actually selling

Barbie Computer, print advertisement

Hot Wheels Computer, print advertisement

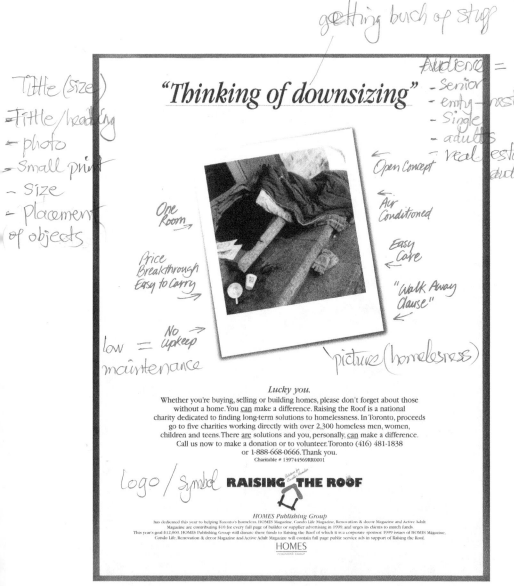

Raising the Roof, public service print advertisement

Handwritten annotations on the page:

this advertise for home

getting bunch of stuff

Title (size)
Title/heading
- photo
- Small print
- Size
- Placement of objects

One Room

Price Breakthrough Easy to Carry

low = No upkeep
maintenance

"Thinking of downsizing"

Audience =
- Senior
- empty-nester
- Single
- adults
- real esta audie

Open Concept

Air Conditioned

Easy Care

"Walk Away Clause"

picture (homelessness)

Lucky you.
Whether you're buying, selling or building homes, please don't forget about those
without a home. You can make a difference. Raising the Roof is a national
charity dedicated to finding long-term solutions to homelessness. In Toronto, proceeds
go to five charities working directly with over 2,300 homeless men, women,
children and teens. There are solutions and you, personally, can make a difference.
Call us now to make a donation or to volunteer. Toronto (416) 481-1838
or 1-888-668-0666. Thank you.
Charitable # 139744569RR0001

logo / symbol RAISING THE ROOF

HOMES Publishing Group
has dedicated this year to helping Toronto's homeless. HOMES Magazine, Condo Life Magazine, Renovation & decor Magazine and Active Adult
Magazine are contributing $10 for every full page of builder or supplier advertising in 1999, and urges its clients to match funds.
This year's goal:$12,000. HOMES Publishing Group will donate these funds to Raising the Roof of which it is a corporate sponsor. 1999 issues of HOMES Magazine,
Condo Life, Renovation & decor Magazine and Active Adult Magazine will contain full page public service ads in support of Raising the Roof.

HOMES
PUBLISHING GROUP

Purpose: get ppl. who have $ & a have a hom
dominate $

You have a home & how ppl. don't have a home

Unit 1: Fiction

Flash Fiction

A Catch Tale, pp. 4–5

1. **Understand:** Look up the definition of *hyperbole*. Reread the story, noting where this literary device is used. In a small group, rewrite the story by eliminating hyperbole. What are the similarities or differences between the two versions?

2. **Apply:** Examine the tale's style, noting word choice and differences in sentence length. Write a paragraph describing the style and how it affects you. How might a more complex style change this tale?

3. **Analyze:** With a partner, use a dictionary to define *comedy*. How does the writer create humour in this selection? Share your examples with a partner.

4. **Think Critically:** What are urban legends? What features do they share with this tale? In pairs, discuss two or three familiar urban legends. Then compare your versions to another pair's. What can you conclude about how urban legends are retold?

A Man Told Me the Story of His Life, pp. 6–7

1. **Understand:** Think about a career you might like to pursue as an adult. Why did you select this particular profession? If someone you respected wanted you to have a different career, how might you react? Why?

2. **Apply:** In this selection, Vicente dispassionately retells the events of his life. Speculate with a partner about how and when Vicente might be emotional about his situation. Then rewrite a section of the story injecting vivid verbs and descriptive adjectives to express these feelings.

3. **Analyze:** Compare and contrast the story's ending with its beginning. What is ironic about both Vicente's assessment of his wife's illness and the doctor's suggestions?

4. **Synthesize:** Imagine that this story is excerpted from a novel. With a partner, write dialogue for the scene in which Vicente and the school official discuss his career choice. Then rewrite the scene, but in this version have Vicente defy the school official's advice, explaining that he'll go ahead and pursue his dream. With a partner, perform each version for the class. Describe the differences in the interactions.

The Dinner Party, pp. 8–9

1. **Understand:** As you read this selection, note the setting. With a classmate, consider its connection to the plot, characters, and themes. If the setting changed, how might this alter the story as a whole?

2. **Apply:** Write a brief explanation of how the young girl, the colonel, the hostess, and the American naturalist are acting according to, or counter to, stereotyped expectations of their behaviour. Compare your responses with those of your classmates.

3. **Analyze:** Write a short story that focuses on a dangerous scenario involving people and an animal. Have the people disagree on what action to take, but resolve the disagreement by the end of the story. Work with a partner to edit and proofread each other's stories.

4. **Think Critically:** In a small group, collect several magazine ads containing pictures of females and males. Look at age groups depicted, clothing worn, roles portrayed, and audiences targeted. Are both genders stereotyped? If so, how? Summarize your conclusions in an oral report.

Gratitude, p. 10

1. **Understand:** Read this selection. How does the title relate to the story? Discuss with a classmate why the character in this story thinks that his life is grand.

2. **Apply:** Use dictionaries to find two or more definitions of the term *anecdote*. What clues in the text reveal that this story is an anecdote?

3. **Analyze:** Shakespeare's Hamlet says, "There is nothing either good or bad, but thinking makes it so." In groups of four, debate whether this statement ·is true. Then divide the class into those who agree with the statement and those who don't. Choose a representative to present your group's position in a class debate.

4. **Synthesize:** What do you think some of the people walking past this homeless man are thinking? Create a cartoon to illustrate their thoughts. Then discuss in what ways the homeless might be stereotyped by others.

The Wall, p. 11

1. **Understand:** After reading, make up three questions to ask Gilles Vigneault about the meaning of his story. Share your questions and responses with a few classmates. How does this discussion help you understand this selection?

2. **Apply:** In your journal, write two short paragraphs commenting on how the making of the wall teaches something about freedom. What might the mason mean when he says, "What pleasure would there be in escaping from a prison that was poorly built?"

3. **Analyze:** In a small group, create a storyboard for a short film based on "The Wall." Include dialogue, directions, and sound effects. Add a description of background music.

4. **Synthesize:** Write a short narrative that describes the scene when the monk arrives at the prison, and the mason departs dressed in a habit and rope belt. Maintain the style of the original in your narrative.

Short Stories

Just Lather, That's All, pp. 12–16

1. **Understand:** In a small group, discuss to what extent each character is a man of action and a man of imagination. Refer specifically to the text to support your arguments.
2. **Analyze:** The narrator says that he is a revolutionary rather than a murderer like Torres. Yet he constantly refers to how easy it would be to kill Torres while shaving him. Is there a contradiction between the narrator's comments and his behaviour? Discuss.
3. **Synthesize:** In the role of Captain Torres, write a monologue explaining your involvement in suppressing your country's revolution. How do you feel about those who oppose your actions, and about those who agree with them? Present your monologue to the class.
4. **Think Critically:** Imagine that the barber is put on trial by the Committee for Revolutionary Justice because he did not harm Torres when given the opportunity. In a group, plan and write a trial of the barber. Choose a prosecutor, defence attorney, barber, judge, and jury. The remaining members of the class can be the court audience. Rehearse and perform the trial.

Dancer, pp. 17–20

1. **Understand:** Before reading, recall an activity that increased your confidence and made you feel valued. What motivated you to take part in it? Why was it important to gain the respect of others? Write your response as a journal entry.
2. **Apply:** What happens to Clarissa's self-esteem and personality? How does learning to dance benefit her and her community? Support your response with examples from the story and share them with another classmate.
3. **Analyze:** In telling Clarissa's story, the narrator reveals a lot about herself. Referring to the story, create a character sketch of the narrator. Consider enhancing it with a drawing or illustration.
4. **Synthesize:** As the adult Clarissa, write a memoir recalling your time with your foster family. Consider starting with a sentence such as, "The year that I remember most is the one in which I learned to dance..." Read your memoir to a partner.

Lifeguard, pp. 21–32

1. **Understand:** In the story, Chris exhibits both selfishness and caring. With a partner, create a T-chart labelling one column "Selfish," and the other "Caring." Under each column, list examples of these behaviours. How do these traits reveal the conflicts Chris experiences?
2. **Analyze:** In a small group, discuss the ending. Does it present an optimistic or pessimistic prediction about Chris's relationship with his father? What does the ending suggest about Mike's and Chris's futures? Chart and compare your responses.

3. **Synthesize:** As the father, write a letter to your son explaining why it has been difficult for you to reconcile with him since the family separated. Comment on your feelings for your son. Share your letter with a partner.
4. **Think Critically:** This story explores the complexities of relationships between families and friends. In a group, discuss how the way we are treated by family members can often dictate how we form and sustain friendships. What are the similarities and differences between these two types of relationships?

The Concert Stages of Europe, pp. 33–52
1. **Understand:** Before reading, recall a time when you felt pressure from an adult to participate in an activity that was unappealing to you. How did you cope with this situation?
2. **Apply:** The narrator often uses humour to deflect the seriousness of his situation. In what ways does humour ease his conflict about playing the piano and living up to family expectations? Support your response with examples.
3. **Analyze:** The mother dictates goals and ambitions to Barclay, but he sees things differently. In a one-page report, compare and contrast the ideas expressed about power and ambition in this piece to those in "A Man Told Me the Story of His Life" in this anthology.
4. **Synthesize:** As a reporter for the local newspaper, write a feature article about "Richy Ryder's CJMT Talent Festival." If possible, format it in columns using a computer. Add a catchy headline. Post your piece on your school's web site or in your classroom project binder.

Tunnel, pp. 53–59
1. **Understand:** In your journal, reflect on why the story is divided into three parts and on what this division indicates about time or place in the story.
2. **Apply:** At the end, Ken looks at the darkness of the tunnel and pulls Ib up the hill into the sunshine. Why would the author conclude the story this way? What might darkness and sunshine represent? Share your response with a partner.
3. **Analyze:** This story effectively combines opposing elements, such as past and present, fantasy and reality, and drama and comedy. In a small group, find examples of these elements in the story. Then discuss how they contribute to plot and character development.
4. **Synthesize:** With a partner, write a script in which Ib recounts the day's adventures to one of her parents. Consider expressing the emotional concerns of both Ib and her mother or father. Rehearse and perform the presentation.

The First Day, pp. 60–64

1. **Understand:** Create a chart showing how each of the characters in this story reacts to the mother, and why they react in the way they do. Compare your chart with a partner's.

2. **Apply:** In the opening paragraph, the narrator recalls in vivid detail her appearance on the first day of school. Using this as a model, clearly and precisely describe in your journal how you looked on a significant day in your life.

3. **Analyze:** "This is my mother" is a cue for indirect characterization of the mother. Read the three sections where this phrase occurs. Then in a small group discuss how this technique helps you to understand the mother in each section.

4. **Synthesize:** Are there clues in the story to suggest that the narrator's embarrassment about her mother has turned to affection? Does the voice of the grown narrator suggest that the mother's pride and courage have been instilled in her daughter? Discuss with the class.

What Language Do Bears Speak?, pp. 65–70

1. **Understand:** Our perceptions of reality are strongly shaped by the images we see. How do the images on the poster shape the children's view of Dr. Shultz' circus? How does this compare to reality? How does it relate to our view of live animal shows, and the humane treatment of animals, today? Write a few paragraphs contrasting the image and the reality.

2. **Apply:** The narrator and the townspeople make a number of assumptions about people who speak a language different from their own. Identify what these assumptions are, and then consider whether you have ever made similar judgments about someone speaking a language you did not know.

3. **Analyze:** Read "The Hockey Sweater" by Roch Carrier. In pairs, create a T-chart, labelling the columns "The Hockey Sweater" and "What Language Do Bears Speak?" List the common elements. Which selection do you prefer? Why?

4. **Think Critically:** The story is told from the child's viewpoint. In a group, discuss whether the story would be as effective if told from an adult's viewpoint. Summarize your conclusions in an oral report to another group.

From How To Write a Serious Novel About Love, pp. 71–81

1. **Understand:** Schoemperlen offers detailed advice about writing novels. Some suggestions are clearly stated, while others are embedded in the selection. Pick out five suggestions and rewrite them in a list called "Notes for Novels." Compare and contrast your list with a partner's.

2. **Analyze:** This selection is written in the second person. With a partner, choose two passages from the selection. One person can rewrite it in the first person and the other in the third. Examine how the changes affect the reader, writer, and tone. What do you conclude about the differences?

3. **Synthesize:** Create a poster or collage based on this piece, and give it a title or message. Include a picture of a woman and a man, as well as other images, graphics, and text from the selection. Then display it for the class.

4. **Think Critically:** Imagine you are the host for a book-review television show that will be featuring Schoemperlen. Consider that you have a fifteen-minute time slot to interview her. Prepare a list of twelve short but relevant questions that you will ask her about the writing of novels.

The Novel

From *Pride and Prejudice, pp. 82–86*

1. **Understand:** Jane Austen often has a character say things that carry a subtext. In pairs, read the sentences below and interpret their meanings within the context of the selection: "I hope *my* dinners are good enough for her"; "I feel it my duty to promote and establish the blessing of peace in all families within the reach of my influence"; "I have great hopes of finding him quite the reverse." Then rewrite each to make the implications clearer.

2. **Analyze:** Austen uses a formal language appropriate for her time. With a partner, select a passage and read it silently, then out loud. Discuss the style and tone of the language. What do you observe about the manners and etiquette of Austen's era?

3. **Synthesize:** Examine both the stated and the implied purpose of Mr. Collins's visit. In the role, and the voice, of Mr. Collins, write a journal entry about your impending visit to the Bennets.

4. **Think Critically:** Jane Austen can paint a clear picture of her characters' personalities using very few words. Reread this selection, making brief notes about her characters. Then write a character sketch or prepare an illustration of one of your favourite characters.

Shinny Game Melted the Ice, pp. 87–89

1. **Understand:** Using contextual clues from this selection, discuss with a partner the concept of a shinny game. How is it different from or similar to a regular hockey game? Include some physical details and dialogue from this piece as well as your own ideas for support.

2. **Apply:** The narrator uses an anecdote or personal story to make a key point in this piece. How does this choice affect the reader? In your opinion, does it enhance or distract from the overall message of the selection? Why do you think the narrator states, "We are all Indians" and does not use the term First Nations, Aboriginal, or Native? Explain.

3. **Analyze:** In this selection, the narrator says, "Nowadays I realize how very much it [the shinny game] was like the development of our brotherhood." What does he mean by this statement? In what ways is the game similar to the brothers' relationship? Explain.

4. **Think Critically:** In a small group, conduct a library or Internet search on the treatment of Aboriginal children in the mid- to late 1950s in Ontario. Look up information on various child-welfare and Children's Aid Society decisions. Then hold a formal debate on the impact these decisions had on Aboriginal families. What conclusions can you draw?

From *Truth and Bright Water, pp. 90–95*

1. **Understand:** Before reading, discuss in a small group how body language often reveals our true feelings. Speculate why people exhibit their feelings in this manner. Is this a useful way to express feelings? Why or why not?

2. **Analyze:** People's feelings and opinions are often revealed as much by their actions as their words. List in your notebook the actions of the mother, father, and child. Then note what these reveal about their respective characters. Compare your notes with a partner's.

3. **Synthesize:** In the selection, note the contrasts between Waterton Lake and the prairies of Bright Water. How do these settings affect the family? Write a formal paragraph in which you examine how the two settings affect the family members and their interactions.

4. **Think Critically:** What does the last paragraph suggest about the boy's feelings for his father? How is the last sentence an effective conclusion for this episode of the novel?

Myths, Fables, Legends, and Folktales
The Fly, pp. 96–99

1. **Understand:** Read the first paragraph of the story. Use contextual clues to explain the meaning of *usurer.* Then find the definition in a dictionary and compare it to your explanation. How did contextual clues help you understand this word's meaning?

2. **Apply:** The boy uses clever riddles when telling the rich man what his parents are doing. Think about daily activities you enjoy. Then create your own riddled explanations similar to the young boy's. Present them to the class, and see if your classmates can identify the activities.

3. **Analyze:** "The Fly" is organized in two ways: chronologically, and by cause and effect. With a partner, make a list outlining each organizational pattern, using examples from the selection for support. Compare and contrast your list with another pair's.

4. **Synthesize:** Design a comic book of "The Fly", and mount it on your classroom bulletin board. Or, rewrite "The Fly" as a children's story suitable for grade one. Illustrate it with highly colourful pictures. Then present it as a gift to a local school or library.

The Cow-Tail Switch, pp. 100–104

1. **Understand:** After reading, discuss in a small group the phrase "A man is not really dead until he is forgotten." What is your interpretation of this phrase? What is significant about it in terms of the events in this legend? Summarize your thoughts and share them with another group.

2. **Analyze:** Death and what happens afterward is a common theme in myths, legends, and fables. Compare and contrast the writer's treatment of this theme in "The Cow-Tail Switch" with "The Death of Balder." Which treatment do your prefer? Why?

3. **Synthesize:** In a group, perform the legend as a readers' theatre. Write a script based on the text from the legend, and also create new material. Use simple props, dramatic make-up or masks, and music or sound effects. Consider videotaping your performance for the class.

4. **Think Critically:** Do you think that Ogaloussa made the right decision in giving the cow-tail switch to his youngest son? Write an essay in which you agree or disagree with Ogaloussa's decision.

The Death of Balder, pp. 105–109

1. **Understand:** Create a story map of the plot of this story and a chart outlining the relationships of the various characters.

2. **Analyze:** In a one-page report, identify and explain the consequences of Balder's death. Why is Balder so important to his country and people? Cite examples from the myth as support.

3. **Synthesize:** In the role of Loki, write a monologue in which you explain your jealousy of Balder and why you plotted his death. Incorporate material from the selection into your monologue. Perform it for the class.

4. **Think Critically:** In a group of four, select one of the following to investigate using a library or CD-ROM search: Raven (from Canadian First Nations legends); Achilles (from Greek mythology); Arthur and Mordred (from English legends). On chart paper, summarize your characters and their stories in point form, and share your summary with the class. Discuss what elements these stories and characters share with "The Death of Balder."

The Rebellion of the Magical Rabbits, pp. 110–119

1. **Understand:** After reading, note how the author has varied the wolf's title or name throughout this fable. Jot down these titles in your notebook. Then explain briefly what these changes indicate about the wolf's personality.

2. **Apply:** A fable presents a lesson or moral. After reading "The Rebellion of the Magical Rabbits," discuss with a partner the lesson it presents. Summarize your response in one or two sentences and share it with your class.

3. **Analyze:** Locate and read several of *Aesop's Fables.* With a partner, make a chart in which you list common features of fables. Then analyze the

way in which the author has used these features to write "The Rebellion of the Magical Rabbits." What are your conclusions?

4. **Synthesize:** Imagine that Captain Torres from "Just Lather, That's All" and Wolf King meet in a café. Write the conversation that would take place between them. Consider using material from both selections in the conversation. Place the finished piece in your writing portfolio.

Unit 2: Nonfiction

Personal Essays and Reviews
The Usual Things, pp. 122–125

1. **Understand:** Before reading the essay, write a journal entry about the importance of traditions in your life. Describe in detail a tradition in your family that is significant. Explain why it is important for you and your family to keep this tradition.

2. **Apply:** In a small group, discuss how those in Canada who celebrate holidays that fall in the winter months might modify their traditions if they moved to a tropical country. List your thoughts on a chart and compare it with another group's.

3. **Analyze:** Notice how the author uses dialogue to show rather than tell you about the various characters' personalities. Pick out five or six quotations from the selection. In your notebook, identify the characters and then explain the personality traits revealed by the quotations. Share your notes with a classmate.

4. **Synthesize:** In a small group, use Badami's essay as the basis for a readers' theatre. Incorporate some dialogue from the essay into the presentation. If possible, include some props, scenery, and music. Present to the class.

Bat Summer Reviewed, pp. 126–129

1. **Understand:** Before reading these reviews, draw up a list of the features you expect to find in a good review. Then look for these features while reading the selection. Afterward, consider whether you need to revise your list.

2. **Analyze:** Look at the vocabulary and language in each review. List examples of both sophisticated and colloquial language in each piece. Who do you think the target audience is for these reviews? Which of these reviews might appeal to a broader audience? Why?

3. **Synthesize:** In a group, create a publicity kit to promote *Bat Summer.* Consider designing a press release, brochure, poster, or web advertisement for it. Use quotations from the reviews in your publicity pieces. Place your finished product in a folder and display it for the class.

4. **Think Critically:** Read the first paragraph of each review. In your notebook, outline the information contained in each lead paragraph. Which review contains a more effective beginning? Look at the opening sentence, the introduction of the main idea, and the clarity of topic. Support your opinion with examples. Then repeat this procedure for the concluding paragraphs.

Reconnecting with the Earth, pp. 130–132
1. **Understand:** Read the title, the author's name, and the first paragraph only. Then predict what you think the selection will be about and how it will be organized.
2. **Analyze:** With a partner, determine the organizational pattern of this essay, and depict it in a graphic organizer. Post it, then have a class discussion about how the way in which Suzuki organized information contributed to the essay's unity.
3. **Synthesize:** In small groups, plan to adapt this essay into the medium of a short video documentary. Write a description of such elements as shooting location, shot and sound directions, narration, tone, dramatization, and use of archival footage.
4. **Think Critically:** In a letter to the editor, summarize Suzuki's overriding concern and then his suggestions for addressing this concern. Evaluate the effectiveness of his solutions, then describe any ideas you have for dealing with the problem.

Journal and Biography
A Country Childhood, pp. 133–139
1. **Understand:** Before reading this selection, note its title. In your journal, describe the tone created for you by the title, and share your response with another classmate. After reading the piece, discuss whether the tone of the title matches the tone of the piece as a whole.
2. **Apply:** Based on your knowledge of Mandela's later life, discuss the similarities and differences between the course of Mandela's life and that of his father.
3. **Analyze:** Compare and contrast the influence Mandela's father and mother had on his development. Find four or five quotations that demonstrate this effect. Then write an essay using these quotations to explain his parents' influence on his overall development.
4. **Think Critically:** In pairs, find and read a biographical piece about Mandela's childhood. Note the differences in style and content with this selection. What are the advantages or disadvantages of a biography versus an autobiography? Create a T-chart in which you list these advantages and disadvantages. Which form do you prefer?

Sunday Dinner for Tourists, pp. 140–143

1. **Understand:** In your notebook, create a graphic organizer of the narrator's family. Include their names and their relationship to the narrator. What basic information do we have about this family?

2. **Analyze:** In your notebook, compare and contrast the personalities of the narrator's mother and father. Design a chart in which you list the positive and negative traits of each. Support your claims with quotations from the selection. Share your chart with a partner.

3. **Synthesize:** In pairs, create a storyboard for a still-photograph documentary of this selection. Decide on which scenes you would like to photograph, and write a caption for each. Display the storyboard for your class.

4. **Think Critically:** With a partner, audiotape an interview with someone who lived through the Depression or whose parents spoke about the Depression years. Include background music or sound effects in your tape, and play it for your class. How has this interview helped you understand this era?

Publishing Anne, pp. 144–146

1. **Understand:** In your journal, describe a time when you had difficulty writing. Explain what you were trying to write, and what factors contributed to your writer's block. Then summarize the strategies you used to overcome your difficulty.

2. **Apply:** Montgomery admits in this selection that she knows very little about publishing. Speculate in a group whether or not this was beneficial for Montgomery, using examples from the selection to support your viewpoint.

3. **Analyze:** At the library, choose any one paragraph from an L. M. Montgomery novel. Compare it to any paragraph in this nonfiction selection. How similar are the writing styles in the excerpts you've selected? Consider such elements as word choice, sentence length, and tone. Write a one-page report detailing your findings.

4. **Synthesize:** Like Montgomery, clip out a noncontroversial newspaper headline of an event. Based on this headline, create a summary of a short story you might write. Give a thumbnail sketch of each character, summarize the setting, and set out the plot. Then describe whether the story is serious or humorous, and write the opening paragraph.

Sowing the Wind, pp. 147–149

1. **Understand:** Read the first paragraph. Pay particular attention to the sentence, "Lots of families live between two cultures in Washington." Explain how families could live in two cultures in one city. Write your response in your journal.

2. **Apply:** Using a Venn diagram labelled "Santiago" and "Washington" compare the two worlds in which the narrator lives. Identify ideas that relate to the narrator's experience in each city, and record them in the appropriate diagram. Discuss your conclusions.

3. **Analyze:** Write an essay comparing and contrasting the style and theme of this nonfiction selection with the fiction piece "Just Lather, That's All" in this anthology. State which selection you prefer, and why.

4. **Synthesize:** In the role of a documentary filmmaker, think about how you would like to adapt this piece to film. Then write a proposal that you would pitch to a production company to persuade them that your film is worth making.

From Into Thin Air, pp. 150–154

1. **Understand:** Some of the vocabulary in this selection may be unfamiliar. Jot down any words you do not know and guess their meaning from context. Compare your guesses with a partner's and then check them against the definitions in a dictionary.

2. **Apply:** In small groups, determine what Krakauer means when he says that "my inner voice resembled Chicken Little." Discuss whether this comparison is effective, and what real dangers he faced in climbing the Icefall.

3. **Analyze:** To examine how Krakauer builds up the sense of threat, work in a small group to list all the words and phrases in this selection that suggest danger or fear. Then construct a similar list of the words that suggest pleasure and security. Compare your lists with those of other groups.

4. **Synthesize:** Write a brief essay describing an experience you have had that was both frightening and exciting, like Jon Krakauer's transit of the Icefall. Choose your words carefully so that your reader can understand both your fear and your excitement. Share your essays in small groups.

Formal Essays and Reports

From The New Ice Age, pp. 155–157

1. **Understand:** Begin reading this selection. Stop when you realize what object is being described. In your notebook, answer the questions: What did you predict the object might be? What specific information confirmed its identity?

2. **Apply:** In your journal, write a paragraph modelled on this selection's introduction, in which you reveal a meaningful object through a series of informative statements. Exchange paragraphs with a partner. At what point did your partner recognize the object?

3. **Analyze:** Compare this selection with a print or television advertisement. Look for similarities in structure and in how the objects are described. Write a short paper detailing the similarities, using examples for support.

4. **Synthesize:** Imagine you are a member of the hockey team that has just won the Stanley Cup. Write an essay for a national newspaper describing how it feels to win this prestigious award.

The Art of Genius: Eight Ways to Think Like Einstein, pp. 158–163

1. **Understand:** Read only the first line of this article. Then in a group of three, brainstorm some suggestions for ways in which geniuses come up with new ideas. How difficult or easy was it to think of these ideas? Explain.

2. **Analyze:** According to the author, we think either reproductively or productively. Explain the differences between these ways of thinking. Then in pairs, design a problem based on either an everyday event or common knowledge. Note which ways of thinking you use to create solutions to the problem. Share it with another pair.

3. **Synthesize:** Choose three people referred to in the article. Then write their conversation as they sit together in a hotel lobby waiting for a conference to begin. What ideas might they agree on? In what areas might they differ?

4. **Think Critically:** In a group of four, debate the concept that genius is a gift and cannot be learned. Assign one person the role of recorder, another that of moderator, and two others to speak for and against the idea. Share your conclusions with another group.

Preventing Conflict in the New Century, pp. 164–166

1. **Understand:** Using contextual clues from the selection, write a definition or interpretation of the following words and phrases: "political will", "conflict-prevention strategies", "intractability", "ethnic war". Compare your definitions with those of others.

2. **Analyze:** Use a graphic organizer to show how the article is organized. Provide examples from the selection for support. Do you think Annan successfully presented his case for preventing conflict? Why or why not?

3. **Synthesize:** Look up the definition of a public service announcement (PSA) in *The Canadian Press Stylebook* or a journalism handbook. Then write a thirty-second radio or television PSA advocating prevention, rather than intervention, in conflicts.

4. **Think Critically:** In a group, discuss reasons why our world is in "an era when 90% of wars take place within, not between, states." Assign one group member to record your ideas on chart paper. Indicate your top ten reasons. Then put the reasons from all the groups together on the classroom wall. Which ideas do all groups share?

Canada's Aboriginal Languages, pp. 167–178

1. **Understand:** First, read only the title and the headings within the article. In your journal, predict what the article might be about. Then read the article and, afterward, consider the accuracy of your predictions.

2. **Analyze:** Notice the vocabulary used in this research report to describe languages that disappear. Words such as "extinct" and "endangered" carry tremendous weight. How might vocabulary choices in a report like this influence the decisions of politicians or other powerful people?

3. **Synthesize:** Imagine that your first language, whether English or another language, is endangered. Write a speech targeting young people who speak your language. Explain your concerns to this audience and suggest how they can help save their language from extinction.

4. **Think Critically:** Using the chart, predict which Aboriginal languages are likely to flourish within the next ten to fifteen years. What were your reasons for choosing these languages? Justify your predictions, citing data and additional examples from the chart and article. Write a one-page report based on this information.

Speeches and Interviews

The Internet and Global Human Rights, pp. 179–182

1. **Understand:** Examine Axworthy's arguments in support of the Internet. Select three that you find convincing and reduce them to short slogans suitable for a sign or billboard. Use your computer to present your slogans in a visually appealing format. Post them in the classroom.

2. **Apply:** Imagine that you are in charge of your school's Internet access, and write out a "Code of Conduct for Internet Users." Consider the restrictions that you would place on time, content, access, and the purposes for which the Internet should be used in school. Compare your "code" with the code already in use in your school.

3. **Analyze:** In a short paragraph, contrast the Internet's potential for good and evil. You must have effective topic and concluding sentences. Make specific references to this selection to support your arguments.

4. **Think Critically:** Communication has always been a human need and compulsion. In groups, brainstorm a list of communication techniques from the primitive to the modern, and from the private to the public: heliograph, smoke signals, the web ... Make a collage that gives insight into human communication. Create an effective title for your collage.

Spinning Facts Into Fiction, pp. 183–186

1. **Understand:** As you read, note any words that are new to you. Look them up in a print or on-line dictionary, then on computer make a visually appealing glossary of words and terms that would help a first-time reader of this piece.

2. **Apply:** Use sources such as the Internet or the library to research one of the figures mentioned in this selection: the Duke or Duchess of Windsor, Rudolf Hess, Joachim von Ribbentrop, or Ezra Pound. Select an interesting incident from the person's life and use it as the basis for a newspaper story. Publish your story in an appropriate format. If you can find an original news story about the character, compare it with your version.

3. **Analyze:** List in point form the "tricks of the trade" that Findley describes he uses to write his novels. In a small group, discuss the following questions: Is it possible to write fiction that does not include facts? Is history always factual?

4. **Synthesize:** With a partner, discuss Findley's "magnet phenomenon" to better understand it. Then select an idea or character that interests you. For several days, keep notes of how this "magnet" attracts other bits of information. Then make a diagram showing the links among the pieces of information that you picked up. Share your "magnetic episodes" with other students.

Family Matters, pp. 187–189

1. **Understand:** What are some of the ways people throughout history, or across different cultures, have chosen mates? Brainstorm a list.

2. **Analyze:** Select and explain in your own words three of the arguments that Abdullah uses to defend arranged marriages. Then consider counter-arguments and write a sentence or two explaining the counter-arguments.

3. **Synthesize:** With a partner, develop a pamphlet entitled "Guide to Healthy Relationships." You can base your ideas on information from articles, the Internet, or interviews. Use desktop publishing to make the pamphlet eye-catching and readable. Share your pamphlet with the class.

4. **Think Critically:** In a journal entry, reflect on how your views on issues such as marriage or dating differ from those of your parents. You could ask your parents how their views differ from their own parents' views, and incorporate these ideas into your journal.

How-To and Reference
Zen and the Art of Stand-Up Comedy, pp. 190–195

1. **Understand:** Read the first paragraph, and make a three-column chart for the primary skills the author claims are essential for writing stand-up comedy. After reading the article, list all the advice you can remember in the appropriate columns. Compare your list with a partner's. Then reread the piece together and fill in any gaps.

2. **Apply:** Select a topic that you and your classmates care about, such as cafeteria food, supply teachers, homework, or the football team, and prepare a one-minute stand-up comedy routine for presentation to a small group. Each group can select their favourite routine to present to the class.

3. **Analyze:** To focus the reader's attention, two of the sections have headings that contain opposing ideas, such as "Clever vs. Funny." For each of the other sections in this text, provide new headings that contain a similar opposition. In a small group, evaluate each other's headings.
4. **Think Critically:** In a group, watch a variety of stand-up comics or sitcoms, and consider such features as their choice of topics. Evaluate the extent to which these comics practise Sankey's principles, and present your findings to the class.

Shapes of Cities, pp. 196–197

1. **Understand:** Make a simple map of your city or a city nearby. In a paragraph, explain which pattern from the selection it most logically fits into. Note how there may be some overlap, if older parts of your city have been surrounded by new areas. Exchange paragraphs with a partner.
2. **Apply:** Imagine you have time travelled into the year 2200. In a journal entry, describe your hometown or city. Include such current details as its physical size, population, transportation, and industries, then create illustrations and diagrams that depict it. Write how you feel about the changes. Present the finished product to the class, and ask for feedback.
3. **Analyze:** Examine the characteristics of each city in this selection, and rank them in order of preference based on where you would like to live. Then, using maps and guidebooks as references, select a city that fits your preferred pattern. In a letter to a friend, explain why you are taking a job in the city of your choice. In a small group, compare letters.
4. **Synthesize:** With a partner, speculate on the future shapes of cities and make diagrams of two possibilities. Include a short description and title for each. Post your material on the bulletin board.

Food Facts, pp. 198–199

1. **Understand:** In a small group, examine the list of facts and use a T-chart to divide them into two categories: those where change can be affected by individual effort, and those where change can only be made by society as a whole. For each entry, discuss the potential consequences of inaction. Choose the food fact that presents the greatest global threat, and compare your choice with other groups.
2. **Analyze:** Each statement in this list is powerful on its own, but by grouping facts, an editor can give each one more power. Which facts are meant to be considered as a group? With a partner, explain how the effectiveness of each fact is increased by its proximity to others.
3. **Synthesize:** Select the fact on this list that most interests you, and use the Internet or another source to add at least four more relevant facts to the original. Then write a letter to the editor expressing your view on these related facts.

4. **Think Critically:** Work with a partner to create a survey of student eating habits at school. You could consider questions such as: How much food brought from home is thrown away? Create the survey and conduct it among class members or in the cafeteria. Calculate the results, and consider what conclusions might be drawn.

Unit 3: Poetry

Narrative

Chance Encounter, pp. 202–203

1. **Understand:** Scan the poem quickly to determine its overall theme. How does it relate to the title? Have you had a similar encounter to the poet's? Write a short journal entry about your experience.
2. **Apply:** Notice the punctuation and line length. How does this affect the mood or overall tone? If Nowlan had structured his poem differently, how might the mood or tone change?
3. **Analyze:** Alden Nowlan has written this piece as a free verse poem. What elements identify it as free verse? Do you think this is an effective style for the poem?
4. **Synthesize:** Write your own free verse poem about the interaction between human beings and nature. You might consider adding drawings or sketches. Share your poem with a partner.

Sarajevo Bear, p. 204

1. **Understand:** In the poem, Pavlich describes how the brutality and trauma of war affected the bear from the Sarajevo zoo. To what war is Pavlich referring? In pairs, speculate about other ways in which wars affect daily life.
2. **Apply:** In pairs, read the poem out loud and then silently. How do the "negative" and "positive" spaces on the page affect your reading? Why do you think the poet created his poem this way?
3. **Analyze:** Compare and contrast the structure and theme of this poem to the poem "Chance Encounter" in this anthology. What are the differences and similarities? Which poem do you prefer? Write a one-page response.
4. **Think Critically:** In a group of four, discuss whether wars are inevitable ends to prolonged disputes between countries or groups. Assign one person the role of recorder, another that of moderator, and have the other two debate the issue. Chart your responses and share your conclusions with another group.

La Belle Dame sans Merci, pp. 205–207

1. **Understand:** In pairs, read the poem silently and aloud. Together, map or list the events that occur. What is their significance? How does a map or list help in your understanding of the poem?

2. **Apply:** Keats intentionally uses archaic language to suggest that the poem takes place in the Middle Ages; certainly some of his expressions are unfamiliar to contemporary readers. With a partner, identify some of these words and phrases. How do they create an atmosphere and mood specific to an historical era?
3. **Analyze:** This poem of twelve quatrains has a specific rhyme pattern. Look up the definition of *quatrain* in the dictionary. Then reread the poem and write a short paragraph explaining its rhyme pattern and citing examples for support.
4. **Think Critically:** In groups, discuss the meaning of the images in the poem. Consider examining the phrases "a lily on thy brow", "a fading rose," and the "death-pale" warriors. Share your conclusions with another group.

To My Son, p. 208
1. **Understand:** From whose perspective is this poem written? What lines or phrases indicate the answer to this question? How might this poem change if another perspective were presented?
2. **Apply:** This poem is written in two stanzas. The situation seems to change from one stanza to the next. What is significant about this change? What words or phrases has the poet used to help the reader understand this transition?
3. **Analyze:** In a dictionary or language handbook, look up the meaning of *foil* and *juxtaposition*. How has the poet used these literary devices to develop contrast? Discuss in pairs.
4. **Synthesize:** Write a poem about your relationship with a family member or caregiver. Focus the poem on a particular memory that has meaning for both of you. Consider enhancing your finished piece with a photo, illustration, or another piece of memorabilia. Display it on the class bulletin board.

Africville, pp. 209–210
1. **Understand:** Based on the information in the poem and in the accompanying author biography, discuss what you know about the history of Africville. Create a list of facts to share with another set of classmates. What conclusions can you draw?
2. **Analyze:** Find examples of personification and metaphor in the poem. How do these literary devices create atmosphere and point of view? How do they add to the poem's overall message? Explain.
3. **Synthesize:** Create a collage to tell the poem's story. Use photographs or drawings from newspapers or magazines, text from the poem, or other materials. Display it on a class gallery wall dedicated to the history of Africville.
4. **Think Critically:** Locate a copy of the National Film Board's short documentary *Remember Africville* (1991). View the film and then write a review, comparing it to the poem. What are the similarities and differences in their messages?

Fifty Below, p. 211

1. **Understand:** In your journal, write about a time when you changed your actions based on comments from others. How did this make you feel? How did this event affect the way you later interacted with these same people?

2. **Apply:** How does the poet use the rhythms of natural speech? What effect does this create? Discuss in pairs.

3. **Analyze:** Compare and contrast the events that occur at the beginning of the poem to those at the end. Why does the young boy change his style of walking? What is significant about this change?

4. **Think Critically:** In the role of the young boy who is now an adult, write a newspaper editorial on how brief events in our childhood can have a great impact on our outlook on life.

Hunger, p. 212

1. **Understand:** After reading the poem, find the stanza in which the man in the poem refers to an event from his youth. What is the effect of this memory on us, the readers? Explain.

2. **Apply:** The speaker states, "My thought/reeled into nothingness,/like run–out fish–line." What is the simile here? Interpret the simile, then use it as a model to write a similar one.

3. **Analyze:** "Vivid" verbs are highly descriptive and show action. This poem uses them to depict the speaker's condition. Pick out three or four lines with vivid verbs. If these lines were rewritten using more passive verbs, how might this affect the poem?

4. **Think Critically:** Do you believe that the man in this poem has lost hope? Write a short essay in which you justify your position with examples from the poem.

The Charge of the Light Brigade, pp. 213–215

1. **Understand:** This is a narrative poem about an incident in a war. It describes physical action and has a straightforward plot line. In pairs, create a plot graph in which you list the rise and fall of events. Share your findings with another pair.

2. **Analyze:** The poem tells of a heroic, but futile, military action. How does Tennyson use imagery to depict these traits? How does the poem's rhythm complement this view? Support your conclusions with lines from the poem.

3. **Synthesize:** Create a six-frame storyboard based on the sequence of events in each stanza. Use text from the poem to support your illustrations of individual scenes.

4. **Think Critically:** In a library or CD-ROM search, find out why the Light Brigade made this famous charge at Balaclava during the Crimean War. Present your findings in an oral report.

Without Hands, pp. 216–217

1. **Understand:** In a small group, consider how you might function daily without the use of your hands. What normal, familiar actions would be difficult or impossible to perform? Write a short journal entry or poem based on your discussion.

2. **Analyze:** This poem is full of imagery related to the workplace and family life. What is the importance of this imagery to Crozier? Why do you think she included these depictions in her poem?

3. **Synthesize:** Trace your hand, or make a large drawing of it, on construction or poster paper. Add pasted images, sketches, text from the poem, or favourite phrases to create a collage on the hand. Then on the back or upper corner of the paper, write an explanation of your image.

4. **Think Critically:** In the nonfiction selection "Sowing the Wind" in this anthology, the writer, Lake Sagaris, presents a different perspective on the 1973 military coup in Chile. Compare and contrast that piece with Crozier's poem. Which style is more convincing? Why?

Lyric

Young, p. 218

1. **Understand:** Recall a childhood experience that seems like "a thousand doors ago," such as changing schools or becoming a stepsibling. What was your reaction? Has it changed with time?

2. **Apply:** This poem contains dramatic, striking imagery. How does the imagery affect the tone and mood? Briefly summarize your response, citing examples from the poem.

3. **Analyze:** In the poem, locate two metaphors that refer to the speaker's parents. What might this indicate about relationships within the family? Discuss with a classmate.

4. **Synthesize:** Imagine you are now a teenager or adult who was once the "lonely kid" in the poem. Write a monologue describing what it was like to change from child to teen. Audiotape this monologue and play it for your class.

In the Almost Evening, p. 219

1. **Understand:** With a partner, read the poem to each other. Jot down some key words or phrases as the poem is read to you. Compare your notes with your partner's. Speculate on the poem's meaning.

2. **Apply:** Why does the speaker decide to listen feverishly by the end of the poem? What is the speaker hoping to hear?

3. **Analyze:** What techniques or poetic devices has Kogawa used to add life-like qualities to this selection? Pick out some lines that best illustrate this. Briefly describe the success of these techniques.

4. **Synthesize:** Write a short poem about the loneliest time of the day. Consider writing it in a similar style to Kogawa's. Or, create a collage

based on some of the images in the poem. Use drawings, illustrations, coloured paper, or other materials.

Justice, p. 220

1. **Understand:** Before you read the poem, discuss in a small group the concept of justice: what it is, who applies it, and how it is used in our society. Chart your ideas in point form.
2. **Apply:** Find the definitions of *justice* and *truth* in a dictionary. How closely linked are these two words? In what ways do people often confuse them? Explain, citing some common examples.
3. **Analyze:** This poem uses adjectives and verbs in a powerful way. In small groups, study what either the adjectives or verbs convey about the poet's interpretation of justice. Summarize her viewpoint.
4. **Synthesize:** Scan the poem and make notes on any imagery dealing with play. Have a class discussion about why the poet might have made this unusual link between justice and play. Then rewrite the poem using a different central metaphor.

Three Strangest Words, p. 221

1. **Understand:** After reading this poem, respond to it in your journal. What message do you think the poet wants to convey? Has he succeeded?
2. **Apply:** Discuss the meaning of *paradox*. Do you think the poem expresses one or more paradoxes? If so, which line(s) contains the best example(s)? Why?
3. **Analyze:** In a small group, reread this poem and "Justice" by Rita Joe in this anthology. They seem quite different, but re-examination may reveal shared characteristics. What are they? Chart your findings and compare them with another group's.
4. **Synthesize:** Use this selection as a model to write your own short, simple poem based on three other "strange" words. Ask other students for feedback on your poem.

First Ice, p. 222

1. **Understand:** As a journal entry or as a series of diary entries, recall a time when you felt that a special relationship was ending. Consider writing about your first indications that the relationship was unravelling.
2. **Apply:** What words or phrases does the poet use to evoke sympathy? Do you think they indicate the depth of her sadness and loneliness? Jot down some additional words or phrases to illustrate the girl's despair.
3. **Analyze:** In pairs, discuss the concept of "first ice." To what do you think the speaker is referring? How can frozen tears be compared to "the first ice of human hurt"?
4. **Synthesize:** With a partner, present a dramatization of this poem. One of you can read the poem, while the other enacts it with movements and

gestures. Rehearse your presentation until you and your partner are confident with it. Perform the reading for your class.

Younger Sister, Going Swimming, pp. 223–224

1. **Understand:** Note the difference between the stanzas that appear in parentheses and the rest of the stanzas. What is different about the two types, and what is significant about the difference? Discuss with a classmate.
2. **Analyze:** Why does the setting appear to be a central component of the poem? Find lines or phrases that describe the setting. How do they help you interpret the poem?
3. **Synthesize:** With a partner, look for clues in the poem to possible character traits of each sister and, in a T-chart, list these qualities. Then, write a dialogue between the two sisters that reveals their personalities. Ask another set of classmates to review the script for clarity.
4. **Think Critically:** Why do you think Atwood introduces writing terms such as "page," "paper," and "these marks I am making on it"? Discuss with a classmate whether these terms are used by the speaker to compare herself to her sister. If so, why?

Sonnet XXIX, p. 225

1. **Understand:** In pairs, look up *sonnet* in a reference guide in order to compare the structure of the two most common forms of sonnets. What type of sonnet does Shakespeare write? Read aloud a few lines from the sonnet to confirm its style.
2. **Apply:** The speaker's attitude seems to change from initial despair to elation by the end of the poem. In your notebook, jot down the words or phrases that indicate these mood changes. Compare and contrast your responses to a classmate's. What conclusions can you draw?
3. **Analyze:** In this poem, Shakespeare has used the preposition "like" four times. In only one case is it used to introduce a simile. Locate the four versions and decide which one is a simile. What is it comparing and why? Discuss with a partner.
4. **Think Critically:** For hundreds of years, Shakespeare's work has stirred imaginations around the world. Speculate with a small group why this is so. What themes does he explore? What are some of the qualities in a writer's work that would make it continue to be appealing and relevant for centuries?

Gurl, pp. 226–227

1. **Understand:** Notice the spelling of the title. Is this a mistake, or deliberate? What might the poem be about, based on the title?
2. **Apply:** How would you describe the tone of this poem? What is the poet's message? Does the tone help or hinder the delivery of this message?

3. **Analyze:** In your journal, list clichés that appear in this poem. How do they add colour and character?
4. **Synthesize:** Create a poster using text and images to convey the poem's overall theme.

Warrior Woman, pp. 228–230

1. **Understand:** In a small group, discuss the concept of a warrior woman. What might she represent? What characteristics would a warrior woman possess? Identify a number of warrior women in fiction or in real life.
2. **Apply:** Who are "the men in grey suits" and "the ones in white coats"? Why are they too busy to deal with the speaker or even acknowledge her? Give examples from the poem for support.
3. **Analyze:** Compare and contrast the thoughts and ideas expressed in this poem to the poem "Gurl" in this anthology. In pairs, create a T-chart with your thoughts under the name of each poem.
4. **Think Critically:** The pink dressing gown is a repeated reference. What is its effect on your reading of the poem?

Kidnap Poem, p. 231

1. **Understand:** Describe the poem's structure. Where do lines and stanzas break? How many spaces are there between each? Why do you think she doesn't use any punctuation? Read the poem to a partner and ask for feedback on your reading.
2. **Apply:** Giovanni's technique is playful and lyrical. Summarize what you like or dislike about this poem. Do you find it amusing, annoying, or confusing? Explain.
3. **Analyze:** How does Giovanni use words that normally describe the language of poetry, such as "meter"? Find the other examples of literary words. What is unusual about using them in this way?
4. **Think Critically:** Poetry does not have to follow the normal rules of punctuation and grammar. This is an example of poetic licence. Discuss in a group why it is important to many poets that they experiment with punctuation, line length, spacing, and language when creating their works.

And I Remember, pp. 232–233

1. **Understand:** In a group of six, choose one member to read the poem out loud, one stanza at a time. Then have the others choose and interpret one stanza. Chart the interpretations and decide on the poem's message.
2. **Analyze:** The poet writes about a carefree childhood affected by powerful images from nature. How does the poet allow us to breathe the air and view the scenery from her childhood? How does she imbue the poem with colour and texture? Support your opinion.
3. **Synthesize:** Recall a favourite place from your past, such as a backyard, a sports arena, a skating rink, or your own room. Write a lyrical poem describing it and the feelings linked with that place.

4. **Synthesize:** In a small group, prepare a choral reading of this poem. Decide how to perform it, such as in unison, cumulatively, or part-by-part. Consider providing some musical accompaniment. Perform it for the class.

My Father, p. 234

1. **Understand:** Respond to this poem in a journal entry. What did you think the poem might be about based on the title? How did your interpretation change after reading it?
2. **Apply:** Alliteration is the repetition of the same sound in a group of words or phrases. Locate the lines that contain alliteration. Experiment with forming alliterations similar to those in the poem. Write a few in your notebook and then share them with a classmate.
3. **Analyze:** Compare and contrast the style and theme in this poem with "And I Remember" in this anthology. Look at the structure, tone, language, and message. Then write an essay in which you explain which poem you prefer and why.
4. **Think Critically:** In a group, reread the last stanza of this poem. Then debate the idea that agricultural lands must be developed to accommodate the increase in population in high-density areas near cities. Summarize your debate for the class.

Concrete and Shape

Point Scored, p. 235

1. **Understand:** Read this poem to a partner. How did you read it—as a line of text with pauses between the words, or in some other meaningful way? Why did you read in the way that you did? Ask your partner for feedback on your reading.
2. **Apply:** Rearrange the words in any format that makes sense to you, such as in two columns or in one straight line. How does this affect the overall impact of the poem? Explain the new structure, and your reasons for the changes, to a partner.
3. **Analyze:** Some words in this poem are used both visually and "kinetically." How does the poet achieve this effect? Is it possible for words to "move" and "dance" on a page? Write your explanation in your journal.
4. **Think Critically:** Because of its simple language and syntax, concrete poetry has been compared to advertising and graphic design. In a small group, brainstorm ways they are similar. List your ideas on a chart and compare charts with another group. What conclusions can you draw?

History, p. 236

1. **Understand:** You may need to read this poem several times, both silently and aloud, to understand the poet's intended meaning. What point is he making? Write your response in your journal.

2. **Analyze:** The poem repeats letters and splits up words, sometimes over two lines. Why do you think the poet did this? What are the advantages or disadvantages in structuring the poem this way? Discuss with a partner.

3. **Synthesize:** Using "History" as a model, write your own concrete poem on the computer. Focus on one word and keep the poem's length to five lines or fewer. Create a separate line for each new word, and use phonetic spelling if necessary. Display the poem on your classroom bulletin board.

4. **Think Critically:** In a group, present a radio phone-in show featuring a "guest expert" who states that history is often presented from the male perspective. One person can be the radio host, another the guest, and the others can be radio listeners who phone in. Perform the show for the class.

Blues, p. 237

1. **Understand:** After reading the poem, discuss in a small group what the relationship is between the title and the poem's content. What are the similarities and/or differences between these two words? Can one be "in love" and "feel blue" at the same time?

2. **Analyze:** The poem is formed from one word, *love*. Yet this one word is broken up and restructured in many different ways. List the variations. Speculate about why the poet chose to structure this poem using such an unusual format.

3. **Synthesize:** Using "Blues" as a model, write a concrete poem that has a different title from its content. Remember to use only one word as the subject of the poem. Share it with a partner.

4. **Think Critically:** The poet T. S. Eliot said: "Genuine poetry can communicate before it is understood." In a personal essay, explain why you agree or disagree with this statement. Consider including the definition of concrete poetry in your essay. Place your finished work in your writing portfolio.

I, p. 238

1. **Understand:** Innovative uses of letters, symbols, and words are a trademark of e.e. cummings's poetry. As you read this poem, notice the words on both the inside and outside of the parentheses. What are these words? What do they represent? Compare your response to a partner's.

2. **Apply:** How often does the word *one* or the digit *1* appear in the poem? What effect do you think the poet wishes to achieve?

3. **Analyze:** Note how the poem's lines are mainly composed of two letters or symbols. How does this structure visually reinforce the meaning of the poem? Write a one-paragraph explanation.

4. **Synthesize:** Reinterpret this poem in a different medium. Consider drawing or illustrating it, preparing it as a mime, or shooting it as a photograph or video. Use your imagination to come up with a unique presentation.

Last Ride, p. 239

1. **Understand:** In a small group, discuss what you know about the disastrous flight of the space shuttle *Challenger*. Think about what you might have felt if you had been a witness to the explosion.
2. **Apply:** How has the poet used irony in this poem? Locate the lines or phrases that indicate this poetic device. In what ways does irony affect the tone and mood of the poem?
3. **Analyze:** Look carefully at the structure of the poem. With a partner, examine and comment on its overall configuration. Do you think "Last Ride" can genuinely be called a concrete poem?
4. **Think Critically:** In the role of a TV news producer, write and present a commentary on how tragedies and disasters are reported. Remember that you have approximately thirty seconds to get your message across to the audience.

Songs
Perfect, p. 240

1. **Understand:** In a small group, discuss why parents or guardians might have high expectations for their children. How might these expectations affect their relationship with their children?
2. **Apply:** Reread the lyrics. Which stanza affects you the most? Copy it into your journal. Then respond personally by writing about a time when you or a friend heard similar remarks.
3. **Analyze:** These song lyrics consist of a series of critical phrases. Why would Morissette use these phrases as the basis for a song? What is her point?
4. **Synthesize:** Create a poster or collage based on the message of this song. Use text from the poem and images collected from magazines or designed by you. Or produce a video commentary about the harmful effects of constant criticism and negative language on the self-esteem of young children and teens. Think about the intended audience and what sound effects, lighting, and props you might use.

The Songs of the Birds, p. 241

1. **Understand:** Read the lyrics of each song out loud to a partner. After each song, pause and ask your partner to summarize what you have read. What is the message in each song? How are they related?
2. **Apply:** Locate other song lyrics or recordings that make a connection between love and nature. List the types of links, considering which are most often used and which you find most effective.
3. **Analyze:** Many cultures celebrate nature or use nature as a metaphor in song. List phrases and words that demonstrate the use of nature in all three songs. In what ways might nature be used to express emotion?

4. **Synthesize:** Using these song lyrics as a model, write your own song or poem about nature. Try to convey a sense of time and place. Remember to use words that create images and evoke emotions. Post your finished piece on your school's web site or in your class's project binder.

Northwest Passage, p. 242

1. **Understand:** Stan Rogers often wrote Canadian folk songs that chronicle the history of Canada. In a small group, discuss the importance of artists who record our country's legacy in songs.
2. **Apply:** With a partner, design a T-chart of the historical allusions in the song. Label one column of the chart "Past Journeys," and the opposite column "Present Journeys." Then jot down the appropriate words or phrases under each. What are the similarities or differences in the columns?
3. **Analyze:** This song is a four-quatrain ballad, with a chorus, which contains a distinctive rhyming pattern. Look up *quatrain* and *ballad* in a dictionary. Then analyze the rhyme scheme in a short paragraph.
4. **Think Critically:** Research information on Stan Rogers's life and recordings in a library or Internet search. Listen to a CD or tape of his work. Then write a review of his recordings, focusing on two or three of your favourite songs. What themes do they share?

Vincent, pp. 243–244

1. **Understand:** This song is dedicated to the post-impressionist Dutch painter Vincent van Gogh. As you read these lyrics, jot down references to art, nature, and emotion. What do these references suggest to you about Van Gogh?
2. **Apply:** In pairs, list the vivid verbs and adjectives that McLean uses to paint a picture of Van Gogh's art and life. In what ways do they allude to Van Gogh's unusual artistic style and inner emotional struggles? Share your response with another pair.
3. **Analyze:** Look at the Van Gogh painting, *The Starry Night*, in this anthology. Analyze its style, colours, and theme. Then compare and contrast this painting to the lyrics by McLean. What is the relationship between the two genres? Write your response as a one-page report.
4. **Synthesize:** Van Gogh's premature death was a tragic loss to his family and the artistic community. What might his legacy have been if he had had access to the resources available today to those suffering from depression and mental illness? Compile a list of resources that are available in your school and community, and on the Internet.

Unit 4: Drama

Microdrama

Treads, pp. 248–249

1. **Understand:** In your mind, visualize this play, concentrating specifically on the setting, the feelings, the thoughts, and the behaviours of the characters. On a sketch pad, draw the scene, skimming the script for details to ensure accuracy.

2. **Analyze:** Analyze the behaviour and attitudes of the Tank Commander, explaining his initial willingness to run over the revolutionary. What factors motivate the Commander to issue the order despite the young revolutionary's "outstretched, pleading" hands and obvious distress?

3. **Synthesize:** What if the men had not recognized the revolutionary as the Commander's son? How might this drama have ended? Write a brief new ending.

4. **Think Critically:** Evaluate the twist at the end of the play. Has the playwright ended the play effectively? Justify your opinion clearly and logically.

A One-Act True Story, p. 250

1. **Understand:** Describe the theme of this play in a brief, well-thought-out paragraph.

2. **Apply:** Create the set design for the play. In pairs, first brainstorm ideas and make notes; then make a sketch of the set. Be sure to include and label every prop that will be used.

3. **Analyze:** David's final statement is extremely significant: "I felt stunned, humiliated. These kinds of acts I can live without." How does this comment reveal David's feelings about himself and his environment?

4. **Synthesize:** How do you think David would have reacted if the Security Guard had been kind and polite to him? If this had occurred, what kind of play do you think David would have written?

Plays

Whale Watch, pp. 251–257

1. **Understand:** Identify three examples in the play that illustrate how Maura is an optimist; then identify three examples that illustrate Ted's pessimism.

2. **Apply:** In groups, discuss the logistics of how this play could be staged. Then write directions to the set designer and prop person detailing your requests. Use the setting description that precedes the play to prompt your writing.

3. **Analyze:** Create a Venn diagram that shows both the similarities and differences between Maura and Ted.

4. **Think Critically:** Ted states, "You animal rights activists make me sick. What about human rights? You Greenpeacers and Save the Whales and Sea Shepherds, you're all nuts. Fanatics. Maniacs." Do you agree with his opinion? Why or why not? Clearly explain your point of view.

The Odyssey, pp. 258–282

1. **Understand:** Describe Odysseus by detailing at least five characteristics of his personality. Explain why Odysseus is truly a "hero."
2. **Apply:** Choose a character in the play who is especially interesting. Pick a scene containing the key lines spoken by this character, and rehearse these lines. Then prepare and present a dramatic soliloquy that would precede and "set up" this scene in the play, and perform it for a small group.
3. **Analyze:** Choosing specific passages from the play, show how the Old Man's narrations help the reader understand the script.
4. **Synthesize:** Two core values in this play are "courage and honour in the face of adversity." Write a short, expository composition showing how Odysseus, the main character, is a role model exemplifying these values.

From Fashion, Power, Guilt and the Charity of Families, pp. 283–288

1. **Understand**: Summarize the main idea or theme of the play, citing specific passages to support your point of view.
2. **Analyze:** Analyze what is meant by the phrase "family on the fault line" and consider whether this is an appropriate description of the family featured in this scene.
3. **Synthesize:** Using the play as a model, compose a free verse poem that reflects concepts contained in the play.
4. **Think Critically:** Do you feel the inclusion of singing is an effective theatrical device? Justify your answer by referring to specific examples in the text.

Monologues

Beatrice, pp. 289–292

1. **Understand:** Reread each section of the excerpt and explain the significance of the title of each one.
2. **Apply:** Identify the meaningful events the narrator refers to in each section. Develop a time line that charts these events chronologically.
3. **Analyze:** Chart both the positive and negative character traits of Roberta and her mother.
4. **Think Critically:** Do you feel that the dramatic form Farrell has chosen is effective as a text to be read? How effective is it as a script to be performed? Explain, dealing with the piece as both a reading and performance text.

Unit 5: Media

Print Media

Birth of a Mavin, pp. 296–300

1. **Understand:** Referring to the article, list five factors that suggest *Mavin* will succeed; then list any potentially negative factors. Share your lists with a partner and together predict the magazine's future.

2. **Apply:** With his or her permission, interview someone whose parents have different backgrounds culturally, ethnically, or geographically from each other. Ask the following question:How have the differences between your parents affected your life? Write an entry in your journal reflecting on what you learned from this interview.

3. **Analyze:** "Knowing that I'm not alone is important. The magazine does that for me." Identify three ways in which *Mavin* helps Matt Kelley feel less alone. Then, as Matt, write a short letter to a friend describing the importance of the magazine to you.

4. **Synthesize:** Examine a magazine intended for people of an ethnic background different from yours. Note the focus of the articles, the nature of the ads, and the products advertised. In a chart compare the magazine with one you usually read. You may find that working with a partner is helpful.

Coming of Age, pp. 301–302

1. **Understand:** Reread the article. In a T-chart, list each wave of change in one column, and the corresponding movement that opposed it in the other. Add pictures illustrating the changes, and display your chart on the bulletin board.

2. **Apply:** In a small group, brainstorm the social changes that may arise from network applications such as e-mail and e-commerce. Referring to the selection, decide whether these innovations are likely to be opposed by individuals or groups. If so, how might this opposition be expressed? Share your ideas with another group.

3. **Analyze:** Imagine you are living in the 1800s. In a short newspaper article, describe the changes arising from the new technology of steam, textiles, and iron, and workers' reactions to these changes. Use the Internet or library to find background information.

4. **Synthesize:** This selection reads like a summary of a longer article or TV show. In pairs, imagine basing a TV documentary on the article. List images, graphics, interviews, and locations you might include to aid viewer comprehension. Present your material as a proposal for a TV program.

How Seventeen Undermines Young Women, pp. 303–305

1. **Understand:** Paragraphs 3 to 7 describe ways in which the writer says *Seventeen* undermines young women. Summarize these paragraphs,

paraphrasing each in one sentence. Compare your sentences to check for accuracy.

2. **Analyze:** In pairs, identify the audience this article is targeting (parents, teachers, teenage girls or boys) and justify your choice. List possible audiences and, in point form, indicate how you would change the article to make it appeal to a particular audience.

3. **Synthesize:** Select a work from a print format other than a magazine (for example, a newpaper) or in a different medium (such as a music video) and write a similar critique using examples to support your case. Share your articles with the class.

4. **Think Critically:** If this article is correct, *Seventeen* is unhealthy for teenage women. Do you agree or disagree? Describe what a revised *Seventeen* Magazine would be like if the criticisms in this article were used to modify it. If such a magazine is available now, read an issue and describe it to a group.

Audio Media

Who's On First?, pp. 306–310

1. **Understand:** The humour of this classic comedy sketch depends on the characters' misunderstanding of the words and phrases: "Who," "What," "I don't know," "Today," "Tomorrow," and "I don't care." Contrast the way each comedian understands the words.

2. **Analyze:** Draw a diagram of a baseball infield and place the players' names at their positions. Compare your diagram with a partner's, and correct any errors in either.

3. **Synthesize:** Using the Internet or library, research the significance of the fact that the team is called "the Cooperstown team."

4. **Think Critically:** Try reading this skit with a partner, and then, if possible, watch or listen to Abbott and Costello perform it. In a few sentences, describe how to achieve a successful performance of the piece. Rehearse and deliver a polished performance of a portion of it.

Do Not Disturb: An Interview with Jane Goodall, pp. 311–317

1. **Understand:** Before reading, write in your journal what you know about Jane Goodall's work. After reading the interview, add what you learned about Goodall to your journal entry.

2. **Apply:** Using Vicki Gabereau's questions as models, create a set of questions to be used in an interview with a scientist who is trying to teach sign language to primates, such as chimpanzees and gorillas. Then try to find answers to some of these questions, and present your questions and answers in a report to the class.

3. **Analyze:** In the interview, Goodall says: "They imitate each other, but not us, fortunately. Otherwise we would really have trouble." Explain what she means.

4. **Synthesize:** Pretending to be Jane Goodall's team, write a proposal to the Canadian government for financial support for your research. In the proposal, explain the nature, purpose, and value of your research. Compare your proposals with those of other groups and decide which is the most convincing.

Visual Media

Eggs, pp. 318–320

1. **Understand:** Write a journal entry describing your responses to this advertisement and considering whether the advertisers want you to react in these ways. Compare your responses with those of others.
2. **Apply:** Draw up a list of appropriate questions the host of a radio show could ask this young woman.
3. **Analyze:** In small groups, design a storyboard for a TV advertisement to encourage people to donate to another charity that specializes in helping people with disabilities cope with everyday life (e.g., the Canadian National Institute for the Blind). Present your storyboard to the class and discuss which storyboards are most effective, and why.
4. **Synthesize:** People may be born without limbs, or may lose them in accidents, or have them severed by landmines or by enemies in wars. Produce a written report on what is being done in Canada and by international organizations to help prevent this from happening and to help people who have never had or who have lost limbs.

BBC film children hoping for adoption, pp. 321–322

1. **Understand:** In a T-chart, identify and summarize the arguments for and against televising appeals from children to prospective parents.
2. **Analyze:** In a small group, clarify the meaning of the following phrases in the context of this article: shop window; some kind of circus; voyeurism; children peddle themselves. Select two and describe the attitude that the word choice is intended to create in the reader.
3. **Synthesize:** "With more than 10 000 British children looking for new families ... the show will debunk the myths about adoption and encourage more people to try it." In a small group, list ways in which this show might make people more comfortable with the idea of adoption. Write a short, personal journal entry in which you explain your attitude to this show.
4. **Think Critically:** Write a letter to the head of daytime programming for the CBC television network, explaining why you would or would not favour a Canadian version of *A Family of My Own*. .

The Making of Pride and Prejudice, pp. 323–330

1. **Understand:** The article describes the challenges of adapting novels for the screen. Summarize these in point form, and in a small group rank them in order of difficulty. Compare your ranking with that of another group.

2. **Apply:** In pairs, discuss the difficulties of speaking Jane Austen's dialogue. Imagine acting in the film, and in several short diary entries reflect on your improvement in speaking your part. Compare your entries with your partner's.

3. **Analyze:** Many people believe movie-making is glamorous, but the "Diary of a Filming Day" shows it is hard work that involves an elaborate team. Analyze the diary in pairs, listing all those who helped create the movie. Remember to include those whose help has to be inferred (for example, "Dogs return to kennels" suggests at least two dog handlers are involved).

4. **Synthesize:** As an accountant working on the film, write to one of your financial backers explaining why you need more money. Base your arguments on your estimate of the number of people involved.

Cyberspace

Buffy's New Gigabyte, pp. 331–335

1. **Understand:** List at least six ways in which Buffy Sainte-Marie has demonstrated her creativity, and state how she has used it to help others.

2. **Analyze:** In a paragraph with specific references to the selection, explain how Buffy Sainte-Marie takes pride in her Aboriginal heritage.

3. **Synthesize:** Isolate the misconceptions about Aboriginal peoples that Buffy Sainte-Marie refers to. Describe how her combination of technology and Aboriginal culture can help correct these misconceptions. With a partner discuss whether a non-Aboriginal person could do this as effectively.

4. **Think Critically:** Find a definition of "cradleboard," and explain why it is an effective name for Sainte-Marie's venture. Design a home page for Cradleboard on paper or on computer, and display your page.

Welcome to Alpine Racing ... With a Difference!, p. 336

1. **Understand:** The title of the web page—"Welcome to Alpine Racing ... With a Difference!"—does not state what the difference is. In one sentence, explain what the difference is and how the photographs make it clear.

2. **Analyze:** Look at the first page of the web site. Allow your eyes to move freely around the page, and note where they move. Draw a rectangle in your notebook and trace the path that your eyes traced as they moved around the page. Noting the lines, text, and photos used on the page, write a brief explanation of why your eyes followed the path they did.

3. **Synthesize:** Investigate other non-traditional activities in which people with disabilities participate. On paper or computer, design a web site to represent their participation in that activity.

4. **Think Critically:** Conduct research to find out what sporting facilities are accessible to and used by disabled people in your community. Write a report on your findings, recommending specific steps that could be taken to make it easier for disabled people to participate in sports.

Researchers Find Sad, Lonely World in Cyberspace, pp. 337–342

1. **Understand:** Summarize in your own words the purpose and findings of the research. In pairs, examine the researchers' hypotheses and confirm or refute them in writing, giving reasons from your own and your friends' experience.

2. **Analyze:** Referring to this article and personal experience, write a short editorial for a school newspaper on the benefits and drawbacks of some form of computer technology. You should give the article a catchy title.

3. **Synthesize:** In the voice of Rebecca, write a letter to your father describing your disenchantment with Internet use and your concerns about the changes you perceive in his behaviour. Exchange letters with a partner, and write Rebecca's father's reply to the letter.

4. **Think Critically:** People's use of the Internet appears to be increasing, not decreasing. With reference to the concerns expressed in this selection, write "Guidelines for Internet Users." In pairs, make a user-friendly pamphlet, including graphics, statistics, various fonts, and other appealing features.

A Virtual Night Out on the Town, pp. 343–345

1. **Understand:** Webcasting is presented as solving at least two problems facing teens and young adults. Find and state the problems, and explain how webcasting offers solutions.

2. **Analyze:** This article has two parts, one describing the appeal and the other the technical challenges of webcasting. In columns titled "Appeal" and "Challenges," summarize each in point form. In a small group, speculate on the state of webcasting in a decade or so, and individually write a short narrative—"A Virtual Night Out in 2015."

3. **Synthesize:** Work in groups of four: two members brainstorm the benefits of the virtual world, the other two the drawbacks. Referring to this selection as well as others in the anthology, make a poster with text and visuals highlighting these pros and cons. Display the poster in the classroom.

4. **Think Critically:** More people watch sports on television than do so live, so sports events are produced for television, and live audiences endure commercial breaks and other sponsorship interruptions. In small groups, brainstorm how the web can solve existing problems with sports broadcasting and live viewing. Imagine you are advertising manager of a sports webcasting studio in 2015, and list ten reasons why fans should subscribe to your web site.

Talk City, pp. 346–347

1. **Understand:** List the links on the web page that are trying to sell you products. Briefly explain how they try to do so.

2. **Apply:** List the elements, such as text and graphics, which comprise the web page. Analyze the appeal and effectiveness of each element. Indicate any changes that you would like to make.

3. **Analyze:** Create three columns on a piece of paper, labelling them "Chat," "Products," and "Services." Place each item from the web page into one of the columns. Share your chart with a partner and resolve any discrepancies.

4. **Think Critically:** Work in pairs to list the functions of this page in order of importance. Browse the Internet and download web pages with different focuses. Make a display of these pages and indicate their primary purposes.

Setting Their Sites on Generation Y, pp. 348–351

1. **Understand:** List reasons why Net marketers have responded slowly to the Gen Y market and explain what they are now doing to attract teens. In a personal response, evaluate the marketers' chances of success.

2. **Apply:** Malls tend to be places where teens meet, but where they are not made welcome. Working in a small group, list ten improvements to your local shopping area, mall, or main street to make it more teen friendly. Share your findings with the class.

3. **Analyze:** Referring to yourself and your peers, write an open letter to a Net marketer confirming or refuting the stereotypes of Gen Y members that the marketers use. Indicate your opinion of the marketing trends described here.

4. **Synthesize:** If a Gen Y marketer designed a successful web site to attract you and sell you products, what would it look like? What information would it provide, and what products would it offer for sale? On paper, design a teen-friendly web page.

The Arts

Oopik Fetching Water, p. 353

1. **Understand:** Imagine if you actually touched this sculpture. How would each of the various textures feel? Include in your description those materials in the sculpture that do not come from the immediate natural environment.

2. **Apply:** As Oopik, write the interior monologue you would have as you go about your daily activities. Refer to your thoughts, the objects you have with you, and your interactions with others. Share the monologues, and read some to the entire class.

3. **Analyze:** A painting is two-dimensional; a sculpture, three-dimensional. Together list and research the following elements of art: *line, shape, colour, value, texture, form.* Then in pairs, place a reproduction of a painting beside the photograph of this sculpture. How does each of the elements on your list differ between the two works?

4. **Synthesize:** Speculate about what feeling the artist is expressing in this work. Share your paragraph with a partner, and comment on each other's ideas.

The Starry Night, p. 354

1. **Understand:** Study this painting carefully. Then put the painting away and make a list of everything you can remember about it. Use this list as the basis for a brief essay about the impression this painting made on you and any questions that it raised.
2. **Apply:** Find colour copies of two different paintings by Van Gogh. Compare their subjects and their use of such features as colour, shape, and texture. Share your comparison with a small group.
3. **Analyze:** In a work of art, *rhythm* refers to the repetition of an element by an artist in order to make a work seem active. In groups, discuss how Van Gogh has used rhythm to generate an exciting and forceful view of nature.
4. **Synthesize:** In your journal, reflect on whether Van Gogh's vision of nature contradicts or complements your own view.

Life's Highway, p. 355

1. **Understand:** In pairs, discuss: What is the main subject in this photograph—the car, the road, the rainbow? What is the point of the image? What feelings does it evoke in the viewer, and which elements of the work contribute to these feelings?
2. **Apply:** In pairs, develop a dialogue between the driver and a passenger. Decide on the identities of the car's occupants and the purpose of their journey. Rehearse and present the dialogue to the class.
3. **Analyze:** Briefly explain the effect of the camera angle both on the sense of space in the photograph and on the meaning of the image. How would changing the angle affect the impact of the picture? Compare your analysis with those of others.
4. **Think Critically:** Consider the title the photographer has given this work. Analyze the title in relation to the photograph. Then discuss what your analysis might reveal about the artist's view on life, technology, or nature.

Child's Tunic from Turkmenistan, p. 356

1. **Understand:** List all the materials used to create this work. In a small group, discuss any materials that surprised you, and consider possible reasons for their use.
2. **Analyze:** Place a ruler in the centre of the image, then use the ruler to analyze, in a few sentences, how the artist has achieved a sense of symmetrical balance in the work.
3. **Synthesize:** One purpose behind the design of this tunic is to demonstrate wealth. Discuss and record what factors beyond practical ones

lead people to buy particular clothing. Using visuals and text, make a poster that expresses "what we wear and why."

4. **Think Critically:** Show the picture of the tunic to students around the school and ask them to describe their emotional response. Record their responses and write a brief summary of them.

Christina's World, p. 357

1. **Understand:** Look at this painting carefully, and make a list of factual information about the subject matter. Record such details as a description of Christina and her surroundings. Afterward, compare your list with a partner's and discuss whether or not it was difficult to keep opinions or speculation out of your list.

2. **Apply:** As Christina, write a monologue from her perspective looking up the slope. Remain true to the mood of the painting.

3. **Analyze:** Many artists strive to include harmonious elements in their works of art in order to achieve a sense of unity in each piece. In small groups, discuss how Wyeth has used texture to create a unified mood. In what ways has he used light, shade, and line to direct the viewer's eyes, and why?

4. **Think Critically:** Show the painting to three people, asking them what they like or dislike about it. Write a short composition in which you detail which common elements in the painting they reacted to, and the similarites and differences in their reactions.

Skaters on the Rideau, p. 358

1. **Understand:** Make notes about all the details in this painting and then describe it to someone who has not seen the picture. Ask this person to sketch a rough diagram of the work based on your description. Then show the sketcher the picture and together discuss how to improve your description.

2. **Apply:** Imagine that you have just bought this painting for your art gallery. Write a brief article for the gallery newsletter, encouraging people to come view your latest acquisition. Emphasize such qualities of the piece as its colour, perspective, and texture.

3. **Analyze:** In small groups, discuss how the artist's use of repetition creates rhythm and unity. Post a copy of the picture with labels attached explaining your group's findings.

4. **Think Critically:** Consider works of art that are not realistic in style. Write an essay reflecting on different reasons that nonrealistic art is appealing to some people and not to others. Include some consideration of the role of art in society.

Tlingit Clan-Emblem Hat, p. 359

1. **Understand:** Study this artifact carefully, then write a clear, concise description of it. Include in your description such elements as line, colour, texture, shape, and medium. Share your description in a small group and compare your observations.

2. **Apply:** Choose the cultural background of your own family, or of someone you know, and then write several paragraphs detailing an item particular to that culture. It may be a type of clothing, household object, or craft. Create a classroom list of all the items, then brainstorm what categories these items could be separated into.

3. **Analyze:** In a few sentences, explain the effect that the hat's various materials, contrasts, and textures have on your overall impression of it. What would you describe as the tone of this hat, or the mood it creates? Discuss with the class in what ways viewers' cultural backgrounds might affect their analyses of the hat's tone.

4. **Think Critically:** Make a poster or pamphlet about hats, illustrating various types and styles, wearers, and uses. Include text and images in your work.

Springtime, p. 360

1. **Understand:** Study the painting, and list any object in the painting that may symbolize something. Write down what you think the object might symbolize, and share your list with a partner.

2. **Analyze:** The proportions and details in this work are not represented in a realistic style. In a journal entry, explore your response to its style. Now, research and make notes on the term *naive art*. Then list naive elements in this work.

3. **Synthesize:** Imagine that you are an artist who creates work in a particular medium and style. Write a letter to a friend in which you describe why you have chosen to work in the medium you do, and why your creations are expressed in this particular style.

4. **Think Critically:** In small groups, choose three famous artists, past or present, and research the selling price of one of their works, noting the year of sale. Discuss with the class what factors contribute to determining the price of a work of art.

Media Images

LYRA Personal Digital Player, p. 361

1. **Understand:** Think of at least three reasons why the mention of "mom" in the dialogue box is an effective advertising tool. Try substituting another relative, such as sister or grandpa, for mom, and discuss the effects of the changes.

2. **Apply:** Using diagrams, work with a partner to consider different layouts for this advertisement. Identify the main components and move them around; discuss the effects of each move. If you think you have made an improvement, post it on a bulletin board.

3. **Analyze:** Imagine that, as the designer of this advertisement, you have to "sell" your design to your employer. Write a report in which you clearly identify the target audience for your ad and the reasons this ad will be effective with that group.

4. **Think Critically:** In a small group, discuss whether you would purchase this item based on this advertisement. Indicate why or why not. List any additional information that would help you in making your decision.

Without Limits, pp. 362–363

1. **Understand:** In a small group, list the qualities you look for in a movie. Apply your list of preferred qualities to the *Without Limits* posters and have members of the group say whether they would pay to see this movie.

2. **Apply:** Look at examples of movie listings in a TV guide. Then write a one-sentence listing for the movie as described in each poster, highlighting the feelings and plot elements you infer from the poster designs. Explain the connection between the design elements and your plot descriptions.

3. **Analyze:** These two posters give two very different impressions of the same movie. Describe the differences and explain what qualities in the poster, such as image, colour, lighting, and text, give you those impressions.

4. **Synthesize:** Create a poster for a movie you know well. The poster must appeal to the target audience—the audience most likely to attend the movie. You may wish to use text and images from the movie or perhaps your own images.

Cab Ride, p. 364

1. **Understand:** "Cab Ride" is a short story in storyboard format. Identify the elements of the short story in this storyboard, and discuss how the format affects the way these are presented. Rewrite this selection as a short narrative.

2. **Analyze:** Effective commercials often add a degree of exaggeration and absurdity to the everyday. List the threats to the laptop and Richard's reactions to them. Decide where the everyday ends and the absurd begins. Compare your analysis with a partner's.

3. **Apply:** Imagine that the Toshiba Laptop is intelligent, and retell the story from the computer's point of view. "Tosh's" reactions will depend on its relationship with Richard. Try to give the computer a style of its own. Share your narratives in a group.

4. **Synthesize:** Richard treats his computer as though it were alive. Compile a list of other commercials, TV shows, and movies that treat computers and machines as living things. Reflect on what this says about society's attitudes toward machines, and analyze your own attitude.

Trix™/Crunch 'n Munch™, p. 365

1. **Understand:** Is the intended audience for these packages children, teens, middle-aged adults, or seniors? In point form, give reasons for your answer.
2. **Analyze:** Analyze the visual impact of such features of package design as colour, shape, text, and layout. Write a paragraph stating which package you find more effective and give reasons for your choice.
3. **Synthesize:** Many breakfast cereals are based on other foods—think of cinnamon toast and graham crackers. Redesign the Crunch 'n Munch package as a breakfast cereal. Make any required changes, but maintain the main ingredients of corn and peanuts.
4. **Think Critically:** Working in pairs, role play the dialogue that might take place between a parent and a child in a supermarket when the child's eye is caught by these packages on the shelf. As the child, be demanding. As the parent, indicate your attitude toward nutrition. Present your dialogue to a larger group.

Barbie™ Computer/Hot Wheels™ Computer, pp. 366–367

1. **Understand:** Imagine that you have to persuade your company to manufacture the Barbie and Hot Wheels computers. Make a speech to a small group explaining how each of these computers will appeal to the intended market.
2. **Analyze:** The hardware components of the two computers are identical, but the colours and accessories are very different. In two sentences, explain how these accessories appeal to specific audiences.
3. **Synthesize:** Adapt these advertisements into a thirty-second radio commercial. Decide whether you will need one commercial or two. Identify your audience and make sure that you choose appropriate sound effects, music, and voices.
4. **Think Critically:** Imagine that you are an eight-year-old or a thirteen-year-old who has received a Barbie or Hot Wheels computer for your birthday. Write an age-appropriate, polite thank-you letter to the relative who sent it to you. You may hint at your feelings if you are less than thrilled with the gift. Confide these feelings in full to your diary. Then share your letters and diaries.

Raising the Roof, p. 368

1. **Understand:** The labels that accompany the picture are used ironically. Clarify the real estate terms that are used and, in a T-chart, explain the literal and ironic meaning of each label.

2. **Apply:** Read the selection entitled "BBC films children hoping for adoption" in this anthology. In groups, create an advertisement that supports this enterprise and a poster that expresses concerns about it, using appropriate visuals. Indicate where the advertisement and the poster could be effectively placed to reach appropriate audiences.

3. **Analyze:** This ad appeared in a real estate magazine that advertises upscale condos and lofts. Describe the audience most likely to read such a magazine, and decide whether this advertisement is appropriate and effective for that market. Present your answer in a short, well-reasoned paragraph.

4. **Synthesize:** In a small group, create a storyboard for a TV commercial directed toward the same audience as the advertisement. Carefully select images, sounds, and narration to elicit a response from the viewers. Decide during which current TV programs you think the commercial should be shown.

act A major section of a stage play, equivalent to a chapter in a novel. An act is often divided into scenes.

adaptation The process of rewriting a text to change it from one genre to another (such as adapting a novel into a movie). A work resulting from such adaptation.

alliteration The repetition of consonant sounds. An auditory device in which consonants are repeated at the beginning of several words that are close together ("And with old woes new wail my dear time's waste"—Shakespeare).

allusion A brief, direct or indirect reference to a figure, place, event, idea, or object from myth, religion, history, literature, society, or popular culture. The writer assumes that the reader is familiar with the reference.

assonance The repetition of vowel sounds. An auditory device in which vowel sounds are repeated within a line of poetry ("In zones of silence they grow tall and slow"—P. K. Page; "And all is seared with trade, bleared, smeared with toil"—G. M. Hopkins).

audience The people who read, hear, or view a literary, nonfiction, or media work. The audience may be limited and specific, such as nuclear scientists, or broader. Effective writers take into account key characteristics of their intended audience, such as age range and background knowledge.

auditory device Any arrangement of letters, syllables, words, and phrases that appeals particularly to the ear. *See* **alliteration**, **assonance**, and **onomatopoeia**.

cast The actors who play the parts or characters in a play or a movie.

character A person in a dramatic or narrative work. *See* **characterization**.

characterization The techniques used to portray a fictional character or an actual person in writing or a media text. These techniques include presenting details of physical appearance; presenting the character's thoughts, actions, and words; and revealing what other characters think of the character.

concrete or shape poetry Poetry in which the arrangement of letters and words on the page visually enhances the meaning by representing an object dealt with in the text.

conflict The struggle of the characters in a story to resolve a problem results in conflict, which often advances the plot. Conflict can be internal (psychological) or external (among characters, or between characters and larger forces such as society, nature, or fate).

couplet Two adjacent lines of poetry, often with an end rhyme ("For thy sweet love rememb'red such wealth **brings**, / That then I scorn to change my state with **kings**."—Shakespeare).

cyberspace A term used to describe the electronic realm of major computer networks, in particular, the "universe" where **virtual reality** is experienced.

dialect A form of a language characteristic of a particular region or social group.

dialogue Conversation between fictional characters or actual people. In works of fiction and drama, dialogue is used for characterization and to advance plot.

diction The type of words chosen by the writer. Categories of diction include words that are concrete, abstract, formal, or informal.

figurative language The use of words in nonliteral ways. Figures of speech such as similes, metaphors, and personification are examples of figurative language.

figures of speech *See* **figurative language**.

first-person point of view When the narrator is involved in the events of the story, he or she is telling the story from a first-person point of view. First-person narrators can be unreliable, so the reader may have to figure out what is actually going on. *See* **narrator, point of view, third-person point of view**.

flash fiction An ultra-short story in which the author focuses on a single point.

free verse Poetry that does not have a regular pattern of rhythm, rhyme, or stanzas, but uses the natural rhythm of spoken language (as in the poem "Younger Sister, Going Swimming" by Margaret Atwood).

genre A broad category or type of literary, nonfiction, or media text, such as short story, drama, essay, biography, documentary, or political cartoon.

home page The first page on a **web site**. This page contains links to all the other pages on the site.

image and imagery In literary and nonfiction works, images are word pictures that appeal to the reader's senses and imagination; imagery refers to all the images in a work taken together.

internal rhyme *See* **rhyme**.

Internet A worldwide network of interconnected computers that allows the movement of electronic information from point to point; often simply referred to as the Net.

irony A statement or situation that suggests the opposite of what appears on the surface. Three common types of irony are *verbal*—saying one thing while implying the opposite; *situational*—expecting something different from what actually happens; and *dramatic*—when the reader or viewer knows something that the characters do not.

lyric poem A fairly short, non-narrative poem expressing the consciousness and emotions of a single speaker.

main idea *See* **theme**.

mass media Modern means of communication that appeal to and reach vast audiences; includes television, film, radio, newspapers, magazines, on-line publications, and web sites.

media text A media message or product, such as a movie, advertisement, photograph, web site, television program, or poster.

metaphor A device of figurative language in which one thing is compared with another by being completely identified with it ("A poem is a small machine made out of words."—William Carlos Williams). *See* **simile**.

metre In poetry, a recurring rhythm of accented (stressed) and unaccented syllables. A metrical unit of one accented and one or more unaccented syllables is called a foot.

modem A device that converts signals from digital to analogue forms and vice versa, enabling a computer to send and receive data over telephone lines.

monologue A long speech delivered by a character or person, often addressed directly to an audience and used to reveal the character's or person's thoughts; often referred to as a soliloquy within a drama. A monologue can also be a play with only one character.

narrative poem A poem that tells a story.

narrator The character or person who tells what happens in a literary, nonfiction, or media text. The narrator describes and interprets the setting, plot, and other characters or people. *See* **first-person point of view** *and* **third-person point of view**.

nonfiction A written prose text aiming to convey ideas or information, primarily by dealing with events or people that are not products of the writer's imagination. Nonfiction includes biographical, reference, informational, philosophical, historical, scientific, and technical texts.

novel A fictional prose story long enough to be published on its own in one or more volumes.

onomatopoeia An auditory device in which the sound of the word imitates the sound of the action or thing the word is associated with (such as buzz, chickadee, or splash).

organization The structure or main method of arranging the content of a work. The most common methods are *chronological*—arranging details in the order in which they occur (a biography); *spatial*—arranging details according to their location (a description of a room); *importance*—arranging details in order of increasing or decreasing importance (a news story); *cause and effect*—arranging details according to cause and effect sequence (an analysis of a problem); and *comparison*—arranging details to show how things are similar or different (a formal essay discussing plays with similar themes).

personification A device of figurative language in which something non-human is given human characteristics ("'Sky, what can you give me?' / and sky said, 'I can give you sunset.'"—Joy Kogawa).

plot The main story of a fictional or dramatic work. The plot usually develops out of the struggle of characters to resolve a problem or problems. *See* **conflict** *and* **subplot**.

point of view This refers to the position or perspective of the character or person telling the story.

props In a dramatic production, movable objects such as furniture and handheld articles that are used to enhance the setting and, often, to advance the plot.

prose Continuous non-metrical written discourse.

purpose The main goal of a work, which generally is as follows: in *fiction*—to entertain, tell a story, or convey insight (as in a short story, a movie, a poem); in *nonfiction*—to describe or explain something (as in an encyclopedia article, a documentary film); in a *media text*—to inform or persuade you (as in a newspaper article or editorial, an advertisement).

quatrain *See* **stanza**.

reference tool A text that provides background or source information.

rhyme The repetition of similar sounds at the ends of words, regardless of spelling (brig**ade**/dism**ayed**, **eyes**/**cries**, st**ate**/f**ate**). In traditional stanza forms, rhymes appear at the ends of lines in a regular pattern, or rhyme scheme. Internal rhyme refers to rhyme within a line of poetry ("In mist or cl**oud**, on mast or shr**oud**"—Coleridge).

rhyme scheme *See* **rhyme**.

rhythm The recurrent alternation of accented (stressed) and unaccented syllables in the words and lines of a poem. This may be regular, in which case it is referred to as metre, or it may be irregular, as in free verse.

scene A self-contained episode in a work of drama or fiction.

sentence structure The types of sentences writers choose to use. Sentences can vary in length and may take the form of questions or commands. Writers may also vary sentence patterns or repeat them deliberately.

sestet *See* **stanza**.

set and set design In a dramatic work, the design and arrangement of physical elements such as scenery, props, lighting, and sound. Sets are crucial for the effective setting of works.

setting The place, time, and social circumstances in which a work is set. The place can be real or imaginary; the time can be past, present, or future, and may be a particular season or time of day (midsummer, or midnight) or a particular occasion (an eclipse, a battle). Setting helps create a mood or atmosphere. In a dramatic work, setting is also communicated by the set and includes such elements as lighting, music, and sound effects.

short story A fictional prose story shorter than a novel, having a plot that focuses on several characters and a single theme.

simile A device of figurative language in which one thing is compared to another using the words "like" or "as" ("Justice is like an open field"—Rita Joe; "the sun wavers on/this page as on a pool"—Margaret Atwood). *See* **metaphor**.

soliloquy *See* **monologue**.

sonnet A single-stanza lyric poem of fourteen lines with a particular rhyme pattern. Each line usually has five metrical units or feet.

spread A story or advertisement occupying two or more adjoining columns of a magazine or newspaper; two facing pages of a publication, such as a newspaper or magazine, viewed as a single unit.

stanza A group of lines making up a unit of a poem, often partly defined by rhyming words and signalled by a blank line in the printed text. Common stanza forms are quatrains (four lines), sestets (six lines), octets (eight lines), and couplets (two lines).

structure *See* **organization** *and* **sentence structure.**

style In written works, a writer's choice and arrangement of words. The main elements of style are **diction, figurative language,** *and* **sentence structure**. A writer's stylistic choices develop the narrator's voice and convey the writer's attitude toward the subject and the audience for a piece of writing.

subplot An author can use secondary action in a fictional or dramatic work to make an independent but related story—a subplot—that enhances the meaning of the main action or plot. (In "Lifeguard," the main plot is about the relationship between the teenager and the young boy; the subplot is about the teenager's relationship to his father). *See* **plot.**

symbol An object or character that represents an idea, value, or condition beyond itself (a dove to represent peace, scales to represent justice).

telegenic Like the term photogenic, a term to describe a person who looks good on a TV screen; suitable for televising.

text The print, oral, or visual form through which content is communicated.

theme The key point, or central message, of a work. This can be either explicit, as it usually is in nonfiction and media works (such as in a research or news report) or implicit, as it usually is in works of fiction and poetry. Also referred to as the main idea or thesis in nonfiction works.

thesis The main idea of a work, used especially with reference to works of nonfiction (such as in formal essays and research reports). The thesis of a work is usually presented explicitly in a thesis statement at the beginning of the work.

third-person point of view When the narrator is not a character or person in the action, and speaks of other characters or people in the story or text either by name or as "she," "he," or "they," the writer is telling the story from a third-person point of view. The third-person narrator is an unseen observer who moves freely though the story, presenting what happens from both the outside (setting and plot) and the inside (the feelings and thoughts of the characters). *See* **first-person point of view**.

tone In writing, a writer's attitude toward a subject or audience, conveyed through the writer's style.

virtual Existing in effect, though not in actual fact, as in **virtual reality**.

virtual reality A simulation of reality created by video and audio programming in which the user experiences and interacts with an artificial environment as though it were real.

voice In writing, a writer's or a character's distinctive style of expression.

web page A page of text and/or graphics within a **web site**. A single data file on the World Wide Web that can include text, sound, and graphics, as well as hypertext links to other files.

web site A location on the World Wide Web consisting of a home page and, often, other files connected to the home page by hyperlinks. Web sites are owned and maintained by organizations and individuals.

World Wide Web A network of linked hypertext files, stored on computers around the world and accessible by the **Internet** using specialized software; "www" is the easily recognized opening of many Web addresses.

ACKNOWLEDGMENTS

Text

"A Catch Tale" by Charlie Slane and collected by Carol Spray. Reprinted with permission of Carol Spray. "A Man Told Me the Story of His Life" from LATER THE SAME DAY by Grace Paley. Copyright © 1985 by Grace Paley. Reprinted by permission of Farrar, Straus and Giroux, LLC. "The Dinner Party" by Mona Gardner, copyright 1942, 1970 SATURDAY REVIEW. Reprinted by permission of Bill Berger Associates, Inc. "Gratitude" by Andrew E. Hunt, reprinted with permission from *The World's Shortest Stories*, edited by Steve Moss, copyright © 1998, 1995 by Steve Moss, published by Running Press, Philadelphia and London. "The Wall" by Gilles Vigneault in Philip Stratford, ed., *Stories from Quebec* (Toronto: Van Nostrand Reinhold Canada, 1974). Translated by Jacqueline de Puthod Stratford. Originally published in *Contes du coin de l'oeil* (Montreal: Nouvelles Editions de l'Arc, 1966). "Just Lather, That's All" by Hernado Téllez, translated by Donald A. Yates, from *Great Spanish Stories*, selected and introduced by Angel Flores, copyright 1962. Dell Publishing Co., Inc. Copyright © 1950 Beatriz de Téllez from *Ashes for the Wind and Other Tales* by Hernando Téllez. Reprinted with the permission of the estate of Angel Flores. "Dancer" by Vickie Sears from SIMPLE SONGS by Vickie Sears published by Firebrands Books, Ithaca, New York. Copyright © 1990 by Vickie Sears. "Lifeguard" by Barbara Scott from *The Quick*. Published by Cormorant Books. "The Concert Stages of Europe" by Jack Hodgins, *Barclay Family Theatre*. Copyright © Jack Hodgins, 1981. Reprinted by permission of Macmillan Canada an imprint of CDG Books Canada Inc. A 30-minute film by Atlantis is available in major libraries. "Tunnel" from *Back of Beyond*. Text copyright © by Sarah Ellis. First published in Canada by Groundwood Books/Douglas & McIntyre. Reprinted by permission of the publisher. "The First Day" by Edward P. Jones from LOST IN THE CITY by Edward P. Jones. Copyright © 1992 by Edward P. Jones. Reprinted by permission of HarperCollins Publishers, +Inc. (William Morrow). "What Language Do Bears Speak?" by Roch Carrier and translated by Sheila Fishman which appeared in THE HOCKEY SWEATER AND

OTHER STORIES, Copyright © 1979. Reprinted with permission of House of Anansi Press Limited. Adapted from **"How to Write a Serious Novel About Love"**, from *Forms of Devotion* by Diane Schoemperlen. A Phyllis Bruce Book, published by HarperCollins Publishers Ltd. **"Shinny Game Melted the Ice"** by Richard Wagamese. Copyright © 1996 by Richard Wagamese and published by Warwick Publishing Inc. Excerpt from *Truth and Bright Water* by Thomas King. Copyright © 1999 by Dead Dog Café Productions, Inc. Published by HarperCollins Publishers Ltd. From **"Pride and Prejudice"** by Jane Austen. **"The Fly"** by Mai Vo-Dinh from THE TOAD IS THE EMPEROR'S UNCLE: ANIMAL FOLKTALES FROM VIETNAM, published by Doubleday, 1970. **"The Cow-Tail Switch"** from THE COW-TAIL SWITCH AND OTHER WEST AFRICAN STORIES by Harold Courlander and George Herzog, with drawings from Madye Lee Chastain. Copyright © 1947, 1974 by Harold Courlander. Reprinted by permission of Henry Holt and Company, LLC. **"The Death of Balder"** from *FAVORITE NORSE MYTHS* retold by Mary Pope Osborne. Copyright © 1996 by Mary Pope Osborne. Reprinted by permission of Scholastic Inc. **"The Rebellion of the Magical Rabbits"** by Ariel Dorfman. Copyright © 1990 by Ariel Dorfman. Reprinted with permission of The Wylie Agency. **"The Usual Things"** copyright © 1999 by Anita Rau Badami first published in *Saturday Night Magazine*, May 1999. Reprinted by permission of the author. *"Bat Summer* **Reviewed"** by Erika Thornton and Diana Brebner. Reprinted by permission of the authors. **"Reconnecting with the Earth"** by David Suzuki from *Time to Change: Essays* Copyright © 1994 by David Suzuki. Reprinted by permission of Stoddart Publishing Co. Limited. **"A Country Childhood"** by Nelson Mandela from MANDELA: AN ILLUSTRATED BIOGRAPHY by Nelson Mandela. Copyright © 1994 by Nelson Rolihlahla Mandela. By permission of Little, Brown and Company (Inc.). **"Sunday Dinner for Tourists"** by Barry Broadfoot, TEN LOST YEARS 1929–1939, Copyright 1973 Barry Broadfoot. Reprinted by permission of the author. **"Publishing Anne"** by Lucy Maud Montgomery from THE SELECTED JOURNALS OF L. M. MONTGOMERY VOLUME I: 1889–1910. Copyright © 1985 University of Guelph, published by Oxford University Press. **"Sowing the Wind"** by Lake Sagaris from *After the First Death: A Journey Through Chile, Time, Mind*, copyright 1996 by Lake Sagaris. Published in Canada by Somerville House

Publishing. Reprinted by permission of the author. From **"Into Thin Air"** by Jon Krakauer. Copyright © 1997 by Jon Krakauer. Illustrations copyright © 1997 Randy Rackliff. Reprinted by permission of Villard Books, a division of Random House, Inc. From **"The New Ice Age"** by Stephen Brunt © 1999. Used by written permission of McClelland & Stewart, Inc. *The Canadian Publishers.* **"The Art of Genius: Eight Ways to Think Like Einstein"** by Michael Michalko, originally published in 5/99 issue of *The Futurist.* Used with permission of the World Future Society, 7910 Woodmount Avenue, Bethesda, MD 20914 www.wfs.org. **"Preventing Conflict in the New Century"** by Kofi Annan from *The Economist, "The World in 2000" issue.* Reprinted by permission of Hutton-Williams Agency. **"Canada's Aboriginal Languages"** by Mary Jane Norris from *Statistics Canada, Canadian Social Trends, Catalogue No. 11-008, Winter 1998, Number 51, pages 8–16. Statistics Canada information is used with the permission of the Minister of Industry, as Minister responsible for Statistics Canada. Information on the availability of the wide range of data from Statistics Canada can be obtained from Statistics Canada's Regional Offices, its World Wide Web site at* http://www.statcan.ca, *and its toll-free access number 1-800-263-1136.* **"The Internet and Global Human Rights"** by Lloyd Axworthy which appeared in CANADIAN SPEECHES, Volume 12, Issue 6, October 1998. Reprinted with the permission of the Office of the Minister of Foreign Affairs. **"Spinning Facts into Fiction: Talking with Timothy Findley"** by Buenavetura and Overbury from *How To Research Almost Anything.* Reprinted with permission of McGraw-Hill Ryerson Limited. **"Family Matters"** by Andy Steiner. Reprinted with permission from *Utne Reader,* May–June 1999 issue. **"Zen and the Art of Stand-Up Comedy"** by Jay Sankey. Copyright © 1998. Reproduced by permission of Taylor & Francis, Inc/Routledge, Inc., http://www.routledge-ny.com. **"Shapes of Cities"** by Vanessa Baird from THE NEW INTERNATIONALIST, June 1999 issue. With permission of *New Internationalist* Magazine. **"Food Facts: What Doesn't Kill You Will Make You Stronger"** from SHIFT MAGAZINE, April 1999 issue. Reprinted courtesy of *Shift Magazine.* **"Chance Encounter"** by Alden Nowlan from THE MYSTERIOUS NAKED MAN by Alden Nowlan, Copyright © 1969. Reprinted by permission of Irwin Publishing. **"Sarajevo Bear"** by Walter Pavlich which appeared in THE ATLANTIC MONTHLY, March 1993.

Reprinted with permission of the author. **"La Belle Dame sans Merci"** by John Keats. **"To My Son"** by Helen Fogwill Porter, Copyright © Helen Fogwill Porter. Reprinted with permission. **"Africville"** by Maxine N. Tynes; Poet, Writer, Teacher, Renaissance Woman. **"Fifty Below"** by Richard Van Camp from STEAL MY RAGE Copyright © 1995 by Na-Me-res (Native Men's Residence). **"Hunger"** by Kingmerut and translated by Tom Lowenstein. Reprinted with permission. **"The Charge of the Light Brigade"** by Alfred, Lord Tennyson. **"Without Hands"** by Lorna Crozier from *Angels of Flesh, Angels of Silence* by Lorna Crozier © 1988. Used by permission, McClelland & Stewart, Inc. *The Canadian Publishers.* **"Young"** by Anne Sexton from ALL MY PRETTY ONES by Anne Sexton. Copyright © 1962 by Anne Sexton, renewed 1990 by Linda G. Sexton. Reprinted by permission of Houghton Mifflin Company. All rights reserved. **"In The Almost Evening"** by Joy Kogawa from JERICHO ROAD, Copyright © 1977 Joy Kogawa. Reprinted with permission of the author. **"Justice"** by Rita Joe from LNU AND INDIANS WE'RE CALLED, Copyright © Rita Joe, 1991. Reprinted with permission of the author. **"Three Strangest Words"** by Wislawa Szymborska from SOUNDS, FEELINGS, THOUGHTS: SEVENTY POEMS. Copyright © 1981 by Princeton University Press. Reprinted by permission of Princeton University Press. **"First Ice"** by Andrei Voznesensky from ANTIWORLDS AND THE FIFTH ACE, Schocken Books. **"Younger Sister, Going Swimming"** from *Selected Poems 1966–1984* by Margaret Atwood. Copyright © Margaret Atwood 1990. Reprinted by permission of Oxford University Press Canada. **"Sonnet XXIX: When in disgrace..."** by William Shakespeare. **"Gurl"** by Mary Blalock appeared in the NEW INTERNATIONALIST, August 1999. Reprinted by permission of the author. **"Warrior Woman"** by Maria Jastrzebska. Copyright © 1994 *What Happened To You?: Writing by Disabled Women*, edited by Lois Keith. Reprinted by permission of The New Press. **"Kidnap Poem"** from THE SELECTED POEMS OF NIKKI GIOVANNI by Nikki Giovanni. Compilation copyright © 1996 by Nikki Giovanni. Reprinted by permission of HarperCollins Publishers, Inc. WILLIAM MORROW. **"And I Remember"** by Afua Cooper from MEMORIES HAVE TONGUE (Toronto: Sister Vision Press, 1992). Reprinted with the permission of the publisher. **"My Father"** by Russell Wallace from LET THE DRUMS BE YOUR HEART, Copyright © 1996 by Joel T. Maki and published by Douglas & McIntyre. **"Point Scored"** by C. Cardenas Dwyer. **"History"** by Peter Park. Reprinted by permission of the author. **"Blues"** by bp Nichol from VANCOUVER POETRY edited by Allan Safarik. Published by Polestar Press. Reprinted with permission of the estate of bp nichol. **"I"** by e.e. cummings. "l(a". Copyright © 1958, 1986, 1991 by the Trustees for the E.E. Cummings Trust, from COMPLETE POEMS: 1904–1962 by E.E.Cummings, edited by George J. Firmage. Used by permission of Liveright Publishing Corporation. **"Last Ride"** by Andrea Holtslander, Copyright © Andrea Holtslander. Reprinted with permission of the author. **"Perfect"** words and music by Alanis Morissette and Greg Ballard. Copyright © 1994 Universal–MCA Music Publishing, Inc., a division of Universal Studios, Inc. (ASCAP) International Copyright Secured. All Rights Reserved. **"The Songs of the Birds"** from TREASURY OF INDIAN LOVE: POEMS AND PROVERBS. Published by Hippocrene Books, Inc. **"Northwest Passage"** by Stan Rogers. Copyright © 1981 Stan Rogers. Used by permission of Ariel Rogers & Fogarty's Cove Music. **"Vincent (Starry, Starry Night)"** words and music by Don McLean. Copyright © 1971 Universal–MCA Music Publishing, Inc., a division of Universal Studios, Inc. (BMI) International Copyright Secured. All Rights Reserved. **"Treads"** by Bill Dempster. Reprinted with permission of the author. **"A One-Act True Story"** by David G. McLeod from LET THE DRUMS BE YOUR HEART, Copyright © 1996 by Joel T. Maki and published by Douglas & McIntyre. **"Whale Watch"** by Colleen Curran first published in *Instant Applause: 26 very short complete plays* © 1994. Reprinted by permission of Blizzard Publishing. **"The Odyssey"** adapted from Homer. By arrangement with Anchorage Press, Inc., New Orleans, Louisiana USA. From **"Fashion Power, Guilt, and the Charity of Families"** by Carol Shields and Catherine Shields © 1995. Reprinted by permission of Blizzard Publishing. **"Beatrice"** by Geraldine Farrell. Reprinted with permission of the author. **"Birth of a Mavin"** by Andy Steiner from the UTNE READER, September–October 1999 issue. Reprinted by permission of the author. **"Coming of Age"** by James MacKinnon from Autumn 1999 issue of *Adbusters*. Reprinted with permission, www.adbusters.org. **"How *Seventeen* Undermines Young Women"** by Kimberly Phillips. Reprinted by permission of the author. **"Who's On First?"** by Bud Abbott and Lou Costello. Cooperstown Baseball Hall of Fame and Museum. **"Do Not Disturb: An Interview with Jane Goodall"** by Vicki Gabereau adapted from "Interview With A Chimp Lady" from *This Won't Hurt A Bit* by Vicki Gabereau. Published by HarperCollins Publishing Ltd. Copyright © 1987 by Vicki Gabereau. **"Eggs"** produced by Abbott Mead Vickers. BBDO. Reprinted with permission. **"BBC films children hoping for adoption"** by Carl Honoré from November 25, 1999 issue of the *National Post*. Reprinted with permission of the *National Post*. From **"The Making of Pride and Prejudice"** by Sue Birtwistle and Susie Conklin (Penguin/BBC, 1995) copyright © Sue Birtwistle and Susie Conklin, 1995. **"Buffy's New Gigabyte"** by Ophira Edut from *Ms.*, August/September 1999 issue. Reprinted by permission of *Ms.* Magazine, © 1999. **"Welcome to Alpine Racing ... With a Difference!"** from Canadian Association for Disabled Skiing. Reprinted with permission. **"Researchers Find Sad, Lonely World in Cyberspace"** by Amy Harmon from August 30, 1998 issue of *The New York Times*. Reprinted with permission. **"A Virtual Night Out on the Town"** by Grant Buckler. Originally appeared in *The Globe and Mail*. Reprinted by permission of the author. **"Talk City"** from Talk City Online Communities. **"Setting Their Sites on Generation Y"** by Kipp Cheng. Reprinted by permission of the author.

Visuals

Page 2 Peter Maltz/The Stock Illustration Source, Inc.; **Page 5** Robert Henno/Spectrum Stock Inc.; **Page 10** Peter Holst/Image Bank; **Page 17** Robert Davidson, *Eagles*, 1991, VAG 94.3 Vancouver Art Gallery Acquisition Fund (Photo: Robert Kezier); **Page 21**, Comstock; **Page 33** Copyright © Bosendorfer Piano Company; **Page 71, 79, 81** Dover Pictorial Archive Series; **Page 82** Copyright Jane Austen Memorial Trust; **Page 99** PhotoDisc; **Page 100, 103** Illustrations from THE COW-TAIL SWITCH AND OTHER WEST AFRICAN STORIES by Harold Courlander and George Herzog, with drawings by Madye Lee Chastain. Copyright © 1947, 1974 Harold Courlander. Reprinted by permission of Henry Holt and Company, LLC; **Page 109** Illustration by Giovanni Caselli; **Page 120** John Lund/Tony Stone Images; **Page 126, 129** Michael Soloman, Groundwood Books/Douglas & McIntyre; **Page 133** McGregor Museum/Duggan-Cronin Collection; **Page 135** McGregor Museum/Jean Morris Collection; **Page 150** Illustration copyright

© 1997 by Randy Rackliff. Reprinted by permission of Villard Books, a division of Random House, Inc.; **Page 155** Courtesy of White Pine Productions; **Page 179** Jan Franz/Tony Stone Images; **Page 192** Copyright © 1998. From ZEN AND THE ART OF STAND-UP COMEDY by Jay Sankey. Reproduced by permission of Taylor & Francis, Inc./Routledge, Inc., http://www.routledge-ny.com; **Page 200** John Martin/The Stock Illustration Source, Inc.; **Page 205** Painting by Sir Frank Dicksee/art.com; **Page 209** Bob Brooks Collection/The Public Archives of Nova Scotia; **Page 213, 215** © Bettman/CORBIS; **Page 223** Peter Finger/CorbisPage; **Page 225** Eugene Delacroix, 1843; **Page 226** Monica Lau/PhotoDisc; **Page 232** Macduff Everton/Image Bank; **Page 244** Andrew Southon/Photonica; **Page 248, 249** Jeff Widener/CP Picture Archive; **Page 258** The Mansell Collection/Time Life Syndication; **Page 294** David C./CORBIS; **Pages 296, 297** Mark Van S.; **Page 301** *The Economist*, February 6, 1999; **Page 303** First Light; **Page 306** © Bettman/CORBIS; **Page 315** © Kennan Ward/CORBIS; **Page 324** Copyright © BBC; **Page 327** *Upper* Copyright Nebille Ollerenshaw, *Lower*- Copyright © BBC; **Page 331**, Raymond Wong: Pacific Light Studios Hawaii; **Page 336** *Upper*-Canadian Association for the Disabled, *Lower*-Kazuji Shimizu; **Page 340, 350** Randy Glasbergen; **Page 353** "Oopik Fetching Water" by Oopik Pitsiulak. Reprinted with permission of the Canadian Musuem of Civilization, image number: S99-43 and with permission of the artist; **Page 354** "The Starry Night" by Vincent van Gogh; **Page 355** "Life's Highway" by Courtney Milne. Copyright © Courtney Milne. Reproduced with permission.; **Page 356** "Child's Tunic from Turkmenistan." Photo by James Austin. From *World Textiles: A Visual Guide to Traditional Techniques* by John Gillow and Bryan Sentance, published by Bulfinch Press, New York.; **Page 357** "Christina's World" by Andrew Wyeth. (1948) Tempera on gessoed panel, 32 x 47" (81.9 x 121.3 cm). The Museum of Modern Art, New York. Purchase. Photograph © 2000 The Museum of Modern Art, New York.; **Page 358** "Skaters on the Rideau" by Molly Lamb Bobak, 1980. Oil on canvas 76.2 x 101.4 cm. Collection: The Robert McLaughlin Gallery, Oshawa, Ontario; Purchase, 1980. Photo credit: T. E. Moore, Toronto.; **Page 359** Tlingit Clan-Emblem Hat. Thaw Collection, Fenimore Art Museum, Cooperstown, New York. Photo credit: John Bigelow Taylor, NYC.; **Page 360** "Springtime" by Maud Lewis. Copyright The Art Gallery of Nova Scotia Photo by Bob

Brooks Illustrative Photography; **Page 361** Lyra Personal Digital Player. Courtesy Thomson Multimedia; **Page 364** "Cab Ride." Courtesy of The Communique Group Inc.; **Page 365** "Trix/Crunch 'n Munch" from *The Look of the Century* published by Dorling-Kindersley Ltd, London. Trix courtesy of General Mills Canada Inc. Crunch 'n Munch is a registered trademark of International Home Foods Inc.; **Pages 366, 367** "Barbie Computer/Hot Wheels Computer" from Mattel; **Page 368** "Raising the Roof." Donald Murphy, Creative Director, Raising the Roof and HOMES Publishing Group.